Roger Dixon,
who was Reader in Architecture
at the Polytechnic of the South Bank in London, was born
in 1935 and educated at Peterhouse, Cambridge, and the
Courtauld Institute of Art, London, where he received his
PhD for a thesis on the Victorian architect James Brooks.
He died tragically after a short illness in 1983.

Stefan Muthesius
teaches the history of art,
architecture and design at the University of East Anglia,
Norwich. Born in Berlin in 1939, he studied at the
Universities of Munich, London and Marburg. He is the
author of *The High Victorian Movement in Architecture
1850–1970* (1972), *The English Terraced House* (1982), *Tower
Block: Modern Public Housing in England, Scotland, Wales and
Northern Ireland* (with Miles Glendinning, 1993) and
Art, Architecture and Design in Poland (1994).

WORLD OF ART

This famous series
provides the widest available
range of illustrated books on art in all its aspects.
If you would like to receive a complete list
of titles in print please write to:
THAMES AND HUDSON
30 Bloomsbury Street, London WC1B 3QP
In the United States please write to:
THAMES AND HUDSON INC.
500 Fifth Avenue, New York, New York 10110

Printed in Singapore

ROGER DIXON
STEFAN MUTHESIUS

Victorian Architecture

with a short dictionary of architects
and 250 illustrations

THAMES AND HUDSON

1 (frontispiece) Putting the finishing touches on Ettington Park, Warwickshire, designed by Prichard and Seddon and built in 1858–63.

© 1978 Thames and Hudson Ltd, London

Second edition 1985
Reprinted 1997

ISBN 0-500-20160-9

Printed and bound in Singapore by C.S. Graphics

CONTENTS

*Throughout this book, a dagger (†) indicates that a building
has been demolished.*

Preface

In this introductory book we explore the rich architectural achievements of the Victorians and investigate the reasons for their many innovations.

The most eminent Victorian architects, men such as Barry, Cockerell, Pugin, Paxton, Scott, Street, Butterfield, Waterhouse, and Shaw, produced designs which may be compared with the best of previous periods. The Houses of Parliament, St George's Hall in Liverpool, the Crystal Palace, Keble College in Oxford, Manchester Town Hall and Cragside are creative achievements of the highest order. Many provincial designers approached their more famous London-based colleagues in competence and originality: we need only look at 'Greek' Thomson's work in Glasgow, Jesse Hartley's docks in Liverpool, Edward Walters' commercial palaces in Manchester, and Chamberlain and Martin's schools, baths and libraries in Birmingham. Further down the architectural scale, the designers of Nonconformist churches, of pubs and of many minor buildings tended to follow the models of the great designers, often with elegance and townscape success. Lastly, there are the polite façades of the houses of the mass of the population from the middle classes downwards, which still form such an important part of the fabric of British towns.

Much of this book deals with the visual appeal of the buildings, the historical style chosen and the artistic development of the designers. The Introduction sets out to give an overall view of the major stylistic revivals and the arguments behind them. It also gives a brief outline of the careers of the leading figures. A list of over three hundred architects with their main works is given at the end. The bulk of the book, however, is divided according to building types, in order to consider, at the beginning of each chapter, the vital question of patronage. What were the reasons for erecting a particular building in the first place? How was it paid for? How was it used? What new types of building evolved? This arrangement also enables the reader to find out something about individual buildings not mentioned in the text: the chapter on monumental public architecture, for instance, will tell him about the kind of events that led to the erection of the nearest Victorian town hall; and the history of domestic architecture may paraphrase the history of his own house.

Our thanks go first to Sir Nikolaus Pevsner, for the guidance that he has generously given us over many years. Paul Joyce kindly read the list of architects and made countless improvements. David Lloyd contributed much useful information. The Scottish regional entries are largely due to David M. Walker and John Gifford. For Ireland our thanks go to Hugh Dixon, F. O'Dwyer and E. McParland. Chris Wakeling helped substantially with Nonconformist churches. Gordon Barnes provided photographs and useful suggestions. There are many more: the Librarian of the RIBA, the City Librarians of Dundee and Aberdeen, Sarah Brindley, Dr S. Cherry, Prof. R. A. Church, Mary Coote, Dr J. M. Crook, Dr C. Cunningham, Dr Andor Gomme, Dr T. Gourvish, Roderick Gradidge, Dr A. Grieve, Richard Haslam, Peter Howell, Edward Hubbard, Dr Derek Linstrum, Dr Priscilla Metcalf, George McHardy, Rory O'Donnell, Willy Payne, Alex Potts, Andrew Saint, Gavin Stamp, Robert Thorne, Ian Toplis, Clive Wainwright, Dr R. G. Wilson and, of course, our students. The staff at Thames and Hudson have been unfailingly helpful and the book owes much to them. Thanks must go to our typists A. Currie and A. Hosier and Janice Malleson. Finally we owe gratitude to our wives for their support and encouragement.   R.D. and S.M.

Introduction

The Britain of Queen Victoria

VICTORIAN ARCHITECTURE is the reflection of unprecedented social, intellectual and technological change. Queen Victoria, who gave her name to the age, reigned for sixty-three years – a period which saw rapid developments in Britain's industrial wealth, political power, and social and artistic life. The Victorian age is in no sense self-contained. When Victoria came to the throne in 1837 the Industrial Revolution had been under way for seventy or eighty years. Five years earlier, the great Reform Bill had swept away the rotten boroughs which had been the symbols of aristocratic power and had introduced a wider franchise, admitting large numbers of the property-owning middle classes to the electorate. Britain was moving to the height of her industrial prosperity and had a rapidly expanding population, which in 1841 numbered $18\frac{1}{2}$ million and by the time of Victoria's death in 1901 was 37 million. The industrial North had risen to challenge the predominance of London, and could boast 'what Manchester thinks today, England thinks tomorrow'. Here was the spearhead of the movement to repeal the Corn Laws; the passing of the Act in 1846 was a symbolic victory for the middle classes at the expense of the land-owning aristocracy. Britain was reaching the zenith of her economic dominance: the beginning of her descent coincided with the agricultural depression of the 1870s, when cheap grain from the American Mid-West flooded into Europe. Soon her industrial production was overtaken, first by America and then by Germany. At the end of Queen Victoria's reign Britain seemed secure in her imperial glory – so magnificently displayed at the Queen's Diamond Jubilee – but relatively speaking her power was already in decline.

Britain had been the first country in the world to industrialize. By the early years of Victoria's reign, industry – freed from its dependence on water power by the steam engine – was becoming concentrated in cities. Birmingham, Manchester, Liverpool, Leeds and Halifax grew up in response to the needs of the iron industry, the cotton industry and the wool industry. Britain not only supplied herself with an increasing range of goods but exported her wares to Europe and America, Africa and Asia.

Improvements in transportation played an important part not only in the development of the Industrial Revolution but also in the subsequent social changes. In the eighteenth century, better roads and the new system of canals, engineered by men such as James Brindley and Thomas Telford, gradually spread across the country. More revolutionary were the railways, which by their speed, efficiency and cheapness were to transform the country completely. Travel, which had previously been the privilege of the rich, became part of the life of a much wider section of the community, including (in the late nineteenth century) the working classes. The railways acted as a unifying force in the country, ironing out regional differences and altering patterns of settlement; they facilitated the suburban development of London and other large cities. Building materials could be transported over long

2 Membership certificate of the Operative Bricklayers' Society, founded in 1848. The certificate,
first issued about 1861, shows gauge work,
bricklaying, brickmaking, and the triumph of
bricklaying in Antiquity (with the Tower of Babel)
and modern times (in London and Rome), all set in a
framework of ornamental polychrome brickwork.
At the bottom are bricklayers' tools.

distances: Welsh slate and cheap bricks began to appear in parts of the country where formerly only local building materials had been used.

The steam engine was perhaps the central invention. It provided power to pump out the mines, which produced the coal that heated the homes of millions and smelted the iron that was used for the new technology. As we shall see in Chapter 3, iron was exploited by engineers such as Telford, Isambard Kingdom Brunel and Sir William Fairbairn to build bridges for roads, canals and railways. It was used by architects to a limited extent for architectural details and for garden structures early in the century. The early railway stations showed what could be done with the material and Paxton's Crystal Palace of 1851 was the culmination of this early development of metal construction. But although it was widely used for structural purposes, its external expression was not accepted by the mainstream of architectural opinion. Steel gradually became available in large quantities following the development of Bessemer's conversion process in 1857, but it did not play an important part in the British construction industry until about the turn of the century. The internal iron frame for factories had been developed in Britain, but the system of steel-frame construction in which the walls are carried by the frame was developed in America, not Britain.

Those who benefited from the unprecedented wealth created by the Industrial Revolution were in the main the owners of capital. Among these were the aristocracy, who profited through the development of their land for coal mining, industry, docks and urban developments, and gained by their investments in new enterprises such as the railways. The middle-class proprietor could also do well, and so could the middle-class professional, who flourished with the increased need for more specialized services. But at the other end of the scale, although the standard of living of many of the working class improved, large numbers lived on incomes which provided them with only the bare necessities and sometimes not even that. The gap between the rich and poor remained great, and indeed tended to widen in the nineteenth century. The Duke of Sutherland, for instance, had four palatial homes – a town palace in London (now Lancaster House) and three other large houses in the country (Trentham [*12*], Cliveden and Dunrobin Castle [*18*]), while in the old centres of the industrial cities many lived in degrading overcrowded and filthy conditions.

The Victorian age can be seen as an age of individualism. Both Tories and Liberals were agreed on a minimal role for the State in the nation's affairs. It was widely believed that if the individual was allowed to follow his own interests, within the law of the land, then general good would result. Victorian Britain was not unconscious of the great division between rich and poor. Most people saw it as an evil, although the ways suggested to combat it were varied. Engels and Marx saw the overthrow of the capitalist system as the solution. Social reformers such as Lord Shaftesbury attempted to work within the existing system. Some saw religion as the answer and believed that by building churches and church schools in slum areas they would defuse a potentially revolutionary situation as well as save the souls of the poor. Most people were averse to official intervention, but eventually, in the name of public health and welfare, there was an extension in the role of local government and the State intervened after 1870 to provide universal elementary education.

The architectural profession

These economic and social developments had important effects on the practice of architecture. There was an enormous increase in public and commercial commissions: town halls, hospitals, museums, banks, hotels, etc. The largest jobs were often allocated by competition. Most of the prominent monuments of Victorian Britain were the products of this system – the Houses of Parliament [*147*], the Royal

Exchange [*135*], the Oxford Museum of Natural History [*149*], the Foreign Office [*152*, *153*], the Albert Memorial [*155*], the Law Courts [*163*, *164*], Manchester Town Hall [*156*] and the Glasgow School of Art [*250*]. Many a Victorian architect first made his name by success in this way. Although there were disadvantages in the system – often the winning design was never built – it did give young and unknown architects an opportunity to display their talents, and it gave wide publicity to new architectural designs.

Secondly, there was a vast increase in the scale of private commissions. The country houses of successful Victorians (whether self-made men or dukes) were palaces, as magnificent as royal residences had been in the past. Private commissions could also include churches, as we shall see, and these could be equally lavish. The great aristocratic patrons often had wide architectural interests and with a talented architect the results were memorable: the association of Lord Bute and William Burges (1827–81) which produced the marvels of Cardiff Castle and Castell Coch is a prime example of such a partnership [*27*, *28*]. Prince Albert had a personal interest in architecture and is credited with contributing to the design of both Osborne [*13*] and Balmoral Castle. The clergy also exercised considerable patronage: the Rev. Arthur Wagner of Brighton commissioned and financed some of the town's most distinguished Victorian churches. Laymen were also important patrons: Dr Robert Brett of Stoke Newington helped the careers of William Butterfield (1814–1900) and James Brooks (1825–1901) with his commissions for churches in the East End of London.

By the start of the Victorian period the architect had emerged as a recognizable professional designing and supervising the erection of buildings. He came to rely on a separate quantity surveyor to supply him with accurate figures on which the builder could base his tender for the work. The architect relied for his remuneration on fees based on the value of work done. It became professionally less acceptable for him to dabble in speculative building or in contracting to supply materials for building, as had Adam and Chambers in the eighteenth century and Nash in the early nineteenth century. The speculative builder took over one function, the civil engineer another. These changes in the profession were marked by the foundation of the Institute of British Architects in 1834, which increasingly became the regulating body of the profession: in 1837 the Institute was dignified by a royal charter of incorporation, and became the Royal Institute of British Architects (RIBA). Another important, though less formal, institution was the Architectural Association, founded in 1847.

It was the individual private practice which was the backbone of the Victorian architectural profession. Most of the offices were small, consisting of one or two architects working with the help of a few assistants, pupils and a clerk. James Brooks by choice designed every detail himself. At the other end of the scale were large offices with numerous assistants, such as that of Sir George Gilbert Scott (1811–78). For many jobs Scott could only have had overall supervision, and many stories are told of his lack of knowledge at times as to which building he was in fact responsible for. The output of his office was enormous: during his career he was concerned with almost a thousand buildings, and at his death over sixty new buildings or alterations to old buildings were being undertaken by his office. The rewards of such professional success were also high: in his will Scott left £130,000.

A number of Late Victorian architects tried to dissociate themselves from this pattern. Rejecting the more professional and commercial concerns of architects, engineers and surveyors, they insisted on architecture as an 'art'. The discussion came to a head in 1892 when the RIBA tried to introduce stricter professional examinations. A number of architects and artists contributed to a volume entitled

Architecture, a Profession or an Art?, edited by Norman Shaw and T. G. Jackson. Some architects left the RIBA; some, such as Shaw, who was a Royal Academician, never joined.

A few of the most prominent architects should be introduced, for their names will recur frequently, as they designed buildings of many different types and were influential on their contemporaries. Perhaps the most successful and characteristic figure of the Early Victorian period – that is from 1837 to about 1855 – was Sir Charles Barry (1795–1860). The son of a prosperous London stationer, he began his architectural education at the age of fifteen when he was articled to a firm of Lambeth surveyors. After travels which took him as far as Greece, Turkey and Egypt, he returned to start his own practice and designed a number of Gothic 'Commissioners' Churches' (see p. 193). In 1836 he won the competition for the new Houses of Parliament [*146–8*], which was to remain his major concern throughout his life. He also worked in the Greek, Italian Renaissance and Elizabethan styles, producing town houses, country houses [*12*, *18*], club houses, including the Reform Club [*65–7*], schools, and Halifax Town Hall. He was knighted in 1852.

Charles Robert Cockerell (1788–1863) represents the virtues of the older generation of Neo-Classical architects. He was the son of the architect S. P. Cockerell. After a period in the office of Sir Robert Smirke (1781–1867), he travelled in Italy, Greece and Asia Minor. Although his practice was not as large as Barry's, he built many public buildings including the Ashmolean Museum in Oxford [*134*], country houses, churches, commercial offices and banks [*117*], succeeding Sir John Soane as the architect of the Bank of England. He was a respected member of his profession and was awarded the first Royal Gold Medal of the RIBA in 1848.

Augustus Welby Northmore Pugin (1812–52), on the other hand, represents the new, intensified fervour for Gothic. His father, A. C. Pugin (1762–1832), an assistant to John Nash (1752–1818), produced a number of publications on Gothic architecture helped by his son, and the young man's knowledge of Gothic was such that Barry used him to design decorative details for the Houses of Parliament [*133*]. A convert to Roman Catholicism, Pugin chiefly designed churches for his fellow Catholics [*180–84*], but his commissions also included schools and country houses [*14, 15*]. His books, particularly *Contrasts* (1836) [*3*] and *The True Principles of Pointed or Christian Architecture* (1841) [*179*], did much to spread the enthusiasm for a revival of Gothic architecture. He worked with a manic intensity and burned himself out, dying, mad, at the age of forty.

Sir Joseph Paxton (1803–65), the designer of the Crystal Palace [*91*], was yet another type of Victorian architect. He began his career as a gardener's boy and rose to be the head gardener of the Duke of Devonshire. The large greenhouses which he designed for the Duke at Chatsworth in Derbyshire served as models for his building for the Great Exhibition of 1851 [*86, 91*]. He also designed many domestic buildings, including country houses [*20*], while continuing his practice as a landscape gardener and designer of public parks.

The Mid-Victorian decades, that is the twenty years from about 1855 to 1875, were dominated by Gothic Revival architects. Sir George Gilbert Scott, as we have seen, was most prolific. The son of a clergyman, he first worked in a number of offices, including those of the architect Henry Roberts (1803–76) and of the London builders Peto and Grissell. Then he set up on his own and was soon designing workhouses and numerous churches [*191*]. Ecclesiastical buildings and restoration work were to be the backbone of his practice, but he also designed buildings of such varied types as the Albert Memorial [*155*], the Foreign Office [*153*] and St Pancras Station Hotel [*71*].

Scott was prepared to produce Classical designs, as in the case of the Foreign Office, but for other leading architects of the

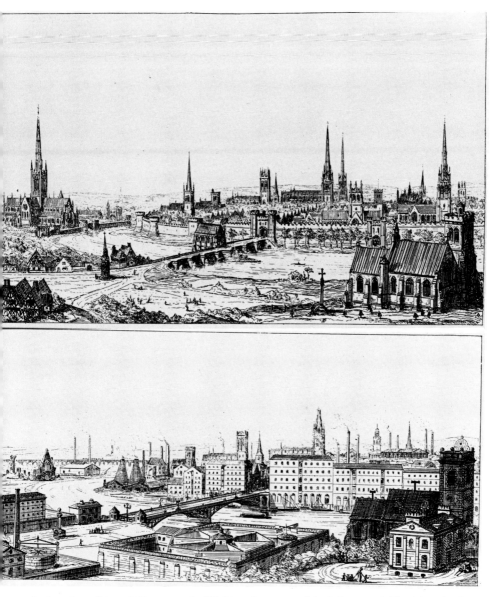

3 In the 1841 edition of Contrasts *A. W. N.* *Pugin shows the same imaginary town in the Middle Ages and at the dawn of the Victorian era. It has* *been ravaged by industry and Classicism; in the foreground now are a lunatic asylum, a gasworks and a prison on the radial plan.*

period, William Butterfield, George Edmund Street (1824–81) and William Burges, Gothic was the only true architectural language. Butterfield's practice consisted mostly of churches [*177, 195–8*], although it included attendant vicarages and schools [*234*], cottages [*57*], one country house, one hospital and a few colleges, such as Keble College, Oxford [*245*]. Street, who worked with Scott, was also essentially a church architect [*193, 194, 200–202*], although unlike Butterfield his career was concluded with a large public building, the Law Courts in London [*164–6*]. Burges built a number of important churches [*206, 207*] but was more involved with domestic architecture: his work for Lord Bute [*27, 28*] and his own house in Kensington show his deep and original study of Gothic.

Alfred Waterhouse (1830–1905), who links the Mid- and Late Victorian generations of architects, was immensely prolific. He was born in Liverpool and began his practice in Manchester, where his Gothic designs won the competitions for the Assize Courts and the Town Hall [*156–9*]. His skill as a planner and his reliability in executing designs led to a flood of commissions for work of a varied character, including public buildings [*170*], churches, schools [*241*], country houses [*25*] and insurance offices. His stylistic variety was great and ranged from Romanesque through Venetian Gothic to French Renaissance. For many of his buildings, such as the Natural History Museum in London [*169*] and the numerous offices he built for the Prudential Assurance Company, he used terracotta. He was a man of great charm, and like Scott he left a fortune and founded a dynasty of architects.

Richard Norman Shaw (1831–1912) represents the more advanced architects of the Late Victorian period, which may be regarded as starting about 1875 and lasting to the end of the reign in 1901. Born in Edinburgh, he was articled to the country-house architect William Burn (1789–1870). In 1859, after a period of foreign travel, which resulted in his delightful *Architectural Sketches from the Continent* (1858), he joined the office of Street as his principal assistant, replacing Philip Webb (1831–1915), who was just starting out on his own. Four years later Shaw began his own practice, sharing an office with William Eden Nesfield (1835–88). Together they evolved a style of architecture based on English vernacular buildings which Shaw was to use for his numerous town and country houses [*40, 51*]. He also designed Gothic churches, and was associated with Bedford Park, a speculative housing development in London [*54*]. His later career was marked by a number of public commissions, including his most famous work, Scotland Yard in London [*174*].

Pupilage was the usual form of architectural education. There were few architectural schools and the majority of Victorian architects learned their skills in another architect's office. A successful architect would attract talented pupils, and there was a certain continuity – a leading office of one generation producing the foremost designers of the next. Among the pupils of Scott were William White (1825–1900), George Frederick Bodley (1827–1907), Sir Thomas Graham Jackson (1835–1924) and Street. Street's pupils, in turn, included Philip Webb, William Morris (1834–96), the designer, and Norman Shaw. Shaw's office was to nurture many of the leaders of the time around 1900, such as Ernest Newton (1856–1922) and W. R. Lethaby (1857–1931).

The building journals were the main agent of the spread of current architectural ideas. *The Builder*, founded in 1842 by Joseph Aloysius Hansom (1803–82), architect and inventor of the Hansom cab, flourished throughout the period, and was later edited by George Godwin (1815–88). It was soon challenged by *The Building News*, *The Architect*, *The British Architect* (a Northern publication), and at the end of the century by *The Architectural Review*. The popular *Illustrated London News* and *Punch* also reported on new architecture.

Builders, building materials, and services

Among the factors that shaped Victorian architecture, the more conventional methods of construction have not received the attention they deserve. Architects enjoyed a fairly high social status, but builders were much lower down the scale: building labourers and brickmakers counted among the poorest and most neglected of the working-class population. The building trade was one of the largest industries in the country, employing about six per cent of the total labour force. Most building firms were small, especially in the field of speculative housing, where some might erect only two to five houses in a year. But very large companies were being formed to build, for instance, docks and railways. Sir Samuel Morton Peto's firm is the best known. He also undertook the construction of prestigious works of architecture, such as the Houses of Parliament. Among housing speculators Thomas Cubitt (1788–1855) was the most successful: to him we owe parts of Belgravia and Pimlico in London, as well as areas of Brighton (see p. 59). In contrast to most other builders he established a permanent work force of over a thousand men, and by the middle of the century in his eleven acres of workshops in Pimlico he used a large amount of machinery. He popularized a new form of tendering, whereby one firm undertook an entire job: traditionally each craft or trade was contracted individually. In addition, competitive tendering was introduced, the client seeking the lowest tender, which led to much cut-throat competition. Gradually municipal building regulations ('bye-laws') were introduced, to ensure standards not only of health but also of quality of workmanship and materials. Later in the Victorian period, the system of comprehensive tendering was applied to individual houses and interiors as well: in the 1890s Trollopes undertook not only the building but all the interior fittings of the new Claridges Hotel in London.

Parallel to this was the growth of large firms of 'decorators', who saw to all aspects of interior decoration in one contract.

The crucial factor in the supply of building materials was the high cost of transport. Thus wherever possible local materials were used. To a large extent, the Victorians maintained the traditional pattern of British materials, from granite in Scotland to serpentine in Cornwall and knapped flint and brick of varying colour in areas without stone. Bricks were made as near as possible to the site. A large railway viaduct might be made of bricks from earth dug up in the cuttings. But, increasingly, builders made use of the canals and especially the new railways, which made the transportation of building materials easier and cheaper. A further spur to the use of non-local materials was the High Victorian craze for varying colours and textures in a façade [*195*]. Finally, the brick tax was repealed in 1850. In London, St Pancras Station and Hotel [*72*] were built in the 1860s of Nottingham red brick, as part of the effort of the Midland Railway Company to promote goods from the Midlands in the South. Brickmaking was gradually mechanized, some machines moulding ten times as many bricks per hour as a man could. The Hoffmann kiln, of Austrian origin, was introduced in the 1850s and used heat more economically. The brick industry in the neighbourhood of Peterborough began to grow rapidly around 1880; the making of ten million Flettons for Westminster Cathedral [*222*], begun in 1895, was one of its biggest *coups*. The price of bricks fell, sometimes due also to the lowering of wages. As a result, from the Late Victorian period onwards bricks appear in parts of the country where stone had previously been used for all purposes.

Other materials also became cheaper and more popular, especially stone for decoration and for gravestones. In many areas the price of Bath stone (with York stone, the most popular) fell by half during the Mid-Victorian years. Towards the end of the century, steam-powered cranes at the quarry and steam-powered saws in the mason's yard helped to speed production, though all the more detailed work continued to be done by hand. Welsh slates replaced tiles in large parts of the country. In carpentry and joinery steam-powered saws, introduced in the 1850s, also did much of the heavy work; and a little later, ready-made doors and windows began to be imported from North America and Scandinavia. Wooden decoration of façades, by bay windows and porticoes, remained popular where not prohibited by law (as a fire risk). Glass also became cheaper, and available in larger sheets. The taxes on glass and on windows were abolished in 1845 and 1851 respectively.

There were other cheap alternatives to stonework for façades. External stucco had been introduced in London in the later eighteenth century and was increasingly used to satisfy the Regency and Early Victorian taste for smooth, evenly-coloured house fronts [11], its cost amounting to about one quarter that of stone. Mid-Victorian fashions, however, as well as the fall in the price of stone, helped to phase out stucco very quickly after 1860. By that time another material for decoration had come into use – terracotta [168, 169]. It was not a new invention, but it was now used extensively and appreciated for its reddish or yellowish colouring. Great durability was claimed, and its price was kept at about that of the cheapest stone. Tiles increased enormously in popularity, whether for floors in hallways, churches and public buildings, or as a sanitary surface in kitchens and bathrooms. By 1840 Mintons had produced the first 'encaustic' tiles, using a cheap and durable method whereby coloured patterns were inlaid rather than painted on the surface. Finally, of course, there were the new industrial materials, to which we shall return in Chapter 3.

Sanitary improvements were almost universal. In a period of growing wealth and status-consciousness, order and cleanliness became synonymous with respectability. At the same time, the growing sciences of statistics and medicine (preventive as well as curative) influenced legislation, beginning with the Health of Towns Act of 1848. All classes were interested in the improvement of houses and the building of modern hospitals and baths, since infectious diseases such as cholera did not discriminate between rich and poor (Prince Albert himself died of typhoid in 1861). The new types of buildings for public health will also be discussed in Chapter 3.

Cleanliness at home depended first of all on a supply of clean water and an efficient drainage system. In the early nineteenth century some better residential districts already had a piped water supply, at least for some hours during the day, but it was only in the mid-1860s that Sir Joseph Bazalgette (1819–91) completed his system of sewage removal for the whole of London (see p. 116). The water-closet, although it had been invented in the sixteenth century, was very rare until the early nineteenth century. By about 1880 every new house had its own w.c. or earth closet. By 1880 also, plumbing had at last become able to cope with the odours involved, and w.c.s began to be fitted upstairs, on the bedroom level, even in smaller houses. A bathroom was usually installed there too. Only the smallest houses – which in the North, however, formed the majority – continued to have outdoor toilets until after 1900.

The other main concern of the Victorians in matters of sanitation was clean air. Many major public buildings boasted comprehensive combined heating and ventilating systems: both the Houses of Parliament and St George's Hall in Liverpool were built with advice from a heating engineer, Dr David Boswell Reid. Hospitals, and even prisons, were in the forefront from the 1840s onwards. Central heating was introduced in some country houses, though ordinary houses had to wait a long time for it. To ensure adequate light and ventilation in all houses, the byelaws specified minimum window sizes for

4 An illustration by James Fergusson showing how a plain structure (far left) may be given progressively more ornamentation and thus be fitted for different types of building – warehouses, plain and fancy (four bays), an office building or bank (two bays), and a monumental civic building (five bays). (Handbook of Architecture, 2nd ed., 1859)

each room, and air bricks where there were no windows.

Finally, passenger lifts, an American invention, found their way into England, first in the 1860s for clubs and hotels, and later for business premises as well. Electric lighting, by means of Swan and Edison lamps, was first used in 1880 at Cragside [*40, 41*], the country house built by Norman Shaw for the Newcastle engineer William Armstrong, and then at the Savoy Theatre, London, of 1881.

Architectural theories and styles

Matters of architectural style, form and theory will arise throughout this book when the buildings themselves are discussed. Here we might summarize them, and compare them to some extent with those of previous periods, in order to understand their origins and development.

First of all, the Victorian age, as we have seen, can be divided into three periods, Early, Mid and Late, each lasting about twenty years – from 1837 till *c.* 1855; from *c.* 1855 till *c.* 1875; and from *c.* 1875 until the beginning of this century. Another term frequently used is 'High Victorian', which also usually covers the middle decades, but denotes a specific style, High Victorian Gothic or High Victorian Eclecticism, to which we shall return.

Classical styles. The style which reigned supreme before the Victorian period was the Classical, which, by Late Georgian times, had become traditional for buildings large and small. Indeed, however much we will emphasize the stylistic varieties of the nineteenth century, quantitatively speaking the Classical – in one version or another – remained the most frequent choice in Western countries up to about the middle of the twentieth century. One of the most important elements in the doctrine of Classicism was what is called the hierarchy of decorum: it meant that the degree of stateliness and the amount of decoration should reflect the status of the client [*4*]. One of the most noticeable developments of nineteenth-century architecture – and this is true for all the revived styles, not only the Classical ones – is the tremendous increase in the richness of decoration. Not only in absolute terms, but also in relative terms: there were types of buildings which at the beginning of the century would have received only very modest decorative treatment, if any at all; now they display a wealth of decoration. This is most noticeable in domestic architecture, related to the growing wealth of the country, and in particular to the rapidly growing wealth of the middle classes. This hierarchical system was finally turned upside down, in that a tradesman's villa could show more architectural display than the municipal buildings of a small town. Much of the early twentieth-century agitation against Victorian architecture was concerned with the rejection of this elaboration of domestic architecture.

Classical forms had been re-introduced into Britain in the sixteenth century: for a whole range of reasons a style of a rather distant past was deliberately revived as the best and only choice, and prevailing Gothic modes were condemned as unsuitable and ugly. The Classical style was perhaps the most comprehensive and most systematic stylistic vocabulary ever evolved. It concerned itself with layout and elevation, as well as with detailed decoration. For the plan, it meant symmetry, simplicity and ordering all the parts into a well composed whole. All measurements should obey detailed laws of proportioning, which assured aesthetically satisfying results. The decorative detail was governed by the rigid system of the 'orders' – columns with their bases, capitals and architraves, of the Doric, Ionic, Corinthian and Composite varieties. Classicism came to stand for ideas of order and harmony in general, which were thought to be derived from nature, God and the universe.

In addition to the traditional Greek and Roman varieties, we have to consider a number of other later stylistic labels, such as Palladianism and Neo-Classicism, which were chiefly meant to be re-juvenations, trying to find a way through the contemporary confusion and practice of the style. Many people remained convinced that the general laws of Classical architecture should form the basis of any style, and that whatever the incidental stylistic varieties, fundamentally architecture cannot change.

By the early decades of the nineteenth century a grandiose Neo-Classicism based on the revival of Greek as well as Roman architecture had firmly established itself throughout Europe. At the same time there was a new and growing demand for large public buildings, such as museums and exchanges and especially town halls of all sizes. Such buildings preferably occupy dominant positions, are placed on high pedestals and display porticoes and grand colonnades [*138, 140, 143*]. Within Neo-Classicism there are numerous varieties. C. R. Cockerell, and many Scottish architects, on the whole adhered to Classical Antiquity. As a scholar, archaeologist and academic, Cockerell fiercely defended the validity of Classical Antiquity when he saw it so frequently attacked in the Mid-Victorian decades.

More frequent, however, since the 1830s, was a new Classicism, which had a less orthodox outlook and included features of the Italian Renaissance or the French Renaissance. Sir Charles Barry adopted the sixteenth-century Italian *palazzo* as the model for smaller buildings, such as club houses [*65*] and offices (see p. 127). It seemed to solve a problem of which the Neo-Classicist had been conscious for some time, namely how to adapt Classical forms of decoration to an ordinary street façade. Barry also liked picturesque vertical accents on the tops of buildings, such as corner pinnacles or chimneys. From the 1850s onwards this device found its way into the composition of many buildings: Cuthbert Brodrick (1822–1905) uses clock towers, turrets, and domes reminiscent of French Renaissance or seventeenth-century architecture [*70*]. The resulting style was sometimes called 'Second Empire', a reference to Napoleon III's exten-

5 Edinburgh about 1890: in the foreground are the Royal Scottish Institution and National Gallery of Scotland by W. H. Playfair, of 1832–5 and 1850–54 respectively (see p. 145), and beyond them is the Gothic memorial to Sir Walter Scott by G. Meikle Kemp, of 1840–44 (see p. 164).

sions of the Louvre in Paris. In addition there are the various forms of English Renaissance which were infused into the general Classical trend, but on the whole these tend to be medievalizing and will be mentioned later. In the 1870s a new version of Classical Revival was adopted, the so-called 'Queen Anne' Revival [10], which had a whole set of new implications (see p. 65). Finally, in the last decade of the nineteenth century and in the Edwardian age Classical architecture was again purified, with a return to basic composition and a reduction in the variety of decoration.

Stylistic variety. The crucial question of the nineteenth century – as has so often been said – is how it became possible for several styles to be used concurrently, and so to speak to have equal rights. To a far greater extent than in other periods different forms of plan and elevation as well as different forms of external decoration were chosen for the same type of building, and were even proposed for the same building (see pp. 161–2). 'Revivalism' is perhaps the best term for this phenomenon.

To begin with, one has to bear in mind that even in traditional Renaissance architecture there are elements of stylistic variety. Very often the different orders were used for different types of buildings: the more heavy Doric would be likely to be used for a prison, or law courts, whereas for a ballroom the lighter and more ornate Corinthian seemed more suitable. These almost common-sense variations of architectural expression apply in a general sense to much of Victorian architecture – as indeed to any period of architecture.

The crucial change came in the eighteenth century. It cannot be explained without looking beyond architectural theory, to a fundamental change in the outlook of historians and of political and social theorists. Traditionally, historians fitted their knowledge of ancient and distant civilizations into a firm, general pattern of world evolution, where each civilization was assigned its place according to how primitive or advanced it appeared. But with the growing enlightenment and liberalism, writers began to stress that each civilization should be judged on its own merits by its own criteria. This was an incentive to search for differences of thought, of manners and of architectural styles. Whereas throughout the Renaissance only monuments of Classical Antiquity seemed worth studying, from the middle of the eighteenth century onwards scholars as well as art-lovers have taken delight in the very variety of forms surviving from the past. Many movements arose, advocating the imitation of one or the other of the newly discovered or revalued civilizations. Winckelmann fought for the Greeks and declared all later Classical styles aberrations; some of the English antiquarians and later the German Romantics began to advocate medieval civilization as the model for the nineteenth century; even China was thought to offer a solution. Rousseau wanted to go back to a period before any civilization had corrupted mankind. Many historicist or revivalist movements have remained influential to the present day. What is important is that the notion of Classical authority or indeed any authority was severely challenged.

There was another important new element in this development of architectural relativism, or breakdown of strict rules: the aesthetic of the Picturesque and the Sublime. Eighteenth-century British philosophers played an important part in the development of a consciousness of our reactions to a work of art, of our perceptions. It was no longer a question of deciding whether a work obeyed established rules. Traditionally, pleasure and satisfaction were to be derived from the correct application of the rules of beauty. But now there were also the elements of variety and surprise. Traditionally again, anything which did not fit the rigid laws of beauty, such as Gothic, was considered

ugly and worthless. Now, irregularity and the unexpected were appreciated in their own right, first in nature and soon in architecture as well. This appreciation and the style of designing that went with it were called 'Picturesque'. The 'Sublime' was related, but here the effects were stronger – not only surprise, but even awe and terror, evoked mostly by exaggerated size or darkness.

The eighteenth century, in its search for 'truth' and primeval qualities, soon linked the Picturesque and the Sublime with the notion of uncorrupted nature, before it was regularized by civilization. This was the spirit in which the landscape garden and its ornamental structures in many styles were conceived, in which Horace Walpole built Strawberry Hill and in which Boullée and his colleagues in late eighteenth-century Paris drew their megalomaniac projects. All these elements permeate Victorian architecture and architectural writing: Jesse Hartley's Liverpool harbour buildings have a Sublime quality (see p. 124), and John Ruskin's 'Lamp of Power' in his *Seven Lamps of Architecture* (1849) reads in part like Burke's *Sublime and Beautiful* of nearly a century earlier. Not one of these categories could be held up as the only valid mode of design: several fundamentally different modes, each corresponding to a different mood, now ran concurrently. And not only were they tolerated: their variety was itself a positive source of delight. As a result we witness a growing speed of change, as nineteenth-century styles follow each other with greater and greater rapidity. At first taste shifted from the Beautiful and Sublime to the Picturesque and back again to the Sublime. Hence the simplicity of Neo-Classical buildings after the exuberance of the Baroque. From the second decade of the nineteenth century onwards the Picturesque gained momentum, and the purer type of Neo-Classical building was increasingly considered stiff and tedious. Now there were attempts to vary, to liven up, to add contrasts of light and shade to Classical façades and to vary the plan and outline of a building to the point of complete irregularity, if necessary by adopting Renaissance or even Gothic forms. Leaving aside the more restricted counter-movements towards massiveness and simple outline, such as the High Victorian Gothic of the 1850s and 60s, the Picturesque reached its peak in the 1880s and early 1890s, when symmetry, and the restriction of decorative forms to any one style, were very unpopular [9]. Again, the Edwardian reaction and much of twentieth-century architecture must be seen as a swing back towards symmetry.

Neo-Gothic and Romanticism. Gothic soon emerged as the most powerful alternative to the Classical styles. Many of the early reasons for reviving it have already been mentioned. The respect for important historical buildings in the Gothic style always existed (see, for example, Christopher Wren and his followers' additions to Westminster Abbey). The antiquarians were concerned with the extant heritage of the Middle Ages in their own country. For Horace Walpole there was the titillation of imagined terror and fantasy and the picturesqueness of Gothic. Houses, especially those which had to be related to landscape gardens, and that means most larger country houses, were built in various versions of Gothic, often mixed and impossible to equate with medieval precedent. Occasionally, for instance in the very influential writings of the great Regency garden designers J. C. Loudon (1783–1843) and Humphry Repton (1752–1818), it was stressed that for houses the Gothic style had practical advantages and was altogether a more natural choice.

Most importantly, Gothic was thought to be a peculiarly national style. Since the late eighteenth century many Western countries had begun to stress not only their political but also their cultural identity. In the competition for the Houses of Parliament both Gothic and Elizabethan were specified as 'national' styles, and the forms of Barry's winning design were taken mainly from Perpendicular Gothic [146],

to harmonize with Westminster Hall and the Henry VII Chapel of Westminster Abbey. The issue of Gothic as a national style is one of the most confusing matters of the nineteenth century. Early in the century many major European countries maintained that they had 'invented' Gothic, and it was not until the middle of the century that they realized this could only be said of France.

In addition there was the idea that Gothic art and architecture were the expression of the Church, not the Church as it had been secularized in the eighteenth century, but the 'true' faith, with all its emotional appeal and its outward splendour of liturgy and mysterious buildings. The yearning for the picturesqueness of chivalry, the grandeur of national superiority, the mysteriousness of the medieval church, are elements of what is loosely called 'Romanticism'. Essentially it is the search for something which did not seem obtainable in the modern world of the nineteenth century.

With the relentless popularization and specialization in architectural history, for instance through the illustrated works of the indefatigable John Britton (1771–1857), architects and critics began to ask which particular variety of Gothic should be used. Thomas Rickman (1776–1841), in his *Attempt to Discriminate the Styles in English Architecture* (1819), had established periods and terms for Gothic architecture that are still used today: Early English, Decorated and Perpendicular. The most widely used version in the early phase of the Gothic Revival was Perpendicular. The reasons for this choice are complicated, but the most important is probably that with its grid-like surface pattern it could easily be used to cover buildings whose massing was basically Classical. Another reason is that many nationally important buildings, such as St George's Chapel at Windsor, were in the Perpendicular style. Pugin's designs, and those of the earlier churches sponsored by the Ecclesiological Society, usually adhered to 'English Middle Pointed', another name for Decorated – the style of the late thirteenth century, with bar tracery in the windows [*177*, *182–4*]. We shall look at this choice in more detail in our discussion of churches (see Chapter 6).

However, these young and enthusiastic designers did not content themselves with the view that Gothic was primarily suited for churches, national monuments and picturesque houses. They claimed the universal validity of their style for any type of building. Pugin and many of his followers, like Scott and Street (see p. 203), influenced by the French Rationalist architects and critics of the eighteenth and early nineteenth centuries, re-examined the fundamentals of architecture, as opposed to its accidental external forms. These fundamentals were no longer proportion and symmetry, but rationalism and structural expression. Pugin in his *True Principles* talks about the 'honest expression' of construction [*179*]. Good buildings, he thought, were the products of structural concern – ingenious constructions of stone vaults or wooden roofs supported by thin stone framework with large traceried windows. Decoration in these buildings was subservient to construction. With his intense moral fervour, Pugin declared that all Classical architecture was 'false'. Pugin was as keen a supporter of the Picturesque as any earlier Gothicist. But for him it was not just a fanciful alternative, but something based on reason and practicality. A building was irregular because functions demanded it. A variety of functions could never be squeezed into a symmetrical frame.

In spite of the keen search for fundamentals, the outward architectural vocabulary changed more and more rapidly. A Gothicist designing in 1855 would tend to reject what he had designed in 1840; in 1870 he would reject both earlier modes; and after 1900 the fashion had changed again. Perhaps it was precisely because of this rapid change that the search for fundamentals was so intense.

The new elements of the High Victorian Gothic of the 1850s and 1860s were brought in by those who admired the medieval architecture of Northern Italy, France and other Continental countries. John Ruskin (1819–1900), the inveterate traveller, sketcher and brilliantly persuasive writer, drew attention, especially in *The Seven Lamps of Architecture* (1849) and *The Stones of Venice* (1851–3), to the Gothic buildings of Verona and Venice. Pugin's demand that building materials not be concealed was turned into something more positive – a new delight in the different textures of materials and, especially, in their colours [6]. (We shall return to Ruskin's ideas in our discussion of churches, pp. 201–3.) Polychromy, inside buildings as well as outside, became the main concern of the more advanced architects. Most important, colour was achieved not only by applying paint, but by combining different building materials. This device, known as 'constructional polychromy' or 'permanent polychromy' [*195*], has only faint parallels outside Britain, and has become, perhaps rightly, a kind of trademark of 'Victorian' architecture as distinct from the style of this or that revival.

The story of colour in architecture in the Victorian period would merit a separate study. At the beginning lay the discovery by some Neo-Classicists – Cockerell amongst them – that many Greek temples were originally painted in bright colours. Later researchers seized upon the coloured decorations of Byzantine churches and Arab buildings. Owen Jones (1806–89), architect, designer and teacher of applied arts at the South Kensington School of Design, was involved in the latter discoveries. Colour was soon demanded for the outside of buildings, but the British climate did not favour painted decoration: the use of varied building materials, as advocated by Ruskin, seemed a satisfactory solution. A further characteristic of High Victorian polychromy is its adherence to flat patterns and simple forms, expressing the two-dimensionality of walls or floors [*177*]. Here again, Pugin, Ruskin, Street and Jones spoke the same language. The lower forms of Victorian architecture, such as the smaller house, were particularly affected by these doctrines, not least because flat patterns are an economical mode of decoration. Many of the more sophisticated church architects, however, turned away from exuberant polychromy in the 1860s, and many of the younger Gothicists defected to something different, yet related, the 'Queen Anne' Revival.

In the early 1860s interest focused on the simplicity of early French Gothic. The leader in this movement was William Burges [*207*], followed by John Loughborough Pearson (1817–97) and James Brooks. At the same time, some church architects were attempting to broaden out and to obtain commissions for public and even commercial buildings. Scott narrowly missed success with his High Victorian design for the Foreign Office [*152*], but had no trouble in getting his hugely expensive Midland Grand Hotel built for St Pancras Station [*72*]. Manchester Town Hall [*156*] by Waterhouse and the Law Courts in London [*163–6*], for which designs in styles other than Gothic were hardly considered, mark a dominance of Gothic Revival design which cannot be paralleled outside Britain.

In the late 1860s, many architects began to turn away from strict Gothic forms, especially in their domestic work, towards the 'Old English', Vernacular, and 'Queen Anne' manners, which will be described below. For churches, there was a revival of the quieter modes of English fourteenth- and fifteenth-century Gothic [*219*]. In general, the use of Gothic became more restricted, and shrank back to its early nineteenth-century range.

The search for a nineteenth-century style: Eclecticism. By the beginning of the Victorian period the coexistence of several styles was accepted. There were attempts to link certain styles with certain types of buildings, such as Gothic with churches (Chapter 6), or, less effectively, Classical with public buildings. But where there

6 John Ruskin in his Stones of Venice *(1851–3) illustrates the dullness of a monochrome, uniform Regency Classical stone surface compared with a medieval wall in northern Italy: the latter has colour that is inbuilt ('constructional polychromy') and an intriguing surface that is due to its age – hence Ruskin's hostility to restoration work.*

*7 A medieval Italian brick style used for a Bristol warehouse: the Granary, Welsh Back, by Ponton and Gough, 1871–3. (*Architect, *1873)*

23

was complete freedom of architectural expression, very soon the question arose: which is the best or most suitable style for this or that type of building, or for the architecture of the nineteenth century in general? One way of tackling the question was complete stylistic freedom and variety. At the other extreme was dogmatism, architects and critics arguing for one particular style, and supporters of different styles clashing violently. There had long been arguments between Gothicists and Classical designers. Heated arguments and pamphleteering arose especially over the designs for the Houses of Parliament. With the Gothicists' claim that their style had universal validity the argument became even more fierce. The most famous case is that of the Foreign Office, in which George Gilbert Scott defended his chosen Gothic style until he had to give way to Palmerston's demand for a Renaissance building (see pp. 161–2).

A further question arose: if each civilization had a style of its own, why was there no nineteenth-century style? Another important new notion of the eighteenth and nineteenth centuries, originality, also supported the demand for a distinctive style. Some critics argued that a new style could and should be 'invented'. Terms such as 'novelty', 'modern style' and even 'Victorian style' were used, mainly in the 1840s and 1850s, when the discussion was at its height. However, these attempts were not considered intellectually respectable by the major practitioners. The relatively little-known architect Thomas Harris (1830–1900), when he published *Victorian Architecture* in 1860, was soon put in his place by critics who pointed out that his architecture was merely a mixture of known revival features.

Eclecticism, a combination of different styles, did indeed seem the best way out of the problem. The method is almost as old as the Gothic Revival. Loudon, in his *Encyclopaedia* of 1833 (see p. 33), gives many varieties and grades between Classical formality and Gothic picturesque. The 'Jacobean' contains more of the former,

the 'Elizabethan' more of the latter. Barry preferred the 'Anglo-Italian' for some of his country houses, such as Highclere in Hampshire, and so did Paxton for Mentmore, Buckinghamshire, where a complicated but symmetrical plan is combined with a lively outline [20–22]. In the 1850s critics argued that the search for new styles was futile and that one had to begin from somewhere. Styles of the past should be studied, carefully combined, and adapted to the needs of the nineteenth century. Even the Gothicists looked at other styles: Scott and even Street played with Classical horizontality. Many of Ruskin's illustrations of architectural features are so simple and basic that a specific stylistic description would be difficult. Indeed, many architectural features were now described as geometrical or massive rather than Gothic or Italian. We can call the result High Victorian Eclecticism.

In general, after about 1860 until the turn of the century, most architects felt free to choose, and to vary their choice and combination of styles from building to building [8]. English sixteenth-century, Italian, French, Dutch and German Renaissance features are mixed with Gothic slenderness and verticality in many of the works of J. J. Stevenson (1831–1908), T. E. Collcutt (1840–1924) [82] and H. T. Hare (1860–1921), and also in some of the designs of Waterhouse and Shaw. A legacy of the Gothic Revival was their interest in exploiting the qualities of different materials: there is an abounding variety and contrast between brick, stone, terracotta, half-timbered work, slates and tiles. Holloway College, Surrey, built in 1879–87 by W. H. Crossland (1823–1909), is one of the most exuberant examples of these exuberant styles [249]. Not surprisingly, these festive modes proved ideal for pubs and music halls.

About 1890 a reaction against the picturesque set in. The more vigorous columns and cornices of English and Continental Baroque provided new models, reflected for instance in the Institute of Chartered Accountants in Lon-

8 Unexecuted design for the Anglican Cathedral at Liverpool by James M. Hay, 1886, combining most known architectural styles: a Byzantine dome vies with Gothic spires, flèches and traceried windows, a Baroque cupola (in front of the dome), and a Neo-Classical body designed to harmonize with St George's Hall, behind (see ill. 140). In the left background is the William Brown Library and Museum by Thomas Allom, of 1857. (Builder, 1886)

don of 1888–93 by John Belcher (1841–1913), or his Colchester Town Hall of 1898–1902 [176]. Like most others, Belcher was soon to turn to the more sober Classical modes.

The Vernacular and 'Queen Anne' Revivals and after. The turn towards the Picturesque and towards 'uncorrupted' nature produced another stylistic variety: the imita-

tion of the primitive rural cottage. The cottages of Nash's Blaise Hamlet near Bristol of 1811, with their purposely rough walls and thatched roofs, are memorable early examples of this genre. Soon there was the 'Swiss cottage', and the 'Scottish Baronial' made use of the same ideas on a grander scale. Simple vernacular building with Gothic overtones was practised by the Ecclesiological architects for their rural parsonages, schools and cottages [57, 234]. A further elaboration of this mode developed in the 1860s, when the 'Old English' style, meaning the imitation of Tudor manor houses with plenty of half-timbering, was used for fairly large country houses [40].

For architects like Philip Webb and George Devey (1820–86) the Vernacular was not just a stylistic alternative to Gothic or Classical, but a complete way of

25

9 J. D. Sedding's Industrial Schools at Knowle, Bristol – the Vernacular Revival at its most picturesque and, like all Sedding's work, highly sensitive to craft traditions. This design of 1890 was only partly executed. (Builder, *1890*)

designing [*36–9*]. They devoted their energies to a small number of buildings, and took special care that each was based on the building customs of the region in which it was built. They were not drawn by the more mundane commissions in cities, and they eschewed publicity, working for a small circle of like-minded patrons, mostly intellectual and artistic, sometimes aristocratic. Webb's most famous client was William Morris [*33–5*]: the two had been friends since their days in Street's office at Oxford, and their interests were shared by some of the Pre-Raphaelite painters. In their emphasis on regionalism, the Vernacular Revival architects were concerned less with formal

variations than with local traditions of building and local materials. W. R. Lethaby called Webb's architecture the 'art of building': it was the art of the local builder, who loved his craft and was not bothered about textbook styles. Most of these architects in the 1880s and 1890s were closely associated with the Arts and Crafts organizations, and their architecture can rightly, though unofficially, be called 'Arts and Crafts architecture' [*9*].

All the major protagonists of the 'Queen Anne' Revival came from the Gothic camp. Although they rejected many Gothic motifs, they continued to insist on 'truth to material': the most essential element of the 'Queen Anne' Revival is the colour of the red brick walls, and its contrast with the other parts of the façade, the wooden window frames and the wooden cornice, painted white. The difference from Neo-Gothic lay not only in the choice of a different historical style, but in the choice of models which were not grand architecture: precedents were provided by the way in which more modest seventeenth- and eighteenth-century builders in England and the Low Countries interpreted the Classical styles. The name 'Queen Anne' was a convenient shorthand, but the movement ranged much farther than the architecture of her reign (1702–14). It is a Classical style without Classical laws of proportion. The most crucial change compared with all previous revivals is that decorative features need have no 'meaning', as J. J. Stevenson, one of the leading architects of the movement [10], affirmed in a lecture of 1874: their function is no longer to express essential elements of the construction, as the Classical and Gothic Rationalists believed, but purely and unashamedly to be ornamental. In the design of domestic buildings, the stress was on 'homeliness' and a greater degree of simplicity, equally suitable for the cottage and the large country house. The leaders were again Philip Webb, Eden Nesfield and Norman Shaw. Their houses will be discussed in Chapter 1; though one of the first major publicized examples of the Revival was Shaw's New Zealand Chambers (1871–3†), an office building in the City of London [129].

Related to the 'Queen Anne' Revival is the Aesthetic Movement, associated with the painter James McNeill Whistler, with Oscar Wilde, with Gilbert and Sullivan, and with the idea of 'Art for Art's Sake', which had important effects on interior design. Its chief exponent, E. W. Godwin (1833–86), who designed a white, asymmetrical house for Whistler [52], held that simplicity, health, practicality and beauty are one and the same. A Gothicist by upbringing, he also worked in the 'Queen Anne' manner, and another major influence behind the simplicity and delicate colours of his interiors was the art and the thin and simple furniture of Japan.

Many of these tendencies survived in Britain almost up to the Second World War. Churches were still designed in English Gothic, powerful yet delicate in their details: one need only think of the Anglican Cathedral at Liverpool, begun shortly after 1900 by Giles Gilbert Scott (1880–1960), Sir Gilbert Scott's grandson. The Vernacular Revival, the respect for the humble old barn with its crumbling walls and mellow colours, is still very important today.

One more major turn in style and aesthetics took place around 1900, as we have seen – the return to the 'Grand Manner', with symmetrical, formal compositions. The chief influence here was the teaching and writings of Richard Phené Spiers (1838–1916), who had studied at the Ecole des Beaux-Arts in Paris and taught at the Royal Academy from 1870 onwards. The new movement aimed at crushing the stylistic varieties of Eclecticism. However, the arguments of the Neo-Neo-Classicists and the Vernacular Revivalists had many things in common: Classical was thought to be suitable because it was the most *traditional* language of architecture. All the major architects of the early twentieth century in Britain liked to call themselves 'traditionalists', and meant this to be distinct from the 'revivalist' attitudes of the nineteenth century. Classical and Vernacular architects, as well as nationalists, met ultimately in the revival of Georgian styles for houses.

Building types and styles. The main part of this book is arranged according to building types, in order to focus on the history of planning and patronage, but stylistic elements will continue to be discussed. The reader might ask: what is the relationship between the history of types and the history of stylistic revivals? There is no simple answer. Clearly, there were many buildings, even highly decorated ones, where practical problems remained paramount and the questions of style seldom aroused much debate, such as hotels and hospitals. But for many others, like country houses and large public buildings, the choice of style was as important as, and often intimately connected with, the process of planning. Thus the story of some types will be concerned mainly with the history of planning and construction, while for others it will be dominated by the whims of patrons and the changing fashions of style; and the section on churches will largely be a chapter in the history of the Gothic Revival.

British influence abroad

One might finally look at the position of nineteenth-century British architecture vis-à-vis that of other countries. As in politics and economics, Britain was relatively self-sufficient, more so than ever before or after. The Picturesque was largely an English invention, and it influenced the Continent strongly even before 1800. Neo-Classicism was very much an affair of a small set of international scholars, in which Britain had a large share. The same is true of the later permutations of the Classical, the many Renaissance revivals. It is often difficult to say which country came first. The English seemed to have looked to France in the 1850s when Napoleon III promoted his 'Second Empire' mode. The Neo-Goths in the 1830s read the treatises of the German and French Catholic Revivalists, just as the Pre-Raphaelites looked at the Nazarenes – but by the mid 1840s Scott obtained the prestigious commission of the Nikolai-kirche in Hamburg, simply because, as his German supporters claimed, he 'understood' Gothic so much better than any of his German competitors. Pugin's books were avidly read by Rhenish, Dutch, Belgian and even French Gothicists. The English in turn admired Eugène Viollet-le-Duc (1814–79), the French arch-Gothicist, for his archaeological expertise, though they thought little of his designs and his restorations of French cathedrals. In the later part of the century, with rapidly growing nationalism, and tech-

nological advances which made it unnecessary for the Continentals to look to England for advice, architectural exchanges were less frequent. Most educated Englishmen travelled, and even left traces of their architecture in many Continental cities, in the form of churches for the English-speaking communities, such as Street's churches in Rome, not to speak of the many Victorian cities throughout the Empire: one of the most splendid of all railway stations is that of Bombay, designed in 1878 by F. W. Stevens. But they found little to interest them in the contemporary architectural production of other countries.

The relationship with the United States was different. Until the 1870s America had been dependent on Europe for architectural styles and talents. But then the East Coast had its own Vernacular Revival, of which some elements, such as the open domestic plan, were taken very seriously by C. F. A. Voysey (1857–1941) [43] and M. H. Baillie Scott (1865–1945). The influence of the Boston architect H. H. Richardson (1838–86), himself deeply indebted to High Victorianism, can be felt in the work of Harrison Townsend (1851–1928) [175] and others. It was not until the very late 1880s and the 1890s that architects in Europe realized what had escaped them about the new English and American development, and tried to catch up. The 'Queen Anne' and Vernacular Revivals, the informality and practicality of English domestic planning, and the Arts and Crafts movement all made a deep impression, and we may conclude with a remark from the first major German book entitled *Das englische Haus* (by Robert Dohme, 1888): 'The historian cannot evade the conclusion that the English way of designing means an advance in civilization.'

10 The 'Queen Anne' style at its beginnings: the Red House, Bayswater Road, London, by J. J. Stevenson, 1871 (see p. 65). (Building News, 1874)

The · Red · House · Nº 3 Bayswater Hill ⊛ John J: Stevenson Architect

1
Domestic Architecture

VICTORIAN domestic architecture is not only more extensive in quantity than that of any previous period, it is also more varied in character. The greater quantity can be accounted for in part by the increased population, but this does not fully explain the variety of Victorian homes.

The social structure of Victorian Britain has few more pertinent memorials than its domestic architecture. Here one can see clearly expressed the hierarchy of society, with the landed aristocracy at the top and the poor at the bottom. For those in between, the key to upward movement was money. The house not only reflected the social position of its occupant: it could also suggest the social position to which he aspired. The simpler houses show architectural features copied from the houses of the social class immediately above, and a feature can thus be traced as it makes its way down the social scale in a generation or two from ducal country house to artisan's cottage. It is thus appropriate to look first at Victorian domestic architecture at the top of the social scale, for it is here that many architectural features originated.

The country house: planning and styles

In Early Victorian Britain the landed aristocracy still retained their pre-eminent social position. The country house was the most important architectural symbol of this pre-eminence. For the newly-monied, or the political adventurer, possession of a country house was the first step towards the high peaks of society. Although the *nouveau riche* businessman could seldom hope to receive full acceptance for himself, he could hope for an aristocratic marriage for his daughter or to establish his son in the landed gentry, with the possibility of a peerage for his grandson. The grandfather of Sir Robert Peel, the Prime Minister, was a yeoman farmer. The Prime Minister's father, Sir Robert Peel the elder, laid the foundations of the family's prosperity with profits made in the cloth industry, and about 1830 built a country house, Drayton Manor in Staffordshire, which was designed for him by Sir Robert Smirke, the architect of the British Museum. Gladstone's father made his fortune out of the slave trade, which provided his son, the Prime Minister, with funds to maintain his own country house, Hawarden Castle, Flintshire, which had been remodelled in the castellated style in 1809–10 by Thomas Cundy I (1765–1825). Disraeli felt that a country house and estate were necessary adjuncts to his ambition for leadership of the Tory party, and with the help of his rich wife and some aristocratic friends he purchased the Hughenden Manor estate in Buckinghamshire in 1848, and had the stuccoed house modernized with an elaborate brick façade by E. B. Lamb (1806–69) in 1863–6.

11 Speculative housing in West London. At the top is the Early Victorian Ladbroke Estate, with its crescents and spacious Ladbroke Square (below the right-hand crescent; see p. 58). The houses are Classical, the church Gothic. At the bottom left are tightly-packed detached houses on the Holland Park Estate, 1860–79 (see p. 61).

Thus although the Victorian nobleman and gentleman were concerned in the main to live as comfortably as possible, their country house was more than just a dwelling. The human frame can be fed and housed satisfactorily in far less imposing surroundings. The size was necessitated by social position and social ambition, and it was important that the symbolism of the architecture should be correct. However, great thought was given to functional considerations.

The large country house was a complex organism. It not only housed the owner and his family but had to be equipped to transact business and to entertain numerous guests. To serve the family and guests there would be a large number of servants, each with his or her carefully defined function and place in the hierarchy of the household. The Duke of Westminster had some fifty indoor servants at Eaton Hall in Cheshire [25]. Guests would bring their own personal servants, and the great country house might contain over a hundred people when there was a large house party.

Victorian standards of propriety required that the complex activities of the house should be separated [17, 21]: the family were able to live apart from the guests, except at set times when they met in the formal reception rooms of the house. People visiting on business had to be segregated from the family and from guests. Servants had their own quarters, and upper and lower servants had different rooms for eating. For the family and the guests, there might be a drawing room, dining room, library, morning room, breakfast room, smoking room, billiard room and chapel. The servants' quarters would include the kitchen, scullery, larder, pantry, coal store, bakehouse and servants' hall. A business room and a gun room might complete the ground floor. The first floor was taken up with bedrooms, approached by a grand staircase for the family and guests, and by back stairs for the servants. The sleeping quarters of men servants were carefully segregated from

those of the maids and in some houses there were separate staircases to avoid them coming into contact. Even guests were divided in the same way, with bedrooms for bachelors being placed in their own part of the house away from those of the unmarried ladies. The importance that the Victorian country-house owner gave to these practical considerations is indicated by the large space devoted to them in books such as *The Gentleman's House; or how to Plan English Residences, from the Parsonage to the Palace*, which was first published in 1864 by the country-house architect Robert Kerr (1823–1904) [21].

The rising standards of comfort throughout the period led to an elaboration of the services. Cold water, and frequently hot water, would be piped all over the house. Open coal fires were the usual means of heating, although systems of central heating, using either hot air or piped hot water for the principal rooms, became increasingly popular. One advantage of open fires was that they assisted the ventilation of gas-lit rooms. Gas lighting was used as early as 1787 and had been installed by Sir Walter Scott at Abbotsford in Scotland in 1823. It became widely used in country houses, which had their own small gas plants to supply the gas; oil lamps however remained common even in the grandest houses, for instance at the vast Thoresby Hall, Nottinghamshire, built in 1864–75.

The country house usually had a liberal provision of water closets: Stoke Rochford Hall, Lincolnshire, built in 1839–41 to the designs of William Burn, had fifteen. The provision of bathrooms was normally less lavish, and although they became more popular, a large house such as Lord Beaumont's Carlton Towers, Yorkshire, had none as late as 1874. The family, guests and servants would wash in hand-filled basins and in hip baths which would be brought into the bedrooms and filled from buckets.

The country house was usually part of a large estate. The eighteenth-century enclosures had largely dispossessed the yeoman farmers and replaced them with tenant farmers paying rent to a large landowner. By 1874, when the population of England and Wales was some 24 million, a quarter of the land of England was owned by a mere 1,200 people.

The landlord often took an enlightened interest in the welfare of his tenants and farm workers. Cottages were frequently built as part of estate improvement [*56–8*], and to provide picturesque objects in the landscape. Various books were published to assist the cottage-builder (see p. 48), of which J. C. Loudon's *Encyclopaedia of Cottage, Farm and Villa Architecture and Furniture* (1833, revised editions 1842, etc.) was one of the best known [*29*]. (George Eliot in *Middlemarch*, published in 1871–2, refers to the careful study of Loudon to gain ideas on cottage construction.) The estate home farm was often rebuilt, again combining the need for efficiency with the desire for a picturesque adjunct to the house. Indeed, in some cases, such as Eaton Hall, the whole estate became dotted with lodges, farms and gatehouses whose purpose was as much to give interest to the landscape as to serve a practical end. In this the Victorians were following eighteenth-century precedent.

Under the influence of John Nash and Humphry Repton, the house itself was seen as a picturesque element in the landscape. Irregularity of outline was one of the main characteristics of the Picturesque, and hardly a single Victorian country house was without some asymmetrical element.

However, as the plan of the house became more informal, there was a return to formality in gardening in the Early Victorian period. Parterres, clipped hedges, fountains and carpet bedding became the fashion. William A. Nesfield, father of W. E. Nesfield, the architect, was one of the leaders of this school of gardening. His work can be seen at Trentham, Staffordshire [*12*], and at Kew Gardens. Tended by numerous gardeners, the formal garden became a mass of colour during the summer, while during the winter conservatories provided shelter for exotic plants. The Victorian period saw an expansion in plant collecting, and the park and garden were frequently embellished with foreign trees, which now, by their contrast with the native trees of the eighteenth-century landscape, give an indication to the traveller that a Victorian improver has been at work. To the Late Victorian gardener the herbaceous borders of William Robinson and the woodland and water gardens of Gertrude Jekyll had greater appeal. They had an informal character that went well with Vernacular Revival architecture, and they required fewer gardeners for their upkeep.

Although the country-house builder was so concerned with practical matters, the architectural style in which his house was built was also carefully considered. The country house, more perhaps than any other building type, gave scope for Romanticism: the patron could re-create the world of the medieval castle and the manor house, the age of Elizabeth I or the Medici of Italy, or even the exotic Orient. The problem of which style to choose was, as Robert Kerr pointed out in 1864, a difficult one for the country-house builder:

A bewildered gentleman may venture to suggest that he wants only a simple comfortable house, 'in no style at all – except the comfortable style, if there be one.'

The architect agrees; but they are all comfortable. 'Sir, you are the paymaster, and must therefore be pattern-master; you choose the style of your house just as you choose the build of your hat; – you can have *Classical*, columnar or non-columnar, arcuated or trabeated, rural or civil or indeed palatial; you can have *Elizabethan* in equal variety; *Renaissance* ditto; or, not to notice minor modes, *Mediæval* in any one of many periods and many phases, – old English, French, German, Belgium, Italian, and more.'

The poor gentleman is merely confused and protests that what he wants is a 'comfortable *Gentleman's House*', and finally settles for 'the style of the passing moment'.

12 Trentham Hall, Staffordshire, remodelled by Sir Charles Barry in 1834–42, seen from the south across the formal garden by W. A. Nesfield. (Only the single-storey arcade at the left end of the house remains today.)

Early Victorian country houses and town palaces

We can find examples of all the styles of architecture enumerated by Kerr. The Greek and Roman Classical rapidly fell out of fashion for country houses, although the Italian Renaissance retained its appeal – particularly among the great Whig magnates. Sir Charles Barry was one of the most prolific purveyors of houses in this style, and he produced a number of very large and expensive examples for noble clients. Trentham Hall, Staffordshire, which he remodelled between 1834 and 1842 for the Duke of Sutherland, was one of the largest [*12*]. Here Barry skilfully combined palace façades derived from the High Renaissance with a belvedere which added a picturesque touch. (The great palace is now gone, but the formal gardens laid out by Barry and W. A. Nesfield survive.)

Trentham was not the Duke's only country house. In 1850–51 Barry was again at work with another Italian Renaissance design, at Cliveden, Buckinghamshire. The house stands high above the Thames, its garden front facing terraces that lead down to a formal garden. The Duke had yet another house in Scotland, also designed by Barry – Dunrobin Castle, which will be discussed later [*18*]. And in London he had the palatial Stafford House, now Lancaster House, which was remodelled for him, also by Barry, in 1838–43. The enormous income necessary to sustain such a way of life came from coal.

Queen Victoria admired the taste of the Duke and Duchess of Sutherland and herself patronized the Italian Renaissance style, although her marine residence at Osborne, on the Isle of Wight, was modest in scale by comparison with the Sutherlands' Trentham [*13*]. The Queen first went to Osborne in 1844 and was delighted with the place; the bay reminded Prince Albert of the Bay of Naples. Plans were drawn up by Prince Albert with the assistance of Thomas Cubitt. The Queen wished the house to be a private residence and that wish, apart from the question of cost, led to the decision not to employ a fashionable architect such as Barry, who was closely connected with a government department. The result is a charming house, built in 1845–51, epitomizing the qualities of the Italian Villa style: the private and public wings are grouped informally together; two asymmetrically placed towers give the necessary picturesque outline. The house is faced with stucco and its details are not very different from those of the terraces that Cubitt was building at the time in Belgravia in London (p. 59).

In spite of such illustrious patronage for the Italian Renaissance style, the Early Victorians for their country houses tended to favour 'English' styles, the most popular of which were English Gothic (in various guises) and Elizabethan.

The Early Victorian Gothic country house can be seen at its best at Scarisbrick

13 The garden front of Osborne House, Isle of Wight, by Thomas Cubitt and Prince Albert, begun in 1845. The private wing is in the background.

Hall in Lancashire, which A. W. N. Pugin remodelled for Charles Scarisbrick, a Lancashire landowner [*14, 15*]. Pugin's work, which was carried out between 1837 and 1845, was an attempt to recreate a real medieval manor house, and the architectural details reflected Pugin's careful study of medieval buildings. Even the planning follows Gothic precedent: Scarisbrick has a great hall with porch and screens passage. The richly carved details, the pinnacles, the chimneys and the lantern on the hall roof give the exterior a sumptuous quality which was repeated inside the house.

Pugin's motive for re-establishing the large medieval hall was romantic and stylistic rather than practical. As he wrote to the Earl of Shrewsbury of another hall he was to build at Alton Towers, in Staffordshire:

As regards the hall I have nailed my colours to the mast – a bay window, high open roof, two good fireplaces, a great sideboard, screen, minstrel gallery – *all or none*. I will not sell myself to do a wretched thing.

14, 15 One of A. W. N. Pugin's proposals for the enlargement of Scarisbrick Hall, Lancashire, c.1837, and his drawing of the Great Hall at Scarisbrick. Here there is a louvre in the roof, a screens passage with minstrels' gallery over, plate on the dresser and armour on the walls. (RIBA Drawings Collection)

The great hall became a feature of many later Victorian houses, although its use was by no means uniform. In some cases it was used for its medieval purpose of entertaining on a grand scale. The Duke of Devonshire gave an annual banquet for local tradespeople and farmers in his great hall at Lismore Castle in Ireland, which was designed for him by Pugin and J. G. Crace. In other cases it served as a grand vestibule to the staircase. If no better use could be found, it could serve as a billiard room, as at Scotney Castle in Kent (1837–44).

For those who wished to take their medieval romanticizing a stage further, there was the Castle style. Peckforton

Castle in Cheshire (1844–50), one of the most impressive examples, stands on top of a hill, its austere walls and massive towers shrouded by trees [16]. The accommodation is skilfully arranged around a courtyard to give the maximum nineteenth-century convenience within the stylistic restraint of a thirteenth-century castle [17]. The designs were by Anthony Salvin (1799–1881), a pupil of Nash, who had an extensive country-house practice. Its owner, Lionel Tolle-mache, later Lord Tollemache, believed that 'the only real and lasting pleasure to be derived from the possession of a landed estate is to witness the improvement in social condition of those residing in it' – a kind of paternalism that recalls Disraeli's novel of the 'Young England' Tories, *Coningsby* (1844). To this end he supplied each of the labourers on his 26,000 acre estate with a substantial cottage and three acres which they could cultivate themselves.

16, 17 Peckforton Castle, Cheshire, by Anthony Salvin, 1844–50: plan, showing the extent of the service rooms, and a drawing by Salvin of 1849, looking along the north-eastern wall towards the great tower (top, in the plan).

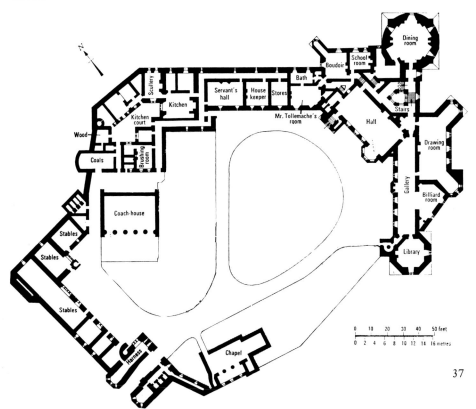

37

18 Dunrobin Castle, Sutherland, remodelled by Sir Charles Barry and W. Leslie, 1844–50.

A variation of the Castle style, the Scottish Baronial style, was popular north of the border. At the same time as Peckforton Castle was being built the Duke of Sutherland was making additions in this style to Dunrobin Castle, Sutherland (1844–50), which he used when visiting his vast estates in the north of Scotland [*18*]. Dunrobin is sited on a commanding height above Dornoch Firth and its towers, tourelles and high conical roofs, designed by Charles Barry and W. Leslie, made a brave show.

In 1848 the Queen had bought an estate at Balmoral, in Aberdeenshire. Between 1853 and 1855 the existing house was replaced in the Scottish Baronial style. Prince Albert again tried his hand at architecture, in this case with the help of William Smith (1817–91) of Aberdeen.

Their most prominent invention was a tall almost detached tower crowned by tourelles. Inside, extensive use was made of tartan patterns for the furnishings.

Closely related to the Gothic modes was the Elizabethan style, which enabled the Victorian architect to combine a picturesque exterior with rich surface decoration. In some cases one feels that the Victorians outshone their Elizabethan predecessors in this respect. Harlaxton Manor, in Lincolnshire, is one of the most exuberant of Victorian houses. The exterior was mainly due to Salvin and was built between 1831 and 1837; William Burn, one of the most prolific country-house architects, added the entrance gates and elaborate interiors, including a spectacular and unusual Baroque staircase [*19*]. The varied skyline and boldly recessed façades compare with Burghley or Wollaton. The Elizabethan style was also chosen by Lord Carnarvon when he decided to remodel his Georgian house, Highclere Castle in Hampshire, to

19 The Cedar Staircase at Harlaxton, Lincolnshire, executed by William Burn between 1838 and 1855.

20–22 Mentmore Towers, Buckinghamshire, by Sir Joseph Paxton and G. H. Stokes, 1851–4. Above: view from the south-east (bottom left in the plan). Above right: ground plan (from Kerr, The Gentleman's House, *1864). The house is on the left, focused on the central hall (A, and ill. 22); the equally large service wing has an open courtyard (B). Below: the central hall.*

bring it into line with Victorian taste. Barry produced designs in the Italian Renaissance style, but Lord Carnarvon, who was a Tory, rejected what might be thought of as a Whig mode in favour of an Elizabethan design. The house was refaced with stonework; turrets rose from all the corners, and a taller tower gave an off-centre accent. The foundation stone of the tower was laid on 24 June 1842 by Lord Carnarvon's son, Lord Porchester, on his eleventh birthday. Mentmore Towers, Buckinghamshire, built in 1851–4 by Sir Joseph Paxton and his son-in-law George Henry Stokes for the financier Baron Mayer Amschel de Rothschild, is another house based on Wollaton [*20–22*]. It has a symmetrical plan centred on a large top-lit hall, and was filled with elaborate Continental furnishings collected by its owner.

The large detached town houses of the rich were less adventurous stylistically than contemporary country houses. Many an aristocrat who regarded his country home as his real home was content to occupy a Georgian terrace house – although one of substantial proportions – as his town establishment. But on occasions the great magnates considered that something more splendid was necessary. The Duke of Sutherland's town palace, now Lancaster House, has been mentioned. Nearby is Bridgewater House, built by Barry in 1847–57 for the Duke's brother, Lord Francis Egerton, who had been created Earl of Ellesmere. The house is named after his grandfather, the last Duke of Bridgewater, who built the Bridgewater Canal to bring coal to Manchester: from the proceeds of the canal the house was built. The design is based on that of an Italian High Renaissance palace; Barry had used this *palazzo* style earlier for his Reform Club [65–7]. The main rooms are arranged around a central hall which is surrounded by arcades. A grand staircase leads up to the principal floor, which is occupied by a state dining room, a state drawing room, both overlooking the park, and a great picture gallery which was occasionally opened to the public. The main fronts are faced with Portland stone and elegantly detailed by Barry in the Italian High Renaissance style. Another very grand London house of this type and style – indeed, an attempt to outdo Bridgewater House – was Dorchester House in Park Lane, built in 1848–63 by Lewis Vulliamy (1791–1871) for the millionaire R. S. Holford. Its sumptuous interior [23], on which the sculptor Alfred Stevens worked, centred on a glazed courtyard from which rose a marble staircase. It was demolished in 1929 to make way for the Dorchester Hotel.

23 *The Green Drawing Room of Dorchester House, London, built in 1848–63 by Lewis Vulliamy and decorated by Alfred Stevens, seen in a photograph of 1905.*

24 *The entrance of Bestwood Lodge, Nottinghamshire, by S. S. Teulon, 1862–4, photographed in 1867.*

Mid-Victorian country houses

The middle years of Queen Victoria's reign, between 1855 and 1875, saw the peak of country-house building. It was financed by agricultural prosperity combined with new industrial wealth. Houses of enormous size were built, which show a confidence in the continued prosperity of Victorian Britain and a belief in an unchanging social structure. The various architectural modes which were employed in the Early Victorian period continued. The modifications that took place reflect the changing currents of taste – the most important of which, as far as architectural style was concerned, was the increasing interest taken in such foreign styles as French and Italian Gothic and French Renaissance.

High Victorian Gothic, with its honest use of materials, its polychromy and its varied outline, expressing a functionally arranged plan, provided the aristocracy and landed gentry with houses which were spectacular and richly ornamented, and which also had the correct historical, religious and moral overtones, as well as increased material comforts.

An early example of this type of house is Milton Ernest Hall, Bedfordshire, which was designed by William Butterfield for his brother-in-law Benjamin Starey and built in 1853–6. It is substantial, but not large by comparison with some of the great houses we have just seen. Butterfield used stone enriched with red brick for the walls, Gothic details, high-pitched roofs and tall chimneys. The garden front is an asymmetrical composition, in which a three-storeyed bay window surmounted by a timber-framed gable provides an off-centre accent; the sash windows have glazing bars.

This forthright and original High Victorian style of architecture was also employed for larger country houses. In 1858–61 George Gilbert Scott built Kelham Hall in Nottinghamshire for J. H. Manners-Sutton. It is a solid house, of red brick banded with stone, incorporating Gothic details from various sources, including Venice. A more assertive and individual Gothic was used by Samuel Saunders Teulon (1812–73) when he built Elvetham Hall, in Hampshire, for Lord Calthorpe in 1859–62. The house has a bizarre appearance with striped walls of red and blue brick, angular roofs and highly original window tracery. Bestwood Lodge, Nottinghamshire [24], designed by Teulon for the Duke of St Albans and built in 1862–4, is in a similarly spiky and harsh brick Gothic. Plate-glass windows, made possible by Victorian technology, are set in a façade embellished with inventive sculptured Gothic detail.

Eaton Hall in Cheshire, as rebuilt by the Duke of Westminster, was even larger – a vast Gothic palace to accommodate one of the richest men in England [25]. The house that was remodelled had itself been rebuilt in the early years of the century, but by 1870 William Porden's Gothic was considered old-fashioned. The Duke entrusted the alteration to Alfred Waterhouse. Between 1870 and 1883 £600,000 was

25 Eaton Hall, Cheshire, by Alfred Waterhouse, 1870–83, photographed in the 1880s. From left to right: the chapel and clock tower (which survive), the low service wing, and the main body of the house.

spent on the rebuilding; but the Duke could well afford it, as his annual income during this period, coming largely from the rents of his London estates, was of the order of £250,000. The house (mostly demolished in 1961–2) had a fine skyline with high roofs, turrets and towers; from a distance, it was reminiscent of a French château. The main block was flanked by a private wing. The chapel, the tall clock-tower and the stable block survive. The park was embellished with numerous lodges and gateways, including the so-called Flemish Gateway of 1882, by John Douglas (1829–1911) of Chester. Bodley built the fine estate church at Eccleston. The whole ensemble of house, garden, park and estate buildings epitomized, better perhaps than any other such group, the setting chosen by a grand Victorian nobleman at the height of Victorian prosperity.

The same vast scale can be seen at Thoresby Hall, built in 1864–75 for Earl Manvers by Salvin in the Elizabethan style, using fireproof construction. Although the house is not so elaborate in its detail as Harlaxton it is more markedly asymmetrical and larger: the east front is 182 feet long and the great hall measures 65 by 31 feet.

While the old aristocracy and gentry tended to keep to the Gothic or the Elizabethan style, the *nouveaux riches*, who wanted something more showy for their money, frequently chose the French Renaissance style. It was particularly popular among bankers and financiers. In 1871–4 Edward Middleton Barry (1830–80), the third son of Sir Charles, built Wykehurst in Sussex for Henry Huth, a banker's son. The exterior is a highly competent re-creation of a sixteenth-century French château. Inside he provided the most up-to-date and luxurious services, including hot-air central heating and a bathroom for each bedroom suite.

The Rothschilds went a stage further for their château at Waddesdon in Buckinghamshire, and called in the French architect Gabriel-Hippolyte Destailleur

26 The south front of Waddesdon Manor, by Gabriel-Hippolyte Destailleur, 1874–89.

(1822–93). The house, which was built between 1874 and 1889, owes debts to Chambord and numerous other châteaux of the Loire Valley. Inside, the walls are panelled with re-erected eighteenth-century *boiseries* from France and the rooms furnished with Louis XV chairs, Savonnerie carpets and Sèvres porcelain.

Castle building was falling out of fashion as the period progressed, but a few more notable examples were built. Cardiff Castle in Glamorganshire and Castell Coch nearby were both built for the Marquis of Bute from designs of William Burges [*27, 28*]. Bute was a young aristocrat of Romantic turn of mind. He was also vastly wealthy, with great estates in Scotland and, more important, large areas of South Wales, including Cardiff docks. Burges was a Gothicist who had begun his career in Ecclesiological circles (see below, p. 214), where he was fascinated with the heavy forms of French Early Gothic. He also had a strong liking for medieval story-telling and symbolism, like some of the Pre-Raphaelites, which could not be satisfied by religious subject-matter, and therefore he explored a wide range of decoration and symbolism inside his castles and houses. The collaboration of Burges and Bute created two of the most opulent Gothic Revival buildings of the period. The exteriors of both buildings owe something to the reconstructions of French medieval castles which appeared in Eugène Viollet-le-Duc's *Dictionnaire de l'Architecture Française du XIᵉ au XVᵉ siècle* (1854–68). Cardiff Castle, begun in 1868 and finished in 1881, is solid and simple in the massing of its walls, but as it rises it becomes more ornate and the towers are crowned by pyramid roofs, turrets, spires and finials [*27*]. The rooms inside are

27 The towers of Cardiff Castle, by William Burges, 1868–81.

28 The Summer Smoking Room in Cardiff Castle.

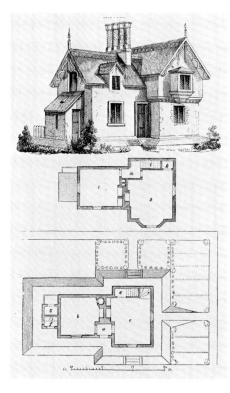

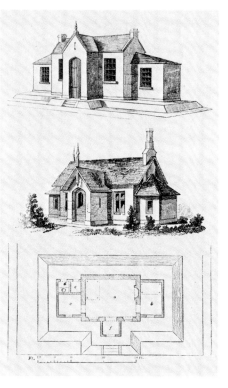

aglow with coloured carvings, panelled walls and painted ceilings. At the top of the tallest tower Burges designed a Summer Smoking Room for the young millionaire [*28*]. The room has a jewelled quality: the walls are elaborately patterned and the great hooded fireplace is richly carved and decorated; a gallery runs round above giving a view of the sea and the distant mountains; from the ceiling hangs a great golden chandelier in the shape of the sun's rays.

Castell Coch (1875–81) is even more in the realm of fantasy. It is set on a wooded hillside and has stout cylindrical towers capped with conical roofs. The austere exterior enhances the bright colours and elaborate decoration of the interior, which like that of Cardiff Castle has a sumptuous quality which can seldom have been equalled in the Middle Ages. There is also

an exotic strain: Lady Bute's bedroom, set in one of the round towers, is covered by a domed ceiling decorated with panels painted with leaves and animals and enriched with oriental motifs. The furnishings are equally bizarre: the posts of Lady Bute's bed are crowned by crystal spheres and her washstand is flanked by embattled towers. As a house Castell Coch was hardly practical, and indeed Lord Bute, who had a number of other houses, seldom actually lived there. Burges's own house in Melbury Road, Kensington, London, begun to his designs in 1876, is a miniature version of these Gothic palaces.

The great age of the Victorian country house came to an end in the late 1870s. The widespread agricultural depression of the mid-1870s, partly caused by the opening up of the American West, lasted with few respites until the end of Queen

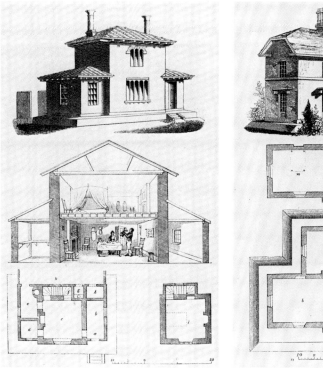

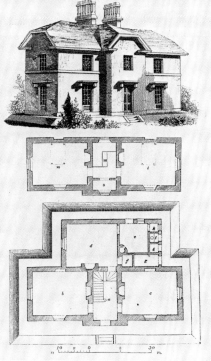

Victoria's reign. As Lady Bracknell says in Wilde's *The Importance of Being Earnest*, written in 1895: 'What between the duties expected of one during one's lifetime and the duties exacted from one after one's death land has ceased to be either a profit or a pleasure.' Country-house building did not cease, but buildings tended to become smaller and were seen more as a retreat from urban life than as the centre of a great estate. The character of the later houses in the country is closer to the smaller, detached house, which had developed on separate lines.

The smaller detached house

Although the aristocracy still had an important part to play in society, and expressed this role in grandiose architecture, the Victorian age became increas-

29 Designs for picturesque cottages from J. C. Loudon's Encyclopaedia of Cottage, Farm and Villa Architecture, *1833*.

ingly the age of the middle classes. Middle-class ideals, middle-class politics and middle-class morals came to dominate a large part of society. Perhaps the most characteristic expression of middle-class ideals was the detached house in both country and suburb. It was the dream of businessman or professional man. The parsonage is a characteristic and influential example of this type of house, reflecting the high social status of the clergy at the time.

The small suburban detached house with its own garden is a peculiarly English ideal. It became popular with the prosperous middle classes in the later eighteenth century and owed something to

47

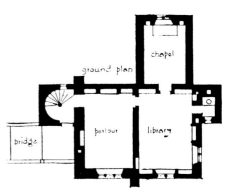

30, 31 St Marie's Grange, Alderbury, Wiltshire, Pugin's own house, 1835–6: the original plan of the main floor, and the house today, looking towards the library (with added bow window) and chapel. (Plan from The Architectural Review, *1904)*

the cult of the Picturesque: Nash's Park Villages near Regents Park in London, begun in 1824, are an important early example of a development containing houses of this kind. Although the Georgian Classical styles, Roman and Greek, survived well into the Victorian period, the Picturesque Italian Villa and Cottage styles were increasingly employed. Both had been popularized by Nash and it is characteristic of much of this type of housing that it follows the high fashion of a previous generation. Books such as J. B. Papworth's *Rural Residences* (1818) and Charles Parker's *Villa Rustica* (1832) provided many a humble architect and speculative builder with models. The houses were frequently asymmetrical and stucco was still widely used as a cheap substitute for stone. Cheltenham in Gloucestershire and St John's Wood and Putney Hill in London became dotted with pale recreations of Tuscan villas, with low-pitched roofs, broad eaves resting on brackets, and sometimes a flat-topped tower; soon soot-laden and ivy-clad, they became models of respectability. Loudon's widely-used *Encyclopaedia* illustrated

examples of the Cottage style, characterized by half-hipped dormer windows and tall chimney-stacks.

Although stucco-covered villas in the Italian Villa style, the Cottage style and even the Gothick style were still going up in the 1850s and even beyond, the leaders of architecture fulminated against their 'sham' nature. Pugin derided what he called the 'resistless torrent of Roman-cement men, who buy their ornaments by the yard, and their capitals by the ton'. He showed how he considered a small house should be designed in St Marie's Grange at Alderbury, near Salisbury in Wiltshire, which he built for himself in 1835–6 [*30, 31, 178*]. It is Gothic in its details, constructed of red brick with stone dressings and a slate roof. The L-shaped plan must have been far from convenient, but it contained on the main floor a parlour, a library and a chapel (pp. 184–5). The air at Alderbury did not suit Pugin's wife and he soon moved to Ramsgate, where he built another house, also called The Grange (1843–4) [*184*]. The features are similar to those of the Picturesque cottage – gables, mullioned windows, bay windows, dor-

mers and tall chimney-stacks – but the handling is different. The simple brick and flint walls have an austere air; morality has replaced the fanciful qualities of the early Picturesque Neo-Gothic. Next to the house Pugin built a church and a chantry chapel, and there he lies buried.

32 Vicarage and school (right) at Boyne Hill, Berkshire, by G. E. Street, part of the group begun in 1854.

Pugin was the main inspiration for a style of Gothic which was developed for small houses, particularly parsonages, in the Mid-Victorian period. Its creators were architects associated with the Ecclesiological movement, most notably Butterfield, William White and Street. The houses are built of the most readily available materials – local stone or red brick. The details are Gothic, but Gothic used to suit nineteenth-century needs. Frequently sash windows with glazing bars are combined with Gothic arches. The planning is informal and the outline of the houses picturesque, but a picturesque coming from strict utility, as Pugin would have wished. Everything is straightforward, honest, and 'real', to use a favourite expression of the period.

One can see major examples of the style in a series of parsonages that Butterfield built in 1853–4 at Cowick, Hensall and Pollington in Yorkshire. In all three villages Butterfield also built very plain brick churches [197] and schools. The vicarages, of red brick too, have wooden window frames, some filled with sash windows. The steep roofs have simple

gables or are half-hipped, as are the dormers. The walls are unbuttressed and although the pointed arch is used it is not stressed in the design. Indeed, the whole style is remarkably unassertive when compared with Butterfield's churches. The vicarages are much closer to the contemporary estate cottages that he built in the mid-1850s at Baldersby St James in Yorkshire [57] (see p. 70).

This simple, earnest, moral Gothic architecture was further developed by White and Street, who both began their careers in Cornwall. White's small house, Penmellyn, built at St Columb Major about 1855, is of stone with slate-hanging, a local feature, used at the tops of the gables and in the spandrels of the windows, which have wooden frames. The chimney-stacks project boldly from the wall; at the side is a small triangular oriel supported on a wooden bracket – a feature frequently found in suburban houses over eighty years later.

Street used a similar style for a number of houses in Berkshire when he became architect to the Oxford diocese. At Boyne Hill near Maidenhead, in 1854, he began

49

an ecclesiastical group comprising a church, school, vicarage, curate's house and almshouse arranged around a court-yard [*32*]. The vicarage is substantial in size, with a varied outline and windows of different shapes placed where they are needed. The red brick walls are patterned with dark brick. One can see here the influence of Street's studies of Gothic architecture in Italy, which he had visited in 1853; he was to publish an account of his journey in 1855 in a book entitled *Brick and Marble in the Middle Ages* (see p. 203).

Street's vicarages tended to become more austere in the 1850s, and in the vicarage at New Bradwell, Buckingham-shire (1857–60), polychromy is abandoned and buttresses are eliminated from the plain red brick walls. Simple wooden sash windows are set under segmental heads.

It was this style that was used by Philip Webb when in 1859–60 he came to build the famous Red House at Bexleyheath in Kent for his friend William Morris [*33–5*]. The house is not large; it is solid, serious and unpretentious outside. Both Webb and Morris had worked in Street's office in Oxford in 1856 and so would have been familiar with Boyne Hill and New Brad-well. Morris saw the Red House as being in 'the style of the thirteenth century'. The oriel of the drawing room derives from Street's book on Italian Gothic architec-ture and the round windows lighting the upper corridor, seen as unfoiled Gothic tracery, were probably inspired by the cathedral at Mantes on the Seine, which Morris had visited when on holiday in France.

The simple exterior concealed a rich interior, embellished with stained glass by Burne-Jones and Webb, coloured wall-paper by Morris, and solid furniture, some painted with medieval scenes. The draw-ing room has a built-in settle at one end, the top of which forms a miniature minstrels' gallery. The Red House has been talked of as a revolutionary building, but it is part of the High Victorian school of Modern Gothic. Its construction is truthful and straightforward, but there is a strong element of Romanticism in its design.

Very soon the Ecclesiological Gothic style of massive walls and brick and stone polychromy caught on in the villas of North Oxford, along the Banbury Road (for instance No. 52 of 1868, by F. Codd), and even in the speculative Norham Manor Estate, laid out by William Wil-kinson (1819–1901) for St John's College from 1860 onwards to meet the needs of married dons and their families.

Later Victorian houses in the country

From the 1870s, architects tended to discard the grand styles of the pattern books and to look toward the more simple and informal qualities of vernacular build-ings for their inspiration. As we have seen, the lead in this direction was taken by the High Church Anglican architects in the 1850s. In the hands of such men as George Devey, Eden Nesfield and Norman Shaw, the vernacular, or regional and homely, architecture of the sixteenth, seventeenth and early eighteenth centuries was adapted to the needs of country-house design. It is significant that all three men were adept at producing superb perspective drawings in the Picturesque tradition. Devey had studied under the watercolourist J. D. Harding; Nesfield's father was well known as a watercolour painter before he turned to garden design, and both Shaw and Nesfield published books of architec-tural drawings.

Although Devey was one of the most prolific Victorian country-house archi-tects, his work was not widely pub-lished. Like William Burn, his practice was sustained by the recommendations of his satisfied clients, who did not wish to have the details of their homes appear in the press. His houses attempt to give the appearance of having grown up gradually over a number of years, even centuries. He used local materials and so handled them as to give the impression that the craftsman rather than the architect determined their use.

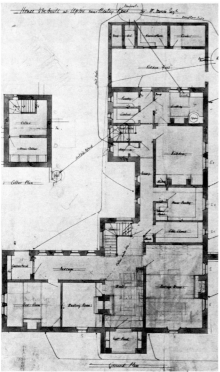

33–5 The Red House, Bexleyheath, Kent, by Philip Webb, 1859–60. Above: view from the south (top left in the plan); the servants' wing is in the left foreground. Left: Webb's ground plan (Victoria and Albert Museum, London). Below: the dining room (bottom right in the plan), with wooden panelling, a built-in Gothic sideboard, and a characteristic brick fireplace with tile cheeks.

36 Betteshanger, Kent, by George Devey, 1856–82, seen in an early photograph.

One can see Devey's technique employed to the full at Betteshanger in Kent [*36*], which he remodelled over the period 1856–82 for Sir Walter James, Bart., who was a friend of Gladstone. It is rambling and picturesque in the extreme – as if designed solely to provide a subject for a watercolour painting. Indeed Sir Walter, like Devey, had studied under J. D. Harding. A low tower, tall chimney-stacks, mullioned bay windows and roofs with Dutch gables combine to compose the picture. The materials Devey used are equally varied: stone, flint, yellow brick, red brick and tiles. They, and many of the architectural features, are local to this part of East Kent. Further opportunities for Picturesque design were offered by cottages on the estate.

Philip Webb, in his country houses, was to make a point of using local materials, but his architectural expression was more individual. He treated each design problem as unique, worrying over the smallest detail. The result is always interesting and often highly original. Although his

37 Clouds, Wiltshire, by Philip Webb, 1879–91.

first allegiance was to the Gothic style, in the Late Victorian period 'Queen Anne' features appeared in his designs, and he even studied the planning of Vanbrugh. Clouds, in Wiltshire (1879–91, now altered), a large house built for the Wyndham family, showed Webb's use of local materials and his mixing of stylistic features [*37*]. Smeaton Manor in Yorkshire (1877–9) was even closer to an eighteenth-century manor house in its style. Standen in Sussex, designed in 1891 and completed in 1894, has 'Queen Anne' sash windows and tall chimneys, but Webb's architecture is so personal that it would be wrong to give it a stylistic label [*38*]. Standen shows a variety of materials – brick, stone, tile-hanging and weatherboarding – combined in a way that is inspired by local buildings. But it also has a number of idiosyncratic features which are peculiar to Webb: windows are recessed in shallow panels, sometimes grouped in pairs with a corbel between them; tall chimney-stacks of simple design are boldly set at right angles to one another to form a dominant element. Inside, Webb's remarkable woodwork, painted white except in the dining room, where it is a soft mid-green, survives intact, as do many of the furnishings by Morris and Co. [*39*].

The picturesque vernacular style which came to be known as 'Old English' was to be popularized by Nesfield and Shaw, who shared an office early in their careers. Shaw's vernacular was based on the houses of the Weald of Sussex, which have tall brick chimneys, tile-hanging, and mullioned windows with leaded lights. An early house, and one of Shaw's best, is Leyswood, near Withyham in Sussex, which he designed in 1866 for J. W. Temple, managing director of the Shaw, Savill Line, which had been started by the architect's brother in the 1850s. (It was for Shaw, Savill that he was to design New Zealand Chambers [*129*].) The planning is more compact than in many earlier Victorian country houses, but by arranging the accommodation around three sides of a courtyard Shaw skilfully contrived to

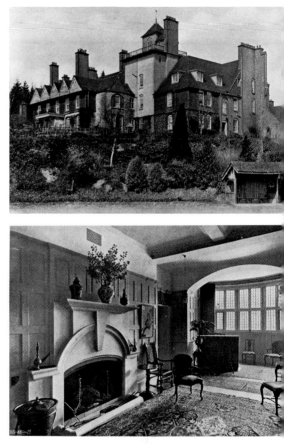

38, 39 Standen, Sussex, by Philip Webb, built 1892–4: view from the south-west, and interior of the hall. (Webb added the hall bow window at the client's request.)

achieve the separation of functions that was still required. It was, however, the elevations that appealed so much to contemporaries. In a brilliant way Shaw made use of gabled roofs, varied fenestration and tall chimneys to create a design which, although based on vernacular elements, is in fact extremely sophisticated. The main part of the house has been demolished, but the gate tower leading to the courtyard fortunately survives. Unlike Devey's architecture, Shaw's was well

40, 41 Cragside, Northumberland, by Norman Shaw, 1870–c.1885. Lord Armstrong is shown (below) seated in the dining room inglenook, in front of stained glass by Morris and Co.

publicized: illustrations of Leyswood appeared in *The Building News* of 31 March 1871 and in Charles Eastlake's *Gothic Revival* in the following year.

Shaw was to build houses of a similar character all over the country, even where the Sussex Wealden style was not the appropriate local manner. His most dramatic house in this vein is Cragside in Northumberland, which he built for Lord Armstrong, the armaments manufacturer [*40, 41*]. He began work in 1870 and extended the house in a series of building campaigns into the 1880s. It is completely isolated and is approached by a long drive through the wooded estate, contrived in such a way that the house is concealed until the last moment. It then rises up above a ravine with a prodigious variety of timber-framed gables to a crenellated tower, itself capped by a gabled roof and extremely tall chimney-stacks. The plan rambles across the hillside, the kitchens and the kitchen court tucked away at the back, leaving the front for the main living rooms to enjoy the magnificent view. The rooms vary greatly in size and character. The dining room, part of the 1870–72 building, is a room of moderate size with a cosy inglenook inscribed 'East or West, Hame's Best' over the fireplace [*41*]. The drawing room, added in 1883–4, is on the other hand a great top-lit room, dominated by an enormous chimney-piece. Lord Armstrong was a friend of Joseph Swan, the pioneer of the use of electricity, and in 1880 Cragside became one of the first houses to be electrically lit.

Related to these houses is Kinmel Park near Abergele in Denbighshire, begun in 1868 to designs by Nesfield for H. R. Hughes, who owed his fortune to a copper mine in Anglesey [*42*]. It is one of the earliest manifestations of the 'Queen Anne' style in country-house architecture. Nesfield had tried out the style in a delightful little lodge at Kew Gardens near London, which he built in 1867. It is of red brick, with pilasters of rubbed brick, and the door is set at the side of one façade. A coved cornice is surmounted by a tall pyramidal roof from the ridge of which a tall brick chimney-stack emerges. The roof contains three bedrooms which are lit by large pedimented dormers. All of these

features are found again at Kinmel, which is one of the largest houses in the style; the plan is irregular, with the service quarters arranged around a courtyard at one end and the reception rooms at the other. An element of formality is introduced in both the entrance and the garden fronts, although in both Nesfield carefully breaks the symmetry with a chimney-stack or a dormer. The high mansard roofs and dormer windows give a slightly French air. Accompanying the house are lodges, estate cottages and a picturesque home farm, complete with dairy and dovecote. Kinmel has a fresh, airy, urbane quality that is very different from the moral earnestness of the great Gothic houses such as Eaton Hall [*25*].

Later, a more personal interpretation of the Vernacular Revival is found in the work of Charles F. Annesley Voysey, who was heir to the traditions of Devey, for whom he worked in the 1880s. Voysey never built a large country mansion. His houses are comparatively small and low, with white, roughcast walls, wide eaves, mullioned windows and large hipped slate roofs. An early example is The Cottage at Bishops Itchington, Warwickshire, of

42 The garden front of Kinmel, Denbighshire, by Eden Nesfield, begun in 1868.

43 One of C. F. A. Voysey's designs for The Cottage, Bishops Itchington, Warwickshire, 1888. (British Architect, 1888)

1888 [*43*]. It has a simple block plan, and the roof sweeps down so that the upper storey windows are treated as dormers. Voysey perfected this style in houses such as Broadleys on Lake Windermere, Lancashire, of 1898, which has a fine site overlooking the lake. Three two-storeyed bow windows light the reception rooms and bedrooms above. Moor Crag, also on Lake Windermere (1898–1900), and his own home, The Orchard, at Chorley Wood in Hertfordshire (1900–1901), are in a similar manner, which was to be copied in thousands of suburban homes all over Britain into the 1930s.

At the end of the Victorian period Sir Edwin Lutyens (1869–1944) designed some of the most brilliant of all houses in the Vernacular Revival style. Lutyens was later to develop into one of the greatest of English Classical architects, but at this early stage of his career he was fascinated by the building techniques of his native Surrey. An early collaborator was Gertrude Jekyll, the gardener, and for her he built Munstead Wood near Godalming in Surrey in 1896. It is not a country house so much as a house in the country; it has the character of a cottage built of local stone. More dramatic is Tigbourne Court, Surrey, of 1899 [*44*]. The details are vernacular, seventeenth-century in character, the material again local, but Lutyens handles them with a baroque swagger which looks forward to his later Classical work and the architecture of another age.

The terrace and semi-detached house, and the speculative builder

The buildings that have been described so far are among the most influential Victorian houses, but they are only a small part of the mass of Victorian housing. Terrace and semi-detached houses are by far the largest group of any Victorian building type, and, more than any other, they determine the character of Victorian cities. They are one of the most characteristic products of Victorian Britain, and they remain in sufficient quantities still to be a significant element in our urban environment.

The provision of housing was normally seen throughout the Victorian period as the responsibility of capitalist enterprise. Although, increasingly, philanthropic organizations, enlightened employers and, at the end of the century, local authorities, were providing some housing for the working classes (see pp. 71–3), the vast majority of houses were constructed by the speculative builder with the aim of selling or letting for profit. He served the needs of all classes of the community. In size speculative houses ranged from mansions such as those built by Cubitt in Belgravia to the one- or two-room tenements of Glasgow, but they all had this in common: the builder had to predict the needs and the tastes of those who were to rent or to buy his houses. On his success in doing this depended his commercial viability.

The role of the speculative builder was well established by Victorian times: nineteenth-century methods are recognizably similar to those of Nicholas Barbon, the great seventeenth-century London developer. But the growth of the population, rising prosperity, the expansion of towns assisted by the railways, all provided ample opportunities for the entrepreneur, large or small, to make his fortune if he was skilful or to go bankrupt if he was not.

The Victorian speculator himself was not a stereotype figure. Most began with skills in an aspect of the building industry: they might be bricklayers, masons, carpenters or plasterers. They would start out in a small way doing such work as they could and sub-contracting the other trades. However, speculative builders also included men such as builders' merchants, shopkeepers and lawyers, who were drawn in by the need to realize bad debts on half-completed houses or attracted by the possibility of high returns. Even clergymen joined in: one of the most notable examples was Dr Samuel Edmund Walker, rector of St Columb Major in Cornwall, who was left a fortune by his father and used it to develop a large area of Notting Hill in west London in the early 1850s. He was caught out by the slump of 1854, and, a near-bankrupt, fled the country in the following year.

The finance for building houses was usually plentiful. The Victorian building industry had a tendency to overproduce rather than to underproduce, and large numbers of unsold, often partly-completed, houses were common on the outskirts of Victorian cities. The industry was subject to the usual fluctuations of boom and depression. When Queen Victoria came to the throne production of houses was increasing, following a slump in the early 1830s. The 1840s ended in a depression, with widespread unemployment in the building industry, but house building was again booming in the year of the Great Exhibition. The slump that followed was in part caused by the shortage of capital as a result of the Crimean War. Further peaks of building activity, as far as the metropolis was concerned at any rate, were in the years 1868–9, 1878–80 and 1898. The low points were 1871–2 and 1891.

The ready flow of capital seeking investment, and the generous credit usually extended by builders' merchants to the speculative builder, made entry in this business activity comparatively easy. The number of speculative builders was therefore high. A study by H. J. Dyos tells us that at the height of building activities in

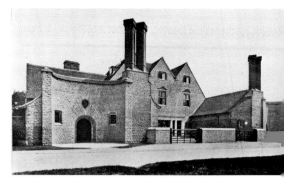

44 Tigbourne Court, Surrey, by Sir Edwin Lutyens, 1899. (Builder, 1901)

the South London suburb of Camberwell, in 1878–80, some 416 builders were engaged in building 5,670 houses. The variation in scale of operations was also large and ranged from the man building one or two houses to the substantial builder employing a large work force and developing whole estates. One of the largest of all Victorian speculative builders was Thomas Cubitt (see below, p. 59). He was responsible for building large areas of London, in particular almost the whole of Belgravia. He was highly successful, widely respected in his day, and able to live in high style: he kept two carriages and three houses – a town residence in Belgravia, a country house in Clapham Park and later at Denbighs, near Dorking in Surrey, and a house in Brighton. On his death he left over one million pounds.

The speculative builder did not normally have difficulty in obtaining land, as the landlord could always get a higher financial return by selling or leasing to a builder than by using his land for agriculture. The pattern of streets in Victorian towns frequently owes less to conscious planning on the part of the developer than it does to the fortuitous arrangements of the original land ownership: in some cases a large estate would be developed in an ordered way, according to a well designed plan, but in other cases the builder might have to contend with a small inconveniently shaped site, which could only with difficulty be joined to existing roads.

Where the land to be developed was sufficiently extensive a coherent plan was often produced. On most large estates it was formulated by the ground landlord who, by means of restrictive covenants, controlled not only the layout of the estate but also the size, type and even design of the houses to be built. This was the policy of the Duke of Westminster when he developed his Belgravia estate in London with the help of Thomas Cubitt. Eton College, the ground landlord of the Chalcots Estate in North London, did the same, hiring surveyors to produce street plans, encouraging the building of churches and other amenities such as public houses, and controlling the elevational treatment of the houses through the leases granted to different speculative builders [45].

The planning of Victorian speculative developments shows a gradual move away from the formal schemes inherited from the eighteenth century towards picturesque layouts with curving roads, which were beginning to appear in the Regency period under the influence of Nash. Much Early Victorian building was carried out to street plans designed before 1837. The formal arrangement of squares and crescents in Belgravia (see below), in Kemp Town at Brighton and Pittville at Cheltenham, of the 1820s, may be compared with a typical Early Victorian layout such as that of the Ladbroke Estate, Kensington [11], planned and built mainly in the 1840s and '50s by designers who included Thomas Allason, John Stevens and Thomas Allom. Although there are still squares and crescents they are treated in a less rigid manner: the garden of Ladbroke Square is not a parallelogram, and on one side it is overlooked by the backs rather than the fronts of the houses. The crescents of the estate follow the contours of the hill, and generous gardens and numerous trees enhance the sense of informality. The increase in size of the private garden led to the gradual abandonment of the shared garden. Finally the curving, tree-lined streets of Bedford Park, laid out in 1875, set the pattern for spacious suburban developments for the rest of the Victorian period (see p. 68).

For the estates of poorer houses the only consideration was to cover the ground with as many houses as possible. In industrial towns landlords were less concerned to ensure high standards of layout or construction, and often found it difficult to enforce high standards even if they wished to. The Duke of Norfolk, who was a strict landlord in London, exerted little control over the development of his estate in Sheffield. The Public Health Acts from 1848 onwards did much to remedy the lack of sanitation, but by laying down a minimum width for streets (the 'bye-law street') they often imposed a dull uniformity on large areas built towards the end of the century.

The Victorian speculative builder was conservative in his techniques: although in other fields of construction great advances were being made, houses kept largely to methods established in the Georgian period. The main external and party walls were built of brick or masonry, the choice being governed largely by cost and the bye-laws. The material was normally local – brick in London and lowland Lancashire, stone in Yorkshire, granite in Aberdeen. For roofing, local tiles were still widely used in areas such as Berkshire and East Anglia, but elsewhere Welsh slates became common, particularly in London, Liverpool and Manchester.

Inside houses, timber was used for roofs, floor joists, floorboards and staircases. Internal walls frequently consisted of timber studs covered with lathes and then plastered. Sash windows were in almost universal use, except for the very cheapest houses. In Early Victorian times they had glazing bars (following eighteenth-century custom), but in the Mid-Victorian period plate glass became common for more expensive houses. During the Late Victorian period glazing bars reappeared, as did casement windows with leaded lights – 'Home, Sweet Home' – as part of the 'Queen Anne' and Vernacular Revivals. The glazing is perhaps the surest guide to the approximate date of a particular house.

For his stylistic ideas the speculative builder might rely on an architect or a surveyor, or he might produce the design himself. At the top end of the market the builder usually employed a reputable or even a famous architect: George Basevi (1794–1845), George Godwin (editor of *The Builder*), Sir James Knowles (1831–1908), Shaw and E. W. Godwin were all prepared to design speculative housing. For cheaper developments the architect might be less distinguished or his design might be modified by the builder to suit the supposed taste of his prospective clients. At the bottom end of the market were houses built without the services of an architect and with little or no architectural embellishment at all.

*Early Victorian terrace and
semi-detached houses*

Thomas Cubitt's development in Belgravia is representative of the upper range of Early Victorian speculative development in both scale and design. Belgrave Square was laid out in 1826 but parts of the scheme were still under construction in the mid-1840s. For the design of the square Cubitt employed George Basevi, who followed Georgian tradition, providing uniform Classical terraces around a large communal garden. Each terrace, built of brick faced with stucco, is treated as a single unit with central and flanking features marked by applied columns. However, the formality of the square was modified by the placing of detached houses at the corners, each of different design. The lease for the south-eastern site was sold by Cubitt to Lord Sefton, who employed Philip Hardwick (1792–1870) to design his house of 1842.

The rest of Belgravia was gradually covered by similar, although mostly smaller, houses. Like Georgian terrace houses,

they have kitchens and service rooms in the basement which look on to an area, railed off in front. The ground floor has a Classical porch sheltering the front door, which leads to the entrance hall and staircase. The living rooms are on the ground and first floors. Bedrooms for the family occupy the upper floors and attics provide bedrooms for the servants. At the rear of the larger houses are mews with accommodation for horses, carriages and their attendants.

This continuation of the Georgian tradition can be seen in most large towns. The grand terraces designed by John Dobson (1787–1865) for the developer Robert Grainger in Newcastle-upon-Tyne are fine examples of the more monumental type of layout. In Brighton grandiose plans were proposed by Thomas Read Kemp in an area of Brighton which came to be known as Kemp Town. The scheme was begun in 1823 but Kemp became over-extended and Cubitt took over, completing in the Early Victorian period a number of houses in Lewes Crescent which had been left as carcases and building the adjoining streets. In style the houses are similar to Cubitt's work in Belgravia.

Cubitt was also involved in building smaller and less expensive houses, which paraphrase the more pretentious dwellings in style and plan. Those that he built in 1836–43 in College Cross Street, on the Barnsbury Estate in North London, are typical. Only two bays wide, they have two floors above a basement with further rooms in the roof. An area protected by cast-iron railings gives on to the basement. The ground floor is faced with rusticated stucco and has two arched openings, one containing a window, the other the door with a lunette over it. There is no porch. The first floor is brick-faced and has two completely plain rectangular windows. Above is a stucco cornice and parapet, behind which is a gutter that drains into a pipe at one side of the house. Cubitt claimed to have put water closets in all his houses built after about 1824, but baths

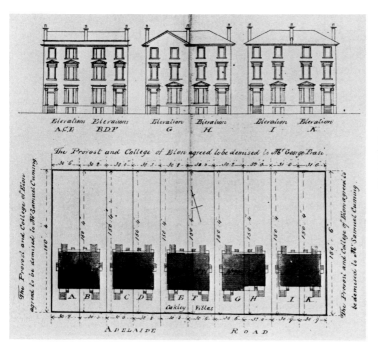

45 *Design for 17–26 Oakley Villas, Adelaide Road, on the Chalcots Estate in London, 1856. (Eton College)*

were not usually provided. From houses such as these the City clerk would set out to walk to his office.

Slightly more elaborate is a terrace of small houses built in South London at Clifton Way, Camberwell, in 1846–7. They also have a stuccoed ground floor with arched openings, and exposed brickwork above, but the two upper-floor windows are joined by an enclosing arched surround. The terrace has a continuous cornice crowned by low pediments which act as a unifying element in the design. The windows have only horizontal glazing bars, an indication of the improved technology of glass-making.

One of the popular features of the more spacious suburban development was the semi-detached house, which shares only one party wall with its neighbour. J. C. Loudon helped to popularize it: in his book of 1838, *The Suburban Gardener and Villa Companion*, he illustrated a pair of semi-detached houses in Porchester Terrace, Bayswater, London, in one of which

he lived himself. The houses, built in 1837–8, have a square plan and simple Classical details. The porches are at the sides and lead to central staircase halls, around which the principal rooms on the ground floor are arranged. A circular conservatory on the front helps to conceal the fact that the building is two houses. Ten years later the semi-detached house was a common feature of suburban speculative developments. The Chalcots Estate in London, already mentioned, has examples dating from the 1840s and 1850s. The principal builder was Samuel Cuming: he had in mind respectable clients who wanted houses that were vaguely Classical and yet not too formal. Designs dated 1856 for large semi-detached houses in Adelaide Road have survived [45]. The basic design – three storeys on a semi-basement, two bays wide – remains unchanged, but there are three variations on this theme. The first pair has a roof set behind a parapet, the traditional roof detail for urban houses since Georgian times.

The others have overhanging eaves, which by the 1860s was to be the standard roof pattern for speculative developments; one arrangement of this group is to have a gable over the front of one house and eaves over the other.

Mid- to Late Victorian terrace and semi-detached houses

With the striking exception of Scotland, where Neo-Classicism continued to flourish at least as late as the 1870s (most notably at the hands of 'Greek' Thomson [46]: see pp. 233-4), the Mid-Victorian builder rejected the austerity of the Neo-Classical styles. The Italian Renaissance proved a more profitable source of inspiration, but builders tended to be less exclusive in their use of style, following, often in an inept way, the architectural theory of Ruskin, Beresford-Hope and Thomas Harris. The bay window also became increasingly popular in all types of houses and all styles of architecture [48a]. Ruskin had written: 'You surely must all of you feel and admit the delightfulness of a bow window.'

In London, stucco remained popular for more conservatively designed houses until the 1870s: it was used to cover the whole façade, but seldom the sides or back. Sumptuous examples can be seen on the Holland Park Estate in West London, built by two brothers, William and Francis Radford, who leased the ground from Lord Holland and undertook to erect 77 detached houses to an agreed design [11]. The houses went up between 1860 and 1879. They are virtually identical and so closely spaced as to appear as a terrace rather than detached houses. Each is double-fronted and of three storeys raised on a basement and topped by an attic storey in the roof. The façades are symmetrical and the centrally-placed door is approached up steps. Flanking the door are bay windows rising from the basement and lighting the principal rooms on the ground and first floors. The entrance leads to a hall, beyond which is a staircase placed centrally at the rear. On either side on the

46 Moray Place, Strathbungo, Glasgow, by Alexander Thomson, 1859.

47 Victoria Square, Clifton, Bristol, by Foster and Wood, 1851.

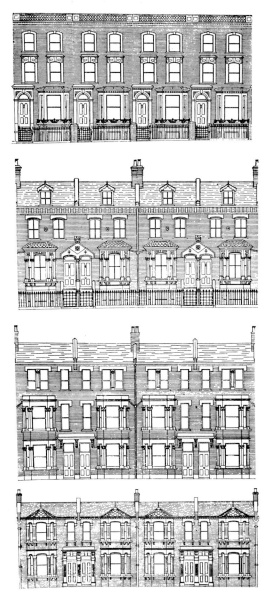

48 *Typical modest London terraces, 1860s–1900. All in Camberwell, from top to bottom they are: (a) 49–52 Vicarage Grove, 1866–8; (b) 90–93 Avondale Square, 1875; (c) 28–34 Sandover Road, 1882; (d) 51–57 Ivydale Road, 1900. (H. J. Dyos, Victorian Suburb, 1973)*

ground floor are large rooms, each with a bay window. The interiors have elaborate plaster cornices and richly carved marble fireplaces. Annual rents were about £340, and the value of the houses about £5,000. They attracted occupants of the most eminent kind: among the early residents were the 4th Marquess of Londonderry, the Maharajah of Lahore and Sir William Fairbairn, the engineer.

Stucco was, however, losing favour with many builders and their clients in London as the principles of Pugin and Ruskin filtered through to them. At the upper end of the market its popularity waned in the early 1860s. Other parts of Britain with good stone at hand, such as Bristol, never took to stucco, and the range of masonry craftsmanship displayed in the houses and terraces of Clifton is astonishing [47].

A grand design in brick appears in two large blocks of houses flanking Cedars Road in Clapham, South London, built in 1860 by a speculative developer to designs by Sir James Knowles. Five storeys high, with attics, they are faced with pale brick and crowned with high French roofs. Their details are neither Gothic nor Classical: the windows have round arches and large-scale leaf decoration of medieval rather than Renaissance character (compare the Grosvenor Hotel: p. 81). In front of the terraces were lamps painted in chocolate and gold in imitation of those of the Tuileries in Paris. Rents were £200–£250 per annum, a substantial sum. The Mid-Victorian fashion for French Second Empire architecture can also be seen in Grosvenor Place, on the Grosvenor Estate west of Buckingham Palace, begun in 1868 by Thomas Cundy III (1820–95). The terraces are stone-faced and grouped as pavilions under separate mansard roofs. The individual houses have bay windows – as we have seen, a common motif.

The Gothic style, which had played little part in Early Victorian developments, grew in popularity. It derived its inspiration from Ruskin and the High Victorian Gothic architects. Polychrome

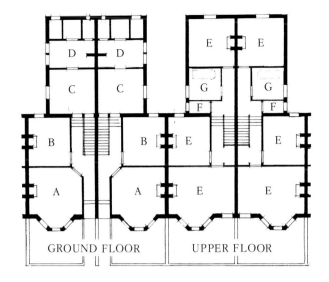

49 *Ground- and upper-floor plans of a typical pair of Late Victorian terrace houses in London (similar to ill. 48d): A parlour, B dining room, C kitchen, D scullery, E bedrooms, F w.c., G bathroom.*

GROUND FLOOR   UPPER FLOOR

decoration in the form of bands of contrasting coloured brick or stone became widespread, and roofs might also have slates of different shades. Leaf carving executed in Bath stone might ape the inspired craftsmanship of the O'Shea brothers on the Oxford Museum of Natural History [150]. Nos. 40–94 Holland Park Road in London, built in 1870–72, are an elaborate later example of the genre, and more can be found in the villas of North Oxford (see p. 50).

A variation on the same theme is that in which similar stylistic features are combined with round-arched or segmental-headed windows and doors. To take one example from many, Lothair Villas in Exeter, of 1870–71, are a pair of brick semi-detached houses, each with two-storeyed bay windows, a gabled third storey and a slate roof. Nos. 90–93 Avondale Square, Camberwell, built in 1875, are terrace houses in a similar style [48b]. Here steps lead up to the entrance floor above a half basement, from which rises a bay window with colonnettes set at its angles. The upper floor has two windows, and a dormer with decorative barge-boards lights an attic room in the roof.

The most common Late Victorian house type developed from this mixed medieval style. In the 1880s in London it took the form of a three-storeyed house, entered on the ground floor, without a basement [48c]. Beside the door, which is protected by a shallow porch, is a two-storeyed bay with sash windows of plate glass. The bay has piers and capitals enriched with naturalistic leaf carving supporting stilted lintels of stone. The bay window above is treated in a similar manner and topped by a parapet. The upper floors above the bay might have a double window divided by a column. A window on each floor above the door completes the fenestration. The slate roof is pitched to the back and front.

The entrance hall gives access – as usual – to a front parlour and a dining room behind, sometimes separated by folding doors. The large front room on the first floor would probably be a bedroom, and behind would be another bedroom with two further bedrooms on the second floor. A long back extension would house a kitchen, washroom and inside or outside water-closet. Nos. 28–34 Sandover Road, Camberwell, built in 1882, exemplify this type of house, which in London may also be found notably in Brixton, Fulham and Shepherds Bush.

By the end of Queen Victoria's reign

the most common houses were two-storeyed, with the bay window capped by a polygonal hipped roof [*48d*]. In place of the third storey, accommodation was added to the 'back addition': above the kitchen, scullery and outside lavatory, on the first floor would be an inside lavatory and bathroom [*49*]. Houses of this type may be seen for instance in Ivydale Road, Camberwell, built in 1900, and Felden Street in Fulham of about the same date. Rosebery Road, Exeter, has houses of a slightly less elaborate, although basically similar design. They were built in 1896–8 and let at £15 a year. For this sum, an artisan could afford an entrance hall, two sitting rooms, a kitchen, three bedrooms, a water-closet and a bathroom. In London such a house could be bought for about

£300 leasehold. Most of the smaller and smallest types of houses in the provinces have no entrance hall: you walk straight into the 'parlour'. They are small by today's standards, but a great improvement over Early Victorian cheap housing. The two-storeyed house might also be built in the form of two flats, each with its own front door, an arrangement known as a 'half-house', 'one up, one down', or 'cottage flats', of which London and Newcastle have many examples.

At the front, the typical house may have low walls topped by cast-iron railings, which sometimes also decorate a small balcony above the porch. The minute front garden was probably planted with a privet hedge by the builder. A tiled path leads up to the door, the upper panels of

50 Back-to-back houses in Leeds, late nineteenth century. Under each roof there are two dwellings back-to-back, in this case on different levels (see the windows in the gable end). Beyond the first three

houses are courtyards containing toilets and coal-sheds. This type of dwelling was so popular with Leeds builders that it was even used – as here – for double-fronted houses.

which are filled with stained glass. The entrance hall is also tiled; an arch resting on plaster brackets – common since the 1840s – gives on to the staircase which would have turned balusters of deal supporting a mahogany rail. The hall and staircase would have a dado of lincrusta, a thick paper with low-relief decoration (mostly produced by the firm of Lincrusta-Walton, on Tyneside). A step or two leads down to the 'back addition' and to a small backyard on a slightly lower level than the front of the house.

Only occasionally do we find variations in the standard plan of the English terrace house. A major example is the back-to-back house [50], found chiefly in the industrial North, and especially in Leeds, where the formula persisted into this century. Two rows of terrace houses are built back-to-back so that each house has a party wall at the back as well as on the sides, and (except at the ends of a terrace) only one outside wall.

'Queen Anne' houses. The final style of the Victorian speculative house was derived from the 'Queen Anne' Revival and particularly from the work of Norman Shaw and others at Bedford Park (see below). It uses red brick, if only for the front of the house, has a tile roof and glazing bars to the windows, bay windows and gabled roofs.

To find the origin of these speculative houses we must trace the use of the 'Queen Anne' style for individual town houses. William Makepeace Thackeray was one of the champions of the revival of eighteenth-century taste. His own house at No. 2 Palace Green, Kensington, London (1860–62), a red brick Classical design by Frederick Hering, has been placed at the beginning of the 'Queen Anne' Revival. A few years later, in 1868–73, a house was built next door at No. 1 Palace Green for the Hon. George Howard. It was designed by Philip Webb and combined many features of the 'Queen Anne' style – red brick, sash windows, rubbed brickwork and asymmetrically placed bay windows

51 *Swan House, 17 Chelsea Embankment, London, by Norman Shaw, 1875–7. (Building News, 1877)*

and gables – although in a characteristically personal way Webb combined these elements with pointed arches. A more publicized example was the Red House at No. 140 Bayswater Road (formerly No. 3 Bayswater Hill), London, which J. J. Stevenson built for his own use (1871,†) [10]. It was a three-storeyed house of red brick (whence its name) and had tall sash windows with glazing bars. A porch at one side and a three-storeyed bay window at the other broke the symmetry of the design. Two gabled brick dormers lit the attic rooms and the roof was flanked by tall chimney-stacks.

Norman Shaw's Lowther Lodge, Kensington Gore (1873–5), now the Royal

52 *A drawing by E. W. Godwin for the White House, Tite Street, London, 1877–9. The high roof covers a studio on the upper floor, lit by windows at the rear of the house. (Hunterian Art Gallery, University of Glasgow, Birnie Philip Bequest)*

Geographical Society headquarters, is another notable early house in this style. It is built on an unusual plan, around an open courtyard, and has an off-centre porch, but with its gables of various shapes, enriched with ornament executed in rubbed and moulded brickwork, it was immensely influential. On the Chelsea Embankment are a group of houses which display variations on the same theme. Swan House

by Shaw of 1875–7 is of red brick and has a varied window treatment [51]. Three large oriels derived from seventeenth-century English exemplars light the first floor; above, tall slender oriels are set between slim segment-headed sash windows; gabled dormers are set in the roof.

Nearby, in Tite Street, E. W. Godwin built the White House for the painter James McNeill Whistler (1877–9,†) [52]. It was of whitewashed brick, an unusual idea in town, and one clearly related to Whistler's interest in making a simple colour the main theme of a painting, as in *The White Girl* of 1864. Godwin and Whistler were the main protagonists of the Aesthetic Movement, which concerned itself with dress and interior design, preaching lightness and simplicity, under the influence of Japanese woodcuts and blue and white porcelain.

Another line was taken by Sir Ernest George (1839–1922) and his partner Harold Peto: the lavish brick and stone decoration of No. 39 Harrington Gardens, Kensington, built in 1882 for W. S. Gilbert (of Savoy Opera fame), is closer in style to the Flemish early seventeenth century [53].

53 Houses in Harrington Gardens, London, by George and Peto, 1880s. On the left, with the stepped gable, is W. S. Gilbert's house.

The house has mullioned windows with leaded lights and elaborately shaped brick gables. This Flemish/Netherlandish style is further exploited in its neighbours, also by George and Peto, and similar houses were soon springing up all over Chelsea and Kensington, notably in Pont Street and Cadogan Square, many by J. J. Stevenson, others by Shaw. Watered-down versions of the style were soon to be used for larger town houses all over the country. For the smaller house in the suburbs designers were beginning to adopt features from these buildings, as well as from smaller detached houses set in the country or in a garden, such as Nesfield's lodge at Kew (see p. 55).

In 1875 Jonathan Carr (1845–1915), a cloth merchant and speculative developer, began to lay out Bedford Park [54], on what was then the western edge of London. It was to be a salubrious suburb, where, in the words of the gently satirical *Ballad of Bedford Park*, 'men may lead a chaste correct Aesthetical existence'. The Gothic style, with its high moral tone, was abandoned in favour of the 'Queen Anne' style, which expressed well the 'Aesthetic' rejection of the showy and the vulgar; Bedford Park attracted many artistic residents. Carr's first architect was E. W. Godwin, but he was soon replaced by Norman Shaw. With help from Maurice B. Adams (1849–1933) and E. J. May (1859–1941), who succeeded Shaw in 1880, houses of varied design were built along tree-lined streets. They are almost all of red brick, mainly two-storeyed with attics but no basements. Shaw built a large house for Carr, a church and the Tabard Inn, as well as giving overall direction for the design of houses. There is a mixture of terrace, semi-detached, and detached houses, each with its own garden. Although Bedford Park was not the first of such spacious suburban layouts it was an influential one.

Carr's own house had wallpapers designed by William Morris; and indeed the whole development looks not unlike the idealized world of William Morris's *News from Nowhere* (1890) which had

54 A prospectus for Bedford Park issued in 1881, proclaiming its healthiness and showing its houses, flowers and church (by Norman Shaw, 1879–82).

BEDFORD PARK, CHISWICK, W.
THE HEALTHIEST PLACE IN THE WORLD
(Annual Death Rate under 6 per Thousand).

Close to TURNHAM GREEN STATION. Trains every few minutes.

The Estate is built on gravelly Soil and has the most approved Sanitary arrangements.

About 500 Houses on the Estate, all in the picturesque Queen Anne style of Architecture.

A Garden and a Bath Room with Hot and Cold water to every house, whatever its size.
A Kindergarten and good Cheap Day Schools on the Estate, and a School of Art.
Also Church, Club (for Ladies & Gentlemen), Stores, "The Tabard Inn," Tennis Courts, &c.
Several houses now to let at rents varying from £30 to £130.

55 *Whitehall Court, Victoria Embankment, London, by Archer and Green, 1884.*

very pretty houses, low and not large, standing back a little way from the river; they were mostly built of red brick and roofed with tiles, and looked, above all, comfortable, and as if they were, so to say, alive and sympathetic with the life of the dwellers in them. There was a continuous garden in front of them, going down to the water's edge, in which the flowers were now blooming luxuriantly, and sending delicious waves of summer scent over the eddying stream.

Flats for the middle classes

Although flats were already common on the Continent and in Scotland in the eighteenth century, they never became popular with the English middle classes in Victorian times. It was perhaps because of their association with working-class housing (see below). Some of the earliest important examples in London were in Victoria Street. In 1853 *The Builder* reported that a Mr Mackenzie had constructed 'residences on flats'. They were built as a speculation, and designed by Henry Ashton. Just nearby, one of the largest early developments of flats was built partly to a design by E. R. Robson (1835–1917), better known as the architect of the London School Board [238]: Queen

Anne's Mansions (1876–88,†) was fourteen storeys high; apart from a Gothic arch leading into a gloomy interior courtyard, the exterior had blank yellow brick walls pierced by unornamented windows.

A far more polished design is that by Norman Shaw for Albert Hall Mansions, built in 1879–86. The block is of red brick in the 'Queen Anne' style, and similar in its details to the houses Shaw was building in Chelsea and Kensington at about the same time [51]. There are sash windows, very large shaped gables and balconies which act as a unifying feature in the design. An alternative Late Victorian inspiration for the design of large blocks of flats was the French Château style, used in 1884 by Thomas Archer and A. Green (d. 1904) for their massive Whitehall Court [55], the high roofs and cupolas of which provide part of the picturesque roofscape of Whitehall as seen from St James's Park.

Philanthropy and paternalism in housing

Although the types of houses discussed so far sheltered the vast majority of Victorians, there remains another important category: housing which was provided by an employer, by a charitable individual, or – at the end of the century – by a local authority for working-class tenants.

56 A lane in Edensor, Derbyshire, by Joseph Paxton and John Robertson, begun in 1838.

57 A cottage pair at Baldersby St James, Yorkshire, by William Butterfield, c. 1855.

The concept of an employer providing accommodation for his servants goes back to earliest times. It must be remembered that the country and town houses of the well-to-do besides housing the family of the owners also accommodated the numerous servants who met their needs. In the same way, on a large estate, lodges and estate cottages would be built for the workers, often, as we have seen, designed as picturesque incidents in the landscape. In some cases whole estate villages were built, as they had been in the eighteenth century. In 1838 the Duke of Devonshire started to move the village of Edensor out of sight of his great house, Chatsworth in Derbyshire. The new village [56] was laid out by Joseph Paxton, who as we have seen was the Duke's gardener, and was to become famous as the designer of the Crystal Palace. He designed a number of the new buildings; the others were by a local architect, John Robertson of Derby, who had worked as a draughtsman in the office of J. C. Loudon. Each house is different, cottages and villas clustering around the church in an informal, Picturesque way that is very much in the tradition of Nash's Blaise Hamlet. In style they range from the Italian Villa to the Tudor Cottage.

The Cottage style, with its gabled and half-hipped roofs, is the basis of Butterfield's remarkably simple estate cottages of the mid-1850s at Baldersby St James in Yorkshire [57], where he also built the church, vicarage and school. His buildings express the ordered social hierarchy of the village: largest and finest is the church, whose tall spire dominates the houses; the vicarage is faced like the church with stone, and is a gabled, two-storeyed building; the school is also of stone. The cottages on the other hand are built of brick and stone, or just brick, and their small scale and simple treatment indicate the humble social position of their occupants. Their plain brick construction, half-hipped gables, dormers and small windows with glazing bars – similar to Butterfield's brick vicarages in Yorkshire – became widespread in estate housing during the middle years of the century, and form the basis of the design of cottage housing estates of later dates.

The Picturesque tradition was revived by Eden Nesfield in estate cottages built in the 1860s and 1870s. Those on the Crewe Hall Estate in Cheshire are particularly delightful. One pair, for instance, dated 1865, is built of red brick with tiled roofs and high chimney-stacks [58]; each cottage has a projecting gable; the upper floor is tile-hung and treated as a half storey; shallow oriel windows overhang a cove decorated with incised pargetting and the crests of the roofs are decorated with metal weather-vanes. Nesfield designed farms and a smithy for the estate in a similar style.

The concept of the estate village was also developed by manufacturers for their workers. One of the first to do this on a large scale was Sir Titus Salt, at Saltaire near Bradford in Yorkshire. By 1854 150 houses were ready: in 1872 there were 820. His architects, H. F. Lockwood (1811–78) and R. Mawson (1834–1904), a well-known Bradford firm, produced substantially built stone terraces with Italianate details, laid out on a rigid plan [59].

Salt had been preceded on a smaller scale in 1849 by Colonel Akroyd, who built a few houses on the back-to-back principle (p. 65) for his workers at Copley, near Halifax. In 1855 he decided on a more ambitious development at Haley Hill, Halifax, which came to be known as Akroydon (now Boothtown). The orig-

58 Stowford Cottages, Crewe Hall, Cheshire, by Eden Nesfield, 1865.

inal architect for the scheme was George Gilbert Scott, designer of a splendid church for Akroyd higher up the hill [191]. He was soon replaced by W. H. Crossland, and building began in 1861. Trim Gothic cottages are arranged in terraces, in a formal layout at the centre of which is a public garden. The later industrial estates

59 Saltaire, Yorkshire, by Lockwood and Mawson, 1851–76. In the foreground, flanking the canal, are the alpaca mills (1851); behind them, the Congregational Church; far right, the beginning of the public park. In the town the large building with a tower is the Institution, facing the school beyond it.

60 Port Sunlight, Cheshire, by William and Segar Owen and others, begun in 1888.

who presided over one of the meetings in 1848. Its object was to erect dwellings for poor families 'so contrived as to unite comfort with economy'. After a few experimental schemes, in 1849–50 the Society erected a block of 'Model Houses for Families' in London in Streatham Street, Bloomsbury [61]. Here Henry Roberts, the Society's architect, produced a highly influential design. The site was in a closely built-up area near the British Museum. The block is four storeys high and the exterior treatment in brick and stucco with minimal Classical decoration, although very plain and solid, is not unlike that of speculative houses of the cheaper kind at the same date. The dwellings are self-contained flats arranged around three sides of a courtyard, which allowed air and light into the rear of the building. Access is by means of open brick galleries with iron balconies, intended – the architect tells us – to give each family the privacy of its own front door, while at the same time separating the flats to prevent the spread of contagious diseases. Gallery access has remained a standard arrangement for cheaper flats in England to this day. Inside, each flat had a living room, one or two bedrooms, a kitchen and its own w.c. Rents were two shillings and four shillings a week – £5.4s. and £10.8s. per annum.

of Bournville, Birmingham, begun in 1879 by the Cadburys for the workers in their chocolate factory (with a larger 'garden city' begun in 1895), and Port Sunlight, Cheshire [60], begun in 1888 by the soap manufacturer Lever, followed the lead, but took the picturesque architecture of Nesfield and Shaw as their model and the spacious layout of Bedford Park (p. 68) as the guide to their planning.

The slums of the Victorian period were in many cases Georgian buildings, although much Early Victorian building of the worst kind soon slipped into this category. A concern for public health, particularly after the cholera outbreaks of the 1840s, led to attempts to provide better dwellings for the working classes. They were inspired by prudence, and by genuine charitable feeling on the part of some of the more fortunate members of Victorian society. The bye-laws, which have already been mentioned, were the most important outcome of this as far as houses were concerned.

A number of associations grew up to deal with the problem, most notably the Society for Improving the Conditions of the Labouring Classes, founded in 1844. Its supporters included Lord Ashley, later Earl of Shaftesbury, and Prince Albert,

Private individuals were also active in building flats for the working classes. One such scheme was Columbia Square, Bethnal Green, in London, financed by Miss Angela (later Baroness) Burdett-Coutts and built in 1857–60 to designs by Henry A. Darbishire. These flats, which are in a robust Gothic style, were arranged around courtyards. Attached to the scheme was the Gothic extravaganza of Columbia Market (see Chapter 3).

Another important private benefaction was that of George Peabody, an American banker who had settled in Britain. In 1862 he set up a trust to 'ameliorate the condition and augment the comforts of the poor . . . of London'. In the next year, with Darbishire as its architect, the Trust started work in a block in Commercial Road,

Spitalfields. By the 1870s Darbishire had evolved a fairly standardized design of mainly five-storeyed blocks with minimal Italianate decorative treatment, built of greyish yellow brick, with small, deep-set windows [*62*]. The Peabody Estate in Greenman Street, Islington, of 1865, is a characteristic example; numbers of these blocks survive.

In spite of these enterprises, purpose-built flats only represented a small proportion of Victorian housing in England. Perhaps the example of Glasgow, where the vast majority of inhabitants were housed in one- or two-room tenements, built in blocks around dark and often unhealthy courtyards, showed the worst aspect of this kind of accommodation.

*62 Peabody Estate, Greenman Street, Islington, London, 1865. (*Illustrated London News, *1866)*

63 Boundary Estate, Shoreditch, London, begun by the London County Council in 1893, seen about 1907.

61 Model Houses for Families, Streatham Street, London, by Henry Roberts, 1849–50: inner and outer façades, and plan of two typical flats. (Roberts, Dwellings of the Labouring Classes, *1867)*

However, towards the end of the period there were a few examples of local authorities providing flats, notably in Liverpool and London. Towards the end of the century the London County Council began a programme of clearing slums and replacing them with blocks of flats, of which the first were the Boundary Estate in Shoreditch [*63*], begun in 1893, and the Millbank Estate near the Tate Gallery, begun in 1897. Built of red brick in a simplified Vernacular or Arts and Crafts style, they have an architectural variety that is lacking in Darbishire's monolithic blocks, which were by that time considered inadequate for all but the very poor. For the rapidly growing numbers of the 'upper' working classes and lower middle classes, the artisans and clerks, the answer to the housing problem was provided not by philanthropic schemes, but rather by cheap train fares and cheap speculative houses in the suburbs.

2

Entertainment

Clubs

THE LONDON CLUBS developed from the seventeenth-century coffee houses and, like them, exist for the sake of conviviality and for people joined by common political or recreational interests. They also provided libraries and newsrooms. With social divisions in the world of entertainment becoming more marked, some clubs became more exclusive. A building for a major club required a number of large rooms – like a stately house – frequented by a relatively small number of people at any one time: library, lounge, smoking room, billiard room and dining room. The kitchen was a very important feature; that of the Reform Club was considered extremely advanced and was often imitated. The Gresham Clubhouse of 1843–4, by Henry Flower, used to bring up 'the dishes from the kitchen to the waiters' rooms by "lifts" '. The club is thus something between a private house and a public building: more precisely, as the contemporary critic W. H. Leeds remarked in his booklet on the Travellers' Club, 'One enjoys in comfort what one might not be able to enjoy oneself singly'; 'the solitary may find society and a home, without the annoyances frequently attached to the latter.' The fashion of a separate stately building for a major club was set by Nash's United Service Club and the Athenaeum by Decimus Burton (1800–1881), built in the late 1820s opposite each other in Waterloo Place, on the corner of Pall Mall, close to Whitehall and the royal palaces [65].

The building which really began the club mania in Pall Mall and St James's was the Reform Club [65–7], begun in 1837, although it had a more modest predecessor by the same architect and in the same style next door in Pall Mall, the Travellers' Club of 1829 [65]. The Reform Club was an institution of the Liberals and its name celebrated the Reform Act of 1832. For the new building, architects of the highest rank were invited to submit designs: Decimus Burton, Sir Robert Smirke, George Basevi, C. R. Cockerell and Charles Barry. Barry had just begun building the Houses of Parliament in Gothic, but he won the Reform Club competition with a Renaissance design similar to his slightly earlier Manchester Athenaeum and Travellers' Club. The Reform Club is almost square in plan [67]. In the centre is a large court [66] top-lit by a glazed roof and surrounded on both the main floors by corridors, an important feature in Barry's work, especially in his country houses. On each floor at the back is a very large room divided into three by pairs of columns placed close to the wall. The order on the upper storey is Corinthian. The decorations are, as usual, largely of plaster. Outside, in contrast to the earlier clubs, the Reform has a Portland stone façade. The cost of the building was originally estimated at £19,000, but amounted to £80,000 in the end.

*64 Savoy Hotel, London, by Collings B. Young, 1884–9: (1) river front, (2) restaurant balcony, (3) courtyard, (4) reception room, (5) 'a pleasant corner', (6) entrance, (7) restaurant. (*Illustrated London News, 1889)

65 View along Pall Mall, London, in 1911 showing the Reform Club in the foreground (by Sir Charles Barry, 1837–41), followed by the Travellers' Club (Barry, 1829–32), the Athenaeum (Decimus Burton, 1829–30), and, beyond Waterloo Place, the United Service Club (John Nash, after 1827).

The Reform Club is of importance as the first major *palazzo* elevation of the nineteenth century in Britain. Changes within the Classical modes are always subtle, and one might at first wonder what the fundamental difference is between the Reform Club and, say, the Athenaeum nearby. The Athenaeum is a product of the English Palladian tradition, with its rusticated ground storey and high *piano nobile*, usually terminating with a simple horizontal line (the attic is a later addition). But the model for Barry's elevation is something more vigorous, the Renaissance *palazzi* of Florence and Rome of the early sixteenth century, notably the Palazzo Farnese. The

building is conceived as one large detached block. Its main divisions are the horizontals of the storeys, and the whole is crowned by a massive projecting cornice. W. H. Leeds gave this kind of cornice the Italian name *cornicione*, to stress its difference from the Greek cornice or entablature. The latter, he says, lacks grandeur if the sculptured frieze is left out: the cornicione is far more useful for nineteenth-century elevations, which in most cases have no columns or pilasters, and rely for their decoration on ornamental window-frames. Another important element of the Reform Club façade is the fact that the ground floor is given equal importance, reflecting the interior. This arrangement was not always followed by the design's imitators, but it proved eminently useful if the building, say a bank, had to be made more open to the street than in the earlier prototype, the Palladian London house. Finally there is one feature which has less to do with the Classical style, but is unmistakably characteristic of Barry: the accents provided by the chimney tops at the corners.

Barry's example was followed almost at once in Glasgow by David (1768–1843) and James (c. 1807–62) Hamilton, among the most noted Scottish Neo-Classical architects: their Western Club, 147 Buchanan Street, of 1841, is a variation on Barry's theme in three and a half storeys.

The unsuccessful competitors for the Reform Club did not have to wait long for similar jobs to come their way. The Conservative Club in St James's, by George Basevi and Sydney Smirke (1798–1877), Sir Robert's younger brother, was built in 1843–5. It reverts to

66, 67 The Reform Club. Right: central saloon, seen from the colonnade near the top of the stairs. The arch on the ground floor opposite is filled with a mirror, and reflects the tiled floor. Below: ground-floor plan (Civil Engineer and Architect's Journal, 1840).

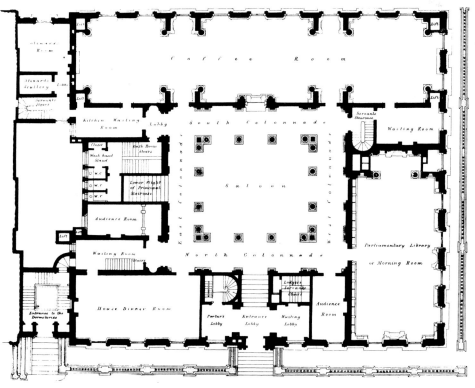

68 Great Western Hotel, Paddington, London, by P. C. Hardwick, 1851–3. In this photograph, taken about 1900, the train sheds can be seen behind the hotel.

C. O. Parnell (d. 1865) and Alfred Smith was similar, but outdid the Carlton in size and in the vigour and three-dimensionality of its features.

By the mid-century, however, the clubs were losing their edge over other ornate Classical buildings, especially in the commercial sphere. Later clubs either continued the old formula, as did the very large Junior Carlton in Pall Mall (1866,†), by David Brandon (1813–97) – an enlarged version of the Reform to relieve the waiting list for the Carlton – or they give up the *palazzo* formula altogether, as does the Constitutional Club in Northumberland Avenue of 1884, by Robert Edis (1839–1927), with its multitude of storeys and giant Dutch gables. The National Liberal Club in Whitehall Place, of the same date, is one of Alfred Waterhouse's most ingenious plans, filling as it does a sharply angled corner site.

In the provinces, where the echo of London Clubland was faint, one might single out the Union Club in Birmingham, built in 1869 at the corner of Newhall Street and Colmore Row, a street noted for its splendid ensemble of Mid-Victorian *palazzi*. It is by Yeoville Thomason (1826–1901), the architect of the Council House [*138*]. The Manchester Reform Club of 1870, by Edward Salomons (1827–1906), is remarkable for its symmetrical Venetian Gothic.

the Athenaeum style, with a rusticated ground floor, Tuscan Doric porches and balustraded cornice; in addition, the main storey has a full Corinthian order. The Carlton Club, the other major Conservative club, next door to the Reform, received an extremely grand new building, also designed by Sydney Smirke (1845–56, later altered,†). Ten years had elapsed since the Reform Club, and we find Smirke selecting the richer Venetian Renaissance of Sansovino's Library of St Mark in Venice. As well as being more outwardly splendid, this design has the advantage of letting in more light – an important consideration for its imitators in Britain. The windows were arched and very much larger than Barry's, and set between half-columns. A balustrade filled the space below the windows on the upper floor and a vigorous cornice with *putti* and festoons, crowned by a heavy balustrade, terminated the building. The Army and Navy Club (1848–51,†), diagonally opposite the Carlton, by the lesser known

Hotels

During the Victorian period there were dramatic changes in the mode, speed and frequency of travelling, and these changes were reflected in the size, planning and structure of hotels. In the early 1800s the speed of travel through Britain had already been greatly improved by the turnpike roads and the stage-coach system. A new group of inns, since about 1830 mostly called 'hotels', grew up quickly. They were soon to be overtaken by the needs of railway travellers: most journeys could be done in one day, and what was needed was

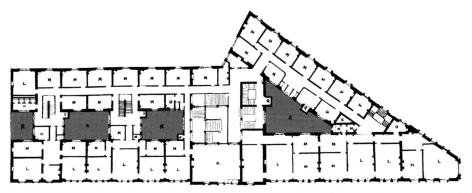

69 *First-floor plan of the Westminster Palace Hotel, Victoria Street, London, by W. and A. Moseley, 1857–8, showing the arrangement of* suites. K ladies' coffee room, L sitting room, M bedroom, N closet, O bathroom, Q lift, R inner court, S ventilation shaft. *(Builder, 1858)*

no longer a rest on the journey but a convenient place at the destination. From the late 1830s onwards huge hotels were built in conjunction with railway termini, most of them financed by the railways or their subsidiary companies.

Although the railway hotels included a great number of cheap rooms, their social standing was about that of the new clubs. In London they could not quite compete with Claridges Hotel (which was then of no special note architecturally, being a group of Georgian town houses), but when the Great Western Hotel at Paddington Station [68] asked for bookings in advance it wanted to ensure a certain class of clientele. The lower floors of the hotels included many sitting rooms and drawing rooms, and on the ground floor there were also sitting rooms which could be hired privately. Enormous decorative display could be found in the main dining and sitting rooms. In their technology and convenience, their large number of bathrooms, private w.c.s and lifts for all purposes, the railway hotels were without rival in the 1860s – with the exception perhaps of the most modern hospitals (see Chapter 3), but with everything crowded on to small sites and consequently on many storeys, construction was infinitely more complicated.

The immediate predecessors of the large station hotels were the resort and spa hotels, such as the Queen's at Cheltenham of 1836–9 by R. W. and C. Jearrad. The Great Western (Hydro) Hotel in Bristol, built in 1837–9 by the local architect R. S. Pope (1791–1884), apparently based on ideas by the great engineer Isambard Kingdom Brunel (1806–59), marks the transitional stage. It boasted 'Baths, warm, cold, vapour and shower in the house', to compete with spas, but its main purpose was to serve the Atlantic Steamship Line and the railway line (soon to come) from London.

The building which started the hotel boom in London was the Great Western Hotel of 1851–3, which forms the main front of Paddington Station [68]. It was designed by Philip Charles Hardwick (1820–90). Hardwick was one of the most versatile architects of the period, and had previously been concerned with Euston Station and its hotel (p. 99). The Great Western had about 150 rooms, and was an immediate commercial success. Large apartments on the first floor, with a private w.c., cost 22s.6d. per day, small bedrooms on the fourth floor 1s.6d. The next major station hotel was the Grosvenor (1860–62), adjoining the Brighton Company's station, later called Victoria Station. It was

70 *Grand Hotel, Scarborough, Yorkshire, by Cuthbert Brodrick, 1863–7. The terrace was originally open.*

designed by James Knowles, senior, with the help of his son, later Sir James (whom we have already met as a designer of houses, p. 62), and has seven storeys in all. After that the fever increased, and we have in quick succession the Cannon Street Hotel (1861,†) and the Charing Cross Hotel (1864), both by E. M. Barry. The Charing Cross had 214 beds. The largest of all, with 400 beds, was the Midland Grand at St Pancras, built in 1868–74 for over £400,000 by George Gilbert Scott for the Midland Railway Company (see below) [71, 72].

Other hotels followed the mode of the station hotels. In London there were vast structures in Northumberland Avenue, and, most spectacular, the Langham Hotel in Portland Place, designed by John Giles, opened in 1865 by the Prince of Wales. It had up to 400 beds plus 36 sitting and drawing rooms, employed 250 servants and cost £300,000. The most important technical innovation since the early 1860s was the hydraulic lift, first used by Elisha Otis in New York in 1857.

Not quite so spectacular was the hotel boom in the seaside resorts. The Clarence Hotel at Dover, Kent, of 1863, by John Whichcord (1823–85), was praised for its lifts and salubrity. The Grand in Brighton, Sussex (1862–4), by the same architect, had five lifts and 'gilded balconies'. It was later outdone in many ways in 1888 by Waterhouse's Metropole nearby. The best known of all the seaside hotels is the Grand in Scarborough, Yorkshire (1863–7) [70], by Cuthbert Brodrick, of Leeds Town Hall fame [143]. It is topped by high mansard roofs and prominently sited on a cliff.

Although British hotels were outshone by American ones as regards size and convenience, and by the French as regards cuisine, the reputation of English hotel designers was high, at least when hotels had to be built for a predominantly British clientele. Even in Germany, as late as 1878, an Englishman is said to have designed the plumbing in the large Central Hotel in Berlin.

Only the very largest office buildings could compete with the later station hotels in size and splendour. From the point of view of architectural style and elevational treatment there are many similarities. The most common modes of decoration were the Classical and Renaissance styles. The Great Western Hotel in Bristol relates to the post-Georgian terraces of Clifton; Hardwick's Great Western, with its stuccoed front, has many features in common with the largest terraces of Paddington [68]. But by 1850 most architects were searching for new, hitherto unused historical styles, or combinations of styles. The Paddington hotel was called 'Louis XIV', referring to its flanking towers and mansard roof. They correspond closely to what was to be called the Second Empire style, after Napoleon III's extensions to the Louvre – a somewhat impure and ornate version of palatial architecture, with a smattering of the Picturesque and French Renaissance in the use of towers and roofs. As in office buildings, the problem arose of how to squeeze the growing number of storeys into the traditional framework of the two- or three-storeyed Classical elevation. Knowles, at the Grosvenor Hotel, got round this by playing down the divisions between the storeys, and by having a very pronounced main cornice and a massive curved roof which dominates the building. Thus the proportions of a Classical building remained basically the same, although the whole is very much larger. In addition, Knowles was to some extent a follower of Ruskin and his theories on decoration, and provided a lot of carved vegetation as well as sculptured heads of famous politicians. The hotel was thus elevated into the realm of modern 'art' architecture. E. M. Barry, on the other hand, at Charing Cross, did not try to pull the numerous storeys and windows together, but left the observer with picturesque fuzziness. The Langham, like the Grosvenor, exhibits bare brick walls, but with its projections and recessions lacks the grandiose unified blocklike structure of Knowles's building.

Scott's Midland Grand at St Pancras (1868–74; now offices) is memorable for its brick elevation decorated by arcaded Gothic windows with polished granite shafts [72]. The clock tower resembles the Big Ben tower at the Houses of Parliament [148]. St Pancras Station with its hotel, costing in all nearly £1,000,000, was a public building of the first order [93]. Its curved façade is cleverly adapted to the irregular site. Inside there were lavish public rooms [71] and a most dramatic staircase, supported on exposed iron beams and still today covered with the original Axminster carpet. Externally the staircase is expressed by very large windows breaking through the division of the storeys. The skyline, one of the most elaborate of the age, gives life to its humdrum surroundings. Gothic hotels, however, remained rare. Aberystwyth Hotel, a fantastic pile begun in 1864 by J. P. Seddon (1827–1906), was abandoned and became the University College of Wales before it was finished.

The very top category of London hotels

from the 1880s to the early 1900s reflected a change in attitude: the new principle was sophistication rather than splendour, quality rather than quantity. Refinement meant especially that women were allowed more and more into the reception rooms of the hotels [*64(4)*]. Modern conveniences were developed further: the number of bathrooms grew. An early example of this new breed of luxury hotel was the Savoy in London [*64*], built in 1884–9 for Richard D'Oyly Carte, the aesthetically and technologically enlightened patron of the adjacent Savoy Theatre (p. 91). The architect was the youthful Collings B. Young, the builder/engineer G. H. Holloway, whom D'Oyly Carte also employed for his Royal English Opera House (p. 92). (There the architect was T. E. Collcutt, who succeeded Young

at the Savoy and extensively remodelled it.) The Savoy Theatre had been the first theatre to have electric light; the hotel too was lit by electricity, and had 67 bathrooms. An early manager 1890–97 was the famous Swiss *hotelier* César Ritz. The first hotel in London where every bedroom had a bathroom was the Carlton of 1891–9, by C. J. Phipps (1835–97). Another hotel in D'Oyly Carte's stable was Claridge's, which he had rebuilt in 1894–7 by Sir Ernest George and Yeates.

The stylistic movement that corresponded to these efforts was the Domestic Revival of the 1870s and 1880s, and more specifically the Aesthetic Movement (pp. 66–7). The interiors were characterized by delicate decoration and colours, and the display of living plants.

Much more outgoing is the terracotta

71, 72 Midland Grand Hotel, St Pancras, London, by Sir George Gilbert Scott, 1868–74: early photographs of the combined hotel and station (with King's Cross beyond; compare ill. 93), and of the Grand Coffee Room (opposite), on the first floor of the quadrant.

73 Midland Hotel, Manchester, by C. Trubshaw, 1898.

decoration of the Russell Hotel (1898), in an arcaded 'Château de Madrid' French Renaissance by C. Fitzroy Doll (1851–1929). The vast pile of the Midland Hotel in Manchester by C. Trubshaw (d. 1917), of the same date, might be seen as the final apotheosis of the Victorian hotel [73].

Popular entertainment

Architecture for serious and not so serious entertainment is probably the least coherent category to be discussed in this book. We shall be chiefly concerned with public houses and with two very distinct types of building: large complex structures providing all kinds of entertainment, and theatres. In addition there are the piers, the characteristic place of entertainment at the newly popular seaside resorts.

The relatively short life of entertainment buildings makes their development difficult to trace, especially in the early part of the period. First there is the story of technological advance – in the construction of large-span roofs, fireproofing, and in heating, lighting and ventilation. Then there is the progress of their exuberant decoration, of terracotta, tiles, mirrors and cut glass. The production of these trimmings became more and more efficient as the century went on, replacing the often more makeshift efforts of the

Regency and Early Victorian periods. In common with the trend in Late Victorian domestic architecture, elaboration of ornament did not mean a rise in social status: on the contrary, there was a growing tendency for the middle classes to stay away.

Public houses

Public houses, or 'pubs', in the nineteenth century form one of the most complicated chapters of social and architectural history. They became a moral and social issue which, given its interplay with the commercial interest of the brewers, led to constant concern on the part of politicians and legislators. Pubs must come second only to dwellings in their frequency and general townscape value, and they are among the most ornate specimens of Victorian architecture. The architectural historian must ask two questions: What were the commercial and legislative developments that gave rise to the vast number of pubs and their extraordinary architectural splendour, and which were the particular styles and methods of decoration adopted in the course of the decades?

To begin with, as with so many other types of building in the nineteenth century, the story is one of increasing differentiation. The inn, the hostel, the restaurant and the tavern producing its own beer were traditionally one institution. By about 1830 several major changes had taken place: the better inns and hostels separated themselves from the coaching inns and began, as we have seen, to call themselves 'hotels' – a term which many pubs confusingly adopted whether they supplied accommodation or not. The 'tavern' became solely concerned with serving drinks to the casual visitor. The beer was no longer brewed on the premises, and the number of breweries became smaller and smaller and competition between them grew. This led to a new feature on the outside of pubs: advertisements for particular brands of drinks. A further

74 The Old King's Head, at the corner of Euston Road and Hampstead Road, London: a largely Mid-Victorian pub, with lanterns, prominent lettering, and marble columns, photographed before demolition (for road-widening) in 1906.

specialization occurred after about 1830 with the 'gin palaces', which served mainly spirits. To serve the interests of the brewers, in 1830 the Duke of Wellington's Government abolished licenses for selling beer: every ratepayer could open a beer house. As a result thousands of drinking resorts sprang up in the next few years.

Another result of all these developments was strict social segregation and stratification. Previously there were no essential differences between middle-class and lower-class establishments. But now the middle and upper classes were attracted to

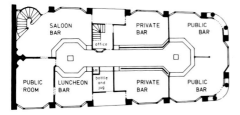

75 *Ground-floor plan of the Elephant and Castle, Newington Butts, London, by John Farrer, 1897, showing the central bar area serving a number of specialized separate rooms.*

the new hotels, and the numerous small new establishments catered for the most numerous customers, the artisans and workmen. Others, who did not like pubs, consumed their drinks at home – an understandable development with the new emphasis on home and family life. The pubs tried to respond to the new stratifications by creating different compartments, saloon, parlour, etc., separated from one another and accessible through up to six separate entrances. Yet by the late nineteenth century most people from the artisan classes upwards would not be seen in a tavern, and the German *Baedeker* for London of 1901 advised visitors to stay clear of the 'numerous public houses', except perhaps to stand at the bar for a quick drink. All these provisions were, of course, even more relevant for women.

Finally there was the growth of the temperance movement. Until the 1830s, no one had thought of beer as dangerous. It was considered wholesome, even for children. But by the 1870s pressure groups, mostly Nonconformists, had obtained sufficient influence through the Liberals to have licensing laws and beer duties reintroduced (in 1872 and 1880 respectively). The number of new pubs increased much more slowly, though they became bigger. In many of the better-class residential suburbs, building covenants already cut down on the number of public houses. In most parts of Belgravia it is difficult to find

a pub at all. Yet another element discouraging trade was the general availability of clean water with the progress in communal supplies.

Like many other new building types in towns, pubs at first did not differ from houses in their arrangement and decoration. On large suburban estates, however, they were planned from the start. Usually placed boldly at the ends of terraces, they brought higher rents to the developer and the ground landlord. Traditionally, the ends of terraces had been supplied with extra decoration, such as a balustrade on top of the cornice and extra rustication. What the pub required in addition was larger windows on the ground floor and on the first floor. Very soon, in the 1830s and 1840s, the new kind of plate-glass shop front was adopted, together with its paraphernalia like narrow pilasters of granite or imitation marble, ornate fascias, bracketed cornices and heraldry, all of which could also be introduced when a new pub was fitted into an older building. What really made a pub look like a pub was the advertisements, on often disproportionately large boards of wood or metal [74]. Usually there were very large gas lamps to illuminate these signboards at night, in considerable contrast to the generally dark streets.

The great majority of pubs were built in the Classical style and its various nineteenth-century interpretations. Examples in London are the Eagle Tavern in City Road (1839,†) and the Balmoral Castle (1856) on the Churchill Gardens Estate in Pimlico, built in the manner of the more ornate dwellings in that district, which was noted for public houses. From the 1860s onwards many pubs followed the fashion for the richer Renaissance modes, especially the 'Second Empire' adopted for hotels. In this style, again in London, are the King Lud in Ludgate Circus (1870, by Lewis Isaacs), rising many storeys on a very constricted site, and the famous Horse Shoe Hotel in Tottenham Court Road (1875, by E. L. Paraire), a large establishment that included rooms for dining. The chaotic character of the earlier and cheaper pub façades was avoided here through a more careful integration of the letter-boards into the fascia. Occasionally there were Gothic and Picturesque versions, of which the best known is the Swiss Cottage, in north-west London, probably first built in this fashion *c.* 1840 and renewed many times.

The inside of pubs changed perhaps more radically than the façade. Traditionally it did not differ from the inside of an ordinary house. Gradually, with more sophisticated machinery to pump beer, a bar, separating those serving from the customers, was required. In the large establishments horseshoe-shaped bars came into use [75]. For customers who wanted privacy 'snob screens' on the bar, of metal lattice or swivelling panes of etched or cut glass, were introduced, while large mirrors (probably from the time of the 1862 London International Exhibition onwards) enabled the publican to observe his customers and also gave the impression of more space. Stucco decoration increased, as well as costly woodcarving on the bar. Pubs became places of the greatest architectural elaboration, an elaboration which a generation earlier even the middle classes could barely afford; yet their customers belonged almost exclusively to the lower classes, for whom they often meant an escape from squalid homes.

The peak in pub building and in architectural and decorative elaboration came only in the last decade of the Victorian period. The temperance war was heating up. During the Liberal administrations there was fear that the country might be 'dried up', but the Tories, in 1886–92 and from 1895 onwards, were openly pro-beer (for instance, distributing 'beerages'). There was frantic development in building, refitting, and buying and selling pubs which became one of the most profitable of all speculations until the boom collapsed, in London at least, in 1899.

Many of the speculative ventures were the work of specialist firms. In London, the

76 *The Rutland Arms, Francis Avenue, Southsea, Hampshire, by A. E. Cogswell, 1898, a half-timbered manor looming over neighbouring terrace houses.*

firms included Treadwell and Martin (the Rising Sun, Tottenham Court Road, 1896), Shoebridge and Rising (the Boleyn, Barking Road, 1899), and Eedle and Meyers (the Angel, Islington, 1901). The exuberance and size of the buildings make them stand out from their surroundings, especially in the suburbs. The artisan terraces of Southsea in Hampshire are dominated by the riotous diversity of A. E. Cogswell's (1858–1934) pubs of the turn of the century [76].

77 *The saloon bar of the Cantons, Cambridge Circus, London. (*Licensed Victuallers' Gazette, *1899)*

78 The Oxford Music Hall, London, by Finch, Hill and Paraire, 1857.

As with most Late Victorian architecture, the nominal style of pubs is difficult to pinpoint. They use English Renaissance half-timbering, 'Queen Anne' and debased Baroque features, which can be traced back to the domestic work of Norman Shaw and Ernest George in the 1870s and 1880s, and they also display a great variety of materials: elaborate stone-carving, contrasting with brick, or complete terracotta facing, as on the Angel. The Rising Sun has slightly more restrained and exceedingly elegant stucco decoration in a sort of Flemish Late Gothic-Art Nouveau. A sign of the firm control of the overall designer is the greater integration of lettering and advertising into the architecture of the façade.

Inside, too, there was growing sophistication and splendour [77]: mirrors with embossed ornament and especially screens with ornamented and 'brilliant cut' glass can still be seen in many pubs, for instance at the Assembly House in Kentish Town, London, of 1896. Many of the decorative motifs recall the exuberant Rococo plant forms seen on textiles in the Great Exhibition of 1851, combined with motifs of popular history and heraldry. The ceilings carry elaborate stucco reliefs, or, more often, imitations of stucco in lincrusta (see p. 65). As Mark Girouard has shown, the wooden bar fittings are reminiscent of the more elaborate sideboards and drawing room mantelpieces of the 'Aesthetic' 1870s and 1880s.

Mixed entertainment, and the seaside

The two largest places of entertainment in London, larger than almost any other building in the country, were the Crystal Palace in Sydenham and the Alexandra Palace on Muswell Hill. The former was the 1851 Exhibition building [85, 91, 92], which was bought by a private company, moved, re-erected and reopened in 1854. Until it burnt down in 1936 it provided innumerable attractions, such as 'industrial courts', cafeterias, orchestras, and natural history and portrait galleries. The most important addition in the new building was central heating, which introduced 'the mild and genial heat of Madeira throughout our cold and damp English winter'. Across London on the north, Alexandra Palace also re-used a large exhibition structure, that of the 1862 Palace of Industries [97]. Immediately after its completion in 1873 the whole structure burnt down; rebuilt by J. Johnson, it reopened two years later. The entertainment, which included waxworks and canoeing, was less cultural than at Sydenham. The building itself still exists, and although it is much smaller than the Crystal Palace and less adventurous to our eyes, in that the outside is encased in Neo-Renaissance stone and brickwork – a reflection of what the 1870s thought about iron architecture (see pp. 106–8) – the inside, especially the central hall, is one of the most impressive of all nineteenth-century engineering spaces.

After the numerous and popular fairs, a more permanent set of structures was to be found in pleasure gardens. They declined in popularity in the early nineteenth century, but the tradition of out-of-town entertainment was maintained along the river Thames· the Star and Garter at Richmond(†) was built in the early 1870s by the versatile C. J. Phipps, in the rich arcaded 'Mixed Renaissance' style of the period on an irregular ground plan. It cost £24,000, served mainly for banquets, and was on the whole a middle-class establishment.

Places mainly devoted to eating were more and more often called restaurants, or cafés, parallel to the adoption of the word 'hotel' for inns. The Holborn Restaurant in London (originally called Holborn Casino and also, misleadingly, Crosby Hall), at the west corner of Kingsway and Holborn, was built by Messrs Francis in a rich and florid Renaissance style (1868, 1873,†). The brothers Frederick John (1818–96) and Horace (1821–94) Francis were best known for their large hotels in Northumberland Avenue. The Café Royal in Regent Street, built in 1865–85 by Archer and Green (decorator R. Lloyd) and still used for its original purposes, has a Grill Room with the most exuberant carved decoration.

Before the middle of the century there was little differentiation between various kinds of entertainment. There were 'supper rooms', 'singing houses', 'music rooms' and 'dance halls'. 'Variety saloons', 'singing houses' and 'music rooms' obtained a boost and clarification of their function when the 1843 Theatre Act, an Act clearly intended to clarify class distinction, divided them into those performing drama, but without a licence for drinks, and those which presented variety theatre and musical shows and retained a licence. The term 'music hall' seems to appear first in 1855. One of the earliest and most popular establishments of this kind in London was the Oxford in St Giles's Circus, by Finch, Hill and Paraire (1857,†). It had a large hall, with long rows of tables and an elevated stage [*78*], and a façade decorated with Corinthian columns between two turrets. Its respectability was somewhat greater than usual, and workmen could come with their families.

In the 1870s, however, the close combination of dancing, drinking and shows came to an end and the large music halls were planned like theatres, with the bars separated from the auditorium. A split-off from the music hall was the concert hall: the best known (apart from the Albert Hall: see p. 174) was the Queen's Hall in Regent Street, London (1891,†), built by C. J. Phipps and decorated by T. E. Knightley (1823–1905). Its façade had a

79 West Pier, Brighton, by Eugenius Birch, 1863–6, at the turn of the century.

80 *The Tower, Blackpool, by Maxwell and Tuke, 1891–4. (*Building News, *1891)*

suspension bridges, was built in 1823 and survived until 1896. Brighton's two other piers are happily still standing – the West Pier [79] of 1863–6 by the great pier engineer Eugenius Birch (1818–84), with later additions, and the Palace Pier of 1898. They are large platforms on a multitude of thin cast iron legs, dotted with a series of low, iron-framed halls with orientalizing decoration no doubt inspired by the Royal Pavilion. The entrances to the piers are especially richly treated, in the form of little kiosks. Later piers tend to be shorter and to have taller buildings with a multitude of turrets and cupolas.

Other buildings in seaside towns tended to be multi-functional: there were, for instance, those devoted to spa activities, like the Baths at Scarborough of 1877–80 by the London architects Verity and Hunt, with exuberant decoration in coloured tiles; or those with a more educational purpose, such as the Aquarium and Polytechnic at Margate in Kent, by A. Bedborough (1876,†), which was basically a glass and iron structure, but masked, like the Alexandra Palace, by a stone frontage in a version of the Second Empire style. The most impressive structures of this type are probably the glazed halls of the Winter Gardens at Blackpool – the Pavilion of 1876–8 by Mitchell and Macleod, and the Empress Ballroom of 1896 by Mangnall and Littlewood of Manchester (decorated with Doulton tile panels designed by W. J. Neatby, somewhat similar to his panels in Harrod's store in London). Each cost over £100,000.

Finally, in some large resorts, the tower became a symbol of gaiety. Blackpool built an imitation of the Eiffel Tower in 1891–4 (by Maxwell and Tuke) [80], only just over a third of the height of the original, but characteristically with much more decoration and built on top of a ballroom. A slightly higher tower of similar design was put up by the same firm in 1897 at New Brighton outside Liverpool, but unlike Blackpool it no longer survives.

curved portico with very widely spaced coupled Corinthian columns and niches containing busts of famous composers.

During the nineteenth century seaside resorts largely replaced the eighteenth-century spas as the place to go for health and entertainment. The Prince Regent's Royal Pavilion at Brighton in Sussex stands at the beginning of the century, and the popular amusements at Blackpool in Lancashire at the end [80]. The most splendid and a unique feature of seaside architecture is the pier. By the early nineteenth century its function as a jetty had become negligible and it was partly or wholly roofed in for entertainment. The Brighton Chain Pier, copying the earliest

Theatres and later music halls

The world of the theatre in England differs markedly from that on the Continent. Two major developments are virtually unknown in Britain: the opera houses of Italy, dating back to the seventeenth century, and the nineteenth-century literary and moral theatre of the German-speaking countries. Although the Theatre Act of 1843 (see p. 89) was clearly intended to raise the status of the theatre by distinguishing it from the music halls, there was hardly any public patronage, whether royal, state or civic. The theatre or opera house as a large and prominent civic building is thus little known in Britain, and there is less external display of the traditional complex organization of this type of building, of its elements of auditorium, proscenium arch and stage tower: usually British theatres appear as just a façade in the street. Because of the restrictions in licensing for theatres, the more representational spaces, such as foyers and main stairways, are poorly developed in England compared with the Continent. The Royal Opera House, Covent Garden, in its present form of 1857 by E. M. Barry, is hardly an exception [81]. There was much progress, however, in practical matters, such as the organization of exits, fire-proofing and the upholstering of seats.

As in all other types of building, decoration greatly increased: as early as 1840 a heavy plaster façade was placed in front of the modest Theatre Royal, Adelphi, in the Strand (1806) to 'give the spectator a correct idea of the entrance to a theatre'. The style of the inside and outside, however, remained conservative. The Criterion Theatre (and Restaurants) in Piccadilly Circus of 1870–4, by Thomas Verity (1837–91), is Neo-Renaissance with a very ornate front, and the London Pavilion opposite, built nine years later by the little-known firm of Worley and Saunders, reverts almost to Neo-Classicism. The Criterion auditorium is entirely underground, and was remarkable for its complicated ventilation devices. (The interior was rebuilt in 1884.) D'Oyly Carte, the great patron of the Aesthetic Movement and of Gilbert and Sullivan, whom we have met as builder of the Savoy and Claridge's hotels (p. 82), claimed to introduce a new style with his Savoy Theatre in the Strand of 1881: it used not 'garish' decoration, but delicate ornaments from the Renaissance and more subtle colours. The great technical innovation here was the first use in a theatre of electric lighting. The exterior was of red brick in a rather vague 'Queen Anne' manner. One of the reasons for this stylistic conservatism was the fact that the architect, C. J. Phipps – who designed many other theatres – specialized in technical matters and was probably far less interested in the rapidly changing stylistic fashions.

81 *Royal Opera House, Covent Garden, London, by E. M. Barry, 1857. The 'crush bar' under the colonnade is a later addition.*

In 1889 D'Oyly Carte began his Royal English Opera House in Cambridge Circus (sold and renamed the Palace in 1892). For the façades he employed the very respected architect T. E. Collcutt, who with small-scale terracotta ornament and curved surfaces cleverly exploited the irregular site [*82*]. But the even more remarkable technical innovations were the responsibility of the builder G. H. Holloway: there were cantilevered balconies (which eliminated view-obstructing pillars), and not only electric lighting but hot- and cold-air ventilation, also powered by the theatre's own generator.

Styles other than Renaissance and Baroque are rare, and usually due to architects who were not theatre specialists. In Leeds, George Corson (1829–1910) applied his favourite slightly medievalizing Quattrocento mode to the Grand of 1878–9, while at Stratford-on-Avon Dodgshun and Unsworth gave the first Shakespeare Memorial Theatre (1876–9,†) a domestic Gothic air, and also gave the various functional parts, like stairs and auditorium, separate roofs.

The most consistent and prolific architect of the later music halls was Frank Matcham (1854–1920). His buildings, mostly in the provinces and in the suburbs of London, equal or exceed in splendour the metropolitan theatres and opera houses. The Empire Palace at Leeds (1898) and the Empire at Hackney (1900) [*83*], one of the poorer suburbs of London, are characteristic. The elaborate London Hippodrome (1899–1900), in an ornate and remotely English Baroque style, had a

82 Royal English Opera House, now the Palace Theatre, London, by G. H. Holloway and T. E. Collcutt, 1889, photographed in 1891.

83 *Empire Theatre, Hackney, London, by Frank Matcham, 1900. (The entrance has been altered.)*

mechanism to flood its circus-like arena for water spectacles. The fantastic Neo-Baroque London Coliseum (opened in 1904), with its 3,000–4,000 seats the largest theatre in London, was advertised as combining the refinement and elegance of a club with the comfort of a café, and being 'the pleasantest family resort imaginable'. Inside these theatres the changes included the elimination of some of the social stratifications of boxes and galleries; the gallery supports were simplified and their great, sweeping curves became more prominent.

As with pubs, there was a boom in theatre-building in the 1890s and early 1900s, at least in the West End of London. But by 1900 the days of over-ornamentation were drawing to an end. For Wyndham's, built in 1899, the prolific theatre architect W. G. R. Sprague (c. 1865–1933) used a more intimate mid-eighteenth-century French décor [*84*].

84 *Wyndham's Theatre, London, by W. G. R. Sprague, photographed soon after its opening in 1899. Notice the cantilevered balconies, and the benches for cheap seating at the back of the stalls and in the gallery.*

3
New materials and new building types

For the great majority of Victorian buildings – houses, churches and civic buildings – there were antecedents going back for centuries. However, the social, economic and technical developments of the period led to the demand for new types of buildings for which there was no adequate precedent – railway stations, large glasshouses, exhibition halls and large-scale market halls – buildings which required extensive, uninterrupted floor areas. In solving these problems Victorian designers were able to use new building materials made available by the Industrial Revolution, and in doing so they created some of the most original and spatially exciting buildings of the period.

The materials were cast iron, wrought iron and, later, steel. All had existed in the Middle Ages; what made them new as building materials was their greater availability and cheapness due to new industrial processes of manufacture. Cast iron was made in increasingly large quantities following Abraham Darby's successful development in 1709 of the process of smelting iron by means of coke. Its first use as a building material in Britain on a large scale was for the iron bridge of 100-foot span near Darby's works at Coalbrookdale in Shropshire, begun in 1777. In the early 1790s it was used for columns, floor beams and window frames of mills in an attempt to make them fireproof. Nash used iron for columns and staircases in the Royal Pavilion at Brighton and Thomas Rickman, working with the local ironmaster John Cragg, employed it for columns, beamed roofs and window tracery in a number of churches in Liverpool. It was

also used by Barry for the roof of the Houses of Parliament, again with an eye to fireproofing. Constructional cast iron became increasingly popular in the 1840s and 1850s, with the building of a series of railway stations and glasshouses that reached a climax with the creation of the Crystal Palace in 1850–51 [*85, 91, 92*].

Cast iron is brittle, and although it is very strong in compression, under tension wrought iron is much stronger, and therefore superior for much constructional work. Wrought iron was however expensive to produce until after 1820, when its manufacture increased using Henry Cort's puddling process of 1784. Sir William Fairbairn (1789–1874) became the great advocate of wrought iron for building. In the 1840s he tested it and then used it in 1845–50 for the Britannia railway bridge across the Menai Straits (see p. 98). Shortly afterwards wrought-iron girders were used by Paxton to span the nave of the Crystal Palace. In 1854 Fairbairn published his influential book, *On the Application of Cast and Wrought Iron to Building*. At the same time there was a demand for railway stations with large-span roofs to enable platforms to be rearranged without disrupting the structure of the building. Wrought-iron girders were developed to meet this need, producing spans of which the greatest was the 243 feet of the roof of St Pancras Station in London (1863–5) [*93, 94*].

85 The transept of the Crystal Palace, London, by Sir Joseph Paxton, at the opening of the Great Exhibition in 1851.

86 The Great Stove at Chatsworth, by Paxton, 1836–40. Two carefully positioned men give the scale.

87, 88 The Palm House at Kew Gardens, London, by Decimus Burton and Richard Turner, 1844–8: exterior, and a view inside the roof of one of the long wings.

In 1855 Sir Henry Bessemer invented a method of making steel in large quantities. His process produced a metal which was stronger and more durable than wrought iron and which cost only one third as much. With steel it was easier to produce I-beams of substantial section and in the 1880s these became commercially available. In 1883–90 the Forth Bridge was erected using steel for its superstructure. English architects were less adventurous than Americans, who led the way with the development of steel-frame buildings in which the internal frame supported the exterior walls, but steel joists were used in the Savoy Hotel in London in 1889, and in 1896 Britain's first steel-frame building, Robinson's Emporium at West Hartlepool, County Durham, a furniture warehouse, was erected by Basil Scott. The first important use of the steel frame in London was at the Ritz Hotel (1905).

Early Victorian glasshouses

Glasshouses had been extensively used in the early nineteenth century to protect exotic plants, a new delight to gardeners, from the British climate. In the Early Victorian period these structures took on monumental proportions. At Chatsworth the Duke of Devonshire erected the Great Stove (1836–40,†), a conservatory 277 feet long, 123 feet wide and 67 feet high [86]. Although an architect, Decimus Burton, was called in to help, the concept and basic design were those of the Duke's gardener, Joseph Paxton. He was the son of a Bedfordshire farmer and, as we have seen, began his career as a humble garden boy; his abilities were recognized by the Duke, who appointed him head gardener at Chatsworth in 1826. The Great Stove was the culmination of a series of conservatories Paxton had built for the Duke. It had an arched metal frame, the central span of which measured 70 feet – a distance greater than any yet attempted by the railway engineers at that time. The central arch rested on cast-iron columns and was buttressed by side arches that covered the flanking aisles. The glass roof which covered the whole structure was of the ridge-and-furrow construction which Paxton had developed on earlier glass buildings at Chatsworth. The general form was almost entirely dictated by its purpose and method of construction. Only the entrances, presumably designed by Decimus Burton, reflected the prevailing historicism of conventional architecture. They were wide enough to allow a carriage to enter, and that was how Queen Victoria saw Paxton's great work when she visited Chatsworth in 1843.

Following the royal visit to Chatsworth a Great Stove was proposed for the Royal Botanical Gardens at Kew [*87, 88*]. Burton was again one of the designers but in this case he was associated with the Dublin engineer Richard Turner, who had considerable experience of building greenhouses. The first with which Turner was associated is the Palm House at the Botanic Gardens, Belfast, begun in 1839. The design was by the Antrim County surveyor, Charles Lanyon; Turner provided the ironwork. The building is of comparatively modest scale but it has delicate detailing. In 1843 Turner built a Palm House for the Royal Dublin Society at Glasnevin near Dublin, which consists of a large rectangular central building articulated by glazed pilasters, linked to lower houses with rounded ends covered by curving roofs which sweep down from a crest of Greek floral design.

Before Kew, Turner worked with Burton on the now demolished Winter Garden at Regent's Park, commissioned in 1840 by the Botanic Society of London. Burton suggested a huge structure 315 by 165 feet in size, larger even than the Great Stove at Chatsworth, which had just been completed with his help. Work began in 1845. The curving roofs, like those of Turner's Irish conservatories, were supported on cast-iron columns. The building was heated by nearly a mile of four-inch pipes. Ventilation was regulated by sliding metal sashes set at the ridge, which controlled from the ground by means of a chain attached to a revolving rod. When it was completed in 1846 the Winter Garden covered an area of 19,000 square feet. In its final form it probably owed more to Turner than to Burton, and indeed the Society's Secretary at the time says: 'this building, constructed of iron, was designed and built by Turner of Dublin'.

In 1844 Burton had begun to prepare sketch designs for the Palm House at Kew. Completed in 1848, it was to be one of the most perfect examples in this great period of glasshouses [*87, 88*]. Burton's first design was rejected for having too many columns. Turner was then approached and presented the Director, Sir William Hooker, with a design for a central house and two wings, accompanied by a model and estimates. Burton criticized Turner's scheme for its 'Ecclesiastical or Gothic style'. His own revised design, based on Turner's scheme, altered the central section so that it resembled that of the Great Conservatory at Chatsworth [*86*]. Turner was given the contract and continued to collaborate on the details with Burton. Thus although *The Builder* credits Burton with the design and Turner with the ironwork, the latter's contribution went further than this.

As built, the Palm Stove at Kew has similarities to the Chatsworth conservatory but also to Turner's Irish greenhouses. Much of its beauty comes from its basic logic and simplicity, and from the clarity of its form. It is 362 feet long, 100 feet wide in the centre and 63 feet high: it is therefore longer than Chatsworth but not so wide, nor quite so high. The centre part has an arched roof resting on columns; the surrounding aisle is covered by a roof formed by half an arch. Joined to this central space are apsed wings covered by a single arched roof of the same dimension as that over the central nave. The curved roofs rise from a low masonry wall and almost all the glazing is set in curving mullions. The main ribs are made of wrought iron. In the central part of the building they rest on cast-iron columns, which also support the balcony that runs around the upper part of the main nave. The ribs are braced together in an ingenious way: there are hollow cast-iron tubes at regular intervals, through which run wrought-iron tie-rods which were tightened when the ribs had been erected, thus knitting together the whole structure. Turner patented this idea in 1846. The smoothness of the glass covering not only expresses the form of the building to great effect but also enhances its translucent quality. The Palm Stove is like a great bubble of glass. In some lights it appears massive and substantial; in others, with the sun shining from behind, it appears light, ethereal and almost magical, with the palms silhouetted through the glass.

Two major cast-iron structures of similar date in London – the Coal Exchange and the British Museum Reading Room – will be discussed in Chapter 5 [*136, 137*].

Early railway architecture

There was a close connection between the construction of the great greenhouses and the construction of early railway stations, which soon surpassed them in size.

The railways themselves were works of engineering of unprecedented scale. Their construction was carried out largely by the manual labour of great armies of 'navigators' or 'navvies'. The great contractors who built the railways, men like Thomas Brassey and S. Morton Peto, made, and sometimes lost, vast fortunes. In the 1840s railway building became a mania. The railways required vast new bridges and viaducts. The bridge over the Thames at Maidenhead, built in 1838 by Isambard Kingdom Brunel, is constructed of brick and has arches of 128-foot span. More radical in its solution is the Britannia Bridge of 1845–50 by Robert Stephenson (1803–59), Sir William Fairbairn and the architect Francis Thompson, which used tubular girders made of wrought-iron plates to carry the railway across the Menai Straits in spans of 460 feet.

The first railway stations had none of the engineering daring of the bridges, and they followed the conventional architectural modes of the period.

The first line to take passengers was that opened between Stockton and Darlington in 1825, but the Liverpool to Manchester railway, opened five years later, produced the first railway stations. The original Manchester terminal, built in 1829–30, survives in Liverpool Road and is a modest stuccoed building of two storeys, five bays wide, with a tripartite entrance; the platform is covered by a canopy. Crown Street Station, the Liverpool terminus of the line, unfortunately no longer exists but its appearance is known through drawings. It was possibly designed by the line's engineer, George Stephenson, without the help of an architect. It consisted of a two-storeyed block of domestic character, in a conventional Late Georgian style, alongside the tracks, with a porch at one end facing a forecourt. The porch gave access to a room serving as both a ticket office and waiting room. The first floor had offices and accommodation for station officials. Between the station building and the track was a platform which was covered by a porch supported on columns, probably made of iron. The tracks were covered by a wooden roof some 35 feet in span, which rested on the columns on the station side and on a brick wall at the other.

The smaller early stations, designed by engineers as well as architects, displayed the current Picturesque architectural styles – Gothic, Greek, Italianate and Moorish. Rural stations were seen as similar in function to the lodges of great estates, and their architecture frequently followed the lead of such buildings. Indeed so successful were Francis Thompson's picturesque designs for the stations on the North Midland Line that they were considered suitable models for villa residences, and as such were reproduced by Loudon in the 1842 edition of his *Encyclopedia of Cottage, Farm and Villa Architecture*. The station at Ambergate, of about 1840, becomes a fanciful Jacobean villa with shaped gables, urns, tall chimneys and a gazebo-like pavilion on the roof. The contemporary

89 Propylaeum of Euston Station, London, by Philip and P. C. Hardwick, 1835–9. The station proper lies behind, its glass canopy roof just visible on the right.

stations built by David Mocatta (1806–82) for the Brighton line showed a similar stylistic eclecticism, Reigate in Surrey being Classical and Horley Tudor Gothic.

The larger terminus railway stations followed the same architectural fashions, but they succeeded in creating forms at once more monumental and more original, and their train sheds were to be unprecedented feats of engineering. The great terminal stations are an expression of the pride the Victorians had in railway companies.

The London to Birmingham Railway, engineered by Robert Stephenson and opened in 1837, was the first great railway of the Victorian age. Its London terminus celebrated with suitable architectural grandeur its engineering achievement. Euston Station (1835–9,†) was designed by the architect Philip Hardwick, working with his son P. C. Hardwick. The platforms were covered by a simple train shed

of metal construction designed by Robert Stephenson. At the side were waiting rooms and a courtyard for carriages. The station was approached through the famous 'Euston Arch', designed by the Hardwicks in the form of a monumental Greek Doric propylaeum or gateway [89]. The juxtaposition of light metal train sheds and massive historicist architecture was to remain characteristic throughout the Victorian age [93]. The cost of the Arch was about £30,000, a large sum for those days, but the railway company gained considerable publicity from the work, and when it was first built it was regarded with wonder, people flocking in omnibuses to see it. In 1846–8 P. C. Hardwick added a Great Hall to the station, a feature regarded during the crisis in railway shares of the late 1840s as an expensive folly.

The western half of Euston Station had originally been planned to accommodate the London terminal of the Great Western Railway, but they preferred to have their terminus at Paddington, which was then an expanding residential suburb on the west side of London. The engineer of the Great Western was Brunel, whose appointment was due to the impression made by his design for the 630-foot-span Clifton

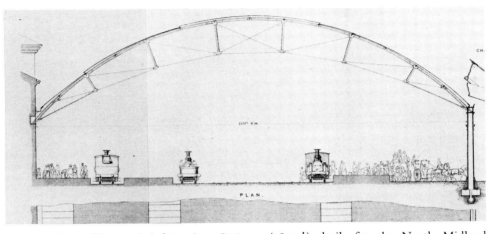

90 *Section of the train shed of Lime Street Station, Liverpool, as rebuilt by Richard Turner and Joseph Locke in 1849–50. (Minutes of the Proceedings of the Institute of Civil Engineers, IX, 1850)*

Suspension Bridge in 1829. He surveyed the route, designed the broad gauge track, built bridges, and cut the Box Tunnel; he also designed monumental entrances to the tunnels – some Italianate, some medieval in style – and the terminal stations at Temple Meads in Bristol and Paddington in London. Brunel chose the Gothic style for Temple Meads, which was built in 1839–40. As a structural achievement the station is remarkable: over the train shed is an arched wooden roof spanning 72 feet – four feet wider than Westminster Hall, the largest span achieved in medieval England. It appears to follow the hammerbeam form of construction, but in fact is a tied, pointed arch. Brunel's Gothic exterior lacks that natural expression of structure which make his bridges and some of his later stations so impressive. It was condemned by Pugin in his *Apology for the Revival of Pointed or Christian Architecture* (1843) as 'engineer's architecture' – 'at once costly and offensive and full of pretension'.

A more successful solution to the architectural problem of station design was achieved at the Trijunct Station, Derby

(1840,†), built for the North Midland Railway by Francis Thompson and Robert Stephenson, who were later to work together on the Britannia Bridge. Two other railways used the station and this necessitated a long platform, fronted by a screen 1,050 feet in length, which was skilfully articulated with Classical motifs. The shed itself had an area of 450 by 150 feet. Apart from the flanking walls it was entirely of metal construction. Slender cast-iron columns by the tracks supported the tie-rod trusses of the roof, of which the centre was filled with broad glass panels.

The central span of the train shed at Derby was a comparatively modest 56 feet. Victorian engineers were soon, however, to rival the achievements of ancient engineers. The first iron roof to cover a terminus in a single span, wider than the dome of the Pantheon in Rome, was at Lime Street Station, Liverpool, as rebuilt by Richard Turner and Joseph Locke, assisted by Sir William Fairbairn (1849–50,†) [90]. Single spans were considered the best form of station roof: they allowed alterations in the track arrangement, and they were safer, since a locomotive hitting a column could threaten a whole roof structure. The Lime Street roof spanned 153 feet; its main element was a 'sickle girder' with upper and lower members connected by cast-iron struts tied diagonally. Locke was the engineer of the railway, Turner the contractor; the girders were made in Turner's Dublin works. Thus we find him working at the same time on what is perhaps the finest of English glasshouses up to that date – the one at Kew [*87, 88*] – and a railway station that achieved an unprecedented span.

The Crystal Palace

By 1850 there was an accumulation of experience in the building of large-scale structures of metal and glass. This experience was largely technical, but with buildings such as the Kew Palm Stove the aesthetic possibilities of the materials were being exploited in a most successful manner. The culmination of this phase of metal and glass construction was the building of the Crystal Palace in London to house the Great Exhibition of 1851.

The idea of the Exhibition had developed out of the annual exhibition of the Society of Arts, of which Prince Albert was President. Henry Cole, an energetic and enterprising civil servant, was one of the prime movers. In 1849 Prince Albert gave his support to the scheme and suggested the site in Hyde Park. A Royal Commission was formed which included

among its members the Prime Minister Lord John Russell, Peel and Gladstone. In a characteristically Victorian way it was proposed to finance this vast scheme by private subscription. Money flowed in: Peto, the railway contractor, gave the huge sum of £50,000. In January 1850 a distinguished Building Committee was formed and an international competition was organized. Over two hundred designs were received. None was considered entirely satisfactory and the Committee, which included the architects Charles Barry, C. R. Cockerell and T. L. Donaldson (1795–1885), and the engineers Robert Stephenson and Brunel, produced its own design. This was also heavily criticized.

It was Joseph Paxton who came to the rescue. He was aware of the latest developments in railway construction, as he sat on the Board of Directors of the Midland Railway to look after the Duke of Devonshire's large investment in the company. While at a meeting of the Board he sketched out his idea for the Exhibition building on the blotting paper. This was on 11 June 1850. Events moved quickly. In eight days he had produced the necessary

91 The Crystal Palace in Hyde Park, by Joseph Paxton, 1850–51, looking from the north-west towards the City. In the right foreground is the steam-engine house.

92 Detail of the west end of the Crystal Palace, photographed in 1851.

The completion of such a colossal building in so short a time required highly efficient organization and close cooperation between Paxton and the contractors. The working details were drawn up by Fox; Henderson organized the production of the ironwork and other necessary materials. The components came from all over the country: the wrought-iron beams to span the central nave were produced by Fox and Henderson in their Birmingham works; the cast-iron columns and girders were sub-contracted to two firms at Dudley; wooden components were made by Fox, Henderson and Company at their mills in Chelsea; and glass was supplied by the Birmingham firm of Chance Brothers. They contracted to produce 900,000 square feet of glass. Ten years earlier that would have represented a third of England's annual production.

The building was sited in Hyde Park south of the Serpentine: it stretched from what is now Exhibition Road as far as Knightsbridge Barracks, with its entrance in the transept nearly opposite Prince of Wales Gate. Its great floor area was 1,848 by 408 feet, and it had three storeys which rose in steps to an upper tier 120 feet wide. In order to avoid cutting down some old elm trees Paxton modified his original design and added a transept, just off centre [85]. It spanned 72 feet and was covered by a ridge-and-furrow roof of glass supported on arched principals of wood. The main structural supports were hollow cast-iron columns which also acted as rain-water pipes. They were placed with their centres 48 feet apart, resting on socketed base plates set in concrete foundations. The columns were braced by cast-iron girders. The upper tier of columns and girders supported the larger girders, made of wrought iron, which spanned the nave and aisles of the building and supported the roofs.

The wooden gutters and glazing bars of the roofs were formed on a special machine developed for the purpose by Paxton. The sides of the building were enclosed by standard wall elements, which had an

drawings. His design was published in *The Illustrated London News* on 6 July. A tender of £150,000 was hurriedly produced from the firm of Fox and Henderson and on 15 July the Building Committee recommended the acceptance of Paxton's design. In nine months the building was completed [85, 91, 92]. On 1 May 1851 the Great Exhibition was opened by the Queen. The building was given the name 'The Crystal Palace' by *Punch*.

Paxton's great structure brought together experience that had been obtained in the 1830s and 1840s in the construction of glasshouses and railway sheds. It was no coincidence that he utilized the ridge-and-furrow system of glazing already proved in his Chatsworth greenhouses: the large sheets of glass had first been employed for the Great Conservatory [86], and the basic exterior unit of the Crystal Palace was an arched panel tried out in 1849–50 in the greenhouse built to house the gigantic Victoria Regia water lily.

arched panel boarded on the ground storey and glazed on the upper two tiers. At the top were louvres which could be adjusted to control the flow of air. The flooring was of wood.

The impression of almost limitless space which the interior must have conveyed was enhanced by the colour-scheme devised by Owen Jones, which was based on his belief that in all great periods of art only primary colours were used. Blue was the predominant colour and was used on the columns and girders. This must have given a misty appearance to the interior. Touches of yellow gave variety and bold

expanses of red, behind the balconies and as a backdrop for the exhibits, provided bright accents.

Paxton's culminating achievement was to design a building that could be taken down and erected on another site. When the Great Exhibition was over the Crystal Palace was re-erected at Sydenham in 1851–4 to a modified design. There, embellished by gardens and fountains designed by Paxton, it served as a cultural centre for South London until it was burnt down in 1936 (see above, p. 88).

Later railway stations

Just as the Crystal Palace drew on the experience of building railway stations, so railway stations after 1851 developed ideas used in the Crystal Palace. In a small way Oxford Station, built by Fox and Henderson in 1851–2, follows the structure of their larger project. On a larger scale King's Cross Station in London [93], built in 1851–2 to designs by the architect Lewis Cubitt (1799–1883), uses for its train sheds

93 Air view of St Pancras Station (left) and King's Cross Station, London. King's Cross and its hotel (the curving building between the two stations) were designed by Lewis Cubitt and built in 1851–2 and 1854. At St Pancras the combined station and hotel by Sir George Gilbert Scott, of 1868–74, fronts the great shed by W. H. Barlow and R. M. Ordish, of 1865–8.

94 Train shed of St Pancras Station, London, by W. H. Barlow and R. M. Ordish, 1863–5. (Building News, 1869)

the techniques of the transept of the Crystal Palace [*85*]. The station, however, is larger: the laminated wooden arches (later replaced by iron) which cover both train sheds – one for arrivals and one for departures – are 105 feet in span. Cubitt's façade consists of a screen of yellow stock brick pierced by two great arched windows lighting the ends of the sheds. Between them is an Italianate clock tower, a feature used by Cubitt at his earlier Bricklayers' Arms Station in London (†). The severe treatment owes a debt to the French architect J.-N.-L. Durand, whose designs for monumental public buildings in a functional Classical style were first published in 1802. The modest ancillary facilities – booking hall, waiting rooms and refreshment rooms – are tucked away to the side.

The integration of the façade of the station and the train sheds is achieved better at King's Cross than in any other major British railway station. The comparison between the expression of the sheds here and their masking behind the hotel at St Pancras has often been discussed [*93*]. King's Cross is an example of that trend in Early Victorian architecture when there was a close integration between architecture and engineering – though this was partly based on economy. On the other hand, the hotel that went with King's Cross was built as a separate structure nearby (in 1854), whereas the St Pancras Hotel [*71*] is more closely integrated with its station shed in that its ground floor is used for passages, booking hall, buffet and waiting rooms. Paddington Station in London shows another attempt to solve the same problem. For a number of years after the opening of the Great Western Railway between London and Bristol, the London terminus in the newly developed suburb of Paddington relied on simple accommodation set between the arches of a road bridge. In 1851 work began on a grand replacement suitable to the company's pretensions. The station was fronted by the Great Western Hotel [*68*], designed by P. C. Hardwick, who after his work at Euston (p. 99) was among the most prominent station architects.

95 *Central Station, York, by Peachy and Prosser, 1871–7.*

Paddington Station itself was constructed in 1852–4. In its design Brunel was assisted by the architect Matthew Digby Wyatt (1820–77). It is symptomatic of the changing climate of opinion that Brunel now sought the assistance of an influential architect and ornamental designer. The collaboration produced a station in which the engineering forms and the architectural details are well integrated. The train shed is 238 feet wide and is covered by three arched roofs of wrought iron. The arches have no ties and rest on longitudinal girders which are supported by metal columns. Wyatt's decorative work, including the capitals of the columns, is highly original and inspired by Renaissance and Moorish models. In places it is fanciful, as in the oriel windows, one of which gives the station-master a view across the platforms. In 1861 William Powell Frith chose Paddington as the setting for his picture *The Railway Station*, in which he depicts the bustle, excitement and human drama which went with this great structure.

The achievements of the railway engineers continued during the period and they concentrated on creating wide spans for stations, which were regarded as desirable not only for the flexibility of operation which they allowed but also for the prestige they attracted. A span of 211 feet was achieved in the train shed of New Street Station, Birmingham (1854,†). It was designed by the engineers E. A. Cowper and William Baker, who used the sickle girder construction which was, as we have seen, employed earlier for the shed at Lime Street, Liverpool [90]. The Birmingham shed was no less than 1,080 feet long. Fox, Henderson and Company made the girders, each of which weighed twenty-five tons, more massive than any of the members they constructed for the Crystal Palace.

St Pancras Station, the most spectacular of all, was the London terminus of the Midland Railway [71, 72, 93, 94]. The directors were late in building a London terminal, and they decided to make up for this by erecting a structure that would eclipse in size and architectural magnificence all previous London stations. In this aim they were successful. The train shed came first and was built in 1865–8 [*93, 94*]. It is 689 feet long and rises to 100 feet. Its span of 243 feet remained the greatest of any building in the world for over a generation. The roof was designed by W. H. Barlow (1812–92) and R. M. Ordish (1824–86). (Barlow was the engineer of the Midland Railway Company and had also helped Paxton with details of the Crystal Palace.) It is supported by lattice ribs which rise in an elegant curve from the level of the platforms to meet in a point. The ribs are tied under the platform and the tracks. The whole shed is raised above cellars which were used to store barrels of beer from Burton, the size of the barrels determining the structural proportions of the building. Across the front of this shed Scott added the great hotel, which has already been described (p. 81) [*71, 72*]. The train shed was nearly complete when construction of the hotel began.

Few of the later Victorian stations were to approach the architectural distinction of

96 An early photograph of the Museum of Science and Art, South Kensington (the 'Brompton Boilers'), by Charles D. Young & Co., 1855–6.

St Pancras, and none rivals the daring of the engineering of its train shed. The present Central Station at York, designed by William Peachy and Thomas Prosser and built in 1871–7, is one of the more successful [*95*]. Its arrangement on a curve is similar to that of Newcastle. The York sheds are neither very high nor of exceptionally large span, but the effect of the curved five-centred ribs of the roof sweeping around over the platforms makes the station one of the most visually exciting of Victorian interiors, just as the massive stone porch or *porte cochère* of Newcastle, by John Dobson, opened in 1850 and completed in 1865, is one of the grandest station exteriors. Perhaps the most important stations of the 1870s are Liverpool Street in London (1875, by Edward Wilson, the company engineer, with later additions), and Manchester Central (1876–9, by Sir John Fowler). The former presents a complicated system of naves, aisles and intersecting 'transept', best seen in diagonal views, while the latter vies with St Pancras Station in size and simplicity.

By 1880 the main railway termini were built and additions to the existing structures provided for increased needs. Moreover, the high confidence which produced the earlier stations was passing, and the high cost of large buildings and wide spans was no longer considered appropriate.

Changing attitudes to iron buildings

One of the features that characterize the transition from Early to High Victorian ideals in the 1850s is a change in the attitude to iron buildings and to the relationship of architecture and engineering. Cast iron was still widely used, particularly for prefabricated buildings, such as temporary churches. Specialist firms like Hemming of Bristol and Charles D. Young & Co. of Edinburgh shipped whole houses, shopping parades and even theatres all over the world. But iron, which in the Early Victorian period had all the appeal of a new, daring constructional material, now became associated in the mind of the public with cheap utilitarian buildings. Thus one of its greatest advantages militated against its use in public buildings. Bishops refused to consecrate iron churches, and the public were unwilling to accept iron-clad structures in their cities. The story of the so-called 'Brompton Boilers' [*96*] is instructive of the changing attitudes of the period.

Following the success of the Great Exhibition an area to the south of Hyde Park – then known as Brompton, now South Kensington – was purchased from the profits, for use as a cultural centre for London. In 1855–6 Henry Cole's Department of Practical Art erected a temporary Museum of Science and Art on the site. Cole, no doubt attempting to be economical as the Crimean War was going on, commissioned a simple structure of metal, which was designed and constructed by Young's of Edinburgh. The temporary museum was rectangular in plan and had galleries looking on to a central space; covering it were light metal segmental roofs. The exterior was faced with corrugated iron. The public reaction was not favourable: the building was dubbed the 'Brompton Boilers' by George Godwin, editor of *The Builder*, and the name stuck. It was eventually moved to the East End of London, where since 1873, decently clothed in a brick exterior wall by J. W. Wild (1814–92), it has housed the Bethnal Green Museum. On the other hand, the court of the Oxford Museum, begun in 1855 by Woodward, shows an attempt by the Gothicists at a more ornate and 'architectural' iron structure [*151*].

Where metal and glass buildings were constructed in the Mid-Victorian period they tended to become less stark, and to be overlaid with architectural decoration. The Floral Hall at Covent Garden, built by E. M. Barry in 1857–8, demonstrates the move in the direction of greater elaboration. Its main iron members owe something to the Crystal Palace in their design, but it is greatly enriched with

97 Exhibition Road front of the 1862 Exhibition building in London, by Captain Francis Fowke, under construction.

applied cast-iron decoration. Other market halls will be discussed below.

In 1860 Kew Gardens began a Temperate House, also designed by Burton, who had been responsible with Turner for the Palm House some fifteen years earlier [*87, 88*]. The Temperate House is larger, consisting of a range of houses 628 feet long, but whereas the Palm Stove is light and airy in its construction with hardly any wall, the later glasshouse has a pitched roof, walls and massive masonry angle piers crowned by monumental urns. It has its attractions, but they are not those of exposed structure and simple form.

The same changed attitude to iron construction can be seen in the contrast between the building for the Great Exhibition of 1851 [*91*] and that which housed its successor in 1862 (†) [*97*]. The building

98 Tower Bridge, London, by Sir John Wolfe Barry and Sir Horace Jones, 1886–94, photographed about 1900.

for the London Exhibition of the Works of All Nations was designed by Captain Francis Fowke (1823–65), the army engineer who was to play an important part in the development of South Kensington (pp. 172–4). Fowke's building had two glass domes, and the roof and galleries were of cast iron, wrought iron and glass. But it was no longer felt appropriate to express all these elements on the exterior: the building was clad in a massive brick skin articulated with pilasters and arched recesses containing windows. After the lightness of the Crystal Palace it appears very heavy and clumsy.

Tower Bridge, built in 1886–94, demonstrates very clearly the Late Victorian retreat from the expression of metal construction [98]. It was designed by the engineer son of Sir Charles Barry, Sir John Wolfe Barry, and clothed in elaborate Gothic detail by Sir Horace Jones (1819–87), the Architect of the City of London. Although it has none of the simple beauty of many of the buildings that have been discussed, it is memorable, and has become one of London's most famous monuments.

In the Late Victorian period Britain was to lose her technological leadership. Her inventions were exploited by other countries; the great roof of the Machinery Hall of the Paris Exhibition of 1889 is a development of that at St Pancras; Chicago was to exploit the steel frame which had been foreshadowed by the cast-iron frame structures in Britain. Indeed the rise of Chicago was a symbol of the increasing prosperity of the New World, which was to challenge Britain's commercial and industrial supremacy and also her technological and architectural inventiveness.

New buildings for public health

New kinds of municipal patronage will be discussed in Chapter 5, but the more utilitarian public buildings belong here, for technical innovations in planning, construction and servicing are the main points to be observed.

Since the Enlightenment in the eighteenth century doctors had advocated greater attention to cleanliness. Older, quasi-alchemical beliefs in the origin of illnesses were discarded. At the same time it was held that the treatment of detainees of any kind, whether lunatics or prisoners, should be made more humane. From the 1820s onwards these ideas were brought more and more to the attention of the general public. If the middle classes tended to turn their eyes away from the squalid parts of their towns they could not help noticing the epidemics which periodically arose out of them. In addition, the new science of statistics brought home the severity of the death rate, infant and hospital mortality and the like. In short, health became the subject of many of the numerous inquiries, reform proposals and Acts which had begun with the Factory Acts which gradually created a more bearable atmosphere in places of work. The Poor Law Commissioners, under the indefatigable Edwin Chadwick, were trying to prove that squalor among the poor was caused not so much by their bad habits as by their surroundings. The effort to ameliorate these surroundings through legal and practical measures, and the cost, would be small in comparison with the beneficial results it would have for the inhabitants; and furthermore, the utilitarians argued, people who are clean and healthy would make better workers and – last and not least – would be less prone to subscribe to Socialist ideas. One has to remember that fears of a revolution were real in Britain in the 1830s and early 1840s.

The first outcome of these reform movements that interests us here is the Poor Law reform of 1834, which created the system of workhouses. It still contained many coercive and corrective elements, which were later softened. At the same time there were attempts to humanize lunatic asylums for the poor, and prisons. In 1848 came the Health of Towns Act, which with its later amendments entitled and forced municipalities to a wide range of measures to improve sewerage, hospitals, cemeteries, and housing (see above, p. 58). Local Boards of Health were to be instituted and new kinds of rates – the 'District Rate' – could be levied. Thus the buildings that we are concerned with here were advocated by tireless scientists and philanthropists, enacted grudgingly by Parliament and implemented by local councils and ratepayers with varying degrees of willingness. Some places, like Manchester and Liverpool, actually beat the legislation with their own earlier measures. In time, most towns did become more salubrious: cholera did not break out again after the 1860s, and cleanliness and respectability became synonymous.

Workhouses, hospitals, barracks and prisons

Workhouses and asylums, hospitals, barracks and prisons almost all have the same distinctive functional requirements. They are preferably situated outside towns, on the edge of open country. They are buildings in which large numbers of people, sometimes over a thousand, live, eat, and even work. The main principle of planning is separation – of functions, of different kinds of people – for various reasons, including ventilation. Thus these buildings consist of groups of separate parts arranged in parallel rows or radiating from a centre. For economy and convenience facilities such as wash-houses and kitchens are usually placed in a central position.

It must be stressed that most of the new plan types were not invented by the Victorians, but went back to the eighteenth century, to French and English empiricists and rationalists, such as the prison reformer John Howard. In their style most of the buildings are very traditional, often based on palace architecture. The architect's task was to show the strict hierarchy of function. The most ornate part of the institution was the chapel, often in a Gothic style. Next in order of importance came the central entrance coupled with the administration block. Larger establishments were often given an ornate clock tower. Sometimes the new workhouse or hospital was regarded as a showpiece for the local authority and therefore had to have a certain amount of decoration. But the particular historical style chosen for this decoration is less important: changes and varieties are slight.

The Poor Law Amendment Act of 1834 reformed the centuries-old English Poor Law by re-instituting workhouses, where 'able-bodied poor' (that is the unemployed) could be 'usefully' occupied. It was administered by a Board of Guardians for the Poor Law Unions. Most districts and towns had built their workhouses by the late 1840s. They are usually two-storeyed buildings consisting of several wings grouped around an open court. The most common style is a simplified Classical, but in the 1840s we find a widespread preference for a vague Tudor or Elizabethan with gables and stone-mullioned windows. In his early career George Gilbert Scott, with his partner W. B. Moffatt (1812–87), designed a number of workhouses in several styles, for example Great Dunmow in Essex, built in 1840 of red brick with yellow brick dressings in a Jacobean style. A second generation of workhouses came in the 1850s. One of the largest was Birmingham's New Workhouse at Winson Green (now the Dudley Road Hospital), built in 1852 by the local architect J. J. Bateman, for about 1,600 inmates [99]. Its cost was £29,000 exclusive of fixtures. There was maximum separation and even isolation of the different kinds of inmates, women, men

and children. Many of the most modern conveniences were provided: heating was by hot water pipes and all the rooms were lit by gas. There was also a separate infirmary, something not generally introduced until the 1860s. Many of these workhouses survive and serve as hospitals.

'Pauper lunatics' were mostly kept in separate departments within the workhouses, but by the 1840s it was generally thought desirable to accommodate them in special institutions, and by 1860 most English (but fewer Scottish) counties had built at least one asylum, for a total of 30,000 or 40,000 inmates. In previous centuries lunatics had usually been kept by chaining them to the building, but since the beginning of the nineteenth century this treatment had been considered inhuman: more and more they were now housed in single rooms, or at least kept there during the night. It was reckoned that a building housing 350 inmates was the best size; it would cost £20,000–30,000. As to the arrangement of the wings, where both ventilation and easy control mattered, a number of different solutions were considered. A few asylums were based on the radiating principle devised for prisons (see below), for instance the Devon Asylum at Exminster near Exeter of 1843–6 by Charles Fowler (1791–1867). As in the case of workhouses and hospitals, however, the arrangement with separate wings at right angles seemed the most satisfactory. One of the largest buildings of its date was the asylum at Colney Hatch in Middlesex, built in 1847–51 (with many later additions) by Samuel Daukes (1811–80), who is best known for his churches. It had about 1,300 inmates and cost over £200,000. In a building longer than the Crystal Palace, it is no wonder that the distance of the wings from the centrally-placed kitchen was criticized. Colney Hatch even had its own railway siding. The restrained decorative details are 'Italian'.

The Lunatic Asylum at St Ann's Heath, Virginia Water in Surrey, generally known as the Holloway Sanatorium, was

99 New Workhouse, Winson Green, Birmingham, by J. J. Bateman, 1852. (Builder, 1852)

built in 1871–84 for 100 middle-class patients, a fact that accounts for its fairly lavish Gothic decoration. It was donated, like the College nearby (see Chapter 7) [249], by Thomas Holloway, who had made his fortune selling Holloway's Pills, a highly popular patent medicine; it cost £300,000. Holloway used the same architect, W. H. Crossland, for both buildings. The Sanatorium is less ornate, but it has a more prominent tower and a more distinct Great Hall, with a very large hammerbeam roof inside.

In addition to these specialized buildings, the traditional type of almshouse continued to flourish in the Victorian period, often with a good deal of whimsical ornamentation, as in the case of Foster's Almshouses, Colston Street, Bristol (1861–83), by John Foster and J. Wood.

The history of hospital patronage is more complicated than for the institutions discussed so far. There were many old-established charities. It was only from the 1860s onwards that care for the sick poor outside their workhouses was made compulsory, and we get the growth of the public 'general hospitals', with departments for paying patients as well. What matters here are the innovations in planning that occurred in the 1850s and 1860s, based on late eighteenth-century schemes. It was not sarcasm when *The Builder* remarked in 1858 that in most hospitals the cure of the inmates was by no means considered a priority: people would have more hope of a cure by 'lying in the open air' than in a hospital. The scandalous conditions of the hospitals in the Crimean campaign drew attention to the problem, and it was there that Florence Nightingale gained the experience which she set out in her book *Notes on Hospitals* of 1859.

The traditional hospital building, often quite large and stately, did not differ in any specific way from other large public buildings. The lack of light and air seemed to be the worst deficiencies. Just those elements were considered the main agents of cure by the Victorians: even in 1906 it

100 Royal Infirmary, Edinburgh, by David Bryce, as designed. The central block was simplified in execution. (Builder, 1870)

was remarked that they were more important than medicines. The problem was to ensure their supply through judicious planning. A focus for the reformers' scorn among recent buildings was the Royal Victoria Military Hospital at Netley, outside Southampton in Hampshire, built in 1856–61 to designs by a War Department surveyor called Mennie. (Only the chapel now survives.) It was a vast and very ornate structure. The fact that it was spread out guaranteed at least some fresh air, but what was criticized was the arrangement of the wards themselves. The windows were placed on only one side of the room, and *The Builder* predicted that many patients would die from lack of ventilation.

The most efficient plan for a hospital was the pavilion model, for which large examples could already be found in France. Each ward has its own building, of not more than two storeys, so that enough light and cross-ventilation were assured. Wards of 25–30 beds were considered ideal, better than the smaller ones which were less well aired and more difficult to supervise. w.c.s, stairs, etc., should be placed at the end of each ward. The individual blocks should be connected by covered walkways, and the kitchen and administration be centrally placed. The maximum size would be 1,000 beds. The different kinds of patients and illnesses should be separated – though separation by kinds of illness was only emphasized from the later Victorian period onwards. Lastly the great advantage of the pavilion system was that it could easily be enlarged when the need arose.

The first large hospital to follow the new principles explicitly was the Herbert Royal Military Hospital at Woolwich, begun in 1860 by a Royal Engineer, Captain Galton. The new St Thomas's Hospital, opposite the Houses of Parliament, was also a model example of the new principles. Built in 1868–71, it accommodated 588 patients in 44 wards and cost £360,000. The wards were arranged in 6 blocks at right angles to the river. Designed by Henry Currey (1820–1900), this succession of blocks with their ornamented fronts was very effective indeed, counterbalancing the continuous but shorter front of the Houses of Parliament. (The old hospital is now being rebuilt.) Of a comparable size is the Royal Infirmary in Edinburgh [*100*], built in 1870–79 by David Bryce (1803–76). Leeds Infirmary (by Sir George Gilbert Scott, 1864–8), is a more compact version, cleverly adapting a Gothic style.

Medium-size hospitals usually chose the H plan, with administration in the centre and wards on either side: an example is the Norwich and Norfolk Hospital of 1879, for which the consultant architect was T. H. Wyatt (1807–80). Butterfield's Royal Hampshire County Hospital in Winchester (1863–8) has a longitudinal arrangement that departs somewhat from the norm. A. Saxon Snell (1830–1904) – who became a specialist for this type of building – designed the St Charles Hospital in North Kensington, London, in 1879 for The Poor Law Board of Guardians. It is a large pile in brick Gothic, with a machicolated tower used for boilers and reservoir. Finally mention must be made of Waterhouse's University College Hospital in Gower Street, London, built in 1897–1906: for the very small, square site the best plan was to arrange four wings in a diagonal cross, just large enough to accommodate four normal-size wards on each floor. The site required a building much higher than usual, and Waterhouse made a feature of this with his corner turrets.

Small hospitals, often called 'cottage hospitals', multiplied after the 1860s. G. E. Street's model design of 1855 for a 'village hospital' for the Ecclesiological Society is as attractive as his schools and vicarages, but its ventilation would not have satisfied the reformers.

Barracks, which are somewhat similar to hospitals in their requirements, can be divided into two very distinct categories: those for officers and those for the men. The Officers' Quarters at Dover of 1856, by George Arnold, R.E. (plan) and Anthony Salvin (elevation), must be counted among the most sophisticated examples of domestic planning of its date; but the conditions in ordinary barracks were worse than in any similar institution. The death rate among soldiers in peace time, it was found, was twice as high as in all other jobs. *The Builder* in 1868 spoke of 'whole-

101 Sailors' Home, Canning Place, Liverpool, by John Cunningham, 1846–52.

sale murder'. A reform of planning based on the pavilion model was advocated, and was implemented to some extent, for example at Knightsbridge Barracks in London, by T. H. Wyatt and others (begun in 1875,†). An interesting early structure of a related kind is the Sailors' Home (1846–52,†) in Canning Place in the centre of Liverpool, by John Cunningham. It was a very high building arranged around a sky-lit court with open metal balconies [*101*]. The outside was in an ornate Neo-Jacobean with corner turrets.

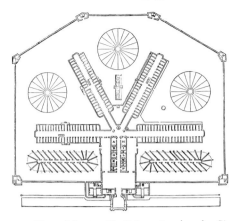

102 *Plan of Pentonville Prison, London, by Sir Joshua Jebb, 1840–42 (Builder, 1847). The wings were lengthened and heightened by one storey in 1865–71.*

The requirements for prisons are even more specific than those for hospitals or workhouses. The most important elements are security and supervision. In addition there were considerations as to the mental and moral state of the inmates. The utilitarians and humanitarians of the later eighteenth century, especially John Howard, turned away from the exclusive emphasis on punishment towards the idea of correction. Several systems were discussed at the beginning of the nineteenth century. The one generally adopted in Britain was that of solitary confinement for most of the day, where the prisoner could 'think over' his problems. Thus buildings with as many small cells as possible were required, combined with a plan which facilitated supervision. The best system was generally held to be the 'panopticon' plan (said to derive from a building Jeremy and Samuel Bentham designed in Russia in the late eighteenth century), in which the accommodation is placed around a central core. Derived from it is the radial plan, in which several wings, each with a top-lit corridor in the centre, stretch out from a central point. The services would be placed between the

wings. The first major example, and the model for Britain, was the Eastern Penitentiary in Philadelphia, Pennsylvania, of 1823. Pentonville Prison in London was built in 1840–42 by Joshua Jebb with architectural advice from Charles Barry [102]. It has four radiating wings forming roughly a half-circle, and a monumental entrance, which remained the pattern for many prisons to come. Jebb was particularly interested in ventilation and heating, and his prison was praised as one of the most salubrious buildings of the time. Each cell was individually heated from above and the foul air drawn off at floor level.

Prisons were relatively expensive buildings and their architects enjoyed a slightly higher status than those of other utilitarian buildings, at least in Early Victorian years, reflecting the importance attached to the issue of imprisonment and reform. As was the case with workhouses, prisons increasingly show medieval features. A striking example is Reading Gaol in Berkshire (of Oscar Wilde fame), built in 1842–4 by George Gilbert Scott and W. B. Moffatt. They used the Castle style, in keeping with the purpose of its walls and gate. The most spectacular prison in this style is Holloway (1849–52,†) [103], in Camden Road, London, by the City Architect J. B. Bunning (1802–63). He chose a bold castellated Gothic style in Kentish rag with Caen stone dressings. The prison accommodated 300 women prisoners in six radiating wings, each four storeys high with top-lit central corridors, at a cost of £100,000. Another variety of the Castle style was Norman, used for the large Walton Gaol in Liverpool (1848–55) by the Corporation Surveyor John Weightman.

In 1865 the central government took over direct control of the running and financing of prisons, and a military engineer, Frederic Du Cane, was placed in charge of the buildings. His Wormwood Scrubs in west London, of 1873–85, was built on the pavilion principle already in use for asylums and hospitals, and that plan gradually replaced the radiating arrangement for prisons.

Cemeteries, pumping stations, baths and market halls

The large cemetery can also be called a major nineteenth-century innovation. Two reasons brought it into existence: sanitation and what has been called the 'celebration of death'. Especially in London, the unsanitary state of the old urban cemeteries had become a menace to the health of all, particularly during epidemics. In the 1840s Edwin Chadwick himself conducted an inquiry into their state and by 1852 Burial Acts had been passed and Burial Boards established, and the first public cemeteries grew up throughout the country. The cult of death and the deceased was something that grew out of the Neo-Classical and Romantic movements, when the old Christian doctrines were set aside and people were beginning to stress their feelings about death and seeking visual expressions for these feelings, such as mourning figures,

urns, and parkland surroundings. Cemeteries became landscaped parks with ornamental graves, and the church was replaced by a chapel treated like a small eighteenth-century park structure.

The first of these parks was Kensal Green Cemetery in London, planned and built from 1830 onwards by a company which found it a very profitable venture. It has a castellated Gothic gate; the chapel was originally intended to look like King's College Chapel in Cambridge, but was finally built in a rich Classical style. The best known of the 'commercial' London cemeteries is Highgate, opened in 1839. In the 1850s the 'public' cemeteries followed, for example the large one at Little Ilford in Essex, opened in 1856, which had its own Great Eastern Railway station. For reasons of health, cemeteries were sited away from town centres.

The forms of the architectural parts of a cemetery had evolved by the mid-century and were repeated all over the country with

103 Holloway Prison, London, by J. B. Bunning, 1849–52.

104 A typical cemetery: Oakham, Rutland, by Armstrong and Hardy of Leicester, 1860. On the right is the gatehouse, in the centre the Anglican and Nonconformist chapels linked by a spire-topped arch.

very little change [*104*]. For obvious reasons, they are among the best preserved examples of Victorian architecture. At the entrance we find the portal combined with the gatekeeper's lodge. The centre is usually taken up by two chapels, for Anglicans and for Nonconformists, which are linked by a porte-cochère carrying a clock tower or turret. The Roman Catholic chapel stands separate and is usually of later date. The chapels are almost always Gothic, as churches in general were from the 1840s onwards; the lodges are also Gothic, inspired by lodges for estates and parks, as well as by the small schools [*234*] and vicarages fostered by the Ecclesiological movement.

Street widening, slum clearance, the provision of sewers and piped water were the most important measures for the improvement of the health of the great mass of city dwellers. As might be expected, with the issue so hotly debated and no expense spared, some of the steam-powered pumping stations for water and sewage are among the most spectacular pieces of Victorian architecture. In London they include Haringey Pumping Station in Green Lanes, built in 1854 by Chadwell Mylne, and Abbey Mills Pumping Station in Abbey Lane, built in 1867 by the engineer J. W. Bazalgette – the former in the Castellated style with asymmetrically-placed battlemented towers, the latter in a Renaissance/Second Empire style with slightly Eastern features. The internal ironwork at Abbey Mills is extremely ornate, and *The Engineer* in 1867 wrote enthusiastically about 'this dainty palace of machinery'. Bazalgette's magnificent Southern Outfall Sewage Works at Crossness near Woolwich, completed in 1865, has similar ironwork [*105*], within an Italianate Romanesque exterior, and has retained its four vast beam-engines made by James Watt.

Liverpool built a large pumping station and water tower at Everton in 1854, under the direction of the City Health Officer W. H. Duncan, in a more sober and very massive Renaissance style. The shaft of the water tower is surrounded by a row of massive arches. Equally massive is the great water tower at Colchester in Essex (by Clegg, 1882), built of magnificent brickwork. A similar landmark for a different purpose is Wild's Grimsby Dock Tower, Lincolnshire (1852), an imitation of the tower of Siena Town Hall over 300 feet high.

The story of bath and wash houses evolved on the familiar pattern of health concern: in 1844 the Commission for Baths and Washhouses was set up and in 1846 Local Bath and Wash Houses Boards were formed. In the vanguard were Manchester, with designs by Thomas Worthington (1826–1909), such as Mayfield Baths, Ardwick, of 1857, and London, with thirteen such buildings by 1855. These establishments were mostly self-supporting, charging 2d. for a 'second-class bath', which was deemed 'within reach of all but the absolute paupers'. Baths were seen as improvers not only of health, but of morals as well – as *The Builder* put it in 1851, 'a great step towards the purification of mind'. Usual facilities included a first- and a second-class swimming bath with dressing rooms, tub baths and facilities for washing clothes.

105 *Interior of Crossness Sewage Works, London, by Sir Joseph Bazalgette, 1865. We are looking* into the central rotunda; beam-engines can be seen on the right and in the background.

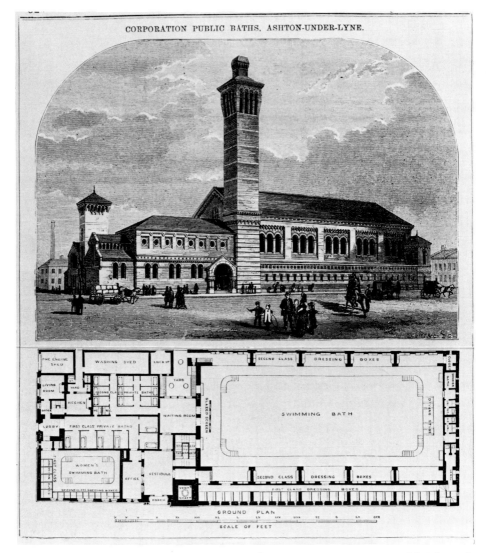

CORPORATION PUBLIC BATHS, ASHTON-UNDER-LYNE.

106 Public baths, Ashton-under-Lyne, Lancashire, by Paull and Robinson, 1870. The building combined a swimming bath, private baths, a washing shed and a shed for a fire-engine. Above were Turkish baths. (Builder, 1870)

Separate entrances were provided for each class, so as to avoid contact. The prominent chimney was always an important architectural feature. Some baths were arranged on a circular plan, such as Banbury Swimming Baths, Oxfordshire (1885,†), and Gilbert Scott's Brill's Baths, Brighton (1866,†), which had a large oval Gothic iron dome. The baths at Ashton-under-Lyne, Lancashire, by Paull and

Robinson (1870,†) [106], included special departments like Turkish Baths, and had a large chimney again treated like a Sienese campanile. Cuthbert Brodrick's splendid Turkish Baths in Leeds of 1866, with their High Victorian polychromy and domed roofs, culminating in a minaret, have unfortunately also been demolished.

Markets had always been amongst the largest secular civic institutions. But despite precedents in Antiquity and some remarkable French buildings of the late eighteenth and early nineteenth century, most markets remained fairly temporary structures. It is to be remembered that even the Royal Exchange in London, built in the 1840s, had an open courtyard until late in the nineteenth century. The demand for covered markets was no doubt stimulated by the growth of arcades and 'bazaars', which sprang up first in Paris and then in London from the beginning of the nineteenth century (see Chapter 4). Bazaars especially come close to the idea of a small covered market: the Pantheon Bazaar in London, which Sydney Smirke created in 1834 from James Wyatt's defunct Pantheon, was a series of large rooms with glazed roofs, lined by shops and with facilities for exhibitions. The most interesting early covered market buildings are pre-Victorian: St John's Market in Liverpool by John Foster (1822), and then, by Charles Fowler – the rationalist architect from Exeter – the two London markets of Covent Garden (1827) and Hungerford (1831–3,†), the latter including an interesting cast iron 'double butterfly' roof, cantilevered out on both sides. Fowler's Higher Market at Exeter of 1837–8 is notable chiefly for its Doric façades.

The Market and Fairs Clauses Act of 1847 laid down standards of cleanliness which these pioneers had already helped to create with their iron structures. Most Northern cities have a large iron market hall, invariably enclosed in heavy stone or brick architecture, such as that at Halifax [107], which is combined with arcades, designed by Leeming and Leeming, who in their public buildings practised a more dignified Neo-Baroque. They also extended the Mid-Victorian City Markets in Leeds (1857,†) in 1903 behind a lively French château exterior. An exception was the large Columbia Market, which formed part of the extensive philanthropic scheme of Miss Angela Burdett-Coutts in the East End of London and was designed in 1866 by her architect Henry Darbishire. The style was a very ornate Decorated Gothic, with innumerable pinnacles and a clock tower. Shops were grouped around a large open court as well as in the aisles of a high, vaulted hall. The whole complex with its close supervision of 'honest dealing' was one of the most remarkable feats of philanthropic patronage, and its destruction in the early 1960s one of the most serious losses of Victorian architecture.

107 Borough Market, Halifax, by Leeming and Leeming, 1895, looking towards the central octagon.

4

Industry and commerce

In dealing with buildings for industry and commerce we have to reverse the method used for domestic architecture of tracing history from ornate buildings to humble ones. The simple and massive utilitarian factories and mills were the first of the new types of building created by the Industrial Revolution. Commercial offices began their architectural ascendancy in the Early Victorian period, as did shops, whereas large stores did not really flourish until later in the century.

Early and Mid-Victorian factories and warehouses

The subject of Georgian and Victorian industrial buildings has been thoroughly explored, at least in pictorial terms. To find their bare walls attractive is a twentieth-century discovery. When the Prussian architect Karl Friedrich Schinkel travelled through England in the 1820s he was overawed by mills and warehouses, but did not think them aesthetically satisfying.

There was little change between 1800 and 1890 in the basic arrangement, construction and exterior treatment of most factories and warehouses, apart from a few specially designed and richly decorated buildings by better-known architects. We may begin with textile mills. Many of the larger buildings are constructed with cast-iron columns or piers supporting segmental arches and brick vaults (for fire resistance). They are massive rectangles, sometimes six or more storeys high, with square or round-headed windows of Georgian proportions. Early mills, such as the famous Norwich Yarn Mill

(Bignold's, now Jarrold's) of 1836, by the local architect John Brown, often carry a small turret or cupola as an 'architectural' feature. More decoration can be found on Sir Titus Salt's mills at Saltaire in Yorkshire, which were built in 1851 by Lockwood and Mawson in conjunction with the model town [59]. Two turrets derived from the Italian Villa style flank the centre on the large block of the mill, and the chimney is ornamented at its base and top. Another huge building of this kind is Manningham Mills, Bradford, of 1871, by Andrews and Pepper [109]. The ornate chimney became a favourite focus for the 'architect's touch' on utilitarian buildings. The most famous example is probably 'Giotto's campanile', an imitation of the tower of Florence Cathedral, on the Tower Works in Leeds, built around 1900.

Perhaps the most remarkable industrial structure of the earlier Victorian period is Temple Mills or Marshall's Mill in Leeds [110,111]. A flax-spinning factory, it was built in 1838–40 for the textile manufacturer John Marshall. It is a one-storeyed building, with high ceilings carried on thin iron supports and plenty of light from glazed cupolas in each bay. The outside was designed by Joseph Bonomi (1796–1878) – son of the Neo-Classical architect of the same name – as a relatively faithful version of Egyptian architecture. Bonomi had first-hand knowledge of

108 Manchester and Salford (now Williams Deacon's) Bank, Mosley Street, Manchester, by Edward Walters, 1860, photographed shortly after its completion.

109 *Manningham Mills, Bradford, by Andrews and Pepper, 1871.*

Egypt, and may also have been advised by his friend Owen Jones.

Among factories, maltings have an additional feature in their kilns, whose pyramidal roofs end in louvered openings. The most impressive maltings and brewery groups are of course to be found at Burton-on-Trent, Staffordshire [113]: they include Bass Maltings (1–7 Shobnall Road), built in 1873–5 at a cost of over £100,000 by William Canning, the company's engineer, and the Clarence Street Brewery of 1883 by Scamell and Collyer. Many towns in eastern England derive their architectural charm from large maltings and breweries, such as the very striking, enormous Bass Maltings at Sleaford, Lincolnshire, by H. A. Couchman (1892–1905).

The term 'warehouse' was often applied very loosely. It could mean mill or factory, as in the case of the Nottingham lace warehouses, where lace was made by machine. These well-preserved buildings are concentrated in one area and form one of the most impressive and least-known groups of large industrial buildings of their period. The most spectacular one, at the corner of Broadway and Stoney Streets,

110, 111 *Temple Mills, John Marshall's flax mill in Holbeck, Leeds, by Joseph Bonomi, 1838–40. The ornate block in the foreground of the exterior*

view (a watercolour of 1849 in Leeds Library) is the office, the plainer wing on the left the mill. The obelisk-shaped chimney no longer exists.

112 Lace warehouse, at the corner of Broadway and Stoney Streets, Nottingham, by T. C. Hine, 1854–5.

113 Bass Maltings, Shobnall Road, Burton-on-Trent, by William Canning, 1873–5.

114 Albert Dock, Liverpool, by Jesse Hartley, opened in 1845.

115 *Detail of a gate pier and the enclosing wall of Stanley Dock, Liverpool, by Hartley, 1850–57. Hartley used a distinctive mechanism whereby a metal door is concealed in one gate pier when open, and slides into a groove in the other pier (seen here) to close.*

was designed by a well-known local architect, T. C. Hine (1813–99), and built in 1854–5 [112]. As in the case of Marshall's Mill, we find the stress on improved working conditions, as well as on external architecture. The structure is very high, with very large windows; the centre and sides project and have ornate doorways, and there is an elaborate balustrade at the top. The whole is reminiscent of the French Château style and the beginnings of the Second Empire style.

Warehouses proper are for the storage rather than the manufacture of goods. The largest are in the docks areas of port cities. A special feature of dock warehouses is accessibility throughout the length of the ground floor, where the buildings may be opened up by colonnades. In the first very large scheme of this kind, Thomas Telford and Philip Hardwick's St Katharine Dock in London of 1825, massive Doric columns of cast iron support brick walls pierced by simple segment-headed openings. In Liverpool, Britain's largest port after London, Jesse Hartley (c. 1780–1860) was Dock Surveyor from 1845 to 1860. His Albert Dock, opened in 1845 by Prince Albert, covers seven acres and cost £722,000 [114]. It follows St Katharine's in the way it encloses an area of water as well as in some of the architectural features, such as the use of cast-iron Doric columns. In the 1850s Hartley continued with Stanley Dock (1850–57) and others, but equally interesting are the subsidiary dock buildings, like the Victoria Tower of 1848 and the Pump House on West Canada Dock of 1858, as well as the entrance to Stanley Dock [115] and other features on the Mersey Wall. For the towers Hartley resorted to the Castellated style, with battlements and octagonal and rounded features built of the same rough and solid-looking masonry throughout. They recall Salvin's Castellated work of the same years [17], but in their details Hartley uses a very personal language of rounded and bulging forms, reminiscent also of the Egyptian vocabulary of the Temple Mills at Leeds [110]. Hartley's work seems to be another aspect of the High Victorian use of the Sublime, combined with the expression of some practical requirements: simplicity and solidity to withstand sea winds and rough use. Hartley thus largely avoided the contrast characteristic of so much practical and commercial architecture, between the functional and the ornamental parts of a building.

Early and Mid-Victorian office buildings

Large structures devoted entirely to the administration of commerce had existed in England for several centuries. There were the Bank of England, the Customs House, and various exchanges. But there were only a few, mainly in London; and because of their size and their importance for the general public they must be classed with large public buildings, which will be discussed in the next chapter. The smaller private business premises – shops and offices – very rarely occupied more than a few rooms in an ordinary dwelling house.

At the time when clubs and pubs were emerging as buildings with architectural pretensions, the commercial office building also began its separate existence. Insurance companies and banks in particular went through a process of rapid transformation in the 1820s and 1830s. Modern company legislation was beginning to be shaped and a sense of security was gained. Whereas in the provinces, and especially in Scotland, banks had enjoyed a fair amount of freedom for some time, the London banks had stood in the shadow of the Bank of England. A series of Acts, the Joint Stock Bank legislation of 1826 and 1833, clarified this relationship: banks could be formed as joint stock companies, though the Bank of England retained the sole right to print money.

Another similar type of building also gained prominence, the so-called 'office chambers', mostly large blocks built by speculators. By the 1860s it was common in the City of London to buy up a number of old houses and erect structures whose total cost was hundreds of thousands of pounds. Rents for offices rose sharply, sometimes to more than £1,000 per year for a suite of six rooms. Often, after a few years of existence these offices had to make way for larger structures, in strange contrast to the permanency and stateliness of their decoration. By the end of the century the process of separating offices from living quarters was nearly complete in the City, and very few people lived there. Such rapid transformation can be paralleled only by the office booms of the later twentieth century.

The façades of these commercial structures were almost invariably Classical, and, as such, did not at first differ very much from clubs and palatial houses. But soon specific requirements were expressed

116 *Commercial Bank of Scotland, George Street, Edinburgh, by David Rhind, 1844–6.*

in the elevations: there was a demand for greater height – more storeys to utilize the precious ground – and larger windows for more light (the use of artificial light during the day was not yet practical). Some differentiation has to be made between the banks and other offices and the warehouse type of building. In the case of the latter the problem of lighting was more acute, and the buildings were usually simpler. Some of the city-centre warehouses of the Northern cities will be discussed in this section because they included the firm's offices and showrooms as well as storage, and are therefore stately buildings. The Classical elevation gave a desired image of solidity, but it also caused problems: there were few precedents for elevations with many storeys and large windows.

Any history of British bank building apart from the Bank of England must begin in Scotland, where freedom for banking had been introduced in the eighteenth century. Both the Royal Bank of Scotland Branch in Glasgow of c. 1827, by Archibald Elliot II, and the Commercial Bank of Scotland in George Street, Edinburgh of 1844–6, by David Rhind (1801–83), are large structures with full

117 Branch Bank of England, Castle Street, Liverpool, by C. R. Cockerell, 1844–7.

pedimented porticos, the former Ionic, the latter an ornate Victorian Corinthian [*116*]. Early bank buildings in English cities include the Royal Bank (of Scotland), now Queen Insurance, in Liverpool, built in 1837 by Samuel Rowland. In Newcastle, several large banks in Grey Street, such as the Bank of England and Lloyds, built in 1835–9 by Richard Grainger with his architects Walker and Wardle, are not distinctive individual structures so much as part of the splendid street architecture.

The first London bank formed as a joint stock company was the London and Westminster Bank, in 1833. For the design of its new building in Lothbury (1837,†) C. R. Cockerell was chosen. Cockerell was one of the most eminent Neo-Classical architects of the younger generation. The reason why he was chosen is clear: in 1833 he had succeeded the ageing Soane as the architect for the Bank of England. The London and Westminster stood opposite Soane's building, and throughout its early life the company was keen to rid itself of

the latter's dominating influence. There was not nearly as much scope for rich architecture as in the 'mother' building opposite, but the general divisions are similar: a linear rustication carried through two storeys of simple rectangular openings to a main cornice, with a smaller third storey set back and crowned by two allegorical figures. Inside, the main banking hall was designed by Sir William Tite (1798–1873) in imitation of Soane's halls in the Bank of England, with a small glazed dome.

A year later, Cockerell built another office block in Threadneedle Street nearby, the Sun Fire and Life Assurance Building (1839–42,†). Here there were four storeys to accommodate. The rustication covered the higher ground floor, which had large stilted segment-headed windows – an influential compromise. Above was a less important first floor and then a giant Corinthian order running through two storeys to a massive cornice, or rather a Renaissance *cornicione* of the type first used in Barry's clubs. The corner of the building was attractively chamfered off.

Cockerell's main contribution to bank design lies in his much more individual solutions for the Branches of the Bank of England. The Bristol, Liverpool and Manchester branches were built during the years 1844–6 [*117*]. Their size and requirements are roughly similar and Cockerell treats them as variations on a complex theme. His combination of Classical splendour and severity with the practical requirements of a bank is highly ingenious. Each building is given a Classical portico with a pediment. However, it is not a full-scale attached portico, but one closely worked into the façade. But for practical reasons three rather than two storeys were required on the restricted sites. While two storeys could be accommodated behind a portico, three would cause much more difficulty according to Classical laws. Therefore Cockerell played a trick: he separated the pediment from the cornices and squeezed the third storey in between.

In Manchester and Bristol he made use of
the intercolumniation of the portico for
very wide windows to light the main
banking hall. But however ingenious
Cockerell's solutions, the *palazzo* type was
to become a more important model for
banks and other commercial premises.

The functional requirements of inner-
city warehouses are somewhat different, in
that a greater number of floors was
generally required – up to five or six, the
most a client could apparently be asked to
climb before the 1880s, when the passenger lift became more common. In addition
large windows were needed, to enable the
client to examine the goods in daylight.
But from the architectural point of view
these various buildings were treated in the
same ornate way and designed by the same
architects. The sudden growth of the
warehouse type was most striking in those
cities where little stately architecture had
been seen before. It is thus fitting to begin
with Liverpool and Manchester.

One of the first buildings to apply
Barry's *palazzo* mode of the Reform Club
[65] on a very large scale was Brunswick
Buildings in Liverpool, by the little-
known firm of A. and G. Williams
(1841,†). It was not quite the first spectacular business structure in that city:
Samuel Rowland's Royal Bank (of Scotland), now Queen Insurance, of 1837 has
already been mentioned. Brunswick
Buildings had three main storeys with
large windows below a massive *cornicione*.
The rustication of the ground floor was
given slightly more emphasis. A variation
on Barry's Reform Club is provided by
William Grellier (1807–52) in his Royal
Insurance Buildings (1846,†), which followed the tendency of contemporary
London clubs in having more overall
ornamentation – in this case Baroque
broken pediments and a heavy balustrade
at the top. The problem of letting in as
much light as possible on the ground floor,
while adhering to the Classical symbolism
of rusticated solidity as a basis for the
palatial floors above, is solved by reducing
the wall to narrow rusticated piers, leaving

large rectangular openings. This feature,
perhaps derived from Cockerell's London
and Westminster Bank, was to become
universal for the type of office building
with which we are concerned [*108*].

Other interesting office structures in
Liverpool include Richmond Buildings
(1857) by J. A. Picton (1805–89), which has
three storeys of round-arched openings
forming arcades, a good solution to the
problem of letting in more light. The
immediate model was the Army and Navy
Club in London (p. 78). The Albany of
1856, a large brick and stone structure with
an open inner court, was designed by an
outsider, J. K. Colling (1816–1905). Colling is chiefly known for his research into
plant forms as patterns for ornament, as
suggested by the theorists of the South
Kensington School of Design, and the
varieties of flat-pattern ornament are the
Albany's most interesting feature.

Turning to Manchester, we find from
the start a number of architects who made
high reputations with their office designs.
Edward Walters (1808–72) was born in
London. He was persuaded to move to
Manchester by Richard Cobden, the
apostle of Free Trade, whom he met in
Constantinople where he was studying the
architecture of the Mediterranean and
supervising work on military buildings.
He started his career in 1839 with a
warehouse for Cobden, No. 15 Mosley
Street, a relatively modest structure only
partly preserved.

Walters' approach to the elevation of
the office building and warehouse was one
of great consistency. He remained strictly
within the Renaissance vocabulary.
Barry's Manchester Athenaeum of 1837,
which was another version of his London
Reform Club [*65*], must have been a
strong influence here. In Walters' Silas
Schwabe Warehouse (1845,†), a brick
structure with stone trimmings, the odd
rustication and the many types of window
surround gave a rather restless, not to say
Mannerist, impression. The J. Brown and
Son Warehouse (1851,†) was one of the
most impressive of all the early *palazzi*

[*118*]. It had six storeys with slight variations in the fenestration. The problem of accommodating them within the *palazzo* formula was solved by placing two storeys behind the 'ground floor' elevation and hiding the sixth storey behind the balustrade. The very large balustrade and the heavy rusticated corner piers were the elements that successfully tied the composition together. It has been suggested that this blowing up of the size of decorative elements was a clever expedient to combat the grime of industrial cities, but one must also remember that the key to Classical façade is proportion, which governs the size of all its elements: as a building is enlarged, so are its details. Walters' last major building before his early retirement was Williams Deacon's Bank in Mosley Street (1860), perhaps the most powerful design of the whole group [*108*]. Earlier, in 1853, the commercial *palazzo* had been elevated to the status of a public building in Walters' Free Trade

Hall, a summing-up of Manchester's political and architectural outlook [*139*].

The work of J. E. Gregan, who died at the age of 41 in 1855, is almost as important as that of Walters. Heywood's (now Williams Deacon's) Bank in St Ann's Square of 1848 is impressive not so much for its size as for the careful handling of its freestone elevation. The rusticated ground floor is pierced by large Venetian windows, and their rhythm is carried on to the right by an arch, which links the bank with the manager's house, treated by Gregan as a simpler *palazzo*. The elevation of his six-storeyed warehouse at the corner of Portland and Parker Streets (1850,†) shows more economy than Walters' designs: most of the windows are simple 'Georgian' openings in the wall, and there is little attempt to coordinate the whole. In his comparatively modest Mechanics' Institute, later the College of Commerce (1854), he reverted to the Reform Club or Manchester Athenaeum formula.

Milne Buildings in Mosley Street (*c.* 1845–50,†), by an unknown architect, showed an unusual combination of two giant orders of the same height placed one on top of the other, each comprising two

118 Warehouse of J. Brown and Son, Manchester, by Edward Walters, 1851. (Illustrated London News, 1853)

storeys. The details are fairly simple and slightly Egyptian in flavour, reminiscent of Marshall's Mill in Leeds [*110*]. Starkey and Cuffley's shops and offices in Market Street (1851,†) had four storeys of arcaded windows of equal height – a point criticized by *The Builder* at the time. Possibly the largest of all the urban warehouses of those years is Watt's Warehouse in Portland Street, built in 1856 at vast expense by Travis and Mangnall [*119*]. The structure seemed too large for a single continuous horizontal cornice, so the skyline is broken at regular intervals. The elevation is enriched by a very great variety in the window forms and applied decoration.

For London, the story is different. Cockerell's pioneering efforts in the late 1830s and 1840s have been mentioned. It seemed impossible for the London counterparts of Walters and Gregan to gain the same eminence, locally and nationally, simply because office building was only one among several major architectural activities in the capital. Also very much less has survived the London commercial booms of later years: almost all the early structures described here are lost. Edward I'Anson (1812–88), who can perhaps be seen as the spokesman for the commercial architects in the city, is chiefly known through his very large and early Royal Exchange Buildings in Freeman's Place (1842–4,†), one of the first of the 'chambers' for a variety of clients. It had a continuous arcade for shops and two and a half floors above.

An architect who did rise to national prominence largely through commercial buildings was John Gibson (1817–92). His Imperial Insurance Office in Threadneedle Street (1846,†) had subtle varieties of rustication all over its three-storeyed façade. Gibson's fame is linked to one patron, the National Provincial Bank of England. The bank's City office at the corner of Threadneedle Street and Bishopsgate, built in 1865 and happily preserved, emulates the Bank of England in being basically a single-storeyed build-

119 *Watt's Warehouse, Portland Street, Manchester, by Travis and Mangnall, 1856, seen in an early photograph.*

ing [*120*]. Large Corinthian columns curve elegantly around the awkward site. Inside there is a very grand banking hall – lit from the top, a feature curiously rare in England at the time, while common in France. Gibson's branches of what is now the National Westminster Bank can be seen all over the country. He carried the basic *palazzo* formula on into the 1880s, by which time his banks often look more restrained and dignified than their more picturesque neighbours.

The Second Empire style, popular for hotels, was also frequently used for offices, such as the mansard-roofed National Discount Offices, Cornhill, in the City of London, built in 1857 by F. and H. Francis. Still in the City, Nos. 191–2 Fleet Street, at

120 National Provincial Bank of England (now National Westminster Bank), Bishopsgate, London, by John Gibson, 1865.

the corner of Chancery Lane (1854–5,†), was an outstanding design by James Knowles, senior, of Grosvenor Hotel fame (p. 81), in solid brick with large round-arched windows.

In Scotland the *palazzo* façade for banks appeared early, and had its own development. In Glasgow, the British Linen Bank at the corner of Queen and Ingram Streets, built by David and James Hamilton in 1840, shows a remarkable variety of Classical features. The office designs of Alexander Thomson (1817–75; see pp. 233–4), known for his Classicism as 'Greek' Thomson, are marked by square 'Grecian'

profiles, generally thin supports between wide openings, and sometimes Egyptian motifs. Grosvenor Buildings in Gordon Street (1859–64) is characteristic. In Edinburgh, David Bryce and others practised in an ornate *palazzo* style, typified by Bryce's British Linen Bank of 1846–51 in St Andrews Square. James Hamilton adorned Belfast, in Northern Ireland, with a very ornate structure, the Ulster Bank in Waring Street (1858–60), where he combined an arcaded elevation with a flat-topped two-storeyed portico [*121*].

All the major English cities adopted the *palazzo* façade for most of their offices and inner city warehouses, although generally not until the 1850s. Often the picture is more one of entire streets than of individual buildings; and in general the story of these formerly proud streets has been a sad one of continuing destruction. In Bradford several firms, including Lockwood and Mawson (whose Venetian Gothic work will be mentioned later), excelled with their warehouses: see especially those in Drake Street (1850s) and Vicar Lane (1870s). The pride of Leeds is, or was, Boar Lane, with its buildings of warehouse type, and Park Row, with its banks and insurance offices, several by George Corson, the outstanding local practitioner in this field, who chose a free kind of Gothic for some of his structures. In Birmingham the north side of Colmore Row presents the best ensemble of Mid-Victorian *palazzo* splendour.

High Victorian variations. By the late 1850s the general relaxation in matters of style made itself felt in office designs. The Italian Renaissance mode was no longer dogmatically put forward as the only one suitable for palatial buildings, nor did the Gothicists maintain the special suitability of their style for churches. The Classical style itself became enriched with motifs from the French Renaissance, resulting, as we have seen, in the Second Empire manner. But it was only very hesitantly that the Gothic architects moved into the commercial sphere. Some, including Butterfield and Street, never took to it. Pugin had published a proposal for a house with shops in 1843, and William White built a parade of shops and houses at Audley in Staffordshire in 1855 and a bank at St Columb Major in Cornwall in 1857. The Italian Gothic branch of the High Victorian movement seemed more promising. Here a symbolic element could also be found: like the *palazzi* of Florence, the Gothic houses of Venice and Northern Italy reminded the Victorians of another vigorous commercial world.

The building generally set at the beginning of this development was in fact not an office building but St Martin's-in-the-Fields Northern District School, London (1849–50,†) [*236*], by J. W. Wild, designer of the Neo-Romanesque Christ Church, Streatham. The school belongs in our last chapter; what matters here is its elevation, based on the arcaded window: two storeys with pointed arches are followed by a third with square-headed windows. In spite of the many openings, the general character of the façade was one of great solidity, due mainly to the uninterrupted horizontal lines and to the use of brick.

Not until the mid-1850s do we find a major office structure with these features in London. The Crown Life Office (1855–8,†) in New Bridge Street was only three bays wide and followed the Georgian proportions of its neighbours. But with its wide semicircular arches and massive piers between the windows it gave an impression of great solidity, set off by rich sculptural decoration. It was designed by Benjamin Woodward (1815–61), of Deane and Woodward, who, partly because of Ruskin's backing, were among the first and most successful architects to apply the new High Victorian style to secular buildings (notably the Natural History Museum at Oxford [*149*]).

Another architect of considerable ingenuity in this field was George Somers

121 Ulster Bank, Waring Street, Belfast, by James Hamilton, 1858–60.

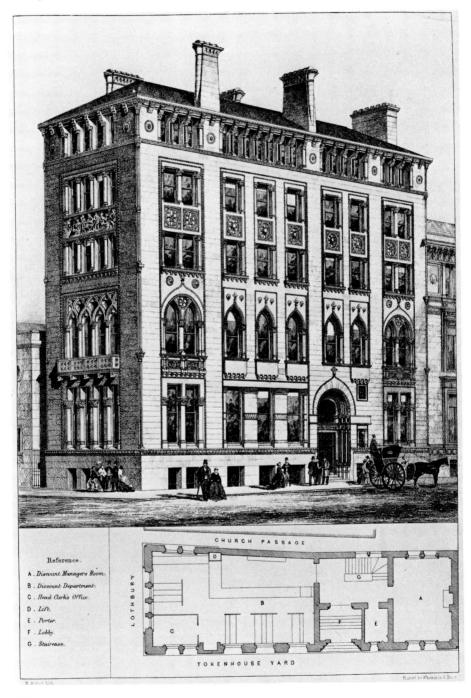

123 Albert Buildings, Queen Victoria Street, London, by F. J. Ward, 1871. Notice the original shopfronts.

Clarke the elder (1825–82). His Printing and Publishing Company in West Smithfield (1860,† a few years later) was a huge pile seven or eight storeys high, with elevations in smooth solid brickwork with a little freestone dressing and brick polychromy. His General Credit and Discount Company, Lothbury (now Overseas Bankers' Club), of 1866, is one of the finest structures in the City [122]. In contrast to the Printing Company with its bulky brickwork, it is all delicately chiselled stone. The windows and the decorative motifs are taken from Venetian Gothic and are grouped together in large flat panels. Large ornate chimneys appear above the slightly pitched roof. Two years earlier in date is Nos. 59–61 Mark Lane, by George Aitchison the younger (1825–1910), with three storeys of round-arched arcades above a ground floor with segment-headed windows.

It seemed a great advantage of this method that the strict proportioning of all parts of a façade no longer mattered, because each storey was a self-contained unit. Two spectacular structures in the Gothic arcaded mode survive in Queen Victoria Street, which was cut through the City around 1870: Mappin and Webb at the corner of Poultry (1870) by J. and J. Belcher, and Albert Buildings, at Nos. 39–49 (1871), by F. J. Ward [123]. The

*122 General Credit and Discount Company offices, Lothbury, London, by George Somers Clarke the elder, 1866. (*Building News, *1868)*

arcades continue around all the main façades, making for very satisfying corner solutions on the irregular sites. A horizontal emphasis is provided by bold cornices of Italian medieval character. But in Nos. 33–5 Eastcheap, of 1868, R. L. Roumieu (1814–77) violently broke through the conventional cornices with his very ornate many-gabled structure, which is one of the most original commercial façades of its time.

Among provincial cities, Bristol produced perhaps the most notable group of buildings, mainly warehouses, in the simple, massive High Victorian style. The manner may have originated in the 1850s with W. Bruce Gingell (1818/19–1900), the chief commercial architect in the city,

124 Warehouse and shop of A. Gardner and Son, Jamaica Street, Glasgow, by John Baird 'No. 1', 1855.

who probably built the warehouse at No. 12 Temple Street, of *c.* 1855. It is of rough masonry with a series of low and massive round arches. A similar design is the Anderson Rubber Warehouse in Stokes Croft (1862), by E. W. Godwin, the famous architect of the Aesthetes who started his career as a Neo-Gothicist here in Bristol. The most impressive structure, in both height and bulk, is undoubtedly the Granary Warehouse in Welsh Back (1871–3), by Ponton and Gough [7]. In this particular type of warehouse very large windows were needed only on the ground floor, so the architect could leave very solid corner piers; the small windows, ranged on seven storeys in all, are treated as a variety of round-arched, square-headed and pointed openings. The whole is of brick, with vivid variation of colour in the arches, and crowned by a massive cornice with butterfly battlements.

Finally, one of the most comprehensive commercial establishments in any city was that of Doulton, the pottery manufacturers, at Lambeth in South London. Built mainly in 1876–7 by Henry Doulton and his architect H. Stark Wilkinson, the whole group of buildings with its exuberant brick and glazed terracotta decoration was an advertisement for the firm's products. The style is a somewhat picturesque High Victorian: the chimney, forming a slim version of the campanile of the Palazzo Vecchio in Florence, was allegedly suggested by Ruskin. Of the complex only the former Museum and Art School are still standing.

Cast-iron and other novel façades. Curiously there is no equivalent in Britain to the 'cast-iron districts' in American towns. Nevertheless, a small number of remarkable exposed iron façades were built between about 1850 and 1880. The first major examples, and the greatest number, are in Glasgow, where the engineer and architect John Baird (1798–1859) specialized in iron construction. His best-known work is Gardner's warehouse and shop, the 'Iron Building', at No. 36 Jamaica Street (1855) [*124*]. It has a fairly heavy framework with wide intervals, which are filled in with narrow arcades on slender piers whose decoration varies slightly. At the top is a moderately projecting cornice. Nowhere do we find the Renaissance heaviness of the later American cast-iron buildings. In many façades, iron and stone are combined. In the Ca' d'Oro in Gordon Street (1872), by John Honeyman (1831–1914), large and very light stone arcades on the ground floor are combined with an iron upper part, in the form of a series of Venetian Gothic windows with complicated tracery. (The mansard roof is a later addition.) A little later in date was Thomas Ambler's warehouse in Basinghall Street, Leeds (1875,†), which consisted of a delicate Gothic framework below a high conventional roof.

Liverpool has a few all-iron façades, but

125 *Oriel Chambers, Water Street, Liverpool, by Peter Ellis, 1864.*

the most remarkable attempts at a new visual and structural solution for the office façade are two buildings by Peter Ellis (1804–84), an otherwise little-known local architect. Ellis seems to have realized early that a light iron framework inside a building made massive external walls unnecessary. He still used stone in the façades of Oriel Chambers in Water Street (1864) [*125*] and No. 16 Cook Street (1866), but the individual members are very thin, reminiscent of Gothic shafts. At Oriel Chambers they frame vertical rows of oriel windows set in very thin ironwork, and end in pinnacles above a narrow

126 *Domed banking hall of the Birkbeck (later Westminster) Bank, Holborn, London, by T. E. Knightley, 1895–6.*

battlemented parapet. It is an abstraction of historical motifs in the service of function and construction analogous to what we saw in Jesse Hartley's docks a few years earlier. The overall impression is one of lightness, paradoxically unrivalled even in the all-iron façades – except at the back of office buildings, where iron is shown much more freely; Ellis's buildings again offer splendid examples.

Late Victorian office buildings, warehouses and factories

Probably no other phase of Victorian architecture shows the same exuberance and variety as the office buildings of the Late Victorian decades. It is increasingly difficult and often impossible to distinguish between historical styles. The Birkbeck Bank (later Westminster Bank,†) in Holborn, London, built in 1895–6 by T. E. Knightley, could perhaps best be classed as mannerist Renaissance [126]. A corner building, it was crowned by an angle turret over the main entrance. Inside and out it was lavishly decorated with Doulton's majolica in many colours, such as a peacock green giant order.

Among the Gothic and exotic buildings one of the most curious is Templeton's carpet factory in Glasgow of 1889 [128] by William Leiper (1839–1916), with its Venetian Gothic windows and its battlemented parapet crowning a large area of coloured brick wall. It is, of course, one of the many British imitations of the Doge's Palace. Somewhat similar, but more Moorish in flavour, is the well-preserved St Paul's House, Park Square, Leeds, of 1878, by Thomas Ambler. Turbulent mixtures of Gothic and 'Old English', that is half-timbering and many other motifs, enliven several streets and corners of central Nottingham: Watson Fothergill (1841–1928) was a local practitioner of great originality.

The Gothic school at its most respected is represented by Alfred Waterhouse. We shall describe the beginnings of his more

127 Prudential Assurance Company, Holborn, London, by Alfred Waterhouse, 1897ff.

fluctuates slightly between, say, Northern Renaissance (Nottingham, 1885), and Gothic (Liverpool, 1886). A small version is No. 1 Old Bond Street, London (1880). Modest at first sight, it reveals upon closer inspection delicate brick and terracotta flushwork.

For the Refuge Assurance building in Manchester (1893–1913) Waterhouse turned to a different style, a florid châteauesque Baroque. Vividly coloured glazed terracotta on huge steel and concrete frames soon spread along Oxford and Whitworth streets, reflecting the new prosperity generated by the Manchester Ship Canal.

Like Waterhouse, T. E. Collcutt was fond of terracotta, but his work is more

relaxed and practical version of High Victorian Gothic in the next chapter. Being mainly based in the North-West, he found commercial work important from the start. His Fryer and Binyon warehouse in Manchester (1856,†) was a clever and practical adaptation of the Doge's Palace on a small scale. Later he became the house architect of the Prudential Assurance Company. Their London headquarters was begun in 1878 at the corner of Brook Street and Holborn, and enlarged and rebuilt in 1897 and later. The façades are very varied, with many gables, turrets and a St Pancras Hotel-like tower over the main entrance. The redorange terracotta which evenly covers the main façades adds an element of unity. Small-scale variation of the façade elements characterizes the many branch offices, where the nominal historical style

128 Templeton's carpet factory, Glasgow Green, Glasgow, by William Leiper, 1889.

129 New Zealand Chambers, London, by Norman Shaw, 1871–3.

seventeenth-century Sparrowe's House in Ipswich. Later, Shaw used his Scotland Yard style, with its strong walls of red brick and horizontal stone bands and its angle turrets [*174*], for instance for the White Star Offices (now Pacific Company) in Liverpool (1895–8), and then went over to the new Edwardian Baroque around the turn of the century.

The new Grand Manner was a style that Shaw had helped to create a decade earlier with some of his houses. Its first major example in the commercial world, Belcher's Institute of Chartered Accountants in the City, came surprisingly early, in 1888–93. This has a very rich and plastic freestone façade with rusticated columns and a sculptured frieze. The overall impression is one of forceful solidity. Strictly speaking, it is not an office building: it belongs, in fact, to the class of the semi-public headquarters of professional organizations, of which some earlier examples will be mentioned below (see p. 147). Their Neo-Classical dignity might well have been influential at this point in the late nineteenth century. Edwardian office buildings were soon to differ radically from most Victorian commercial architecture, rich, but dignified and consistent Classical replacing exuberant variety.

Shops, arcades and stores

By its nature, retail trade – unlike wholesale – places stress on direct and frequent contact with the passer-by. Shop front decoration could be called a branch of advertising, with its demand for splendour, elegance and novelty; and it is the least permanent of all the kinds of architecture with which this book is concerned.

The shop and the shop window as we know them today go back only to the eighteenth century. In London Nash's Regent Street, especially the Quadrant with its covered colonnade, and the Burlington Arcade nearby (planned in 1815) mark the beginning, together with the 'bazaars' which emerged at this time. The best known bazaar was Sydney

restrained and shows the influence of the Vernacular Revival, for instance in the yellowish facing, large windows and curved gables of Nos. 45–57 Ludgate Hill in the City, of 1890. Norman Shaw's New Zealand Chambers (1871–3) in Leadenhall Street [*129*], also in the City, was destroyed in the last war. A very early example of the Queen Anne and Vernacular Revival, it had a more immediate influence on the Domestic Revival than on office buildings. Its large and ornate oriel windows were derived from the

Smirke's refitting of James Wyatt's Pantheon in Oxford Street, carried out in 1834, which provided a large number of shops inside one building. Shopping became a fashionable activity, especially during the early afternoon. The improvement in public transport in the mid-century brought in further customers. By then the usual extension of facilities and decoration to the lesser parts of cities and to the lower classes was also well under way.

The Early Victorian period added and developed two very important elements: iron supports for the building above, and cheap large sheets of plate glass. Regency shops did already have fairly large windows, often bowed, which seemed to open the ground floor to the street and to alienate it from the building above. At their most extreme, such arrangements were possible because the shop fronts projected a little beyond the plane of the upper part of the building (or, to put it another way, the upper part was recessed behind the building line), and thus they didn't need to accommodate any structural supports. Windows could extend freely, and the whole shop front could be altered to suit changing fashions. It is a feature still characteristic of British shopping streets, and not normally seen on the Continent.

Large shop windows in the plane of the building became possible with the introduction of cast-iron piers, which were common in the best shops by 1850. Such windows allowed more room for display, and let more light into the shop itself. Both qualities were enhanced by plate glass. In the eighteenth century it was extremely expensive and used mainly for mirrors, but new manufacturing processes made it generally available in the 1830s, and by about 1850 it was possible to get sheets 8 by 14 feet at less than one-tenth their eighteenth-century cost. Another factor which helped was the abolition of the tax on glass in 1845. One must remember that it was the availability of cheap large sheets of glass that made the Crystal Palace possible in 1851.

130 Two Early Victorian shop fronts, one Rococo, the other simplified Classical, from N. Whittock, On the Construction and Decoration of the Shop Fronts of London, *1840.*

While they tended to see the shop front as an independent unit, architects and decorators also began to apply more and more architectural detailing to it [*130*]. It might be given pilasters or half-columns carrying an architrave which usually served as a fascia to display the owner's name. It might have ornate stucco-work, woodcarving, gilding, veined marble, and so on. A particularly rich example in London was L. Y. Piver's Perfumery Shop at 160 Regent Street (1846), by the otherwise unknown designer Cambon. A greater attempt to integrate shop and façade was made in the large fashionable shopping area of New Oxford Street, created about 1850: here many shops had round-arched windows, set in heavily

131 County Arcade, Leeds, probably by Frank Matcham, 1898–1900.

still further), but towards the end of the century stone arches, round- or more often segment-headed, became ubiquitous, the stone being at times reinforced by iron ties.

The chief characteristics of an arcade, in the sense of a passage, are a glazed roof and access for pedestrians only. Room was provided for a great many small shops. The whole structure was normally a speculative venture by an individual or a company. Most early arcades are to be found in Paris, where the idea was first developed, whereas the most splendid examples in the second half of the century are in Italy. English arcades never developed into the large glazed public buildings that made sense in warmer countries, but there are nevertheless fine ones – often neglected – in many English towns. Of Leeds' eight Victorian arcades, five survive, all situated close together. The earliest, Thornton's Arcade (1878), is rather simple, with an attempt to Gothicize the ironwork; Queen's Arcade (1889) has an attractive iron balcony on the first floor. The County and Cross Arcades (1898–1900) [*131*] were designed for the Leeds Estate Company, probably by the well-known music hall architect Frank Matcham (see Chapter 2): they have gay terracotta work, and the County Arcade has a central dome clearly inspired by the Galleria Vittorio Emanuele II in Milan of 1865. One of the pleasantest smaller arcades is the Royal Arcade in Norwich of 1898, by the renowned local architect George Skipper (1856–1948). It has decorated white tilework and Art Nouveau motifs of female figures and flowers.

A remarkable large urban speculation related to the arcade and a predecessor of the modern shopping centre was Victoria Buildings in Victoria Street, Manchester (1874,†), built by the local architect William Daws for the 'Corporation Property Company'. It covered a large triangular plot; inside was a spacious glazed courtyard lined with shops, and there were shops also around the outside. In addition the complex included a large hotel and office chambers. The style of the exterior

stuccoed façades. Apart from straightforward Classicism, the fashionable style seemed to be 'Louis XIV', which usually meant Rococo Revival.

After 1850 some designers tried to advocate more serious historical styles, as well as greater care in the choice of style. One of the many pattern books for shop fronts, V. Delassaux and J. Elliot's *Street Architecture* of 1855, prescribed 'dark chestnut or ebony (or the imitation of these woods) with a portrait of the Queen in imitation marble' for a jeweller's shop, and a Gothic cast-iron front for an ironmonger. Inside shops, glass was also more common, chiefly in the form of large mirrors. At the same time, critical voices were heard. Pugin and Scott roundly condemned the plate-glass shop front as a deception because you could not see how the weight of the building above was carried. Asprey's shop front in New Bond Street, London, of *c.*1865 consisted of large arches with very thin vertical supports (the windows were later enlarged was a hybrid of Second Empire and Gothic, with segment-headed windows.

The origin of the department store in Britain is somewhat diffuse: here too France deserves the credit for invention and popularization. Department stores began to replace arcades for fashionable shopping in the mid-nineteenth century. What made them so popular was, apart from the quantity and variety of goods displayed, the absence of any pressure to buy, and the system of fixed prices. The latter was pioneered in the rapidly developing co-operative shops. The large London stores developed essentially out of the large drapers' and novelty shops. One of the first drapery firms to build a structure that emphasized the unity of the shop was Marshall and Snelgrove: their new building in Oxford Street by Oc-

tavius Hansard (1876,†) was free-standing and somewhat French in flavour. A little later, in 1877, the first Bon Marché opened, at Brixton in South London.

Here too our story can end with a particularly exuberant specimen, Harrods in Brompton Road [*132*]. The family had begun with a very small grocery shop on the site, and by 1889 had formed a limited company. The present building was built by Stevens and Hunt in *c.*1897–1905, but the $4\frac{1}{2}$-acre site was not covered until 1911. The exterior is entirely faced with Doulton's yellow terracotta, and culminates in a dome which stresses the building's aspiration to be almost a public monument. Inside there is a further display of multicoloured terracotta and glazed tile pictures, made by Doulton's to designs by W. J. Neatby (who had done similar panels for the Empress Ballroom at Blackpool). The Harrods principle was not only to sell but also to entertain: there are numerous restaurants and even a hairdresser. Finally, the store provided the first public escalator in Britain.

132 Harrods Store, Brompton Road, London, by Stevens and Hunt, c.1897–1905, photographed about 1910.

5

Monumental public architecture

IN NINETEENTH-CENTURY Britain government was regarded as a necessary evil. But the influence of government on everyday life, although modest by today's standards, grew rapidly, and so too did the number of ordinary people who had a say in the decision-making. The history of the large public building mirrors these constitutional developments. Before the late eighteenth century, the notion of buildings for the general public sponsored by central or provincial governments hardly existed: Sir William Chambers' Somerset House in London could easily be mistaken for a large domestic palace. Because parliamentary rule in Britain evolved more gradually than in other countries, there is no great burst of buildings for central government such as we find from the late eighteenth century onwards in some Continental countries and especially in the United States. There is no equivalent to the prominence of the American Federal Capitol and its many replicas in the individual state capitols. The domestic architecture of the Crown is hardly a compensation. London's Houses of Parliament [133, 146–8], especially the 'Big Ben' clock tower, can be called a national symbol. But the Royal Courts of Justice, the Law Courts in London [164–6], although a highly successful and beautiful building, cannot remotely compete with the contemporary Brussels Palace of Justice in its domination of the city. The architectural effect of county (as opposed to local) administration in England in the nineteenth century is negligible. It was not until the Edwardian period that English architects, town planners and patrons began to ask for, and to practice, a more monumental approach in large government buildings.

Museums and picture galleries had been considered of equal importance with government buildings since the Neo-Classical period. London and Edinburgh have their share of grand Neo-Classical museum buildings [5], though the completion of some of them dragged far into the Victorian period. Large theatres and opera houses hardly ever reached the architectural prominence of some of their European counterparts (see Chapter 2). In South Kensington, London had a complex of museums, colleges and concert hall which rivalled that of any European capital: but there the motive was mainly educational [167–70]. Schools and colleges, before 1870 at least, were predominantly the result of private patronage and will be considered later (see Chapter 7).

The situation is rather different when we look at civic buildings, which were the result of patronage by municipalities. Here, constitutional and economic change, and therefore architectural change, was rapid. Until the nineteenth century English towns were as a rule dominated by the aristocracy and gentry who resided mostly in the country, and many towns were hopelessly underrepresented in Parliament. It was the rapid rise of the industrial cities in the Midlands and the North that helped the change. The

133 The throne end of the House of Lords, designed by A. W. N. Pugin and completed in 1847.

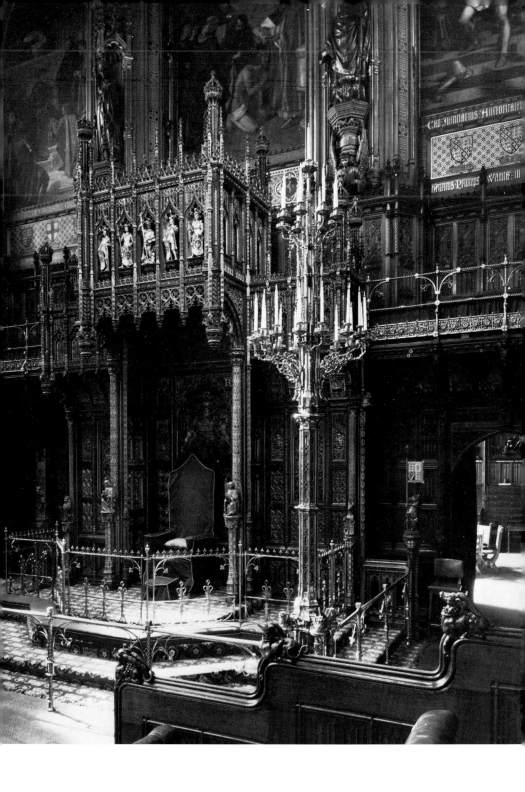

repeal of the Corporation and Test Acts in 1828 made it possible for Nonconformists, who already dominated life in many of these cities, to take part in government. The 1832 Reform Act extended the franchise to the new industrial rich. In 1835 the Municipal Corporations Act followed, which meant the beginning of more democratic and more efficient administration of the towns themselves. One of the chief tasks of the reformed corporations was the various works of public health which have already been discussed. The speed of implementation varied greatly. Much of Parliament's legislation was permissive, rather than compulsory. The initiative still lay largely with each individual town – its ratepayers, its committees, and its 'civic élite'. This fact is of great importance, since decisions and efforts towards architectural splendour were seen as efforts of those civic bodies: a new town hall or exchange was a direct outcome of the new civic pride. Intense rivalry between cities, especially in the North, also helped to foster large and ornate civic buildings.

A civic building usually served a whole group of different functions. It contained first of all a large hall, for public meetings, concerts and so on, based to some extent on the eighteenth-century assembly room. Then it accommodated the municipal offices, with a town clerk's office, a treasurer's office and a council chamber as the minimum requirement. On the outside, one symbol of the public nature of the building was the clock tower or turret [*143, 156, 172, 176*], which in many cases followed the outline of the Big Ben tower at Westminster [*148*], a fact which can be taken as a symbol for the new franchise. Other functions often housed in the municipal buildings, especially in smaller towns, were the courts, which were in part administered by the central government. It was not the responsibility of the local government to provide an exchange, but in many towns the group of manufacturers and merchants who relied on the exchange were the same men who controlled the municipality. Separate exchange buildings (basically large public halls, related to open markets) competed with town halls in splendour.

The museum and the public library, sometimes combined, were an innovation in most towns. It was only after two Acts of Parliament in 1845 and 1850 that municipalities were empowered to levy a special rate to build and maintain such buildings. They were often prefixed with 'free', to distinguish them from some 'public' libraries which were in fact private, commercial subscription libraries (though there might be charges in the 'free' libraries as well). They often operated in conjunction with the mechanics' institutes for the education of the working and lower middle classes, and with government-sponsored schools of art. On the whole, finance and architectural display remained modest, often more so than in the large municipal 'Board schools', which began to spring up after the 1870 Education Act (see Chapter 7).

'Possessing wealth is the prelude to architectural display', *The Builder* maintained in an article on town halls in 1878. Architectural display and the variety of styles, and as a secondary factor ingenuity of planning, have governed the selection of buildings in this chapter. It goes with the nature of monumental architecture that one concentrates on the most expensive and ornate buildings. For civic structures in smaller, less affluent places, the basic requirements were the same – a place for assembly, a town clerk's office, a market or exchange – but they were often combined in a single building, leading at times to very interesting planning solutions [*162*]. In the matter of display, small towns tended to construct miniature versions of the grand designs of the period.

Neo-Classical public buildings

A number of grand public buildings commenced in the previous two reigns were still under construction when Victoria came to the throne. Most were in the Greek Revival style, which was rapidly

134 Ashmolean Museum and Taylorian Institute, Oxford, by C. R. Cockerell, 1841–5.

becoming old-fashioned. The foremost was the British Museum, by Sir Robert Smirke: although building started in 1823, the great entrance front with its portico of Ionic columns was not begun until 1842. In Scotland enthusiasm for the Greek Revival was kept alive longer, especially in the public buildings of Edinburgh, proud of its claim to be 'the Athens of the North'. A number of them are by W. H. Playfair (1790–1857), who had worked for a time under Smirke in London. His Royal Scottish Institution (1822–6, enlarged and remodelled 1832–5) is a massive Doric structure. Beside it, at the National Gallery of Scotland (1850–54), Playfair used an Ionic order [5]. Both buildings are treated as single-storeyed structures dominated by grand colonnades. Like the British Museum, they belong to the international Neo-Classical tradition that stretched from Boullée and Ledoux in late eighteenth-century France through Schinkel and Klenze in Germany to Smirke. They are solid and earnest, but in their modelling

and detail they have more variety than Smirke's more uniform design with its repeated columns.

In England one of the last important examples of the revival of Greek architectural forms in public architecture is the Ashmolean Museum and Taylorian Institute at Oxford (1841–5) [134]. The building was to house the university's collection of antiquities and accommodate an institute to teach foreign languages which had been endowed in 1788 by the architect Sir Robert Taylor. A competition was held: the scholarly design chosen was by C. R. Cockerell, who had travelled extensively in Greece in pursuit of his studies of ancient Greek architecture. Among his discoveries was the Temple of Apollo at Bassae, which contained Ionic capitals of a curious form (rounded at the top) that he was to use in his Oxford design and elsewhere.

Cockerell's Greek Revival was very different from that of Smirke or Playfair. Although his main motifs are Greek, he also uses details and ideas from other periods. The façade of the Taylorian Institute has Ionic columns with Bassae capitals, but they appear in a composition based on the Roman triumphal arch: they stand free from the wall and their entablatures break forward boldly above them; each order is crowned by a statue, and linked to its neighbour by an arch. The general effect of the building recalls English Baroque. Cockerell adds further to the variety by using stonework of subtly contrasting colours. His design, in spite of its chaste Greek details, is Victorian in its eclectic sources of inspiration, the lively modelling of its façades, and its use of colour.

The Fitzwilliam Museum in Cambridge is another indication of this change in taste, among both architects and the public, towards richer architectural effects. It was built to house a fine collection of pictures left to the university by the 7th Viscount Fitzwilliam in 1816. He also left £100,000, and the accumulated interest on this sum allowed building to begin in 1837. The

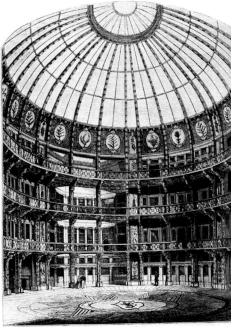

136 Coal Exchange, London, by J. B. Bunning, 1847–9. (Builder, 1849)

135 Royal Exchange, London, by Sir William Tite, 1841–4, showing the clock tower on the rear façade. (Illustrated London News, 1844)

architect was George Basevi. The museum fronts on a comparatively narrow street and its architectural rhetoric is therefore slightly out of place. It is, however, a design of great power. A portico of eight Corinthian columns in the centre is flanked by colonnades that terminate in richly modelled pavilions. Inside is a staircase hall of monumental proportions which occupies nearly a quarter of both floors – a lavish use of space for a comparatively small museum. On Basevi's death, Cockerell took over the interior decoration; and the entrance hall was given an added richness, and its present marble staircase, by E. M. Barry in 1870–75.

In London, the craft guilds and the more modern professional organizations had for some years provided the younger Neo-Classical architects with important commissions for their large headquarters build-ings, such as Goldsmiths' Hall in Foster Lane (1829–35) by Philip Hardwick, and the Royal College of Surgeons in Lincoln's Inn Fields (1835–6) by Charles Barry. They are especially important in constitut-ing a link between corporate public and private commercial architecture, which as we have seen was soon to rise to such prominence in the 1840s.

In 1839 Cockerell entered the com-petition to rebuild the Royal Exchange, the corporate expression of the immense wealth of commerce in the City, which had been destroyed by fire in the previous year. The conditions called for a stone building, in 'Grecian, Roman or Italian style'. Cockerell submitted a magnificent design based on the theme of a Roman triumphal arch. Six Corinthian columns are placed across the façade, the central ones framing three arched entrances. The entablature breaks forward above the columns and supports statues set against an ornate attic storey. The rich sculptural treatment of the façade as a whole is reminiscent of Sansovino's work in Venice. Perhaps the City assessors found the design just a little too exciting, for they eventually chose a project by the worthy but uninspired Sir William Tite. His building (1841–4) is more conventional, with a grand temple front, though for the side and rear elevations he permitted himself a more elaborate treatment. The east front has a clock tower, quite a novel feature in a Neo-Classical building [*135*].

In 1845 Charles Barry was called upon to complete Sir John Soane's unfinished buildings for the Board of Trade in Whitehall. The impetus came from the great increase in the Board of Trade's work that resulted from the railway boom of the 1840s and Gladstone's attempt to regulate it by the Railway Act of 1844. Barry removed Soane's porticos and in-creased the height of the building to three storeys. Although he re-used Soane's half-columns, he changed the character of the design, making it somewhat Italianate. The columns are set on a rusticated ground

137 Round Reading Room of the British Museum (now British Library), London, by Sydney Smirke, 1854–7.

storey, and chunks of entablature break forward above them; at the top Barry placed a balustrade crowned by urns. He was perhaps happiest designing in an Italianate manner, although his most famous building is in the Gothic style. (Another building by Soane in Whitehall was an important precursor of Barry's Italianate manner: the State Paper Office in Whitehall, of 1828, which soon had to make way for the new Foreign Office.)

The enthusiasm for exposed metal architecture was at its height in the late 1840s, but it later faded, as we have seen. The most important Early Victorian application of this method of construction to a public building was the Coal Ex-change in London (1847–9,†) [*136*], by the City Architect, J. B. Bunning. An Ital-ianate exterior hid an internal rotunda of great boldness and ingenuity. It was constructed of cast iron and surrounded by galleries supported on delicate brackets. Thin ribs rose to support a glazed roof 74 feet above floor level. Decorating the rotunda were panels depicting mining and the fossil plants found in coal. This remarkable structure was demolished in 1962 to make way for road-widening.

The rotunda in the City was followed by an even larger one at the British Museum, also of metal construction but less clearly expressed [137]. In 1837 Anthony Panizzi had been appointed librarian of the Museum: as a result of his efforts the library had expanded rapidly, and in 1854 work began on a circular domed reading room sited in the quadrangle. It was designed by Sydney Smirke, and was opened in 1857. The metal construction of the dome and book-stacks was suggested by the need for fire pre-vention, which had been the impetus behind the similar iron roof erected over the Halle au Blé in Paris in 1808–13. Metal construction was also used by Henri Labrouste (1801–75) for his additions to the Bibliothèque Nationale in Paris, of 1862–8: he had visited the British Museum when he was designing them.

Civic Classicism in the industrial towns

By the 1820s most of the new industrial towns could afford small or medium-sized town halls or exchanges. They were soon to be vastly outdone by their Victorian successors. The story of Victorian town halls begins with Birmingham. A long time before Joseph Chamberlain made it the 'model corporation' in Britain, its citizens sought a monumental expression of their new industrial wealth in a temple

138 Chamberlain Place, Birmingham. Left to right: the 'Big Brum' tower, City Museum and Art Gallery and domed Council House, by Yeoville Thomason, begun in 1874; the Gothic Chamber-lain Memorial by J. H. Chamberlain, 1880 (see p. 170); the Town Hall by J. A. Hansom, begun in 1832; and the Midland Institute by E. M. Barry, of 1855 and 1863.

139 Free Trade Hall, Manchester, by Edward Walters, 1853, photographed about 1860.

structure of quite unusual size [*138*]. It has even been said that the Town Hall itself helped to form the feeling of civic importance. A competition was advertised in 1830 and won by the unknown young Joseph Hansom, a man of various talents, who later built Roman Catholic churches in Gothic style (e.g. Arundel in Sussex), founded *The Builder*, and invented the Hansom cab. The building history is by no means straightforward: funds and subscriptions were very slow in coming in and the Town Hall, begun in 1832, was only finished in the early 1860s. Its total cost was about £25,000, a relatively modest sum. It is a town hall in the literal sense of the word, in that it only contains one large room for concerts and the like (not preserved in its original state). The outside is completely surrounded by Corinthian columns, on the model of the Temple of Castor and Pollux in the Roman Forum.

The Town Hall stands in isolation in the centre of an area that originally contained several public buildings, all of which took account of it in their elevations. The first major structure to join it was the Midland Institute and Public Library, which also housed the first Museum, built by E. M.

Barry in 1855 and 1863 (recently demolished). A rusticated ground floor carried a giant order of Ionic half-columns roughly corresponding to the Town Hall, but in contrast to the Town Hall's angularity both ends of the Midland Institute were rounded off – an unusual and effective feature. The interior contained a number of very spacious halls with wide segmental roofs supported by thin granite columns. On the other side of the Town Hall, the massive Council House [*138*] for municipal offices was erected from 1874 onwards by Yeoville Thomason (whom we have met as the architect of the Union Club). Like the Town Hall it has a giant Corinthian order, but this is now expressed by pilasters and piers as well as columns. It is altogether a larger, more complicated and more heavily decorated structure, and cost some £120,000. It extends back along Congreve Street, where it was joined in the early 1880s by the larger and even more ornate City Museum and Art Gallery, also by Thomason. The far corner of the whole group is marked by 'Big Brum', a Renaissance version of Big Ben at Westminster. The Post Office (1891) by Sir Henry Tanner

149

(1848–1935) completes this magnificent forum on the other side. Birmingham's Classical buildings well reflect the course of Classicism in the Victorian period, from stark Neo-Classical beginnings to a flexible, ornate and free version of the Renaissance. But by the 1880s Classical was on the way out, and when we return to Birmingham to look at other works built during the mayorship of Joseph Chamberlain we shall find them to be Gothic.

In Manchester the Neo-Classical style was supplanted by the Neo-Renaissance much earlier. Charles Barry moved from the Neo-Classical of his Manchester Royal Institution of 1824–35 (now the City Art Gallery) to the Reform Club-like manner of his Manchester Athenaeum in 1837. As we have seen, the latter must have helped the Manchester *palazzo* fashion on its way. The culmination of this fashion was Edward Walters' Free Trade Hall of 1853, where, in the Italian sixteenth-century manner of Palladio and Sansovino, the rich arcading and decoration are framed by a massive horizontal cornice [*139*]. The other major Victorian Classical building is the Royal Exchange (1869–74) by Mills and Murgatroyd, a somewhat picturesque version of Leeds Town Hall [*143*]. By that time, however, the authorities of Manchester had already turned their back on the Classical modes, in favour of Gothic (see pp. 165–8).

Liverpool's major public buildings adhered more faithfully to the Neo-Classical ideal. The city has two centres of civic buildings. The first is around the eighteenth-century Town Hall (an unusually prominent building for its period), which was joined in the nineteenth century by the Municipal Offices (1860–66), by John Weightman and E. R. Robson, and the large Exchange building (1865) by the busy T. H. Wyatt, both in a rather rich Second Empire manner. The second, the new 'Forum', was set up outside the old town centre, on a slope to the east called the Plateau. At the top of the open area stands the first and largest of this splendid series of civic buildings, St George's Hall

[*140–42*]. The scheme goes back to 1836, when the Corporation, obviously in competition with Birmingham, proposed the building of a concert hall by public subscription. In 1840 it was decided to combine it with the Assize Courts – the highest court that could be held in a provincial town. The competition was won by the young London architect Harvey Lonsdale Elmes (1814–47). Work began in 1841. The strain of designing and supervising so large a building was, however, too much for his health, and Elmes withdrew and died of consumption in 1847, leaving the building to be completed in 1856 by C. R. Cockerell, with the help of the engineer Sir Robert Rawlinson and the heating specialist D. B. Reid.

Elmes and Cockerell were among the most knowledgeable Neo-Classicists of their time, as regards both Antiquity and contemporary European architecture, and St George's Hall can be seen as a summing-up of Neo-Classicism in Britain. The first impression one gets is of a very large and simple mass, but the more one studies it, the more it reveals itself as a very complicated and multiform structure. The plan, it must be remembered, had to accommodate three main functions, public hall, courts and concert hall. At the centre is the large public hall [*142*], which is flanked by two courts; the concert hall is placed at the north end. Looking at the building, one might be puzzled to know which is its main façade. The main entrance to the hall is on the long side [*140*], facing Lime Street Station. It is marked by a huge portico of sixteen Corinthian columns, and is crowned by a windowless attic masking the roof. On either side of this centre part square pillars continue the Corinthian order. Behind them are the halls of the two courts. The other side of the building, facing St John's Gardens, has less architectural display [*8*], and its centre is enriched by pillars similar to those at the sides of the Lime Street front. The short sides, facing north and south, again differ: the south end has a large pedimented portico, the entrance to

*140–42 St George's Hall,
Liverpool, by H. L. Elmes
assisted by C. R. Cockerell,
1841–56: exterior, ground plan
and Great Hall. The plan
centres on the hall; flanking it
at either end are the two courts,
while the apse contains the
circular Concert Room.*

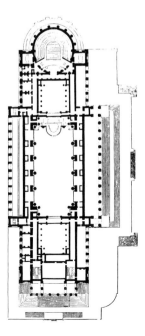

the courts, while the north end, containing the concert hall, is semi-circular and ornamented with half-columns. There is ingenious variety within the order, which remains uninterrupted below its massive cornice.

The interior of St George's Hall is equally splendid. Inside the Great Hall [*142*], the Corinthian order of the exterior is repeated in a series of red granite columns that support part of the elaborately coffered vault, 20 feet wide, inspired by the Baths of Caracalla in Rome. Altogether, in its richness of detail and colouring, especially the multi-coloured Minton tiles on the floor, the inside is much less severely Neo-Classical than the outside. This is especially true of the very elegant Concert Room with its wavy-fronted balcony, designed by Cockerell.

On the north side, the Liverpool 'Forum' is flanked by a row of further civic structures, all for cultural and educational purposes. The pivotal point is the Picton Reading Room (1874), which marks the angle of William Brown Street with a circular Corinthian portico. To its right is the Walker Art Gallery (1875), designed by the same architect, Cornelius Sherlock. To the left is a similar structure, the William Brown Library and Museum of 1857 [*8*] by Thomas Allom (1804–72). Further to the left and right, the Sessions House of 1882 by F. and G. Holme and the College of Technology of 1896–1902 by E. W. Mountford (1855–1908) form the ends of this splendid group. Finally, the 'Forum' is graced by a large Tuscan column carrying a figure of the Duke of Wellington, erected in 1862 to the design of the Glasgow architect G. A. Lawson.

St George's Hall presents sophisticated planning behind a severely simple exterior: Leeds Town Hall, on the other hand, presents exuberant decoration on a disarmingly simple frame, and is (like the Fitzwilliam Museum) a clear statement of the move away from the Neo-Classical interpretation of Classical architecture [*143*]. The competition was won in 1852 by a young and unknown architect from Hull, Cuthbert Brodrick. The building was erected in 1853–8. Just as Liverpool wanted to emulate Birmingham, so Leeds wanted to rival Liverpool. Much of the interior is taken up by the Great Hall; the rest is occupied by courts and municipal offices. The giant Corinthian order with its massive cornice, carried right round the building, also recalls Liverpool. But here the similarity ends. In plan Leeds Town Hall is basically a simple square, and in elevation (setting aside the tower) it is a rectangle, concealing the division of the interior. The main entrance is not under the usual attached portico, but recessed behind a row of columns. Most of the other elevations carry long rows of pilasters. It is this adherence to a block-like form with the decorative elements moulded close to the surface that justifies the term Renaissance rather than Neo-Classical. Leeds Town Hall is essentially a *palazzo*, not a combination of temples. If one looks for immediate stylistic predecessors, one finds the Paris Bourse and Tite's Royal Exchange in London (which also has a tower [*135*]), and also designs by Charles Barry, whose country houses in particular are recalled by the four projections at the corners [*12*]. Barry was, in fact, the juror who most enthusiastically supported Brodrick's design. The urns that dot the top balustrade again recall Barry; Brodrick produces a continuous *fortissimo* by placing an urn above each of the serried columns and pilasters. The tower, which serves partly to mask the high roof of the Great Hall, exemplifies the growing fashion for belfries and clock towers. Brodrick provided it with another large Corinthian colonnade, and crowned it with a dome-like structure whose curved outlines and exuberant decoration recall Continental Baroque, and perhaps, nearer home, the English Baroque tower of St Philip's, Birmingham, by Thomas Archer. In the Great Hall Brodrick again followed Liverpool [*142*], but characteristically his vaulted roof is now supported not by single but by double rows of columns.

143 Leeds Town Hall, by Cuthbert Brodrick, 1853–8.

Two other major buildings by Brodrick in Leeds survive, and show his approach, whereby a simple basic form is clothed with rich but consistent decoration. The Corn Exchange of 1861–3, one of the most appealing of all Victorian buildings, is a simple oval inside and out, reminiscent of early nineteenth-century French designs. A two-storeyed ring of offices surrounds a large central space, covered with a light iron and glass roof. The exterior has regularly spaced round-headed windows and is covered throughout with sharply-cut diamond-headed rustication. The large Mechanics' Institute (now the Art School), built a few years later in 1865, returns to the simple square form. It has a massive entrance arch flanked by two piers, and a series of round-headed windows on both sides, again flanked by the same square piers. One other prominent building by Brodrick, the Grand Hotel in Scarborough, has already been mentioned [70].

In his last building, Charles Barry himself had the opportunity to design a large civic structure: this was Halifax Town Hall, built in 1859–63. Here Mid-Victorian eclecticism is carried many

144 *Todmorden Town Hall, Yorkshire, by John Gibson, 1860–75.*

local industrialist E. R. Harris. Plan and elevation are similar to Leeds and Bolton, but more of the details, such as the square piers, are taken from Liverpool, and instead of a clock tower we find a square structure rising from the centre of the building above a circular central hall.

In 1860–75 the comparatively small Yorkshire town of Todmorden was able to build a magnificent town hall [144], thanks to a gift of £40,000 by the local industrialist Samuel Fielden and his family. It is a simplified version of St George's Hall, a plain rectangle with an apse at one end, surrounded by a giant attached Corinthian order. The designer was John Gibson, whom we have met as the architect of Renaissance banks [120].

The severity of the Preston library points to Scotland, and in particular to Glasgow. The city is rich in Victorian architecture, but it differs from English towns in being a city of private and corporate rather than municipal magnificence. There is also less distinction between public or semi-public buildings, commercial premises, and even churches. Glasgow's, and probably Britain's, greatest Neo-Classical architect of the Victorian period was Alexander 'Greek' Thomson: he has been mentioned in connection with houses and commercial buildings, and will be discussed more fully in the section on churches [230–32]. The purer Classical styles usually prevail. The pedimented portico remained the chief element of decoration, as in the Royal Exchange, later Stirling's Library (1828–30) by David Hamilton, and the County Buildings and Courthouses in Wilson Street (1842–71) by Clarke and Bell. Thomson's successor as the chief Classical architect was James Sellars (1843–88). For his very severe St Andrew's Halls (1873) he went back far beyond St George's Hall to the geometric Neo-Classicism of the very early nineteenth century [145]. Glasgow City Chambers in George Square (1883–8) came unusually late as an expression of municipal pride for so large a British city. The design remotely

stages further. As in some of his country houses, Barry combines Renaissance arcading and half-columns with the Gothic verticality of a very ornate, heavy tower with a pointed spire. His son, E. M. Barry, added a mansard roof.

The example of Liverpool and Leeds was infectious. The closest followers of Leeds, and the two most impressive Classical civic structures of the later Victorian years in England, are Bolton Town Hall (1866–73) and Portsmouth Guildhall (1886–90). Both were designed by a little-known architect from Leeds, William Hill (1827–89). They are so similar that it is difficult to tell them apart: both are basically square in plan (Bolton was enlarged later), and their elevations consist mainly of a giant Corinthian order, with a clock tower above the main entrance. In many ways, for instance their pedimented porticos, they revert to Neo-Classicism.

The only other later Victorian Classical building of similar size in England is the Harris Library and Museum in Preston, Lancashire (1882–93), also built by a relatively little-known architect, James Hibbert (c. 1833–1903), and paid for by the recalls the Leeds group, with a central tower behind the main portico and corner accents, but the elevation follows Italian sixteenth-century precedents much more closely. Significantly, the designer was not a Glaswegian but a London Scot, William Young (1843–1900). The interior is particularly rich in its use of different materials. A Glaswegian who also began his career in the 1870s was J. J. Burnet, whose early work could be seen in the very Grecian former Fine Art Institute, No. 171 Sauchiehall Street, of 1879. Burnet studied at the Ecole des Beaux-Arts in Paris, and provides the link between early nineteenth-century and Edwardian Neo-Classicism.

Of the countless smaller municipal buildings, two may be chosen to illustrate the range of planning solutions. Loughborough Town Hall (1854–5), by the London architect William Slater (1819–72), has a fairly ornate façade squeezed in between other buildings, crowned by a slim central clock turret. The main rooms are an assembly hall doubling as a corn exchange and the mayor's suite on the upper floor. Corn exchanges seem to have become *de rigueur* for even the smallest towns in Southern England. Diss, a pleasant little market town in Norfolk, had fewer than 4,000 inhabitants when in 1854 the local architect George Atkins built a large Corn Hall capable of holding about 300 people, with magistrates' room and library attached. The front displays a full stuccoed portico, that sign-post of a public building, consisting of two sets of coupled Ionic columns.

Gothic symbol for the nation: the Houses of Parliament

On 16 October 1834 a fire destroyed most of the old Palace of Westminster. Only Westminster Hall and the cloisters and undercroft of St Stephen's Chapel survived. In the competition which followed in 1835, Gothic and Elizabethan were specified as the only possible styles for the

145 *St Andrew's Halls, Glasgow, by James Sellars, 1873, soon after completion.*

new building. Both were considered at the time to be peculiarly British and thus appropriate for the national Houses of Parliament. There were 97 entries; all but 6 were in the Gothic style. The winning design was by Charles Barry. A brilliant series of drawings, executed with the help of A. W. N. Pugin, helped in his success.

The foundations of the New Palace of Westminster [146–8] were begun in 1837 and the first stone of the superstructure was laid in 1840 by Barry's wife. The House of Lords was opened in 1847. The clock tower was completed in 1858 and the Victoria Tower in 1860, the year of Barry's death, though work continued until 1867. In 1850 there were 300–400 men working on the building. On its completion it covered 247,200 square feet. The estimate was for £707,104, but the final cost was about £2,000,000. For the fabric Barry chose a magnesian limestone from North Anstone in Yorkshire, which has not weathered well.

Barry's solution to the complex planning problems presented by the numerous functional requirements of this vast building is masterly [146]. It resembles, in its central cruciform layout, the plan of

Fonthill, James Wyatt's great Gothic house for William Beckford. The two main axes of the plan meet in an octagonal central lobby. This lobby is approached from an entrance porch to the south of Westminster Hall, that leads through a gallery on the site of St Stephen's Chapel. The main axis runs at right angles, and comprises the Royal Gallery, the House of Lords and the House of Commons, together with their lobbies. The river front is parallel to the main axis and contains libraries and committee rooms looking on to a terrace. The Speaker's House is set at the north-east corner.

146 The Houses of Parliament, or New Palace of Westminster, London, by Sir Charles Barry and A. W. N. Pugin, 1837–67, seen before the embankment of the Thames about 1870.

Barry was a child of Neo-Classicism, and this axial arrangement owes something to the tradition of Classical planning, as does his elevational treatment [*146*]. Indeed, Barry himself would have preferred to have built the Houses of Parliament in an Italianate style. For all its Gothic detail, it is far from Gothic in the principles of its design. The regular fenestration is carried round the building regardless of the internal arrangement: staircases can be seen mounting behind windows whose design pays no attention to their existence. Pugin, although he contributed so much to the detailed design of the building, did not approve: he remarked to a friend when passing the building, 'All Grecian, Sir: Tudor details on a classic body.'

But Pugin never saw the building completed. The two great towers, the

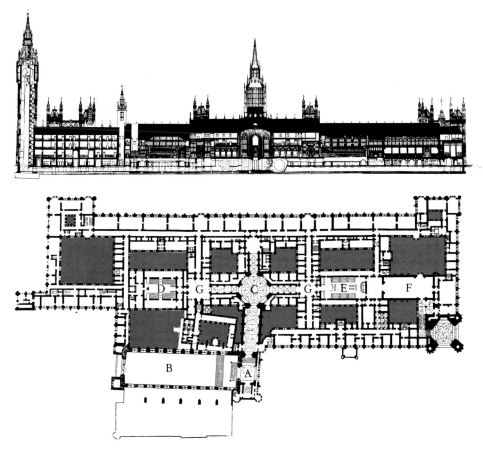

147 *Section from west to east and matching plan of the Houses of Parliament. Big Ben is at the left, the river front at the top of the plan. A entrance porch, B Westminster Hall, C central lobby, D House of Commons, E House of Lords, F Royal Gallery, G lobbies. The river front contains the Commons' and Lords' libraries, separated by committee rooms.* (Building News, *1858, and A. Barry,* Life and Works of Sir Charles Barry, *1867)*

spire over the central lobby, the pinnacles and the numerous turrets, many of them outlets for the ventilation system, give the Houses of Parliament a varied, picturesque and quite unclassical appearance. The two

towers are both masterpieces of Neo-Gothic design. The clock tower, containing the bell Big Ben, is one of the most potent and influential architectural images of the Victorian period [148]. It rises sheer from the ground, unobstructed by any surrounding building which would diminish its apparent height, and points like a great arrow bolt to the sky. The lower part of the tower has no large windows and is covered with blank panelling; at the clock stage it widens to accommodate the clock faces, which are of suitably gigantic size; above is an open bell stage covered by a pyramid roof, the gentle upward curve of which is broken by an open lantern. Pinnacles, lucarnes and the crowning finial

157

148 Detail of the Big Ben tower of the Houses of Parliament, London.

secular structure in Britain. It was to dominate this part of London for a hundred years, until it was overtopped by the nearby Millbank Tower.

In spite of his disapproval of the overall design, Pugin continued to produce sheets of detailed designs for the Houses of Parliament. To him we owe the wealth of decorative detail, of which the chief examples are in the House of Lords and the Queen's Robing Room. The Lords' Chamber is a double cube (90 by 45 by 45 feet), the same Palladian proportion as Inigo Jones's Banqueting House in Whitehall, but it is transformed into a Gothic chamber of enchanting richness. The focal point is the throne, which is set beneath a canopy covered with a profusion of medieval ornament; the woodwork is gilded and enlivened by touches of red and blue [133].

Only one major public building paid for by the State was to follow the Perpendicular Gothic style of the Houses of Parliament – the Public Record Office (1851–96) in Chancery Lane, London, by Sir James Pennethorne (1801–71). Its most interesting feature is, perhaps, its fireproof construction: the basic module is provided by the individual cells for documents, constructed of wrought iron with shallow arched vaults of brick.

create a light and fanciful climax. Features of the design are reminiscent of the tower of the Gothic Cloth Hall at Ypres, although in its placing – in an almost detached position – it follows Italian rather than Northern Gothic precedent. Pugin had designed a similar clock tower, on a smaller scale, for Scarisbrick Hall [14]. The Victoria Tower, although less spectacular, is a splendid design [146]. Its base forms the Royal Entrance to the Palace. Above are two tiers of great windows set in a filigree of stonework. Massive octagonal corner buttresses rise to openwork pinnacles, and crowning everything is a flagpole with elaborate supports. The tower is 337 feet high and on its completion was the tallest

High Victorian Gothic: the Foreign Office and the battle of the styles

Barry's design for the Houses of Parliament can certainly be seen as a success for the Gothic cause, but the building was a very special case. The Gothicists did not really have to fight, because all the competitors had to choose a 'national' style for this unique building. Although it was so prominent a building, the Houses of Parliament had little immediate influence on the style of other public or major civic structures – excepting of course the idea of a clock tower – for by the time it was completed its Perpendicular Gothic style was considered old-fashioned in advanced architectural circles.

In the mid-1850s things began to change, due to a concerted effort by many parties. There were the High Tories, such as Beresford-Hope and Lord John Manners; there was the High Church Movement, strongly supported by the High Tory nationalists; there were the young Neo-Gothic architects themselves, who had been happy with their small churches and schools so far but who began to aspire to more; and there were the critics and the architectural publications. But the kind of Gothic these younger people advocated was no longer the restricting English Perpendicular of the Houses of Parliament, but the new High Victorian Gothic eclecticism, which allowed much wider scope by admitting French, German and Italian Gothic, brick and marble, and even Classical elements such as strong horizontal lines and mansard roofs. Street, influenced by Ruskin's recently published views on Gothic, began to advocate this new style in lectures and pamphlets and in outline proposals for a natural history museum in Oxford, put forward in 1853. Shortly afterwards a competition for the museum was launched. Ruskin's influence on his Oxford friends helped the decision to appoint as architects two Irishmen, Sir Thomas Deane and Benjamin Woodward. The building was begun in 1855 and finished in 1860 [*149–51*].

Woodward was the designer of the partnership, and had clearly shown his understanding of Ruskinian principles in the Museum of Trinity College, Dublin, which he had designed in 1853. Although the plan is similar to Barry's Reform Club, with rooms grouped around a central glazed courtyard, the interior walls are faced with stone and the details are Venetian Early Renaissance. Round arches are carried on capitals of a naturalism only paralleled in the paintings of the Pre-Raphaelites, with whom Woodward was friendly. The carvings were executed by James and John O'Shea, sculptors of the highest abilities, who were to work on the Oxford Museum [*151*].

Woodward's designs for the Oxford building were Gothic, but Gothic of a very different character from that of the Houses of Parliament [*146, 149*]. The origins of its

149 University Museum, Oxford, by Deane and Woodward, 1855–60, photographed soon after completion. *The laboratories pavilion on the right has since been altered.*

features are varied: details from Venice catch the eye; the use of constructional polychromy is also Italian Gothic. However, the high slate roof with its metal finial that crowns the central tower is of French or Flemish Gothic inspiration, and the laboratories at the side are based on the fourteenth-century Abbot's Kitchen at Glastonbury in Somerset.

The main façade is relatively flat, and its sheer walls are enlivened with bands of stone of different colours, rather than by mouldings. This is the Gothic surface praised by Ruskin in his *Stones of Venice* [6]. In the centre of the main front, above the entrance porch, is the tower; the windows are placed slightly asymmetrically, as if to emphasize their functional relationship with the rooms they light.

151 *James O'Shea carving the jamb of one of the first-floor windows of the University Museum, Oxford.*

Each window was intended to have different capitals. Ruskin himself entered with enthusiasm into their design ('*such capitals as we will have*'), and is said to have designed some himself. They are carved with leaves, animals and birds, and they make clear – as they were intended to do – the function of the building as a natural history museum.

Inside, Woodward developed the idea of a glazed courtyard on a large scale [150]. The delicate Gothic ironwork is by Skidmore of Coventry, who was also George Gilbert Scott's favourite metalworker. Surrounding the open centre are cloisters on two storeys, their column shafts of different British stones or marbles, all carefully labelled, each with its individual capital.

Perhaps the most formidable effort of propaganda by one architect in favour of his own design in a particular style was Scott's campaign for his Government Offices (Foreign Office, Home Office, etc.) in Whitehall. The outcome of the competition of 1856 was ultimately tied up

150 *Interior of the University Museum, Oxford.*

with the vagaries of British politics, with the prejudices of the Liberal Prime Minister Lord Palmerston, and with the ambitions of Scott.

Palmerston's increased activities in the Foreign Office and the War Office reinforced the need for new buildings. The site chosen flanked Downing Street and stretched from Parliament Street to St James's Park. Of the 218 designs submitted, only 19 were Gothic. The winning designs were in a Classical style and by little-known architects: for the Foreign Office that of H. B. Garling (1821–1909) was chosen; for the War Office that of H. E. Coe (1825/6–85) and his partner Hofland. They revealed a careful study of the New Louvre.

Scott's Gothic designs clearly owe something to the new Oxford Museum [152]. The façade of the Foreign Office, on St James's Park, was to have a central tower with a high roof, Gothic windows ranged on either side on three storeys and gabled dormers and high chimneys punctuating the roof. But whereas the windows at the Oxford Museum are asymmetrically arranged [149], Scott's façade is completely regular. Both the War Office and the Foreign Office are U-shaped blocks with a central entrance leading from the courtyard into a grand staircase hall. The arrangement of the plan is roughly symmetrical, and although the elevations are covered with Gothic details there is nothing about the massing of the building which would prevent their replacement by Classical details – as indeed was to happen.

Palmerston did not like either of the winning designs and proposed that Pennethorne, the Board of Works architect, be given the job. When he heard this, Scott, whose designs had been placed third in the Foreign Office part of the competition, felt at liberty to start lobbying for their acceptance. There were many in the House of Commons who wanted a Gothic

152 *Sir George Gilbert Scott's competition design for the Foreign Office, London, 1857: façade to St James's Park. (RIBA Drawings Collection)*

153 Scott's Foreign Office as built, 1862–73, seen from St James's Park.

building. In February 1858 Palmerston fell from power and Lord Derby formed a Tory Government. The romantic High Tory Lord John Manners, one of the leading protagonists for a Gothic design for the Government Offices, became First Commissioner of Works. After the question had been considered by a Parliamentary Committee, Lord John appointed Scott the architect. The scheme was changed to include an India Office and to exclude the War Office; Scott prepared a modified Gothic design.

However, the triumph of the Gothic faction was short-lived. In June 1859 Derby's Government fell, and the sprightly Lord Palmerston returned to power. He would have nothing of Scott's Gothic design, which smacked too much of High Church and High Tory. Scott, who had recently published his *Remarks on Secular and Domestic Architecture, Present and Future*, which was an apology for High Victorian Gothic, made a valiant attempt to get Palmerston to change his mind. But when the Prime Minister hinted that perhaps another architect would be better for the job, Scott swallowed his principles and produced new designs. The first was in a 'Byzantine' style: Palmerston rejected it as a 'regular mongrel-affair'. Eventually Scott gave in and produced designs in an Italian sixteenth-century Renaissance style. 'To resign', he commented, in his *Recollections*, 'would be to give up a sort of property which Providence had placed in the hands of my family.' Aided by Matthew Digby Wyatt, the official architect of the India Office, and by Cockerell, he designed the buildings which we see today [153]. Work began on the Foreign Office in 1862 and the whole complex was finished eleven years later.

The change in style required little change in plan. The buildings are grouped around courtyards. Classical details of Venetian richness, executed in Portland stone and coloured granite, clothe the façades. That to Parliament Street is symmetrical, that to the Park asymmetrical, with an Italianate tower making a picturesque eyecatcher [153]. A grand staircase [154] leads up to the office of the Foreign Secretary, overlooking the Park, from which for a generation or two Britain continued to dominate the world.

Although Scott had been deprived of the opportunity to build a secular Gothic Foreign Office, his designs were in-

154 Staircase in the Foreign Office.

fluential: the Canadian Houses of Parliament at Ottawa (1859–67), by Fuller and Jones (rebuilt after a fire in the twentieth century), are perhaps the most important derivative. Scott himself soon won a massive, and easy, victory with his design for the St Pancras Station hotel [71], perhaps the most successful High Victorian building, certainly the most exuberant one. Even before that he had been given the chance to design a Gothic monument of national importance. In 1861 Prince Albert died and the following year a number of distinguished architects were asked to submit designs for a memorial. Scott's was chosen by the Queen. Money was raised by public subscription, Parliament granting £50,000. The memorial was erected in 1863–72 and in the end cost £120,000 [155].

The basic concept of Scott's design – a statue under a Gothic canopy – had been used before [5, 160], by G. Meikle Kemp (1795–1844) in his monument to Sir Walter Scott in Edinburgh, of 1840–44, and also by Thomas Worthington, whose designs for an Albert Memorial in Manchester were published in *The Builder* more than six months before Scott's were accepted. But Scott's work has a lightness, a greater richness, and a more Italian Gothic character than either of these earlier designs. He described his idea as 'a colossal statue of the Prince, placed beneath a vast and magnificent shrine or tabernacle, and surrounded by works of sculpture illustrating those arts and sciences which he fostered'. The inspiration comes as much from medieval metalwork as from Italian tombs such as those at Verona beloved by Ruskin and praised by Street.

The four extremities of the monument are marked by sculptural groups representing Asia, Europe, Africa and America. Steps lead up to a podium decorated with a frieze depicting 169 men who had excelled in the arts: the four Victorian architects represented are Pugin, Cockerell, Barry – and Scott [1]. At each corner the podium projects to carry groups symbolizing Agriculture, Manufacture, Commerce and Engineering. All of this sculpture is carried out in white marble. The statue of Prince Albert, by John Henry Foley, is of bronze; it is framed by arches carried on columns of red and grey granite and enriched with carving and cabochons of coloured marble. Above them are gables decorated with mosaics by Clayton and Bell. Carefully hidden from view is a massive cruciform box girder of wrought iron set above the vaulting, which supports a crowning metal flèche executed by Skidmore. The canopy work of the flèche ends with four angels, which, in the words of Scott, are 'in attitudes suggestive of the resignation of worldly honours; while those above and surrounding the base of the cross suggest aspiration after heavenly glory'.

Civic Gothic

During the first two Victorian decades few major civic structures in Gothic were built. The Guildhall in Broad Street, Bristol (1843), is perhaps the most remarkable, an ornate Perpendicular front with statues of English kings and a gate tower in the centre, by R. S. Pope. (The Assize Court front in Small Street was designed by T. S. Pope and J. Bindon in 1867.) By the mid-1850s Scott was advocating Gothic for civic buildings, in his first design for the Foreign Office and in his book, *Remarks on Secular and Domestic Architecture* (1857), where he especially recommended the Gothic of Italy, the Low Countries and Germany. In 1854 he had entered the competition for Hamburg Town Hall with a combination of quiet horizontals and massive central tower that is one of the key designs of High Victorian Gothic. The design was based on the medieval Cloth Hall at Ypres. The medieval civic architecture of the Low Countries, Scott argued, would provide the best models for Victorian England. In 1857 he submitted a Gothic design for Halifax Town Hall, but was defeated – as we have seen – by Sir Charles Barry. In 1862 he was able to build the town hall at Preston, Lancashire (†), a

155 Albert Memorial, London, by Sir George Gilbert Scott, 1863–72.

medium-size building with a Big Ben type clock tower on one corner of the main block.

By 1860 the younger Gothicists began to compete for this kind of job. Edward Godwin first made his name with Northampton Town Hall (1860, later enlarged), which largely follows Scott and also Woodward's Oxford Museum [*149*], with a central tower over the façade. It was particularly influential in its Ruskinian display of sculpture, which illustrates the history and industry of Northampton in the setting of English history. Two other examples of the medium-size town hall in Gothic style are those of Chester (1864) and Barrow-in-Furness, Lancashire (1878–87), both by W. H. Lynn (1829–1915) of Belfast.

The city where the new Gothic manner was most successfully applied was Manchester. This was perhaps due to its desire to differ radically from its great rival, Liverpool; though Manchester, as we have seen, had its own Classical-Renaissance style. Much of the Gothic was due to Alfred Waterhouse, who was born in Lancashire and did much of his work there, building his reputation on Gothic as well as sound planning. He was scarcely known when in 1859 he won the competition for the Assize Courts (1859–64,†). In its general symmetry and fairly restful horizontality, as well as in the design of the windows, his building resembled Scott's first project for the Foreign Office [*152*]. Only the tower is placed asymmetrically. Inside, the arrangement was equally straightforward: two courts of the same size and a large public hall in between, close to the main entrance. The planning of courts, like that of most buildings, was in fact becoming more and more complicated: it became customary to provide separate corridors and access for the general public, the lawyers, the judges and the accused. The Assize Courts were highly praised at the time, even by Ruskin, who rarely spoke favourably of contemporary Gothic.

In 1867 a competition for the Town Hall was held. It attracted a large but not particularly distinguished set of designs. The established Gothicists and Classicists did not take part – perhaps for political reasons. Waterhouse obtained the commission largely on the merits of his plan. The building was erected in 1868–77 [156–9]. Apart from the great public hall [158], it is entirely taken up by municipal offices. A lot had to be crammed on to the irregular site, and Waterhouse gained the maximum of accommodation by placing the public hall in the centre as a quasi-independent structure and grouping three wings around it. The main front faces Albert Square (where Worthington's Albert Memorial stands [160]). The main

156 Alfred Waterhouse's second design for Manchester Town Hall, 1868. The Albert Square façade is on the right. (We are looking from the lower corner in the plan, below.)

157 Final plan of the principal floor of Manchester Town Hall. The public rooms are on the main front (right); the council chamber is at the top; in the centre is the Great Hall; the long sides of the triangle accommodate offices. All open off a fire-resistant vaulted corridor. (RIBA Transactions, 1877)

158 A drawing by Waterhouse for the Great Hall in Manchester Town Hall, slightly different from the final design. (Victoria and Albert Museum, London)

traceried openings [159]. The Great Hall [158] has an elaborate hammerbeam roof and frescoes by Ford Madox Brown on the historic and scientific progress of Manchester.

With his Town Hall design Waterhouse turned away from his earlier Scott-influenced symmetry and, in a way, returned to the Picturesqueness of Pugin's work of the 1840s. It was a crucial change and a very influential step to take: much of the later Victorian Picturesque aesthetic and the idea of flexible planning are based on it. This element of flexibility was

159 Interpenetrating staircases in Manchester Town Hall (bottom in the plan, ill. 157).

door, under the clock tower, leads to a very spacious entrance hall. The mayor's suite is also on this front on the first floor, signposted by its large windows. The other sides of the building are by no means inferior in treatment. The windows are often large, their size varies considerably, there are many bay windows and projections from the façade, and the outline is much more lively with gables and chimneys. One of the most exciting features of the elevation is the corner to Princess Street [156], where by a number of odd angles and bay windows Waterhouse manages to soften considerably the acute angle in the plan. The designers of other Gothic schemes in the competition simply placed a turret on this sharp corner. But this would not do for Waterhouse, who produced a more thoughtful solution. Inside, there are a number of interesting details, such as the way in which the smaller and larger staircases are placed next to each other and visually linked by

160 *Albert Memorial, Manchester, by Thomas Worthington, 1862–7, seen from the site of the Town Hall. The photograph probably dates from the 1860s.*

perhaps also the crucial factor in the initial choice of style. In an article on town halls in *The Builder* in 1878 it is argued that Gothic is more suitable than Classical for a building with a multiplicity of functions. To the people of Manchester, according to the contemporary *Description* of 1878 by E. A. Axon, the Town Hall symbolized not only 'the opulence of the city, but also the great principle of self-government'. In fact part of the building's cost, in all £775,000, was paid from the profits of the municipal gasworks.

Second in line of the Manchester Gothic architects is Thomas Worthington. Like Waterhouse, he wanted to combine Gothic expression with practicality. His Albert Memorial (1862–7), which as we saw preceded Scott's, is in a sort of Anglo-Venetian Gothic [160], and parts of the elevation of the Memorial Hall (1864), a multi-functional building also in Albert Square, are taken from the Ca' d'Oro in Venice. His most important building in the city is the Police Court (now Magistrates' Court) in Bloom Street, of 1868–71: its front is similar in many ways to Waterhouse's Assize Courts, and it has in addition a large Big Ben type clock-tower. Finally, among the Gothic buildings of Manchester, there is the privately-endowed John Rylands Library (1890–99) by Basil Champneys (1842–1935), who is usually a man of the 'Queen Anne' Revival. While the façade is in a somewhat whimsical Late Gothic style, the interior is a very impressive space, consisting of a wide nave sumptuously vaulted, the books being stored in small bays off the main space and on the gallery.

What Brodrick was for Leeds and Hull, the firm of Lockwood and Mawson were for Bradford. In the 1850s they won their fame with Saltaire [59] and with St George's Hall in Bradford (1851–2), a smaller version of Liverpool's St George's Hall. Their work in the 1860s was heavily influenced by Scott, that is it is Gothic, but a very Southern kind of Gothic, with horizontal Florentine machicolated cornices, Venetian windows and Sienese clock towers. The two major public buildings of Bradford, the Exchange of 1864–7 and the Town Hall of 1869–73, are of this type. Both are very rich buildings: the original part of the Town Hall, which contains just the municipal offices and a court, cost over £100,000. While the Town Hall has a more irregular and picturesque plan, the Exchange displays richer pictorial decoration, mostly representing nineteenth-century men of trade and technology.

A building of a more specifically Ruskinian character, in that it adheres to the Doge's Palace in Venice, is the City Museum in Bristol (now the University Refectory), by Foster and Ponton. The most impressive building in a more picturesque variety of Gothic is the town hall of Rochdale in Lancashire, of 1866–71. It was designed by W. H. Crossland, who had been a pupil of Scott and had worked for him in Halifax (see p. 71). Rochdale Town Hall is a free-standing building, with each part under a different roof, including the very grand staircase. The large public hall is in the centre, its roof parallel to the main front, flanked on both sides at right angles by the council chambers and other offices, whose roof gables form the ends of the façade. A tower (rebuilt by Waterhouse after a fire in the 1880s) stands to one side. Crossland's design is also remarkable in that it is an early departure – like Manchester Town Hall – from High Victorian heaviness in detail and constructional polychromy. The effect is now determined by one colour of stone, with all its gradations and weatherings. Inside, the building seems again to vie with Manchester in its lavish painted and sculpted decoration.

Gothic buildings become rarer in the later 1870s. Middlesbrough's ornate Town Hall (1883–9) by G. O. Hoskins is a late example. The new Late Victorian mixed styles were catching on rapidly. One of the most ardent believers in Gothic for civic buildings in the later decades was J. H. Chamberlain (1831–83) in Birmingham, with his partner William Martin (d. 1899). About 1875 they built the School Board Office (now the Treasurer's Department), and in 1881–5 the College of Arts and Crafts nearby, England's first municipal school of art [161]. Chamberlain, who had been an enthusiastic supporter of Ruskin since the 1850s, had by the 1870s adopted the Late Victorian mode of providing as many windows as possible and livening up

161 *College of Arts and Crafts, Birmingham, by Chamberlain and Martin, 1881–5. This early photograph shows the polychrome decorative details. (Birmingham Library)*

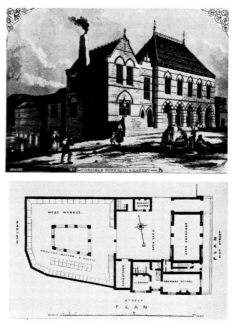

162 *Municipal Buildings, Cardigan, by R. J. Withers, 1859.* (Building News, *1859*)

163 Design for the Law Courts in London by William Burges, 1866–7, looking east along the Strand. (Builder, 1867)

mention only one example, the Municipal Buildings at Cardigan of 1859 [162]. The front range contains a corn exchange, a grammar school, a library, the council room, a urinal and a fire station, crowned by a small clock turret. At the rear, where the ground slopes down, is a large covered market with store rooms underneath. The exterior is of local stone left fairly rough, and there is little other ornamentation except for the occasional use of constructional polychromy. The total cost was under £5,000. This vernacular Gothic building was designed by R. J. Withers (1823–94), a relatively minor follower of the Ecclesiologists, applying the principle of 'picturesque utility'.

The Law Courts

The last great national monument to be built in the Gothic style was the Royal Courts of Justice or Law Courts in the Strand, London. Paradoxically, it represents both the triumph and the ultimate decline in popularity of the style for public buildings. All the entries for the 1866 competition were Gothic. Among those who submitted designs were E. M. Barry, Burges, Lockwood and Mawson, J. P. Seddon, Street, and Waterhouse. Scott's design has a regularity in plan and elevation that recalls his first Foreign Office scheme [152]. By contrast, Burges produced a brilliantly picturesque design, which if it had been built would have given London a re-creation of a thirteenth-century dream world and a skyline of great inventiveness, pierced by towers and turrets [163]. Seddon's design, although more compact, has a splendid skyline and a grand vaulted hall. A great central hall was also a feature of Waterhouse's scheme, but his solution was more adventurous and his hall was to have had a great metal and glass roof. Eventually, after considerable wrangling, Street was pronounced the winner. It was not until 1874 that work began (to modified designs), and not until 1882 that the building was completed [164–6]. Street was dead by then, and the

the façade with gables and elaborate window-frames. More in the High Victorian mode is his Chamberlain Memorial of 1880, celebrating the Mayor, Joseph Chamberlain [138]. The two were not related, but seem to have been on friendly terms, and Chamberlain built the Mayor's large suburban house, Highbury, at King's Heath (1879).

Another medievalizing style is the Scottish Baronial, a castellated manner characterized by round corner turrets placed high up and covered with conical roofs, plain walls and square-headed windows. This was the mode chosen by J. D. Peddie (1824–91) and C. G. H. Kinnear (1830–94) for Aberdeen Town House, begun in 1868. The building is punctuated by a clock tower placed asymmetrically.

In smaller civic structures Gothic seems to have been less frequent, and one might

164–6 The Law Courts, London, by G. E. Street, 1874–82. Above: the Strand front. The main entrance is through the large arch on the left. Below: plan of the court floor (Building News, 1882). Right: Great Hall.

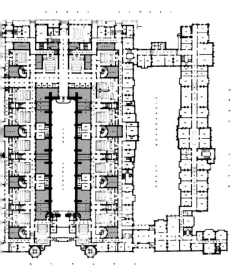

final supervision was by his son, A. E. Street (1855–1938), and Arthur Blomfield (1829–99).

Street's building has many fine features. The front to the Strand is varied – a composition to be seen in perspective as one walks along the road [*164*], not a grandiose façade whose symmetry can only be appreciated in the drawings. The central internal feature is a great vaulted hall 230 feet long and 82 feet high, which has an austere dignity suited to its purpose [*166*]. From it, a complicated range of corridors and numerous staircases connect the different small courtrooms with each other and with the Great Hall. There are attractive views through the stairs, which have openings into the hall. And yet, in spite of these excellent features, the Law Courts are often said to lack architectural coherence. Many details show Street's inventiveness, but in places they crowd upon one another without functional or aesthetic justification. Moreover, the use of Portland stone, only sparingly relieved by other materials, gives the building a cold precision which contrasts with the delightful liveliness of many of Street's earlier and smaller works. The lawyers were said to be dissatisfied with it as a place of work.

Street normally designed every detail of his buildings himself. But although this could be done by someone with his capacity for work in the case of a church, a building of the scale of the Law Courts taxed even his remarkable energies, and when he died at the age of 57 in 1881 it was generally agreed that it had broken him. He is commemorated by a very dignified seated statue in the Great Hall, by H. H. Armstead, put up in 1886.

Eclecticism at South Kensington

It would be wrong to see all Mid-Victorian architecture as a battle between the Goths and the Classicists. Scott, as we have seen, was prepared to have a foot in both camps, and Waterhouse eventually developed a free style that owed more to his own interpretation of the past than to any one period. The style displayed in the group of buildings that grew up in South Kensington after the Great Exhibition of 1851 might best be called Mid-Victorian eclecticism.

The idea of a cultural centre for London came from Prince Albert. With the unrelenting drive of Henry Cole the idea became reality. A collection had been formed of objects bought at the Great Exhibition. It was shown by Cole's Department of Practical Art at Marlborough House, with such success that the Prince Consort and Cole decided to enlarge the collection and seek a purpose-built home for it. In 1852 the Gore Estate, south of the site of the Crystal Palace, was purchased.

The first, unhappy, venture was, as we have seen, the building of a temporary museum, which became known as the 'Brompton Boilers' [*96*]. It was soon followed by permanent buildings, which form the basis of the present Victoria and Albert Museum. Work on that complex began in 1859. Most of it was designed by Captain Francis Fowke, whom we have met as the designer of the 1862 Exhibition building [*97*]. On his sudden death in December 1865 he was succeeded by another army engineer, Lieutenant-Colonel H. Y. D. Scott (1822–83), and the most important part, the Quadrangle, was finished by 1872. Fowke was helped on the decorations by Godfrey Sykes (1824–66), a sculptor and pupil of Alfred Stevens. Fowke and Sykes represented the success of the Government-run Schools of Design and Schools of Art. Many other decorators and designers were also employed: they included E. J. Poynter (Grill Room, 1866–73) and William Morris (Green Dining Room or tea room, 1866–70).

The style of the Quadrangle is Italian Renaissance, but of a very different kind from that used by Barry for his clubs and country houses: not Florentine or Venetian but from the North of Italy. The elevations are of fine red brick and buff terracotta, with ornamented piers and

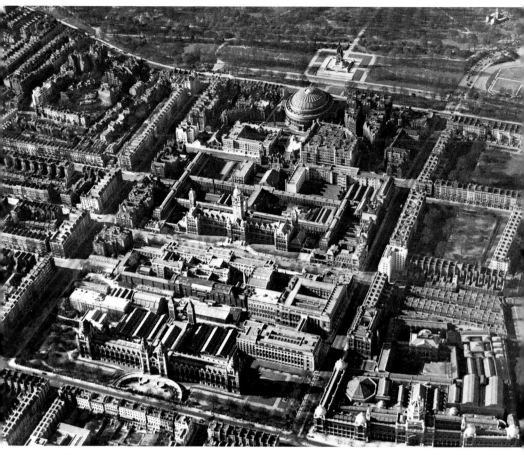

columns dividing the many arches [*168*]. Large terracotta panels decorate the walls and fill the pediment. (Fowke had employed both the materials and the style in 1861, for the arcade with which he embellished the gardens of the Royal Horticultural Society, west of the new museum.)

The monument to Prince Albert by Gilbert Scott [*155*] was to be erected in Kensington Gardens due north of the 1862 Exhibition building (which, unlike the Crystal Palace, was not in the park). As part of the memorial it was also proposed to erect a public hall, between the monument and the Exhibition site [*167*]. Fowke produced designs in 1864, but his death

167 Air view of 'Albertopolis', the cultural district in South Kensington, taken in 1939. At the top is the Albert Memorial (see ill. 155); south of it the rotunda of the Albert Hall (by Lieutenant-Colonel H. Y. D. Scott, 1867–71); south of that, the tall tower and symmetrical wings of the Imperial Institute (by T. E. Collcutt, 1887–93); farthest south, the Natural History Museum (by Alfred Waterhouse, 1873–81). Exhibition Road, running north–south, divides this group from the Victoria and Albert Museum, bottom right (the main front by Aston Webb, 1899–1909, and behind it the original front, now part of the Quadrangle, by Captain Francis Fowke, 1859–72: see ill. 168). Immediately north of the Victoria and Albert Museum is the Huxley Building (by H. Y. D. Scott and others, 1867–71).

168 *Detail of terracotta work on the original façade (now in the Quadrangle) of the Victoria and Albert Museum, London, by Captain Fowke and Godfrey Sykes, completed in 1872.*

prevented their execution and Henry Scott again took over. His scheme owes much to Fowke's conception. The Albert Hall, begun in 1867 and opened in 1871, is a vast amphitheatre seating an audience of 8,000 below an elliptical roof measuring 219 by 185 feet. The exterior is of red brick, again enriched by buff terracotta, notably in the form of a continuous frieze depicting the triumph of the Arts and Letters. At the same time, Scott worked with J. W. Wild and others on the Huxley Building in Exhibition Road (1867–71), which is in a similar style to the Quadrangle of the Victoria and Albert Museum. It is particularly impressive in its juxtaposition of blank brick walls and concentrated areas of pale terracotta decoration.

Fowke was also connected with the other major museum in South Kensington, the Natural History Museum. In 1864 he won the competition for the building, which was to be on the site of the 1862 Exhibition. (Other competitors included Greek Thomson from Glasgow, whose design consisted of a series of Greek temples.) Again, his death prevented the execution of his design, and in 1866 the job was given to Alfred Waterhouse. He produced new designs; work began in 1873, and the museum was finally completed in 1881 [167, 169, 170]. The cost was £395,000.

Waterhouse's design has certain features in common with his project for the Law Courts, including an entrance flanked by twin towers, high roofs, and a glazed central hall. The façade to Cromwell Road, 675 feet long, is boldly punctuated by central towers which rise to 192 feet and by massive high-roofed pavilions at the ends. It is entirely faced with terracotta, which was not only widely used in the other South Kensington buildings, as we have seen, but was also a material that Waterhouse specially favoured. The walls are yellow, enlivened with bands of bluish-grey, and appropriately decorated with figures of animals (some prehistoric) [169]. Between the central towers is a great arched portal which leads into a glazed hall [170] giving access to the galleries. Elements of the design are Romanesque, but the massing and details are a long way from the originals of that period, and Waterhouse's Romanesque is not far removed from Fowke's Renaissance style.

The last major public building in 'Albertopolis' sought its inspiration from the châteaux of the Loire. The Imperial Institute was the outcome of the Colonial Exhibition of 1886, and was built by T. E. Collcutt in 1887–93 in honour of Queen

Victoria's Jubilee [*167*]. Only its tall tower, capped by a copper dome, survives. The Institute had much of the quality of the buildings it emulated: it was rich, regal, and yet small-scale and charming, given a fanciful air by numerous gables and cupolas. The material was Portland stone, decorated with narrow bands of brick used sparingly as if it were some precious material. It is a characteristic example of the Late Victorian mode for public and civic architecture, which must now be discussed in greater detail.

169, 170 Natural History Museum, London, by Alfred Waterhouse, 1873–81: beasts in terracotta and iron (right) and the main hall.

Late Victorian 'Free' styles

There was a continuing need for municipal buildings, as local government administrations grew out of their Late Georgian or Early Victorian buildings. The variety of styles in later Victorian decades is great, and often it is difficult to find a label for them. The intensity of symbolism, the identification with the ideals of some chosen past age, is much weaker. Like the advanced domestic architecture of the period, civic buildings adhere in some vague sense to the *genius loci*, to the customs and materials of the particular region in which they are built. Generally they become more human, less grand and forbidding, and their planning appears more sophisticated and flexible. In their details they freely mix elements from Renaissance styles in Britain and abroad; characteristically the details are small-scale and treated in an informal manner.

One of the most important variants of the 'Free Renaissance', the 'Queen Anne' Revival, popularized by Nesfield and Shaw, was quickly becoming accepted for public buildings. As we have seen, it took elements from the English Renaissance and combined them with an informality of planning, and a truthful expression of both materials and function, which were derived from the Gothic Revival. It was, as H. S. Goodhart Rendel pointed out, the reverse of Pugin's dictum about the Houses of Parliament: 'Classic details on a Gothic body'.

One of the earliest manifestations of this style is Leicester Town Hall, built in 1874–6 to the design of F. J. Hames, a local architect. The design has all the easy informality of Nesfield and Shaw. It is of warm red brick with lively stone details, and large sash windows with thick wooden frames painted white. The composition is basically symmetrical, apart from the clock tower on the side, but by strict Classical standards the different parts are awkwardly put together and the windows are far too large, creating an impression of domestic informality. Large windows are also the characteristic feature of the town hall of Wakefield in Yorkshire (1877), by T. E. Collcutt. The main front is articulated by three very large oriels with rounded corners, which reach up three storeys right into the roof and end in Jacobean gables. The tower in its verticality is more reminiscent of a Gothic belfry.

A more ornate example of the Late Victorian mixture of styles is the Victoria Assize Courts at Birmingham, perhaps the outstanding civic structure of the 1880s, in the period when Joseph Chamberlain was mayor [*171*]. It was built in 1886–91 to designs by Aston Webb (1849–1930) and Ingress Bell (1837–1914). Waterhouse was one of the assessors of the competition and praised the choice of materials – terracotta and brick – as 'undoubtedly . . . the best materials for Birmingham'. The terracotta work, by W. Aumonier, provides a unifying factor in an otherwise varied design, both outside and in. Because the building is mostly seen from odd angles, it appears much less symmetrical than it actually is. There is a characteristic Late Victorian restlessness in its very rich detailing, with very few features capable of definition in conventional stylistic terms. Windows are neither semicircular nor pointed. All are very heavily mullioned and transomed.

Civic authorities were not slow to realize the attractions of the Free Renaissance, and in 1890–97 Sheffield built a town hall in that style [*172*]. The architect, E. W. Mountford, combined English, French and Flemish details and placed a tall gabled tower on one corner. In 1893–7 the town hall of Oxford was rebuilt by H. T. Hare. It has Elizabethan gables and transomed windows, used in a manner popularized in Oxford by T. G. Jackson [*246*]. There is sculpture on the exterior, again by Aumonier. Hare produced a series of

171 Detail of the Great Hall of the Victoria Law Courts, Birmingham, by Aston Webb and Ingress Bell, 1886–91.

172 Sheffield Town Hall, by E. W. Mountford, 1890–97.

magnificent interiors: the Great Hall has a low elliptical coffered ceiling, and lively plasterwork in high relief enriches spandrels and the fronts of balconies.

One of the most significant contributions of the last Victorian decades, reaching into the Edwardian period, was the provision of smaller libraries and branch libraries, a hitherto neglected service. It was felt that books ought to be brought to the people rather than the people to books. A great many of these buildings were partly or completely funded by the munificence of Andrew Carnegie, the Scottish-born steel magnate from Pittsburgh, Pennsylvania, and the newspaper publisher Passmore Edwards. Stylistically they are usually in one of two modes – the Late Victorian terracotta

picturesque, or the Baroque grand manner on a small scale, such as the Passmore Edwards Library in Pitfield Street, Shoreditch, one of the poorest parts of London, which was designed in 1897 by H. T. Hare [*173*].

During the late 1880s and 1890s there was a move away from the pretty Free Renaissance towards a more Baroque style: it can be seen in Norman Shaw's New Scotland Yard, built in 1887–90 for the Metropolitan Police [*174*]. Shaw combined details derived from the Baroque of Wren with tourelles to give a lively, slightly 'defensive' quality to his building. The lower part of the walls is faced with granite, above which Shaw used Portland stone and red brick in alternating bands. The design met with some criticism in Parliament but was widely supported in the architectural press. In his reply to his critics, Shaw made

*173 Passmore Edwards Public
Library, Shoreditch,
London, by H. T. Hare, 1897.
(*Architectural Review, *1898)*

*174 New Scotland Yard,
London, by Norman Shaw,
1887–90.*

play with the fact that it was a 'genuine building – in which we have no sham or show front, all is of the same quality and in the Court it is the same'.

An even more original style, combining Renaissance with Arts and Crafts and Art Nouveau elements, was used by C. Harrison Townsend for a number of small public buildings. The Bishopsgate Institute in London (1892–4) has a remarkable narrow façade with characteristic foliage carving in shallow relief and octagonal angle turrets reminiscent of Waterhouse as well as H. H. Richardson, the American architect [*175*]. The Whitechapel Art Gallery in London, designed in 1895 and executed in 1897–9, is a modified version of the Institute. The round-arched door is set off-centre in a Norman Shaw manner. In 1898–1901 Townsend built his most original public building, the Horniman Museum in South London. Its façade is dominated by a curving pediment, beneath which is a large mosaic by Anning Bell. The entrance is at the side, set in the base of a tower of unusual design, whose rounded corners rise to cylindrical pinnacles decorated with leaf carving.

Late Victorian Baroque

By the 1890s many of the younger architects were trying to rid themselves of the indiscipline of these 'Free' styles, in order to design something more imposing and permanent which they thought would be more suited to the expression of a public building. One of the first examples of this new mode is Battersea Town Hall (1892) in South London, by E. W. Mountford. It stands across the road from his Public Library, and is more serious. It has a formal, tripartite façade on two storeys: in the centre of each block is a tripartite window, above which, set in the parapet, is a curving pediment filled with low-relief sculpture. The entrance has a semi-circular columned porch. Stone dressings are combined with the red brickwork.

In 1893 Aston Webb produced his design for the completion of the Victoria and Albert Museum. In his very rhetorical façade (1899–1909), built of red brick and Portland stone, informal elements of Early Renaissance character are combined into a design of Baroque swagger, crowned by an elaborate octagonal cupola. A far more successful essay in the Baroque Revival is the town hall of Colchester in Essex (1898–1902), by John Belcher [*176*]. Above a ground floor faced in Portland stone with banded rustication rises an

175 Bishopsgate Institute, London, by Harrison Townsend, 1892–4, soon after it opened.

elaborate composition in brick and stone, articulated by giant columns that support one triangular and two segmental pediments, the whole a riot of Baroque architectural decoration and allegorical sculpture. From one end rises a tall, slender tower that is a landmark for miles around.

Official architecture at the close of the century turned to a Wren-inspired Baroque. Its beginnings can be seen in Leeming and Leeming's undistinguished design for the Admiralty in London, won in competition in 1884 and built in 1894–5. J. M. Brydon (1840–1901) produced one of the most prominent, if not perhaps the most exciting, of these Neo-Baroque structures – the large block of Government Offices fronting Parliament Street and Parliament Square (1898–1912). For some of his ideas, including the circular central courtyard, he went back to Inigo Jones's plan for Whitehall Palace. The front to Parliament Square has a crushing symmetry and an overbearing scale. The War Office, also begun in 1898, is a more lively and attractive design in the same vein by William Young, the architect of Glasgow City Chambers. The stone domes which crown its corners add another picturesque element to the view of Whitehall from St James's Park.

To see Late Victorian Baroque at its best it is necessary to go to Cardiff. It says much for the wisdom of Alfred Waterhouse, the assessor of the 1897 competition for the city hall and law courts at Cardiff, that he was able to recognize the merits of a design which differed so radically from anything that he could have produced himself. The winners were Lanchester, Stewart and Rickards. Their buildings were admirably planned, it is true, but the elevations were in a Continental Baroque style of extraordinary maturity and brilliance. The exuberant Portland stone ornament inspired by the Baroque of Vienna we owe to E. A. Rickards (1872 1920). A tall tower, which rivals Belcher's at Colchester [176] in the ingenuity of its architectural decoration, adds a vertical accent more characteristic of Victorian than of genuine Baroque civic

176 Colchester Town Hall, Essex, by John Belcher, 1898–1902.

buildings. Lanchester and Rickards went on to build Deptford Town Hall in South London (1900–1903), and to set their mark on much of the Edwardian architecture that followed. Their Cardiff design brings to an end the Classical stream of Victorian public architecture which, ever since Cockerell's Ashmolean Museum and Taylorian Institute [134], had played with Baroque elements and Baroque massing.

6
Churches

EVEN TODAY, for most people, Gothic and churches go together. But this is entirely a nineteenth-century way of thinking. Like all Victorian stylistic revivals, Neo-Gothic was bound up with certain cultural and political attitudes – perhaps more so than the others, as it was thought of as a more distinctive and controversial style in itself. Gothic Revivalists always fought harder than the supporters of other styles. Many of them fought for a religious cause as well. But why *should* a post-medieval church hark back to the Middle Ages? The reasons are many and have been touched on in the Introduction – antiquarianism, nationalism, the search for emotive appeal, the greater opportunity for pictorial decoration. They were largely a part of Romanticism. The Church had to meet the challenge of scientific method. Belief in the Bible had been eroded and even theologians had begun to doubt; but a new tendency arose in the early nineteenth century which by-passed these attacks. Poets like Wordsworth and Coleridge, partly under the influence of the German Romantics, were converted from rationalism to belief. The new theologians, Catholics as well as Anglicans, maintained that the chief concern of the Church was not politics and society but spirituality, and the expression of this spirituality in services and church buildings. There is a new emphasis on 'real presence', on the sacraments, and consequently a stress on liturgy, on ritual rather than preaching, and on all the visual and decorative elements that went with the ritual: altars, vestments, and older forms of church music. Models were found in the Middle

Ages: theologians and designers were filled with enthusiasm by pictures and written accounts of medieval church services. Most Gothic Revival work was carried out by the Established Church, spurred by the Anglican Revival, but the Roman Catholic Revival occurred first. The Nonconformist churches were less involved with Romanticism and will be discussed separately.

The Catholic Revival and Pugin's theory of Gothic architecture

The revival of Roman Catholicism was well under way when Victoria came to the throne. Liberal legislation in the 1820s and 1830s lifted some of the social and political restrictions on Roman Catholics, and the full Church hierarchy was re-established by 1852. The Catholics' primary aim was to regain some of the ground they had lost since the Reformation. But they were mostly concentrated in the North-West of England, and it was only in the later nineteenth century that most towns in Britain had a large enough congregation to warrant a Catholic church.

Intellectually the movement was rather varied. Of primary interest to us here are the followers of Romanticism, such as the two Cambridge undergraduate converts, Kenelm Digby and Ambrose Phillipps de Lisle, who, back in the 1820s, had been struck by the richness of Catholic art on the Continent. Phillipps returned to support the Catholic Church ardently in his

177 All Saints', Margaret Street, London, by William Butterfield, 1850–59 (see p. 206).

native Leicestershire, with the help of his very wealthy friend the 16th Earl of Shrewsbury, who resided in neighbouring Staffordshire. Much of A. W. N. Pugin's work went up under their patronage, including Alton Towers for Lord Shrewsbury (see p. 35).

Conversion to Roman Catholicism was a decisive moment in the lives of many Romantic artists and writers of the nineteenth century. It was a determined and conscious step from indifference or disbelief to faith and conviction and gave a tremendous boost to every thought and every activity. One of the first of the spectacular cases was the German writer Friedrich Schlegel, whose ideas on religious art were beginning to be known in England in the 1830s. The overwhelming reason for Pugin's conversion, in about 1835, was that he found the visual arts of his day lacking in 'truth' and 'life'. In architecture a 'grand' and 'sublime' style could only be restored by the Catholic Church; the whole of architecture and decoration should be subservient to or related to the Church.

In his first major publication, *Contrasts, or a Parallel between the architecture of the Fourteenth and Fifteenth Centuries and Similar Buildings of the Present Day* (1836), Pugin talks about the religious devotion of the architect to his work as opposed to the contemporary pursuit of architecture as a business. Pugin believed, as did his contemporaries, that architecture was a reflection of the period and culture of those who built it; but just as he had much stronger preferences among different periods of history, extolling the Middle Ages and despising the modern age, he had much stronger preferences among architectural styles. Classicism seemed to him the language of paganism, and especially of Utilitarianism, for which he, together with Thomas Carlyle, William Cobbett and Kenelm Digby, felt a profound disgust. Naturally, he fiercely condemned the desecration of medieval buildings since the Renaissance. His writing was influenced by the sharp satirical style of the

day and ranged between the humorous and the vitriolic. His illustrations, in which he compared splendid medieval churches, inns, towns and almshouses with mean and utilitarian-looking modern structures, were even sharper [3].

He was able to pay for the publication of *Contrasts* himself when he was only twenty-five, because he was born into a well-to-do family, the only son of Augustus Charles Pugin, a French nobleman who had fled from the Revolution, and Catherine Welby, who came from an established Lincolnshire family. His mother, a strong Evangelical, was protective as well as strict towards her precocious and demanding son. A. C. Pugin had studied at the Royal Academy and become a draughtsman with a reputation for accuracy in details of scenery and architecture. Nash employed him as designer for some of his Gothic decorations, a method, as we have seen, not uncommon at the time. He also published numerous illustrated books on Gothic and picturesque kinds of architecture in France and Britain. Thus Welby was imbued with Gothic already as a child. Before his father's death in 1832 he had acquired an immense amount of antiquarian knowledge and produced designs for a variety of objects, including plate, furniture for Windsor Castle, and stage sets for a production of *Kenilworth*.

His first architectural jobs, the design of Gothic details for Charles Barry at the King Edward VI School in Birmingham (1833–7) and at the Houses of Parliament, are mentioned elsewhere (Chapters 7 and 5). What Pugin really wanted to do was to build churches. In those years opportunities were limited, and the first building entirely built to his designs was his own house, St Marie's Grange at Alderbury near Salisbury [30, 31, 178]. Its importance for the beginnings of the domestic revival has been discussed. But it also reveals his ideas about religious architecture very clearly. In an inscription he emphasized the religious aspect: 'Hanc domum cum capella edificavit Augustus de Pugin sub invoc[atione] beatae Mariae anno christi 1835 laus deo' (A.P. built this house with a chapel dedicated to the Blessed Virgin Mary in the year of Christ 1835. Praise to the Lord). The chapel [*178*] with its prominent traceried window and its bell-cote appears as the most important part of the house. For Pugin the house was an example of the fusion of belief, art and life: he originally intended to execute the sculpture for the chapel himself, and on occasions he helped to officiate at services in a surplice he had himself designed. His total commitment is reminiscent of the fantastic ideas of the writers of 'Gothic' novels in the late eighteenth century, figures such as William Beckford, who dreamed of enacting chivalrous, mystic events in the setting of their Gothic Revival architecture. But for Pugin Gothic was not a stage one occasionally reverted to for titillation, or to supply decorative motifs for varying purposes. It was a complete way of life and building, synthesized from many quarters of architectural theory and practice. Not surprisingly, convents, with their detailed plan and organization, are among his most interesting designs (p. 241 and ill. *184*).

Before going on to a discussion of Pugin's designs, his architectural views as he developed them in his books must be considered. In his *True Principles of Pointed or Christian Architecture* (1841) he defended the merits of Gothic more assertively than any of his predecessors. First of all he emphasized the national argument. Renaissance architecture belonged to Italy, the Swiss Cottage was suitable only for Switzerland, and so on. Then there were practical arguments, such as the fact that for a wet climate a steep roof was considered advantageous. And above all there were religious arguments. Gothic was deemed to be the ecclesiastical style for the true Catholic Church: it is chiefly verticality, Pugin argued, that expresses the Christian concern with upwardness. A Classical church symbolizes worldliness. As to the more detailed and more literal elements of Christian symbolism, such as

178 *A drawing by A. W. N. Pugin of the view from the library into the chapel at St Marie's Grange, Alderbury, Wiltshire, 1835 (compare the plan, ill. 31).*

the instruments of the liturgy, Pugin was convinced that anything Classical must be pagan and thus utterly unsuitable for Christian churches and a Christian society.

As we have seen, within medieval architecture there were a number of styles from which one could choose (pp. 21–3). The simplest Gothic style, Early English, was often seen in relation to Romanesque (or Norman), and writers stressed its simplicity and primitiveness. Pugin rarely used the Romanesque but made ample use of Early English. It was generally looked at as a more economical version of Gothic, for it did not require tracery for the windows. Because of its narrow, single-light windows it was often called the Lancet style. Pugin and other architects thought Early English suitable for particularly remote and therefore 'primitive' areas, such as the West of Ireland, and in general for projects with limited funds [*181, 193, 194*].

179 Good and bad stonework for a Gothic building, from Pugin's True Principles, *1841: irregular coursing and window surrounds (left) are to be preferred to the large, even blocks used by the early Gothic Revivalists.*

The variety of Gothic that Pugin and most of the Anglican architects in the circle of *The Ecclesiologist* seemed to prefer for the next ten or twenty years was Decorated or 'Middle Pointed', that is the style of Westminster Abbey [*183, 198*]. The reason for this preference was that Perpendicular, the style revived for the Houses of Parliament [*146, 186*], was beginning to be considered too 'late'. There was a notion that any late style meant decay: the Renaissance was already creeping in. It was also found too ornate, whereas Early English was considered too simple for many purposes.

Many accounts of Pugin's work and ideas stop at this point. It is said that he initiated the serious imitation of Gothic work, his predecessors having produced mere pastiches. But that is not the full picture. Pugin was hardly dead by 1852

when pure English Gothic and the faithful imitation of one period of Gothic went out of fashion. The new elements of Pugin's architecture are more than a particular set of decorative and symbolical forms: they concern most aspects of architectural practice. Architecture in Britain was never to be quite the same again whatever the style.

The first element is conviction and sincerity: a devotion to particular principles and a particular mode of design. It is the image of the Gothic architect devoted to his church architecture, of which we shall meet many more exponents. Later in the century this kind of architect was more concerned with particular modes of domestic design. The second element is 'propriety'. This is rather a vague term and was defined in various ways. For Pugin it meant a place in a hierarchy of decorum, whether ecclesiastical or social. The most common demonstration of 'propriety' was in the ornateness of churches: the chancel had to be the richest part, and within the chancel ornament concentrated on the area around the altar [*182*]. At the other end of the scale, church naves or the utilitarian parts of a monastery might be left absolutely plain. The concept itself had developed in the Renaissance and was commonly observed in nineteenth-century buildings: the organism of a large country house is an example. But Classical architecture had long ceased to be consistent: large façades hid poor buildings; mass-produced decoration diluted the social hierarchy. Pugin railed against all this, and in his criticism lies the beginning of the decrying of most of the architecture of the nineteenth century as inappropriately ornate.

But the real difference between Pugin's approach and the Classical approach to propriety lay in the fact that the Classicists would tuck the less important parts of a building away and give their appearance as little thought as possible: for Pugin, on the contrary, the simpler parts of a building are not something to hide, but something that exists in its own right, and even has a positive aesthetic value. Simplicity must not be disguised: it is a matter of *truthfulness*. 'Truth' was for the Neo-Gothic architect of the mid- and later nineteenth century the most important principle. It was clearly related to the notion of sincerity of artistic expression, and has remained up to this day (or almost) one of the key ideals in architecture. But of course 'truth' is not just an abstract ideal. It is concerned with the particular expression of practical function and materials in construction.

To take the first element: Pugin harshly criticizes the way in which the typical 'Gothic villa' of the nineteenth century uses the elements of fortified architecture without reference to their particular functions: watchtowers are used as chimney-tops, and so on. The fact that these towers are evocations of the past is not a valid reason: as you hardly need private watchtowers in the Victorian age, you must do without them. The flues in Pugin's secular and monastic buildings look like flues: they are usually placed on the outside, and regularly break through the main roofline [*31*, *184*]; similarly, the large windows which light the staircases of large houses cut through the divisions between storeys. In fact the Classical concept of a unified façade, which had been applied to all buildings, whether Classical or early Gothic Revival (one has only to think of the river front of the Houses of Parliament [*146*]), is given up in favour of an agglomeration of different parts, each clearly defined by its individual function. A Pugin church is always a combination of at least three or four different elements – a chancel, a nave, a porch and a tower [*181*, *183*]. They do not have to be arranged symmetrically and they present no 'façade'. In this way they differ radically from the later Nonconformist churches, which took up Gothic decoration but almost always remained aligned with the street or the street corner on which they are placed. Pugin's buildings are generated from the inside out. Of course irregularity had been appreciated for some time by those advocating the Picturesque, but again for Pugin it was not just a fanciful alternative to Classical regularity: it resulted from practical considerations.

The other element pertaining to 'truth' is honesty of construction. The designer must not disguise but should stress how a building is put up – whether it be of inexpensive rough stonework or brick or of more elaborate masonry. Pugin feels very strongly about this, and compares examples of good and bad practice which might at first sight appear rather finicky and meaningless: a wall, for instance, must not be covered with large regularly-cut facing stones [*179*]. There is an idea of the Picturesque behind this liking for rugged walls as opposed to Classical smoothness. But, as the Ecclesiologists were soon to add, a wall should not be faced with too large and too obviously irregular blocks either. Again, a principle of the Picturesque has been reformulated on the basis of 'truthfulness', contempt for disguise, and practical considerations.

Many things followed from these tenets. The most important was the effect on the applied arts of the new respect for different materials. In a well-appointed early nineteenth-century Classical church the interior tends to uniformity: the walls, iron piers, galleries, balustrades, organ case, etc., display the same decorative motifs and are even painted the same colour. From Pugin onwards, different materials – iron, wood, fabrics, precious metals, painted decoration, and so on – received different treatment. Pugin designed objects in all these materials, and so did most of his followers. The most conspicuous result of the change of outlook was the revival in churches of open wooden roofs, which during the Classical period had been disguised by plaster ceilings.

It is these principles of picturesque utility in planning and undisguised materials in construction that form the basis of most of the buildings to be discussed from now on.

Roman Catholic churches, 1837–1870

Into the short span of his career Pugin crammed the design and most of the execution of over one hundred buildings. The great majority of them are churches. In most cases we know a lot about the history of each particular building, and in most cases the story is of a complicated struggle between Pugin and his patrons. Pugin considered that few of his major buildings fully reflected his original intentions – a symptom of the early stage of the revival of church building, but also of his own erratic ways.

Perpendicular Gothic stands at the beginning, with St Marie's at Derby and St Alban's at Macclesfield, Cheshire, begun in late 1837 and late 1838 respectively. The emphasis is on vertical linearity, even elegance: high nave and aisles, tall arcades, slender piers, and a central western tower (in both cases unfinished). There are large windows with rich Perpendicular tracery. In many ways these buildings are still reminiscent of the earlier Gothic Revival of Rickman and the 'Commissioners' Churches' built after 1818: for instance, their chancel does not form a very distinct

space. (Pugin would of course have loathed the comparison.) Both churches have open wooden roofs.

The second mode is the Lancet, or Early English style. Pugin used it for churches in remote parts of the country and where economy was necessary. St Wilfrid's, Hulme, in Manchester (1839–42) is a fairly large church in a populous district, and comparatively little money was available [*180, 181*]. (After bomb damage and rebuilding, the church today is not as attractive as one would expect so historically important a building to be.) The Lancet style had been used before, but even in the cheapest design there would have been some pinnacles and other small embellishments, at least on the west front. That was not Pugin's way of designing. For him, as we have seen, simplicity was a positive feature, rather than something that had to be disguised. Of St Wilfrid's Phoebe Stanton concludes, in her book on Pugin, 'In the struggle with circumstances Pugin had made a statement based on principles.' Pugin himself had proclaimed, in his *True Principles*, that 'the picturesque effect of the ancient buildings results from the ingenious methods by which the old builders overcame local and constructional difficulties.' Which are the new principles here at Manchester? The emphasis is on massive treatment throughout. The material is brick. What little stonework there is is confined to copings, battering and the openings, which are far fewer and smaller than hitherto. The facing of the windows lies flush with the wall and shows a picturesque, rugged contour. The plan is compact, but asymmetrical, the tower being placed over the north aisle. The proportions of the interior are low, and the arcades rest on short, heavy piers. The windows lie almost in the plane of the outer wall, with a wide splay inside, which again adds to the effect of massiveness. The roof is of wood, with hardly any decoration. The chancel is now very clearly separated by a low chancel arch. There, much more ornament can be found – a reredos behind the altar, sedilia (seats for

180, 181 St Wilfrid's, Hulme, Manchester, by Pugin, 1839–42. (Exterior and plan from Pugin, The Present State of Ecclesiastical Architecture in England, 1843)

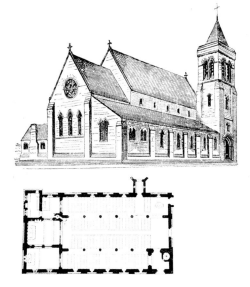

the clergy) on the right, and richly coloured stained glass. The description of this modest church can be applied word for word to thousands of churches, both Catholic and Anglican, built in the next decades.

A number of buildings in this Early English manner can be grouped together. Most are larger and more important ecclesiastically, notably the cathedrals at Nottingham and Killarney, begun in 1841 and 1842 respectively. They have a more elaborate plan and a soaring verticality (especially Killarney), but they show the same reliance on the masonry surface for effect (at Killarney, rough local stone) and the same simple wooden roof inside.

Finally, Pugin's use of Decorated tracery can be said to begin with St Chad's Cathedral in Birmingham (1839–41), the first Roman Catholic cathedral to be built in Britain since the Middle Ages. The exterior is brick, again rather neatly contoured, with very little stone decoration. The interior is of great height with very slender supports. The rich fittings have been altered drastically in the last few years. They included a large choir

183 *St Giles's, Cheadle, from the east.*

screen – a highly important feature in the revived medieval interior, marking as it did the separation of the chancel from the nave. At St Oswald's, Old Swan, Liverpool (1840–42), Pugin combined Decorated tracery with a return to the massiveness, if not quite the simplicity, of St Wilfrid's. (All but the tower was recently demolished.)

In the same year, 1840, Pugin began designs for St Giles's at Cheadle, Staffordshire, the Earl of Shrewsbury's own church [182, 183]. Built in 1841–6, it was to be his most elaborate and expensive commission, costing between £30,000 and £40,000. The overall squatness and heaviness of his earlier buildings are retained, but against them he sets the soaring height and sharpness of the spire. In his external detailing he also seems to want to make things as solid-looking as

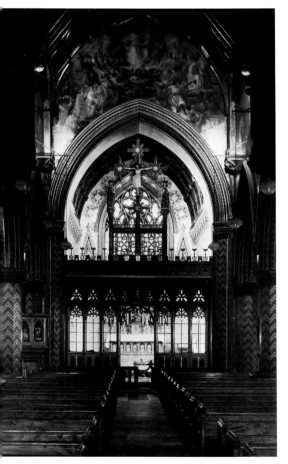

182 *Looking towards the chancel in St Giles's, Cheadle, Staffordshire, by Pugin, 1841–6.*

possible: the profiles and the ashlar work are big and heavy. The interior is richly decorated with coloured and gilded diaperwork, a choir screen, and an ornate roof (apparently more to his patron's liking than to Pugin's).

In his later churches, for instance St Augustine's at Ramsgate, Kent (1845–51) [*184*], where he himself was the patron, there is always a fair amount of elaboration in the tracery, but little else in the way of decoration on the outside, where rather more sharply profiled stone mouldings are contrasted with rough walling (he seems to have specially liked knapped flint).

There is no sign that Pugin would have taken part in the High Victorian movement that began in the years around 1850 (see pp. 22, 201–3), except perhaps for his habit of omitting buttresses, thereby emphasizing the continuous surface of the walls.

At the time of Pugin's death in 1852 there were very few Roman Catholic church architects of prominence. Joseph Hansom (of Birmingham Town Hall fame [*138*]), himself a Catholic, designed the large church of St Walburga at Preston (1850), with its very high and acutely pointed spire, St Philip Neri at Arundel,

184 Pugin's drawing of the complex of St Augustine's, Ramsgate, Kent, from the south-east. On the left is The Grange (1843–4: see pp. 48–9), *in the centre the church (its spire was never built), behind it the cloister and sacristy. (Victoria and Albert Museum, London)*

185 St Patrick's Cathedral, Armagh, begun in 1838 by Thomas J. Duff of Newry, continued after 1853 by J. J. McCarthy, and dedicated in 1873. The nave arcade is to Duff's design, the rest by McCarthy. The fittings are by Ashlin and Coleman, 1900–1904.

Sussex (1870–73, for the Duke of Norfolk), and the Holy Name at Manchester (1869). His churches excel in their spaciousness, a quality not familiar in Pugin's work. Pugin's son, Edward Welby Pugin (1834–75), produced the exuberantly tall, spacious and ornate church of St Francis, Gorton, Manchester (1864). Following in his father's footsteps, Edward

Pugin was also active in Ireland, where a magnificent series of large Roman Catholic churches were built. Cobh (Queenstown) Cathedral, of 1868–1919, was designed by E. W. Pugin in partnership with G. C. Ashlin (1837–1921). The most prolific Irish church architect was J. J. McCarthy (1817–82), the designer of Monaghan Cathedral (1861–92). These buildings lack the reticence of the elder Pugin's churches in Ireland, as well as the sophisticated polychrome simplicity of the Anglicans of the Ecclesiological Society. On the other hand, many show a decorative brilliance and exuberance which links them with Neo-Gothic churches on the Continent. Closer to the Ecclesiologists' heavy style of the 1860s was George Goldie (1828–87), the designer of St Wilfrid's at York (1862–4).

To Pugin's dismay, not all Catholics accepted Gothic. Cardinal Newman, the most famous convert from High Anglicanism, was closely involved with two buildings which are interesting additions to the variety of styles in Victorian churches. The University Church in Dublin (1856), by J. Hungerford Pollen (1820–1902), is in a very plain round-arched style reminiscent of the early medieval brick buildings of Ravenna, with marble slab decoration of the type that Ruskin advocated, while the cloisters of the Oratory in Birmingham (1860), by Henry Clutton (1819–93), a convert to Catholicism, are in a heavy Romanesque style with massive stone vaults. When it came to building the most prominent Roman Catholic church in London to date, the Brompton Oratory, the competition of 1878 prescribed the Classical style (see p. 224).

The Anglican Revival and the Ecclesiological Society

Although for our purposes the Catholic and the Anglican Revivals had much the same results, the story of the latter is very much more complicated. In the eighteenth century the Established Church had degenerated in many places into little more than a sinecure, but things seemed to be poised for change in the 1830s. The Evangelical Movement, which had recently sprung up, offered an example of piety, morality and pastoral concern which seemed to be sadly lacking in the Anglican Church. It was a time of liberalism and reform, and a Church which abused privileges and money had to put its house in order or face a severe reduction in its functions and power. Some curtailment seemed inevitable. Acts in the 1820s lifted restrictions on Dissenters and, as we have seen, on Roman Catholics. In the next two decades the registration of births, marriages and deaths with the Church ceased to be mandatory. Finally, in 1868 compulsory rates for the Church were abolished.

On the other hand, in 1818 Parliament had voted £1 million for the building of new churches, especially for the rapidly expanding towns in the North. Apart from meeting the challenge of the Nonconformists, these 'Commissioners' Churches' were meant to save the working classes from the twin dangers of atheism and revolution. Smaller amounts were voted later, but equally important was the stimulus for the Church to organize its finances in a more businesslike way, especially in a more equitable distribution around the country. The Ecclesiastical Commissioners (now the Church Commissioners) were convened in 1835. The most astonishing achievement of the Church was the number of new buildings erected – an average of 100 churches per year between c. 1840 and the late nineteenth century. Their typical cost was something like £3,000. In addition, almost all the existing churches were restored and scores of schools and vicarages, colleges and other institutions were erected. The bulk of the finance came from private donations, but the old system of buying pews was greatly reduced, and many seats became 'free'.

The patronage remained predominantly middle- and upper-class. The new political faction of George Smythe, the 'Young England' Tories, rejected Utilitarianism, upheld 'faith', and favoured, in conjunction with a powerful old-established aristocracy, an 'almsgiving church', 'protecting and cultivating the affection of the dependent peasantry'. Many new rural parishes sprang up as a result. The squire was frequently the patron; often he was identical with the incumbent, and sometimes he was the architect as well. In many cases the new religious and architectural ideas were picked up at Oxford or Cambridge by undergraduates who returned with missionary zeal to their remote country areas. But there still remained a shortage of churches in cities, especially in the poorer districts. In fact, the proportion of churchgoers among the poor and very poor seems never to have been particularly high, notwithstanding the valiant attempts by some patrons and vicars to get involved in social work. The considerable contribution of the Church to education will be examined in the next chapter.

After the threat of liberalism had receded another challenge arose, with the growth of scientific discovery. But here too, as we have seen, tendencies manifested themselves which countered the attacks. The influence of Romanticism has already been mentioned. In 1833, spurred by John Keble's Assize Sermon at Oxford, a group of theologians began to fight against liberalism and the new science. Their crusade became known as the Oxford Movement. Their *Tracts for the Times* (whence their name, Tractarians) stressed the elements of tradition and continuity in the Church, its 'Catholic past' in the Middle Ages. They pleaded for adherence to the Book of Common Prayer and insisted on the importance of the sacraments, especially Holy Communion. They set out to create – or to re-create – a Church that was chiefly concerned not with social and political influence but with spirituality and its expression through ritual, as had been the concern of the Catholic Revival.

The term 'Ritualism' gained circulation; 'High Church' or 'Anglo-Catholic' denoted a high degree of Ritualism in a particular parish, as opposed to 'Low Church', which was more Evangelically oriented. This speaks of a fair degree of tolerance within the Church, but some of the most ardent Anglo-Catholics in fact took the final step to Rome, among them John Henry Newman. Other extreme Ritualists were accused of 'Popery', sometimes physically attacked, and in rare cases imprisoned. It was only after the 1870s that the controversy died down. The great majority of Anglicans, including the Queen and Prince Albert, classified themselves as 'Broad Church', that is somewhere in the middle between High and Low, with a fair amount of Evangelical moralism and less stress on ritual and the altar. What was of great importance from the point of view of every parish was that the vicar now actually lived there and personally looked after his flock within an active institution.

While the Oxford Movement stood for the doctrinal reform of the Church of England, the Cambridge Movement saw to the reform of liturgy and church building. John Mason Neale, its founder, Benjamin Webb, its secretary, and their fellow undergraduates all espoused the new Tractarianism. It began around 1836 as the Cambridge Camden Society (named after William Camden, the famous sixteenth-century antiquarian), a typical undergraduate society whose main purpose was outings to local churches. Constituted in 1839, it changed its name in 1845 to the Ecclesiological Society, after a crisis and several conversions to Rome. Its members became known as Ecclesiologists. (It still exists, although its later history is of little importance here.) The influential Conservative MP Alexander J. Beresford-Hope (1820–87) became its president. Like his father, the Regency connoisseur and designer Thomas Hope, he was to lavish his fortune on advanced architectural designs.

In its beginnings the Cambridge Camden Society differed very little from other local antiquarian and archaeological societies, but from about 1841 its numerous publications started to propagate a new line. *The Ecclesiologist*, begun in that year, must be considered one of the most important English architectural periodicals, and remained a forum for discussion until it ceased publication in 1868. Numerous pamphlets, such as *A Few Words to Church Builders* and *A Few Words to Churchwardens on Churches and Church Ornaments*, also began to be published in 1841. The booklets cost sixpence or a shilling; tens of thousands were sold, reaching almost every parish in the Kingdom.

These publications were not concerned with theology or even with architectural history. They simply gave prescriptions for the building of churches of various sizes and degrees of elaboration, which were basically the same as Pugin's. It was taken for granted that the altar was the most important feature. The chief requirements of a church were nave and chancel, separated by a chancel arch, and differentiated by the degree of ornamentation and, on the outside, different roofs [193, 194]. The other essential features were the porch, attached to the side of the nave, and the sacristy or vestry, attached to the chancel but expressed by its own roof on the outside. All other features were optional. There could be aisles on both sides of the nave, but one would be sufficient. If a tower could be afforded it was welcomed, but for small churches an extension of a gable, either on the west front or over the chancel arch, crowned with a little bell-turret would be enough. Galleries (usual in Georgian and Nonconformist churches) were strictly forbidden. Like Pugin, the Ecclesiologists gave up the idea of symmetry and façade. The tower, for instance, could have many positions – at the west end of the nave, in the middle of the nave (over the crossing or chancel arch), or at one side, where its ground floor might serve as porch.

In addition to these basic features, the

Ecclesiologists went into complicated arguments about more narrowly doctrinal symbolism. This sometimes conflicted with practical considerations: transepts were advocated, as symbolic of the Cross, but in practice they were often useless and were turned into store-rooms. Hence they were not recommended for smaller churches. By the late 1840s these theological and symbolic arguments had lost force, but the Church of England never returned to the Georgian simplicity of plan. As in Pugin's churches, the fittings, such as altar rails, reredos and, especially, coloured glass in the windows, became a vital concern for the architects [*198, 200*] and for firms specializing in church fittings – Minton for tiles, Hardman for stained glass and metalwork, etc.

Early Victorian Anglican churches

Anglican church building in the 1840s, when the number of new buildings increased dramatically, is a reflection of the general architectural situation: a multitude of factions and styles. Perpendicular was by far the most popular style until about 1845. The 'Commissioners' Churches' built after the 1818 Act were based on designs by Nash, Soane and Barry, and later by Thomas Rickman, the greatest expert on Gothic before Pugin (see p. 21). Bishop Ryder's Church in Birmingham (1837,†) by Rickman, and Holy Trinity, Gloucester Terrace in Paddington, London (1844–6, partly †) [*186*], by Thomas Cundy II (1790–1867), are typical, with long and high naves and small chancels. The interiors are relatively simple and very spacious, with thin piers and galleries, but the exteriors are characterized by rich and elegant tracery, battlements, numerous buttresses terminating in elongated pinnacles, and a dominant west tower containing a lavish west portal and crowned by four pinnacles or by a piercingly slender spire. There are also more individual solutions: St Peter's at Leeds (1839–41), by R. D. Chantrell (1793–1872), has a tower at one side; St Peter's at Leamington Spa, Warwickshire, begun in 1844 to designs

186 Holy Trinity, Paddington, London, by Thomas Cundy II, 1844–6, photographed by Fox Talbot soon after completion.

by its vicar, John Craig, is largely modelled on Cologne and Regensburg Cathedrals. Edmund Sharpe (1809–77) of Liverpool made his name with economic terracotta decoration (hence the label 'pot churches'): St Stephen's, Lever Bridge, at Bolton-le-Moors in Lancashire (1842) is an example. The Catholic Apostolic or Irvingite church in Gordon Square, London (now the University Church), was designed and built in 1851–5 by John Raphael Brandon (1817–77) in a very lavish English cathedral style.

One architect whose work represents a different trend of Early Victorian Gothic is Edward Buckton Lamb. We met him first as the remodeller of Hughenden for Disraeli (p. 30); Loudon's *Encyclopaedia* included illustrations of his extremely Picturesque villas. Lamb remained faithful to Late Gothic modes, and did not adopt many of the Ecclesiologists' planning features: his churches are 'Low' or 'Broad'. He remained above all Picturesque and fanciful in all his work right up to

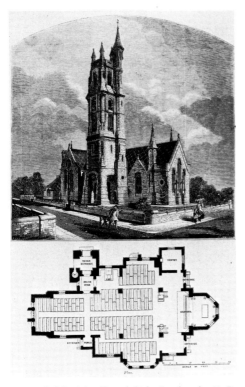

187 St Martin's, Gospel Oak, London, by E. B. Lamb, 1862–5, seen from the south-west and in plan. (Builder, 1866)

his death in 1869, to the continuing displeasure of *The Ecclesiologist*. He did, however, adopt some fashionable features in the 1840s and 1850s, such as a low contour and a general heaviness of effect, and the use of contrasting materials both inside and out. On the whole he preferred centralized plans, which produced the wide spaces that he covered with extremely complicated open timber roofs, especially in his later churches of the 1860s such as St Martin's, Gospel Oak in London (1862–5) and St Mary Magdalene, Addiscombe, Croydon, Surrey (1868) [*187, 188*]. Their jagged outline, the restless

relief on the surface, the continuous chamfering and the nervous contours of the stone facing earned for Lamb in the twentieth century the title of 'Arch-Rogue' among Victorian architects. He himself in 1860 was quite conscious of the way in which he antagonized the High Victorian architects, with their preference for severe, unmoulded surfaces [*195, 201, 211*]. Thus his buildings, apart from giving delight, demonstrate the range of conscious formal possibilities in the Victorian period.

Several other architects have been classed as 'Rogues'. Woodyer and Teulon will be mentioned below; in the 1860s among the most original were Bassett Keeling (1837–86) and Thomas Harris (see p. 24).

A relatively new mode for churches in the 1840s was the 'Round-arched' style. It had many sources: Norman architecture had, for instance, been revived as part of the Castellated style, as at Penrhyn Castle in Wales, of 1827–37, by Thomas Hopper (1776–1856), and it was popularized for churches by G. E. Hamilton's *Designs for Rural Churches* (1836). Italian Early Christian, Byzantine and Romanesque architecture was rediscovered, and cultivated especially by the Germans: thus the name *Rundbogenstil* gained currency. St Mary's at Wilton, Wiltshire, of 1840–6, is the most prominent example [*189*]. It was promoted by Sydney Herbert and designed by T. H. Wyatt and David Brandon, who were to go on to excel in other fields. Apart from its splendid free-standing Italianate campanile, the chief element of this very lavish church is its dark interior, rich with paintings and fittings which came in part from Italy. The other most notable church in the *Rundbogenstil* is Christ Church, Streatham, in South London (1840–2), by J. W. Wild [*190*]. Unlike Wilton, it was a relatively cheap building, and economy was probably the main reason for its rather bare yellow brick exterior. The courses are however very carefully laid, and different-coloured bricks are occasionally inserted, fore-

188 St Mary Magdalene, Addiscombe, Surrey, by Lamb, 1868.

189 St Mary's, Wilton, Wiltshire, by T. H. Wyatt and David Brandon, 1840–46.

190 Christ Church, Streatham, London, by J. W. Wild, 1840–42.

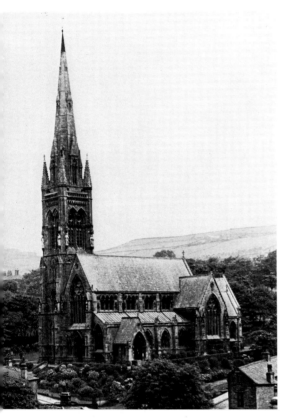

191 All Souls', Haley Hill, Halifax, by Sir George Gilbert Scott, 1855–9.

and his office. His first major work was St Giles's, Camberwell, South London, begun in 1842. With its prominent chancel, separated from the nave by a tower with a high spire, its large porch and early Decorated tracery (or Geometrical, before the introduction of the double curve), it could be said to derive from Pugin's earlier designs. Other elements, such as the relative simplicity of the interior, are similar to contemporary designs by Pugin. In general Scott dispensed with elaborate pinnacles and picturesque skylines, seeking an effect both sturdy and plain. This effect appears in the cathedral at St John's, Newfoundland (begun in 1846), and at St Anne's, Alderney (1847), a small and remote church, plainness is intensified to the point of roughness. In 1844 he won an international competition for the Nikolaikirche in Hamburg with a design which still included an ornate crest of pinnacles. It had a far greater influence in Germany than in England. (Only the spire survived the Second World War intact.)

But if Scott eventually dispensed with trimmings, unlike Pugin he seldom eliminated the buttresses: he thought them essential, as an expression of solidity and as a means of stressing the basic symmetry and regularity of a design (though structurally they are less important in wooden-roofed churches than in those rare buildings vaulted with stone or brick). His later churches, unlike his secular work, show little development towards High Victorian Gothic. Moreover, to the displeasure of the Ecclesiological Society, he remained basically a Broad Church architect – or, as many said, a compromiser. St George's, Doncaster, Yorkshire (1854), he rebuilt somewhat on the lines of the original elegant fourteenth-century church. All Souls', Haley Hill, at Halifax in Yorkshire (1855–9), built for the industrialist Colonel Akroyd (see p. 71), Scott called 'on the whole my best church' [*191*]. Its elements are beautifully grouped, Scott's strength, and dominated by a soaring spire. St Mary Abbots in Kensington, London (1869–72), is one of

shadowing High Victorian work of a decade later. The elaborate coloured decoration inside by Owen Jones, the great authority on polychromy in architecture (and Wild's brother-in-law) survives in part.

Some of these churches were on their way to 'correct' Ecclesiology. The first and most important of the more strictly Ecclesiological, Puginian architects was undoubtedly George Gilbert Scott, who was a year older than Pugin. Important works by him have already been mentioned; but to the Victorians he was above all a church architect. Many hundreds of churches were built and restored by him his many medium-size parish churches. Finally, he won the competition for Edinburgh Cathedral, held in 1872–3.

Churches built with more direct supervision from the Ecclesiological Society begin modestly enough, with the small church at Kilndown, Kent (1840), by Salvin, where Beresford-Hope had fittings designed by Butterfield and Carpenter and stained glass imported from Munich.

Richard Cromwell Carpenter (1812–55) had been experimenting with Tudor Gothic façades on terrace houses in Lonsdale Square, Islington, in London (1838–42), and got his first major commission from the Ecclesiologists in 1846. The building was St Paul's, Brighton, Sussex, and the patron Father Wagner, one of those stoned for their Ritualistic and 'Popish' convictions. Carpenter's best-

192 Chapel of the House of Mercy (now St John's Convent), Clewer, Buckinghamshire, by Henry Woodyer, 1880–81.

known church is St Mary Magdalene, Munster Square in London (1849–52). Like Scott's early work, these churches are very much in the manner of Pugin. St Mary Magdalene has a rough, irregular stone facing of Kentish rag, which made it seem a primitive, rural intruder into the white plastered elegance of Regency and Early Victorian terraces. In the 1850s, before his premature death, Carpenter was mainly occupied on large schools in Sussex, including Lancing College [240].

Of the many adherents to Ecclesiological principles, perhaps the most inventive is Henry Woodyer (1816–96), who worked briefly with Butterfield in 1844. His love of sharp angles and refined, unorthodox tracery, and his inventive use of materials, are displayed in his very ornate church at Highnam, Gloucestershire (1847–52), with accompanying vicarage, school and lodge, commissioned by the collector Thomas Gambier-Parry, who painted a mural inside the church. Other characteristic works are the House of

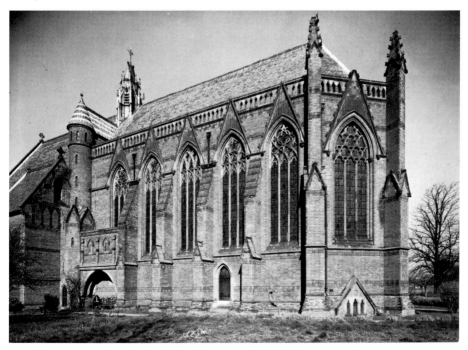

193, 194 St Mary's, Par, Cornwall, by G. E. Street, 1847.

Meicy at Clewer, Windsor (begun in 1853) [*192*], and St Michael's College at Tenbury, Worcestershire (1854–6).

The furtherance of rural simplicity in design was perhaps the greatest architectural contribution of the early Ecclesiological movement. In a paper of 1843 entitled 'On simplicity of construction, especially in Churches of the Early English style', *The Ecclesiologist* advocated a low contour and 'rough masonry', even going so far as to say: 'Let mean materials appear mean.' Plainness and 'reality' are the highest aims. Pinnacles and parapets are superfluous; projecting eaves much more appropriate. Many of the Ecclesiological architects began their careers with simple churches of this kind in remote parts of the country: such are the Cornish churches of Street (Par, 1847 [*193, 194*]) and William White (St Hilary, 1853), and the minute churches of R. J. Withers in the Welsh countryside around Cardigan. The ideal was in fact a combination of features from the *cottage orné*, the purposely primitive rural building, with moral and religious justifications to make it suitable for many other types of building. It helped to prepare the way for the next phase of the Gothic Revival, High Victorianism.

High Victorian Gothic churches: the influence of Ruskin

In the matter of style, 'Middle Pointed' remained very popular, but there was also a strong liking for Early English, or better still a style with massive masonry, few windows and hardly any decoration. However, during the 1840s another type of medieval architecture attracted attention: that of the Mediterranean. Byzantine and Romanesque art were rediscovered; there was a growing liking for medieval painting (the 'Primitives'), and a new interest in coloured decoration. In the 1840s and early 1850s the Rev. John Louis Petit (1801–68) publicized the massiveness and simplicity of the Romanesque churches of France. The churches of St Mary's at Wilton, Wiltshire, and Christ Church,

Streatham, in South London, are early examples of the Romanesque Revival in England [*189, 190*]. In 1845 the Secretary of the Ecclesiological Society, Benjamin Webb, reported on his journey to Italy in a lecture entitled 'Tropical Architecture as adapted to tropical climates'; and in his book, *Sketches of Continental Ecclesiology* (1848), he praised in particular the simplicity of Italian Gothic churches in planning and detail, their flat wall surfaces and their colour. Horizontality was no longer a vice. Webb was extremely fond of the flat-topped campanile of Florence Cathedral. He also liked brick, for the massive effects it could produce and for its bright red colour. Another medieval building greatly admired by many Ecclesiologists in these years was the cathedral at Albi in southern France, a very solid (indeed fortified) fourteenth-century brick building, with buttresses placed on the inside of the walls, giving a sheer outer surface.

The first cautious advocations of brick and strong polychromy appeared in *The Ecclesiologist* in the late 1840s. In 1850 the Society began to build All Saints', Margaret Street in London, to a design by Butterfield, as a fully-fledged example of the new mode [*177, 195, 196*]. At the same time Street propagated it in a semi-official letter to the Ecclesiological Society on 'town churches'. A parallel approach can be found in the writings of the greatest art critic of the time, Ruskin.

Architecture was only one of Ruskin's many interests; but it dominated his thoughts during the years around 1850. His starting point in architecture, like Pugin's, was travelling and sketching picturesque old towns, architecture, landscape and cottages. (In the 1830s he wrote a series of articles on cottages.) Like many others around 1845, he was overcome by the effects of colour in Italian medieval architecture, Romanesque as well as Gothic. At the same time, he began to prefer the Italian 'Primitives', such as Fra Angelico, to the Renaissance painters. He also began to make watercolour studies of details of buildings, in which he records with almost photographic precision stones and the state of stonework – cracks and fissures as well as colours [6]. (In 1845, he tells us, he discovered the uses of photography for the study of nature and architecture.)

Ruskin had no interest in the practical matters of architecture, in plans and functional arrangements. And although he always argued with great religious and moral fervour, he had no specific denominational axe to grind. In his books, *The Seven Lamps of Architecture* (1849) and *The Stones of Venice* (which came out in three volumes, in 1851 and 1853), many passages were concerned with describing sculptural decoration and paintings adorning architecture, rather than the structure. He often stressed (especially from about 1851 onwards) that the *art* of architecture lies in these decorations. But logic and consistency were never his strong points, and he in fact says many things about the aesthetics of structure that are of vital importance in the context of High Victorian architecture.

The most important sections of *The Seven Lamps of Architecture* are those on the Lamps of Truth and of Power. In 'The Lamp of Truth' Ruskin takes his starting point from the Gothic Revival in his insistence on honesty of construction and truth to materials. But he is in many ways less doctrinaire than Pugin, for he allows the covering of walls with paint, whitewash or stone slabs, provided there is no deception: gilding an object is acceptable as long as it is not held to be gold all the way through. What Ruskin is really after is colour, the colours of the materials themselves (see especially his glowing descriptions of Italian multi-coloured marbles). He also indicates an essential connection between his liking for colour and his preference for smooth surfaces: colour is most effective when not disturbed by light and shade, when its contours are simple. His preferred form of decoration for architecture is inlaid marble and stone, where everything lies flush with the surface. Such 'permanent' or 'constructional' polychromy also met the demands for structural truth. It is one of the most characteristic features of High Victorian architecture.

In 'The Lamp of Power' Ruskin goes back to the eighteenth-century concept of the Sublime. The most important element in architecture is size, combined with simplicity of outline – 'vast flat surfaces gathered up into a mighty square', bounded by continuous lines as much as possible and crowned by a vigorous cornice. He admired massive medieval cornices with their series of projecting corbels, or machicolation. Another feature that he especially liked was the arcade, with its seemingly endless repetition of the same element. Repetition is a device that is praised in eighteenth-century aesthetic writing (such as Burke's), and one much used by Neo-Classical architects. Thus Ruskin helped to turn the tide from Picturesque variety towards massive uniformity.

The first volume of *The Stones of Venice* is an immensely complicated investigation of masonry and simple architectural decoration. What interests us here is the elaboration of points we have already noted in the *Seven Lamps*. Masonry is essentially a matter of horizontal layering (Ruskin here draws an analogy with geology), and this fact should be shown as clearly as possible by introducing differently coloured materials [6], for instance by alternating layers of brick and stone. Ruskin's principle of layering applies to the whole of a façade: he despises all kinds of 'attached' vertical divisions, such as shafts or pilasters, and allows only those that actually support the masonry above, such as columns supporting an arcade. (The importance of the 'structural' colonnade as a device in commercial architecture has already been stressed in Chapter 4.)

Ruskin then deals with all manner of openings in the wall. Basically, he regrets any interruption of a beautiful coloured surface; but you can show the mass of masonry and its coloured materials by the shapes of the openings. He prefers the simplest kinds of openings, with bold chamfers and severe outlines. He greatly likes buildings seen in bright southern light, for, he says, it creates deep shadows and strong contrasts between light and shade. This dividing line between light and dark must always be as sharp as possible: therefore, again, sharp contours and deep recesses are necessary for windows and doors. The decorative frame of a window ought to lie flush with the wall. He greatly prefers the plate tracery of North Italian Gothic, which often lies flush with the wall surface or is only slightly moulded, to other Gothic tracery with its elaborate profiles and thin members.

Ruskin himself soon lost interest in these aspects of design, and never showed great interest in the new High Victorian style of architecture that he had helped to create.

Of all the High Victorian critics, Street in his writings, many published in *The Ecclesiologist*, was perhaps the most vigorous. We miss some of Ruskin's sensitivity, but Street offers more clarity and practical usefulness. His views on massiveness, contour, colour, tracery, and so on are very similar to Ruskin's. He also makes some interesting remarks on the spatial arrangement of buildings in relation to windows and light sources (something we would never find in Ruskin): lights should be unevenly distributed, groups of windows should be concentrated in some places, while other areas of the walls are left blank. He pleads for integration of interior space rather than complication, as the Picturesque taste of the 1840s preferred.

A lecture that Street gave in 1852 was entitled, in the good Puginian tradition, 'On the true principles of Pointed Architecture' – but he characteristically added, 'and the possibilities of its Development'. By 'development' he meant that we should not have to stick to English Gothic, as Pugin and his immediate followers had maintained, but could borrow freely from the medieval styles of other countries, especially Italy, and even from Classical architecture (for instance the strong horizontal line of a cornice). In fact, he declared in true rationalist fashion that Gothic is not a symbol of 'this or that nation or this or that age'. Symbolism is a matter of controversy, whereas Gothic is a matter of rational construction, and the pointed arch is the best of all forms of construction. Thus Street carried on Pugin's rationalist arguments while purging them of symbolism. In his book *Brick and Marble in the Middle Ages: Notes of Tours in the North of Italy* (1855) he elaborates all these views. He was one of the most indefatigable of architectural travellers, and indeed, considering his experience of Italy, Germany and later Spain, and of English medieval architecture, he was perhaps the most knowledgeable medievalist of his day. In the accounts of his travels we realize that he makes full use of the modern railway: on his annual holidays – as he tells us – he would rush round dozens of churches until dusk, then travel at night and start again in the morning.

High Victorian Gothic in the strict sense lasted into the 1870s. By that time most practitioners were moving towards less assertive Late Victorian varieties of Gothic. About eight major church architects can be singled out whose work, taken together, spans the decades from 1840 to 1900. Butterfield (b. 1814) is the great protagonist of the early 1850s, and carried on in essentially the same vein until the end of the century. Street (b. 1824) comes next, his major works grouped around 1854–65. The masterpieces in brick of William White (b. 1825) date from the same years. William Burges (b. 1827) began his major contributions in the later 1850s, initiating the even more severe style of the 1860s. James Brooks (b. 1825) follows, with his distinctive severe manner, in the 1860s through to the 1870s and later. Pearson (b. 1817), somewhat older, was active from the 1840s onwards, but only really came into his own about 1870. Bodley (b. 1827), after a brilliant beginning in the High Victorian style, turned his back on it as early as the mid-1860s, initiating the predominant mode of the Late Victorian period.

Butterfield

Among all the eminent nineteenth-century practitioners William Butterfield has always been considered the most notoriously 'Victorian'. At the height of the Neo-Georgian and Modern Movements in this century phrases such as 'sadism' and 'deliberate ugliness' were used to characterize his forms. The intention in the pioneering writings of John Betjeman and John Summerson was not so much to decry Butterfield's architecture as to draw renewed attention to him. Paul Thompson in his recent study firmly refutes the notion of such a psychologically-motivated 'viciousness' of style, pointing out that Butterfield's forms must be seen in the context of the High Victorian style and its system of decoration. Yet Thompson has to admit that the criticism is not just a twentieth-century prejudice: it accompanied Butterfield's work almost from the beginning of his career. As we have seen in many cases, especially with Lamb (pp. 195–6), there was considerable room for variety and changing fashions even within the same historical style, and consequently there were many different critical dogmas – picturesque irregularity versus simple massiveness, stricter adherence to historical forms versus greater freedom, and so on. Butterfield himself was acutely aware of the frequent criticism of his work and reacted in true nineteenth-century fashion, seeing himself (at least later in his career) as the lonely artist understood by very few.

Butterfield reacted against many new elements of the architectural profession: he did not take part in competitions, because he thought they would upset concentrated work, and he objected to elegant perspective drawings, because they did not represent a true picture of the proposed construction. In all these matters he was stricter than any other major architect of the period except Philip Webb. On the other hand, he was the most scrupulous professional. Estimates, designs and execu-tion were minutely controlled. Variety and individuality of form, together with precision of execution, characterize his work: his is no longer only the art of the overall architectural designer but the art of the mason and the master bricklayer.

Butterfield was born in London into a fairly well-to-do Evangelical background, and Evangelical morality had a strong influence on him throughout his life. He never married. In 1831 he began his architectural education by being apprenticed to a builder, and then to a lesser-known architect, E. L. Blackburne. In 1840 he set up office in London. He tried hard to enter Ecclesiological circles, and published letters in their journal. Finally in May 1844 he was elected a member of the Society. Immediately the first major commissions came in, and thereafter he devoted himself almost exclusively to the Church of England. His patrons were High Church and mostly young gentry. Beresford-Hope, President of the Society, was probably the most generous, paying for St Augustine's College at Canterbury, Kent [243], and for most of All Saints', Margaret Street in London [177, 195, 196], but the story of this patronage is also one of lack of understanding and eventual hostility. Another important figure was the 7th Viscount Downe, who paid for many small churches in Yorkshire. Occasionally Butterfield showed his devotion to the cause of a particular client by designing without a fee, as in the case of a convent at Plymouth in Devon.

His major buildings of the 1840s are the church and vicarage at Coalpitheath near Bristol and the rebuilding of St Augustine's College at Canterbury, both begun in 1844. They differ in no essential way from contemporary designs by Pugin and Carpenter. A number of restorations followed, as well as small vicarages and schools [234]. During the years 1849–52 commissions multiplied. Among the most important are All Saints', Margaret Street, the semi-monastic complex of Cumbrae College (1849–51), romantically situated on an island in Western Scotland, St

Ninian's Cathedral at Perth in Scotland, and St Matthias's, Stoke Newington, in North London. They have many things in common. It goes almost without saying that their planning fulfils the ritualistic demands of the Society. Stylistically too they scarcely depart from the Puginian Ecclesiological principles of the day: the churches have soaring spires, lofty naves over high arcades, and high steep roofs. Butterfield was especially praised by *The Ecclesiologist* for his ingenuity, indeed his love of solving special planning problems. Another striking feature is his insistence on showing not only the symbolic but also the practical elements of churches: a vast chimney is boldly displayed on the side of Perth Cathedral.

All Saints', Margaret Street was built as the model church of the Society [*177, 195, 196*]. It took nine years to build, from 1850 to 1859 (the walls were up by 1852), and cost £70,000. The most important church of the Society and the whole new Anglican movement is squeezed on to a small site in a modest London street, without any townscape impact except for its tall spire. Butterfield placed the church at the rear of the plot, leaving a courtyard at the front, which is encroached on from both sides by the school and the vicarage. The tower is at the west end of the south aisle, and the porch is pressed into a corner of the yard. But the real novelty of All Saints' lay in its decorative treatment: it is in fact the first High Victorian building, and it was planned by the architect and the patron as a novel structure almost from the beginning. The basis of the High Victorian style is the emphasis on the surface properties of each material. Thus the choice of brick stands at the beginning of the design of All Saints'. Undisguised brick was not a material that Regency and Early Victorian architects, including the early Ecclesiologists, would have used for more expensive buildings, because of its colour and because to them it looked mean. Butterfield chose a special red brick which was far from cheap. (London soot has since made it more sombre.) He used Bath stone

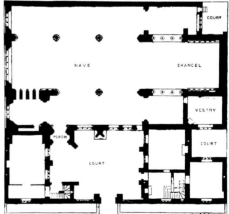

195, 196 All Saints', Margaret Street, London, by William Butterfield, 1850–59. Top: exterior. The church lies at the back of the courtyard, its porch just visible; on the left is the choir school, on the right the clergy house. Above: ground plan (Builder, 1853).

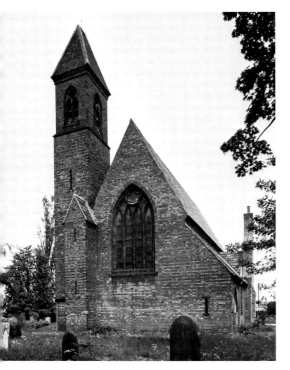

197 St Paul's, Hensall, by Butterfield, 1853–4, from the west.

and grey glazed tiles, and black and red mastic inlaid in pale stone or terracotta. The floor is covered with tiles, more richly patterned in the chancel. Again the structural features are differentiated, through different materials and different kinds of decoration. The piers are of polished red granite; their carved capitals are left unpolished. All this is a very dramatic step away from the Georgian smoothness of a surface either ashlar-faced or painted over in non-committal light hues. It is also a step away from Pugin's treatment of St Giles's, Cheadle, with its coat of painted plaster [*182*], though many of the actual decorative motifs with their geometric figures are similar in both buildings. Indeed, there are so many experimental varieties of form in All Saints' that it is perhaps lacking in harmony and coordination; certainly critics from the later 1850s onward thought so.

During the next few years Butterfield only rarely used such bold constructional polychromy. At the chapel of Balliol College, Oxford (1854–7), regular stripes of red stone are embedded in the brown masonry, producing an effect that was soon christened the 'streaky bacon style'.

In the mid-1850s Butterfield began to receive more small commissions, and certain formal characteristics first seen in All Saints' become more and more apparent. He develops a sense of neat continuous contour, ultimately reminiscent of Ruskin's commendation of smooth, flush surfaces in the *Seven Lamps*, and, like Ruskin, he applies it specially to towers. The number of buttresses and their size diminish: Baldersby St James in Yorkshire (1855–7) marks a mid-point, while at Bamford, Derbyshire (1856–60), only minute buttresses are left at the bottom of the tower, and there is no break between tower and spire, resulting in a

only for mouldings and stringcourses, profiles and other more complicated decorative details. In addition he patterned the wall with black bricks, and inserted horizontal stripes in some parts of the church: where they connect the features of the windows, they also serve to stress the flatness of the wall, by showing that the window-frames are flush with the wall surface. There is a growing sensitivity to the characteristics of a wall: we get a greater feeling both of the massive weight of the wall and of the flatness of its surface. A similar development was noted in Pugin's later churches.

The interior of All Saints' is also highly significant [*177*]. The walls are decorated with geometrical flat patterns in several colours and techniques – red, black and off-white bricks and tiles, green, yellow

198 Chancel of All Saints', Babbacombe, Devon, by Butterfield, 1865–74. All the furnishings except the hanging lamps were designed by the architect.

199 Font in St Mary's, Ottery St Mary, Devon, by Butterfield, c. 1850.

lent itself to a smoother treatment. Like Pugin, Butterfield designed all the decoration and fittings of his churches himself [*198*], and in each case the specific character of the material is emphasized. Even in country churches, which have little added decoration, there is always a surprising amount of variety, especially in the treatment of open timber roofs and the shape of fonts [*199*]. He scrupulously observed his principles but he never repeated himself.

The later 1850s again saw a number of large urban and suburban churches, typified by St Alban's, Holborn in London (1859–62; only Butterfield's tower survives). Polychrome patterns of tile and painted inlay reappear, but the motifs are no longer as large-scale and varied as at All Saints': there is a more even distribution of decoration, together with more delicate profiling and more complicated bar tracery. Indeed, Butterfield was the first of the High Victorians to abandon the vigour of heavy walls and square or simple chamfered profiles.

Butterfield's works of the 1860s and early 1870s seem to be his most individualistic, of a polychrome splendour often defying description: the two churches of Penarth in Glamorgan (begun in 1864) and Babbacombe in Devon (1865–74) [*198*], Keble College Chapel in Oxford (begun in 1867) [*245*], Rugby School Chapel (1870–72; see below, p. 242), and St Augustine's, Queen's Gate in London (1870–77). Outside Great Britain, he built St Mark, Dundela in Belfast in 1876–91, and in 1877 he designed the Anglican cathedral at Melbourne in Australia. The latter is his largest church, with a very long nave, transepts and a two-tower west front; but he resigned halfway through the building campaign, and the spires and many of the furnishings are not to his design.

Architecturally, Butterfield's churches lack the solidity and sense of spatial volume found in many works of the 1860s, such as those by Brooks [*208*], although in the 1870s he adopted a more restricted set

very elegant yet solid form. Neat contours and squareness characterize most of the other parts of his churches as well, and increasingly he emphasizes the massiveness of the walls by using plate tracery in the windows. Major examples of this manner are the three groups of church, school and vicarage in South Yorkshire, all begun in 1853 – Pollington (Balne), Cowick and Hensall [*197*]. The churches are all of brick with very subdued polychromy and hardly any stonework except in the east windows; but all differ in the arrangement of their elements, such as tower and porch.

The design of Butterfield's small churches is always basically determined by the choice of material: at Langley near Maidstone (1854–5) the Kentish ragstone is left rough, while at Milton near Banbury (1854–6) the fine yellow Oxfordshire stone of larger features which help the clarity of the composition. He maintained his vivid polychromy after the late 1860s, when most other architects had begun to give it up, and in the profusion of coloured stone inlay and the bold forms of the interior walls at Babbacombe [*198*] we can perhaps see the culmination of his style.

Street and White

Street's career was not as unified as Butterfield's. His outlook was much broader, he took part in many competitions, and he designed public buildings (most notably the Law Courts [*164–6*], though he did little residential work (that is outside church commissions) and no commercial work. But although he comes much closer to the normal professional type of architect, about four-fifths of his career was devoted to the Church of England. He worked in the office of Scott from 1844 to 1848 (at the same time as White and Bodley), and in 1847 he built his first church, at Par in Cornwall [*193, 194*], which has already been mentioned. His career developed rapidly: like many Ecclesiological architects he was placed in charge of a diocese – Oxford; in 1855 he published his influential book, *Brick and Marble in the Middle Ages*, and in 1856 he finally moved to London.

In his earliest village churches he shows a liking for massiveness and simplicity, and for sparse but always very carefully cut ashlar work. In his writings of the early 1850s he followed the lead of Ruskin and Butterfield, shown also in his own church at Boyne Hill, Maidenhead (begun in 1854). The opportunity to make a name came with several important competitions, where conditions favoured a High Victorian victory. The first, in 1855, was for a new cathedral at Lille in Northern France, where brick was recommended, and the second, in 1856, was for a Crimean War Memorial Church in Constantinople. At Lille the first prize went to the young Burges and his partner Henry Clutton, an expert on French medieval architecture, and the second prize went to

Street, relegating the design of the Frenchman Lassus to third place. At Constantinople Burges and Street again won first and second prize. Street's Lille design is a clever combination of many elements, reconciling a full French cathedral plan, including ambulatory and radiating chapels (of which few English competitors seemed capable), with a fabric of brick with stone dressings. The whole composition has a calculated roughness, gradually enriched towards the top, but even there we find nothing of the small-scale detailing of Lassus's design: compared with the new English High Victorian style as it had developed in the past few years, Continental Gothic Revival seemed frilly and unnecessarily ornate – as *The Ecclesiologist* indeed pointed out. Street's Constantinople design (eventually simplified and built in 1863–8) showed a massive buttressed chapel-like building with a few selectively placed vertical accents.

In the mid-1850s constructional polychromy had begun to appear in Street's designs. He had many small commissions, but, like Butterfield, he was known to spend an equal amount of care on every detail in all his designs. The small church of Howsham in the East Riding of Yorkshire (1859) is extremely heavy and massive, with a semi-circular apse, a tower placed to one side, and a few strong horizontal bands of decoration. In 1859 he also began the first two of his major urban churches, St James the Less, Westminster, London [*200, 201*], and St Philip and St James in Oxford. Though quite spacious inside, they are not very large, or at least any impression of size is counteracted by the impression of the greatest weight and solidity. St James's is of red brick; rough stone with ashlar facing is used at Oxford. There is much polychromatic decoration inside and out, especially in the London church. But where Butterfield goes in for more sensuous linear arrangements, for instance in the clustered shafts of his piers and in the moulded profiles of arches [*177*], Street uses polished monolithic columns and

square profiles. In the windows he uses
plate tracery, most unusually curved in the
apses. Like Butterfield, he varies the
position of his towers: that at Westminster
stands squarely on its own, like a North
Italian campanile, while at Oxford it
grows out of the western part of the
chancel – an arrangement suggested inside
by the powerful low chancel arch and the
curious narrowing of the nave towards the
arch.

In Street's churches of the 1860s we find
the same characteristics, and, in addition, a
greater sense of spaciousness that reflects
the new ideal of the 'town church' (see
below). His very large urban churches of
this period include St John's at Torquay,

*202 St Mary Magdalene, Paddington, London, by
Street, 1867–73, from the east. This view would
have been impossible when the church was first built,
in an area of densely packed small houses.*

*200, 201 St James the Less, Westminster,
London, by G. E. Street, 1859. Opposite: the
junction of nave (on the left) and chancel, showing
the use of polychrome bricks and tiles, marble and
granite columns, and patterns inlaid in the stonework. The furnishings are by Street. Above: the
round apse and free-standing tower (The Ecclesiologist, 1859).*

Devon (1861–85), the magnificent All
Saints', Clifton, at Bristol (begun in
1864,†), St Saviour's at Eastbourne, Sussex
(1865–72), and St John the Divine, Kennington, in South London (1871–88). In
some of them he experimented further
with the device of narrowing the building
towards the chancel, stimulated by churches he had seen in Spain. St Mary
Magdalene, Paddington, in London
(1867–73) [202] is generally lighter, with
more vertical forms and more elegant

203 South porch and nave window of Christ Church, Smannell, Hampshire, by William White, 1856.

204 St James's, Leckhampstead, Berkshire, by S. S. Teulon, 1858–60, from the south-east.

details. Street seems now to be interested in clear contrasts between broad and slim forms – here, the bulky brick body of the church juxtaposed to its slim banded tower and slender spire entirely of finely carved freestone. The same contrast appears in his contemporary design for the Law Courts. Later, the church at Kingston, Dorset (1873–80), shows a return to sturdiness.

William White, a year younger than Street, was in Scott's office at the same time. His early buildings in Cornwall have already been mentioned (pp. 49, 131). All Saints', Notting Hill in London, begun in 1852, shows interesting spatial arrangements but little polychromy yet. Smannell in Hampshire (1856) [203] is built of chalk, brick and stone with tracery that lies completely flush with the wall. By 1858, White had built the lavish church at Lyndhurst, Hampshire, with plenty of polychromy, a strikingly vigorous form of notched decoration around the arches, and decorations by noted sculptors and painters of the day, including Lord Leighton. His masterpiece is St Saviour's, Aberdeen Park, in London (1865) [205]. Like many of the most beautiful Victorian churches it is small but rich, and richness means intricacy or ingenuity of design, not necessarily outward splendour. St Saviour's is built of red brick and decorated with brick of other colours, in an infinite variety of sizes and patterns but a subdued range of tones (partly due, perhaps, to age); the interior is of brick which is relieved by lightly stencilled patterns.

Many other architects' careers show the same pattern, of small churches in the 1850s and larger buildings in the 1860s and '70s. S. S. Teulon in 1858–60 built the very vividly polychrome brick church at Leckhampstead, Berkshire [204], and in 1868–71 the large and lavish St Stephen's, Rosslyn Hill, in London.

205 Chancel of St Saviour's, Aberdeen Park, London, by White, 1865.

206 *Detail of the chancel in Studley Royal Church, Yorkshire, by William Burges, 1871–8.*

Burges and Brooks

Many churches of the 1860s have already been mentioned, but there were new men whose work was even more important in that decade. Eastlake, in his *Gothic Revival* of 1872, which is very much an apologia for the Gothic of the 1860s, uses the term 'muscular': where forms had been round or polygonal in the 1850s, they were now square; where piers had been clustered, they were now massively cylindrical. There is less use of vivid surface polychromy and the whole character of the designs is more 'archaic'. Architects looked at the Early Gothic of Northern France, such as the cathedrals of Chartres and Laon, rather than Italian Gothic.

One theological issue which was frequently discussed among the Ecclesiologists around 1860 was the idea of the 'town church'. It was felt that more should be done for non-church-goers in large cities, especially in the poorer areas. In his book *The English Cathedral of the nineteenth century* (1861), one of the most useful summings-up of current architectural views, Beresford-Hope advocated cathedral-like churches – large buildings of imposing height, with a simple plan, high naves lit by clerestories, and in general a clear, unobstructed interior space. The first major example of this type was St Peter's, Vauxhall, in London, designed by Pearson in 1860 and built in 1863–5 [211, 212], to which we shall return in the context of Pearson's main work.

We have already met William Burges and seen his secular work (pp. 44–6 [27, 28]). His church work is not essentially different in form and outlook. Most of it comes early on, because the Ecclesiologists had more understanding for his individual and radical ideas. Burges first made a name with his prizewinning entries for the Lille Cathedral and Constantinople Memorial Church competitions of 1855 and 1856. His primitivism comes out strongly: the forms are heavy and square, the columns thick (one gets the impression that their diameter exceeds their height), and everywhere he introduces horizontal bands and cornices. Yet his interiors are clear and lofty, lit by clerestories which usually show large lancet-shape windows. His manner could be seen as a continuation of the heavy Early English of the 1840s, with the important difference that the latter was reserved for 'primitive' country churches. He only built one fairly large church in this style, St Finn Bar's, the Anglican cathedral at Cork in Ireland, begun in 1863 [207]. It is one of the few Victorian churches completely modelled on a French Gothic cathedral with a two-towered west

207 *St Finn Bar's Church of Ireland Cathedral, Cork, by Burges, begun in 1863.*

208 James Brooks's drawing of the complex of St Columba's, Kingsland Road, London, mainly built in 1865–74. The east end of the church, dominated by the crossing tower, appears on the left, and the school – the first building on the site – at the far right. (RIBA Drawings Collection)

209 The Transfiguration, Lewisham, by Brooks, begun in 1880. The chancel is on the left, the nave with plate-traceried windows on the right.

front with three portals, a crossing tower, a transept, an ambulatory, and a triforium between arcade and clerestory in the very high and narrow interior. The small church at Studley Royal in Yorkshire (1871–8) is a concentrated example of Burges's exuberance and invention, paid for by Lord Ripon, to whom it served as a private estate church [206].

However important Burges's purely architectural contribution, his main concern was for the fittings in his buildings. Following Ruskin, he argued that craftsmanship, as well as the figurative aspects of decoration, should be 'one of the main concerns, if not the main concern' of the architect. Street shared his opinions, and in a lecture to the Ecclesiological Society in 1858 maintained that architects' efforts ought to be seen in the same light as those of the Pre-Raphaelites. The Albert Memorial [155] and the decorating firm founded by William Morris, however different from each other, have to be seen as products of this tendency. Burges himself tirelessly researched into subjects of decoration, such as leadwork and the iconography of 'paganism in the Middle Ages'. At Cork the stonework and sculpture of the pulpit, the woodwork of the canopy and the painted roof, and the ironwork of the gates, show the greatest elaboration and individuality [cf. 28].

The greatest exponent of the 'town church' in the 1860s and 1870s was James Brooks. His most important contribution is the series of brick churches in the East End of London, which were backed by the organizational ability of Robert Brett, a doctor from Stoke Newington, and the money of Richard Foster, a rich City merchant. The churches have wide naves, narrow aisles and lofty roofs. In the earliest, St Michael's, Shoreditch (1863–5), and St Saviour's, Hoxton (1865–6,†), Brooks employed Butterfieldian polychromy. St Saviour's was apsed and its nave and chancel formed a single space; it had no tower, but its unbroken roofline was surmounted by a flèche. At St Chad's, Haggerston and St Columba's, Kingsland

210 *All Hallows', Gospel Oak, London, by Brooks, begun in 1892, showing the intended stone vaults.* (Academy Architecture, 1896)

Road [*208*], nearby, both built in 1868–9, polychromy was abandoned for plain red brick, laid with the utmost care. Very large plate-traceried windows punctuate unbuttressed walls. Almost all the elements are reduced to simple geometry; there is hardly any ornament outside, and inside only the chancel is enriched. At St Columba's the site accommodates not only the church and the vestry (over the entrance porch) but also the parsonage (on the corner) and behind it a mission house and school; the compact composition expresses the complications of the plan, yet binds the various elements together successfully.

Brooks applied similar principles to his London suburban churches of the Ascen-

sion, Lavender Hill (begun in 1876), and the Transfiguration, Lewisham (begun in 1880) [*209*], which are among the most elemental of all Victorian churches. He could be equally impressive building in stone, as at St Andrew's, Plaistow, in Essex (1867–70). His final masterpiece is All Hallows', Gospel Oak in London, begun in 1892. It is a hall church, built of ragstone: in the austere but impressive interior [*210*], slender columns rise without capitals to a vaulted roof (alas, unfinished).

Brooks's work is the supreme example of the aesthetic of the Sublime in Victorian church architecture. Only one other church tried to rival the size and massiveness (though it has not the care for detail) of his designs: St Bartholomew's at Brighton, built in 1872–4 by the local architect Edmund Scott (d. 1895) for Father Wagner, the High Churchman who had earlier sponsored Carpenter's St Paul's, Brighton.

Pearson

John Loughborough Pearson's work spans
nearly six decades. A very high degree of
competence and quiet assurance characterized his career, which lacks the notoriety
of Butterfield's or Scott's. Born in 1817 in
Durham, the son of an artist, he was
articled in 1831 to Ignatius Bonomi (d.
1870), then worked in London with
Anthony Salvin and Philip Hardwick, for
whom he supervised the building of the
rich Tudor Gothic library at Lincoln's
Inn, before setting up his own practice
in 1843. Up to the early 1850s, his churches
are dominated by the influence of Pugin
and the Ecclesiologists. In St Mary's at
Dalton Holme, Yorkshire (1858–61), he
combines High Victorian vigour with the
elegance of the Decorated style, especially
in the soaring spire. His very small church
of Appleton-le-Moors, Yorkshire
(1863–6), is one of the most impressive of
all essays in the very heavy 'Early French
Gothic' manner. By that time his first big

*211, 212 St Peter's, Vauxhall, London, by J. L.
Pearson, 1863–5: apse (above), and interior,
looking east.*

213 Truro Cathedral, Cornwall, by Pearson, 1880–1910, from the north.

church of the new generation of 'town churches' was going up, St Peter's, Vauxhall, in London [*211, 212*], already mentioned. It consists of one long rectangle with very little division between nave and chancel, terminating in a semicircular apse, whose massive brick drum is especially memorable. The aisles are small, the clerestory high, and the roof brick-vaulted throughout. There was to have been a tower and lavish internal decoration, but neither was completed. With its massive unbroken brick walls, strict horizontals and general heaviness, St Peter's belongs to High Victorian design proper; but the vault – a great rarity in Britain at the time – and the simplicity of the plan also point to Pearson's final style from 1870 onwards.

It is hard to select from the great number of large churches of Pearson's maturity. Perhaps the most remarkable are St Augustine's, Kilburn in London (designed in 1870 and begun in the following year) [*214–16*], St Michael's at Croydon, Surrey (designed in 1876), and Truro Cathedral in Cornwall (1880–1910) [*213*]. They all show restful horizontals, continuous rooflines, sharp contours, square sections, undisturbed rectangular profiles. Pearson very rarely employs diagonally placed buttresses and uses little in the way of battering or tapering. But the overall emphasis is on the vertical, not on the horizontal or on the gradual building up of masses (as in many of Brooks's churches). To begin with, Pearson likes to surround the main body of his churches with a variety of small buildings, narrow aisles and chapels. Their purpose is to emphasize by contrast the size and height of the main parts. He usually intended a tall tower, though funds were not always available to solid-looking, usually built of stone, and with relatively simple corner pinnacles. The main subsidiary vertical accents are the massive corner piers which flank the chancel and the west end of the nave – occasionally (as at Kilburn and Truro) curiously hemming in the west and east windows [214]. Pearson's windows also reflect his concern for verticality: they are almost all elongated lancets, with only

214 *St Augustine's, Kilburn, London, by Pearson, from the west. The church was built in 1871–c.1877, the spire completed in 1898.*

build it. In its design he stresses the square contour, and keeps the enrichments at the top within this square outline, as was often the case in the Early Gothic of Normandy. Between tower and spire is a fairly thin cornice. Pearson's horizontals are always decisively drawn, but he never uses bulky string-courses or projections as does Scott [191]. The spire, neatly fitted on to the tower, is sharply pointed but still fairly

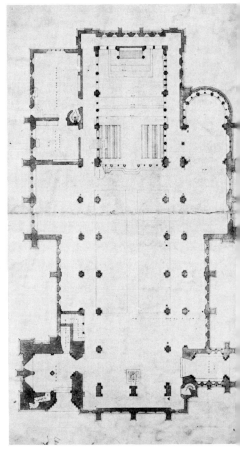

215 *Pearson's ground plan of St Augustine's, Kilburn. The north-east corner (top left) contains vestries, balanced on the south by the apsed Lady Chapel. As built, the nave is one bay longer. (RIBA Drawings Collection)*

occasionally some fairly elemental plate tracery. The exceptions are the frequent very rich rose windows.

The interiors of many of Pearson's churches are dominated by their stone or brick vaults [*212, 216*]. As a rule these are simple quadripartite rib vaults, carried on shafts that go right down to ground level. Thus High Victorian solidity, horizontality and variety of materials are abandoned in favour of elegance, a multiplication of thin shafts along the walls and of pointed ribs in the roof. The effect is accentuated by the multitude of slim lancet windows. One of the most striking results of these combinations of different pointed arches is the way in which the arches of the vault cut across the lancets at the east end, at least from certain viewpoints (for instance at St Augustine's, Kilburn [*216*]). As with the exterior, the interior is also characterized by a contrast between the large main spaces of nave and chancel and small subsidiary spaces, such as narrow passages without particular ritual use. Nowhere is this element stronger than at St Augustine's, Kilburn [*215*].

Entering from the porch under the tower, one finds oneself at first in a narrow aisle that is hardly more than a corridor. In front of it, towards the nave, runs another low and narrow passage which carries a gallery. Going further in, one discovers that the vault over this narrow gallery does not lie where one would expect it, about halfway up the elevation of the nave, but is almost as high as the main vault [*216*]. The gallery bays are separated from each other by what might be called internal buttresses – a feature that was to characterize several other striking later Victorian churches, such as St Augustine's at Pendlebury by Bodley, also of 1870 [*217*], and St Clare's, Sefton Park at Liverpool, of 1888, by Leonard Stokes (see below, p. 224). The effect of the buttresses is to conceal the sources of light, especially as one looks down the centre of the nave, contributing to the subdued, even illumination that is characteristic of all Pearson's churches. The stained glass has darkened, but the

216 *St Augustine's, Kilburn, looking south-east from the upper gallery. On the left is the chancel with its stone screen, in the centre a view into the south transept, crossed by the gallery like a bridge.*

small-scale decoration on the nave walls, and some of the wall-paintings in the transepts designed in an Italian Quattrocento manner by Pearson himself, have recently been cleaned.

Pearson also had his own methods of applying sculptural decoration inside his churches: reredos and screens, usually in a whitish stone, are neatly fitted into the lines of the architecture. Unlike most other Victorian architects, he tried to play down the contrast of different materials in walls and fittings.

217 *St Augustine's, Pendlebury, by G. F. Bodley, 1870–74, looking east.*

The return to English Late Gothic: Bodley

In strong contrast to Pearson and Brooks, George Frederick Bodley began his mature phase of work with an apparently sudden change of style which dominated his views until his death in 1907. In the 1840s he was in Scott's office with Street and White. In the late 1850s and early 1860s he produced what Eastlake called 'muscular' designs, for instance for St Michael's, Brighton (1858–62, with additions by Burges after 1865), and St Martin's on the Hill at Scarborough (1861–3). In 1861 he also made a design in the same vein for All Saints', Jesus Lane in Cambridge. Before building had begun,

however, about 1863, he completely changed his design to something closely resembling works by Pugin of the 1840s – a modest English parish church consisting of a nave with only one aisle and a narrow chancel, divided off by heavy arches supporting a central tower from whose battlemented top rises a thin spire. There is little of High Victorian heaviness, and nothing of its concentration and simplicity of space. Inside, any tendency at unification of space is further counteracted by ornate stencilled patterns. (All Saints' was also one of the first major churches to display large amounts of stained glass made by William Morris's then very young firm.) Anticipating a new wave of nationalism in church and domestic architecture, *The Ecclesiologist* wrote in 1864: 'English Gothic is homely and sweet.' Bodley's first full statement in the

218 *Chancel of Holy Angels', Hoar Cross, Staffordshire, by Bodley and Garner, 1872–6.*

219 Holy Angels', Hoar Cross. The nave is on the right, the chancel (see ill. 218) on the far left, almost hidden by the north transept.

English fourteenth-century parish church style came in 1868, with St John's, Tue Brook, in Liverpool. It repeats most of the elements seen at All Saints', Jesus Lane, but is larger and on the whole more ordered.

Then, in 1870, comes the surprise of St Augustine's, Pendlebury, near Manchester [*217*]. It was paid for by the banker E. S. Heywood and, like Pearson's large churches, it must be connected with the 'town church' movement. It is a single large space: there is no transept and scarcely any stress on the chancel inside or out; the tower (never built) was to be free-standing. Like St Augustine's, Kilburn [*216*], Bodley's church has internal buttresses, but here there are no galleries, just arches cut through at ground level forming passage aisles. Again, the buttresses have an important effect on the lighting, in that the windows cannot be seen when one looks down the centre of the nave. The boarded wooden roof and complicated late Decorated flowing tracery are very different from Pearson, as are Bodley's wood sculpture and his decoration of rood-screen, reredos and organ case in a heavily gilded and painted Flemish or German Late Gothic style.

In 1869 Bodley had entered into partnership with Thomas Garner (1839–1906), an arrangement which lasted until 1897. In 1872 they began to build Holy Angels' at Hoar Cross in Staffordshire, given in memory of Francis Meynell Ingram by his wife [*218*, *219*]. A spreading church in a country setting, it is a complete contrast to Pendlebury: it has a nave with aisles, a tall flat-topped crossing tower panelled in the Perpendicular manner, transept arms, and a high aisleless chancel with ornate tracery in its windows, most of which are square-headed (as elsewhere in the church). Inside, the space is compartmentalized, as in Pugin's work, by means of heavy arches and the crossing itself; the individual parts are treated differently and their height varies. There is much stone decoration, superbly executed – complicated panels of tracery and statuettes on the walls and intricate ribs on the vault. The final enrichment comes from the reredos and screens.

Another church in a similar situation was that built by Bodley in 1886–9 near Clumber House in Nottinghamshire. Larger, but not quite so rich, it has a central tower with a spire which rises inside an openwork crown linked to the corners by flying buttresses, in the manner of the Perpendicular spire at Patrington in Yorkshire. The interior is again divided by deep crossing arches and a screen.

In 1902 Bodley began Holy Trinity, Prince Consort Road in London: it is more elaborate in its decoration, with rich Perpendicular tracery, but it shows a curious, no doubt conscious, lack of verticality and elegance. Finally, in 1906, he was commissioned to design the large Episcopal Cathedral at Washington, D.C., in the United States. It is still under construction, though to modified designs, and marks the apotheosis of the English fourteenth-century manner, with its square-topped, pinnacled central tower. Bodley's particular form of Gothic was extremely influential, not only on the next generation of English church architects (for instance Leonard Stokes and Ninian Comper), but also on the American Gothicists working in the early twentieth century.

Other Late Victorian churches, Catholic and Anglican

Late Victorian churches have not received the same attention as those of earlier decades. The number of competent Roman Catholic architects increased rapidly, and Catholic churches were also designed by Anglicans. The competition of 1880 for the Brompton Oratory in London, that magnificent freak among English churches, was won by a little-known outsider, Herbert Gribble (1847–94). His Roman Baroque design looks the more authentic because it is so unfamiliar in England. Most Catholic churches were, however, dependent on the style of one of another of the major Anglican architects. Edward Goldie (d. 1921), the son of George Goldie, shows strongly the influence of Pearson in his tall and serious St James's, Spanish Place in London (1885–90).

Scott's sons, George Gilbert Scott the younger (1839–97) and John Oldrid Scott (1841–1913), built a number of churches, of which the best known is St John's in Norwich, now the Roman Catholic cathedral, a large and rather austere and heavy building begun in 1884. Like several other rich churches of the period, it was entirely paid for by one patron – here the Catholic Duke of Norfolk, in memory of his wife.

Leonard Stokes (1858–1925), who had worked with Street and Bodley, handled Gothic with great freedom, setting traceried windows in an un-medieval frame of verticals and long-drawn-out horizontals. At St Clare's, Sefton Park, Liverpool (1888) [*220*], he used a variation on the St Augustine's, Kilburn theme of recessed nave windows above a gallery. Stokes also built a number of smaller Roman Catholic churches that are squat and solid-looking with irregular plans, exemplified by Our Lady Help of Christians at Folkestone in Kent (1889). Similar characteristics appear at All Saints' Convent, London Colney, Hertfordshire (1899), and in other colleges designed by Stokes.

John Francis Bentley (1839–1902) is the

most important of late nineteenth-century Catholic architects because he designed Westminster Cathedral, the most important Catholic church in England [222]. He had trained with Clutton in the late 1850s, and went through several phases of Victorian Gothic. His Holy Rood at Watford [221], north of London (begun in 1883), shows the inspiration of Bodley in its segmental arches and early Perpendicular tracery, and the superb handling of the masonry of flint with stone stripes. In 1894 he began to design Westminster Cathedral (built 1895–1903), where Cardinal Vaughan had considerable say, especially in the choice of an 'Italo-Byzantine' style [222]. In plan this very large church is basically a simple rectangle, from which only the east end projects; even the campanile on the south side does not step outside its confines. Three shallow domes roof the nave and a fourth, the only one pierced with windows, covers the sanctuary. In the nave the buttresses are again internal and linked by a gallery (as at St Augustine's, Kilburn), but here the source is Byzantium; between them at ground level there are side-chapels. The nave windows are out of sight, and in addition filled with rather dark glass, and the brick of the walls is not yet covered with the intended facing of white and coloured marble (begun in the chancel): the interior is thus very dark indeed – a darkness that is in itself very impressive. The external walls are on the whole flat, because all the major supports are inside. Towards the top the red brick is relieved with stripes of white Portland stone. Most of the major flanking turrets and the tall tower end in small domes, and they give the building a typically Late Victorian ambiguous, and in places even gaudy, character.

In the North Midlands, the Anglican firm of E. G. Paley (1823–95) and H. J. Austin (1841–1915) tended to follow Bodley's style of rich late Decorated and early Perpendicular English Gothic, as in their very late St George's, Buxton Road at Stockport in Cheshire (1893–7).

220 St Clare's, Sefton Park, Liverpool, by Leonard Stokes, 1888. (Builder, 1889)

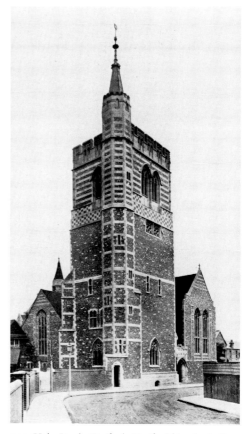

221 Holy Rood, Watford, Hertfordshire, by J. F. Bentley, begun in 1883.

222 Westminster Cathedral, London, by Bentley, 1895–1903.

Finally, in the story of Victorian church building, there are those architects for whom churches came second to their domestic commissions, and who often adopted the new elements of the Domestic Revival. Nowhere is this more obvious than in Norman Shaw's St Michael and All Angels (1879–82) at Bedford Park, the garden suburb in west London [54]. A few Gothic features survive, but they are mixed up with vernacular Renaissance turrets and gables. Inside, most of the woodwork is painted light green, one of the colours favoured by the Aesthetic Movement. In his remote country churches Shaw used an entirely different mode. The church of Richards Castle near Batchcott, Shropshire (1890–93) is late Decorated; but where Bodley would have put the emphasis on elegance and linear pattern, Shaw uses massive rough walling, stumpy vertical accents and blunt outlines.

John Dando Sedding (1838–91) was closely involved with the Arts and Crafts movement of the late 1880s. In his relatively short career he designed buildings in a multitude of styles, ranging in London alone from the Holy Redeemer, Clerkenwell (1887) [*223*] to Holy Trinity, Sloane Street (begun 1888) [*224*]. The Holy Redeemer, which stands in a poor part of the city, looks like a simple early Renaissance church with a tall campanile, and is built of plain stock brick with a few stone bands and details in a flat Roman type of red brick. The church was completed and the campanile built by Sedding's pupil Henry Wilson (1864–1934), of whom more below. Holy Trinity, on the other hand, in a wealthy neighbourhood, is in a most refined early Perpendicular style, with delicately chiselled stone tracery, battlements and turrets. The interior, one of the most elaborate of its time, is vaulted, and even though the decoration was never completed it can show a variety of sumptuous Arts and Crafts fittings.

224 Holy Trinity, Sloane Street, London, by Sedding, 1888–90: view into the nave showing some of the fittings by members of the Arts and Crafts movement – chancel rails, pulpit, hanging lights and carved corbels – and the free Decorated tracery.

223 Holy Redeemer, Clerkenwell, London, by J. D. Sedding, 1887. The campanile was built later by Henry Wilson.

A number of other architects were associated with the Arts and Crafts movement, and produced designs in a new abstract Gothic, based on familiar historical styles, or in the alternative Byzantine manner. Such were Temple Moore (1856–1920), with St Cuthbert's, Middlesbrough, Yorkshire, of 1900; W. D. Caröe (1857–1938), with St David's, Exeter, begun in 1897; Beresford Pite (1861–1934), with Christ Church, Brixton

227

Road, London, begun in 1898; and Charles (later Sir Charles) Nicholson (1867–1949), with St Alban's, Southend-on-Sea, Essex, also begun in 1898.

Henry Wilson might provide a fitting end to the story. He completed several buildings for Sedding, but he was mainly known through his exuberant designs and projects published in the journals of the time. His major work of the 1890s is the decoration of the High Victorian St Bartholomew's at Brighton (see p. 217), which illustrates both the 'Arts' aspect of the movement, in its rich use of painting and sculpture, and the 'Crafts' aspect, in its dazzling display of materials (marbles, semi-precious stones, hammered silver and copper, etc.) and excellent workmanship.

Church restoration

Even the briefest account of Victorian church architecture would be incomplete without a glance at church and cathedral restoration, which probably occupied about as much of architects' and builders' time as new work. The busiest designers were also the busiest restorers, and the busiest of all was George Gilbert Scott.

Restoration work has always been the most controversial aspect of Victorian architecture. We must try to understand the restorers' motives: many medieval buildings were in bad repair, or had fittings or additions in a later style. They felt a duty to preserve these buildings, and they felt that they were capable of doing it, and that they were the first generation who really understood the history of medieval architecture as well as the techniques of medieval construction. In addition, their training led them (as it had earlier restorers) to demand an appearance of completeness and perfection in a work of architecture – something which few large medieval buildings, having taken so long to build, ever in fact had. In each case, Scott and his contemporaries decided which was the main style of the building, or, in the absence of a clear answer, which was the finest period in medieval architec-

ture, and they restored, rebuilt and refitted accordingly. At Lichfield Cathedral, for instance, where Scott began his extensive restoration work in 1857, most of the window tracery is his.

Very soon, however, the more sensitive observers rebelled. Ruskin, in his *Seven Lamps of Architecture* (1849), roundly condemned this kind of restoration. For him, as we have seen, the 'art' of a building (apart from its sculpture) derived almost entirely from the material with which it was built. Restoration was thus impossible: 'What copying can there be of surfaces that have been worn half an inch down?' Street shared his opinion, though he did do restoration work. The new gospel of preservation or protection gained acceptance only very slowly, until the time of the formation in 1877 of the Society for the Protection of Ancient Buildings (SPAB). (The stimulus for the foundation of the Society itself was William Morris's horror at Scott's proposed restoration of Tewkesbury Abbey.) It was the new attitude associated with the Arts and Crafts movement, which saw architecture as the art of building, that led people to find pleasure and aesthetic significance in untidy, crumbling walls of different dates, and fittings from different periods. Understandably, early examples of this new kind of restoration – or better, preservation – are hard to spot, and they are not strictly speaking works of Victorian architecture. Inglesham Church in Wiltshire was discreetly repaired in 1888, and an inscription tells us that the work was done 'through the energy and with the help of William Morris who loved it'.

The other essential step towards modern attitudes to preservation was government legislation. Surprisingly, Britain was a latecomer: it was not until 1882 that a beginning was made, with the Ancient Monuments Protection Act. This was almost exclusively concerned with prehistoric monuments; the amended Act in 1900 extended protection to some medieval buildings.

Nonconformist church architecture

Nonconformist churches are one of the most neglected areas of nineteenth-century architecture. It must be remembered that they outnumber Anglican churches by far and that they are in many ways much more characteristically Victorian institutions. We are well informed about the few pre-Victorian chapels, thanks to the delight the Neo-Georgians took in simple structures of the past: conversely, their contempt for ornate nineteenth-century architecture hit later chapels especially hard. Among historians of Victorian architecture, the main reason for the neglect of Nonconformist buildings is, no doubt, the fact that few of them were designed by the major architects of the age. If our vision is conditioned by the churches of Butterfield and Pearson, the massing and detailing of almost all Nonconformist architecture will be found wanting. If, however, we are interested in practical planning considerations and in townscape, we will find that chapels often surpass the Established churches, especially in their greater involvement in the street scene. In the 1870s there was something of a change in this pattern: the churches and the facilities attached to them became much more complicated in plan and more inventive, and many more renowned architects became involved in their design.

Before the early nineteenth century religious activities outside the Established Church carried disadvantages. The repeal of the Corporation and Test Act in 1828 gave the vote to many Nonconformist citizens, although the last social barriers were not removed until the 1880s. Nonconformism was shaped by pressures from within and without. There was the desire to compete with the Establishment – socially, especially politically, and of course architecturally as well. In many of the new large cities the Nonconformists rapidly ousted the old order. Within the various denominations, new shades of opinion were constantly being asserted, resulting in the founding of new branches and sects. The building of a chapel was more of a local affair than in the Church of England. Members and their ministers usually formed a Chapel Committee which directed the building in all its aspects. Finance was obtained from collections, subscriptions, and also mortgages. Some seats were still rented, not free. In the 1850s several national bodies were established to help with finance and to give directions as to the design and running of chapels.

Of the major denominations, the Congregationalists and Unitarians, though fairly small in number, were often important in political and social life, and produced many prominent buildings. Baptists often came from the world of commerce; their chapels required a special feature, the immersion font, but it was not significant architecturally. Wesleyan Methodists tended to be lower middle-class. They and the Presbyterians were closer to the Church of England in their ritual, with a greater emphasis on the altar table. The most exclusively working-class denomination was the Primitive Methodist Church, which had many small chapels.

However, for the broad purposes of chapel architecture, the differences between denominations do not matter very much. The basic functional requirements were the same. First of all, a large congregation had to be housed as cheaply as possible – usually much more cheaply than in the Established Church. Then, because the sermon was the most important part of the service, the chief requirements inside were that everyone should hear and see the preacher. The accommodation problem was solved by the use of galleries on three sides, generally supported on iron pillars. The fourth side was usually given over to the pulpit or to a more elaborate affair on several levels with stairs, the 'rostrum', and often held the organ as well. In some ways these features are a continuation of the eighteenth-century church type, which the Tractarian and Ecclesiological reforms had obliterated within the Church of England. In addition there are entrances and exits, stairs to the gallery, and a porch

225 *Capel Siloa, Greenfach, Aberdare, 1855.*

or foyer. The main entrance is a major feature, almost invariably placed in the façade and not at the side. A chapel did not have to have its altar at the east, as did an Anglican Church, so it could easily be fitted into an existing street line.

For most chapels, the façade is the only part of the exterior given any 'architectural' treatment. By the early nineteenth century it was usually on one of the short ends of the building [225], the long sides being concealed and handled much more simply. The elevation is usually two-storeyed, denoting the gallery inside, with windows of Georgian proportions, often round-arched. The chief feature is the gable, which in somewhat richer chapels is treated as a pediment. There were many possible variations for the portal. A round window is frequently placed over the door or in the gable. In addition, the name and date of the building are often boldly inscribed. As in ordinary Victorian houses, these features must be seen as survivals of Classical architecture, and they continued to be used into this century. Country chapels tend to be simpler versions of the more spectacular urban chapels with which we shall be concerned here.

The Early Victorian decades saw a spate of large Nonconformist churches, a few of them designed by major architects. Charles Barry designed Upper Brook Street Chapel in Manchester (1837–9), in the Middle Pointed style. Nonconformist buildings in the 1840s reflect the stylistic variety and individualism of that decade. At Hull in 1843, Lockwood and Allom built the spectacular Great Thornton Street Chapel (Independent), with a Corinthian portico flanked by colonnades and wings projecting towards the street. At Leeds in 1847, Bowman and Crowther designed the Mill Hill Unitarian Chapel in Park Row in Decorated Gothic with a large transept. These features displayed the architects' command of historical styles, but had little to do with the needs of the church. The Cavendish Independent Chapel at Manchester (1847–8,†), by Edward Walters, the architect of the Free Trade Hall, was in a more sober Middle Pointed style with an asymmetrically placed tower, and looked like some of Scott's churches of the same date. In Leicester Joseph Hansom, who was beginning to specialize in Roman Catholic churches, built the Particular Baptist Chapel in Belvoir Street (1845, now part of an adult education centre). It has a Classical exterior and an oval plan, with circular staircases leading to the galleries. John Tarring, who worked exclusively for the Congregationalists, supplied a kind of Commissioners' church with a high central tower for the Clapham Congregational Church, Grafton Square, London (1850). Finally, the Central Baptist Chapel in Bloomsbury Street, London (1845–8), by John Gibson, is in the *Rundbogenstil*, and remarkably early in its use of exposed brick with thin ornamental stone stripes. The façade brings us back to the more usual Nonconformist arrangement, with its circular windows and central gable. The church has accommodation for over 1,000 worshippers under a roof of 65-foot span.

By the 1850s, with the consolidation of Anglo-Catholicism, divisions between the churches became stronger again. Nonconformist denominations began to employ specialist architects as well as the more respected local architects. Many also tried to fix a more binding architectural policy. In 1850 the Wesleyan Methodist architect F. J. Jobson published *Chapel and School Architecture*, a book which recalls the Ecclesiologists' earlier *Few Words*. He maintains that chapels are not concert halls or theatres, and should not look like warehouses either. He speaks of 'the house of God', and 'scriptural holiness'. Gothic, he says, has the added virtue of giving the best value for money; but he reiterates the traditional functional demands of the Dissenters, hearing and seeing, and he rules out one important feature of Anglican churches, the passage down the middle of the nave. The Wesleyan Methodists were perhaps the most consistent users of Gothic. Even their colleges were built in a Puginian mode, such as Westminster College in Horseferry Road, London

227 French Congregational Church, St Helier, Jersey, by Poulton and Woodman, 1854. (Builder, *1855*)

226 Square Congregational Church, Halifax, by Joseph James, 1855–7. On the left is the Georgian chapel that it replaced.

(1849,†), by James Wilson (1816–1900) of Bath.

The most outstanding architect working for Nonconformists in the 1850s – to judge by the standards of High Church architecture – was Joseph James (1828–75). Almost all his Congregational chapels are Gothic, starting with the very flamboyant flowing Decorated designs in Yorkshire at Barnsley (1854–6) and Halifax (1855–7) [*226*], whose tall spires dominate their towns. The latter was the church of Crossley, the textile king. James then most competently adopted the High Victorian manner of flat surfaces, massive brick- or stonework, and Geometrical tracery, as in his Cemetery Road Congregational Chapel at Sheffield (1859,†). The very busy firm of Poulton and Woodman of Reading were slightly less sure of contemporary trends, and in many ways adhered to the spiky Gothic of the earlier

228 Congregational Church and Schools, High-bury Quadrant, London, by John Sulman, 1880–82. The Sunday school is at the back (right).

decades. Their interiors, however, as in the French Congregational Church at St Helier, Jersey (1854), show very interesting attempts at combining Puginian open timber roofs with the requirements of a centralized auditorium [227].

In the 1860s and 1870s there seems to have been some reaction against Gothic: wooden roofs had disadvantages acoustically and many favoured the use of much richer, bolder and more varied Classical and Renaissance forms. An example of this trend is the Hanna Street Congregational Chapel in Cardiff, with an attached portico, built in 1867 by Habershon and Pite, another busy firm.

There was no going back on the architectural splendour which had increased continually since the 1840s. And from the 1870s onwards interest in different forms of plan became more widespread. There was a greater sense of freedom and experiment, just as within the Anglican Church there had been a slight relaxation of rules and the acceptance of some new elements, such as wide spaces. James Cubitt's book *Church Designs for Congregations* (1870) supported the idea of centralized plans with transept arms containing spacious galleries, which would

not interfere with the large central space. His Union Chapel in Compton Terrace, Islington, London (1876), shows such a plan, covered by an octagonal wooden roof and styled in a somewhat Pearsonian Early English. In a similar manner he later built the Welsh Presbyterian Church in Charing Cross Road, London (1888).

Many of the large churches were now trying to escape the restrictions of the cross or longitudinal plan, especially inside. Two London chapels by Waterhouse, always considered one of the great planners among Victorian architects, provide interesting variations. The Congregational Church in Lyndhurst Road, Hampstead (1883), is polygonal, the effect being that of an auditorium in a large theatre. The King's Weigh House (Congregational) Chapel in Duke Street, Mayfair (1889–91), is a simple rectangle in plan, but with an oval gallery and roof, shown also on the outside. Both are of brick and terracotta.

An essential feature of Nonconformist architecture is the provision of subsidiary facilities [228]. Especially in the larger Late Victorian establishments there are many utility rooms, rooms for the preacher, and often a flat for the sexton. Increasingly a church hall is provided, for lectures and other activities, often underneath the church. Since the late eighteenth century

229 Islington Congregational Chapel, Upper Street, London, by Bonella and Paull, 1888. (Building News, 1889)

Nonconformists had organized Sunday Schools, which were one of the chief educational institutions before the Anglicans turned to primary education on a larger scale in the 1840s. After the 1870 Education Act, Sunday Schools increased in importance as providers of religious education. Many church groups built separate buildings for the schools, often as large – though not as ornate – as the churches themselves. These complex combinations of church and school are frequently masterpieces of planning, especially when the site offered additional complications. The Wesleyan Methodist Church in Corporation Street, Birmingham, was built in 1886 by the local firm of Osborne and Reading on a narrow, irregular and sloping site. The church is on the first floor, facing the main street, and the Sunday School is behind, with a lecture room above it. Much of the ground floor space is let as shops – a fairly rare practice. Other combinations can be found in the work of Paull and Bickerdike (Christ Church, Westminster Bridge Road, London, 1873,†) and later Bonella and Paull (Islington Congregational Chapel, London, 1888 [229]), John Wills (Baptist Chapel, Queen's Road, Wimbledon, Surrey, 1897), G. Baines (Congregational Church, Little Ilford, Essex, 1903), and John Sulman (Congregational Church and Schools, Highbury Quadrant, London, 1880–2 [228]) – to name but a few busy chapel designers. John Sulman (1849–1934), later Sir John, worked in London from 1870 to 1885, then emigrated to Australia, where he was especially active in town planning. Aesthetically, some of these firms have their own trademarks – in the case of Baines, a fussy Art-Nouveauish Late Gothic or Perpendicular that recalls Henry Wilson (p. 228), and in the case of Sulman a survival of High Victorian heaviness.

Finally, there are the buildings which tell of a renewed evangelical interest, the missions. Towards the end of the century there was an attempt to attract the masses with over-ornateness. Perhaps the most characteristic example is the Leysian Mission in City Road, Finsbury, London (1903), by Bradshaw and Gass, a Wesleyan Methodist establishment near the eighteenth-century chapel of the great Evangelical preacher. The huge building looks more like one of the showy office structures in the area, while its dome and exuberant Art-Nouveau Gothic terracotta decoration make it a competitor to Frank Matcham's contemporary music halls in the West End.

Churches in Scotland: Alexander Thomson and others

The story of the Church and church architecture in Scotland is very different from that in England. The Scottish Episcopal Church, the Anglican Church in Scotland, was and is a minority denomination: a few of its churches were designed by English architects, and some have been mentioned above. The Church of Scotland and most other sects were Presbyterian. The Tractarians and Ecclesiologists thus had little influence on planning, and most Scottish churches remained basically preaching boxes. Unlike the Nonconformists in England, Scottish Nonconformists were the establishment, and did not have to assert themselves against anybody. In one important way the two countries were alike: there is the same indecision as to the architectural style to be used. Indeed, lack of experimentation and eclecticism in Scotland made for an even greater clash between Classical and Gothic.

The most singular and remarkable of the Scottish Classical churches are those by Alexander Thomson. Thomson, whose domestic and commercial work has been mentioned (pp. 61, 130), was born in 1817, the same year as Pearson. He never travelled much beyond Glasgow, but he believed in the use of Greek forms above all else, and his nickname, 'Greek', has stuck with him. Whether most of his forms are actually Classical Greek in origin or not, he differed markedly from the other Scottish Neo-Classicists, such as

230 United Presbyterian Church, Caledonia Road, Glasgow, by Alexander Thomson, 1856, photographed in the 1870s. The tenements on the right are also by Thomson.

231 United Presbyterian Church, St Vincent Street, Glasgow, by Thomson, 1858. The tenements on the left are again part of the church development (c. 1860,†).

David Hamilton and Charles Wilson (1810–63). In his three United Presbyterian churches in Glasgow, Caledonia Road (1856) [*230*], St Vincent Street (1858) [*231*] and Queen's Park (1867,†) [*232*], as well as in his design of 1864 for the Natural History Museum in London (p. 174), he wants to present not a box with a portico but a complete temple structure. The temple contains the upper part of the auditorium of the church. It is made more conspicuous by being placed on a large podium, at least one storey in height: at the St Vincent Street church, built on a steep slope, this podium contains additional subsidiary rooms and entrances. Thomson's compositions are not usually a true reflection of the rooms inside. At the Caledonia Road church, the large portico above the entrance lights both the church and the foyer. As regards Thomson's towers, no architect since Wren and Gibbs has been so successful at creating out of Classical elements a spire-like diminution of the top. The towers consist of a large and very simple rectangular block (remotely reminiscent of High Victorian work) crowned by a 'spire' which is made up of forms not so much Greek as Egyptian, perhaps even Hindu, including oddly rounded shapes. In all his buildings, Thomson's trademark is the band of square-headed windows, usually separated by square piers with very simple capitals, that recalls the earlier Neo-Classicism of Schinkel and Smirke. There are few columns and no round arches in his architecture.

There were also 'normal' Neo-Classical churches in Glasgow: the latest major example is St George's in the Fields, built by Hugh Barclay (1828–92) and David Barclay (1846–1917) as late as 1886. It has a large Ionic portico and a pediment filled with sculpture.

Most of the Gothic churches of Glasgow are characterized by extremely thin and high spires that contrast with the broad mass of the nave: the Lansdowne United Presbyterian Church of 1862 by John Honeyman is typical.

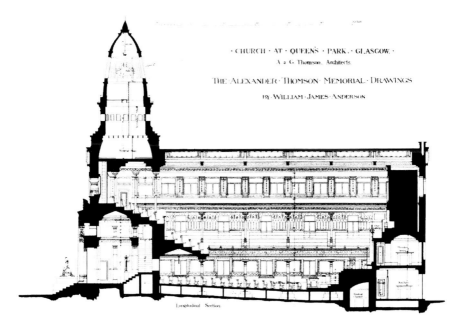

232 Longitudinal section of the Queen's Park United Presbyterian Church, Glasgow, by Thomson, 1867. The entrance is at the left, the reading desk and choir gallery at the right. A gallery along the side is continued around the west end, where it is extended upward under the tower. Ancillary rooms at the right are the vestry, kitchen and heating chamber. (Building News, *1888)*

In Edinburgh, F. T. Pilkington (1832–98) shows more influence from the English High Victorian movement, including something of the 'rogue' quality of E. B. Lamb [*187*] and perhaps William White in the odd juxtaposition of parts and profusion of ornament. His masterpiece in the city is the Barclay Church (1862–3) [*233*]. In the 1870s some architects began to take up major trends of English church design, more boldly than any of their English Nonconformist contemporaries. The Lancet mode of J. J. Burnet's Barony Church in Castle Street (1886) recalls Pearson (who was one of the assessors in the competition), but it is also distinctly Scottish, for it is based on the sober thirteenth-century Dunblane Cathedral.

233 Barclay Church, Edinburgh, by F. T. Pilkington, 1862–3. The church is entered on the right; its 'auditorium' lies under the sharply folded roofs.

7
The architecture of education

THE ESTABLISHMENT of a system of elementary education available to all the country's children was one of the great achievements of Victorian Britain. Before the Elementary Education Act of 1870 it was haphazard. Secondary education was available for the more fortunate; higher education was reserved for the privileged few.

In Early Victorian times illiteracy was widespread, as witnessed by the crosses instead of signatures on many documents. The churches played an active part in dealing with the problem, and the parish schools were the most important providers of elementary education. They were usually built with donations from private individuals, many prompted by genuine charitable feelings, others by the belief that education was an antidote to revolution. Government grants became available later in the period for all denominations, including Roman Catholics.

Parish schools

The parish school was usually small and relied on one teacher, whose small house was usually part of the school buildings. The schoolmaster might be assisted by an unqualified 'pupil-teacher'. There was a shortage of trained teachers, and the planning of schools reflected it: most of the instruction was done in a large schoolroom, off which there might be one or two classrooms used for teaching smaller groups. A school of above minimum size might have separate schoolrooms for boys and girls. A porch, cloakrooms and lavatories made up the rest of the simple requirements.

School design was one of the many architectural matters with which *The Ecclesiologist* concerned itself. In an article in 1847 it advocated a separate roof for the schoolroom and the master's house, with the classroom set at right angles, and a lean-to cloakroom. Separation of the sexes was also considered desirable whenever possible. The school should be 'the prettiest building in the village, next to the church'. The Ecclesiologists, of course, expected schools to be in the Gothic style; Henry Kendall, in his *Designs for Schools and School Houses* of the same year, also advocated Gothic.

The principles of the Ecclesiologists were influential in the designing of the smaller type of parish school. Their ideas on school building were foreshadowed, as so often, by those of Pugin. His small Roman Catholic school at Spetchley in Worcestershire (1841) is a model of its kind [235]. It is built of red brick with mullioned windows and a gabled roof. The chimney-stacks project from the walls and combine with a charming bellcote to produce a picturesque skyline for the little building. A two-storeyed house for the teacher is attached at one side.

High Anglican architects such as White, Butterfield, Street and Brooks took up these ideas and produced a series of parish schools which combine simple planning and construction with the details that they had developed for church architecture

234 Model design for the simplest village school, combining school room and master's house, by William Butterfield, published in 1852 in Instrumenta Ecclesiastica.

236

School Room and Masters House

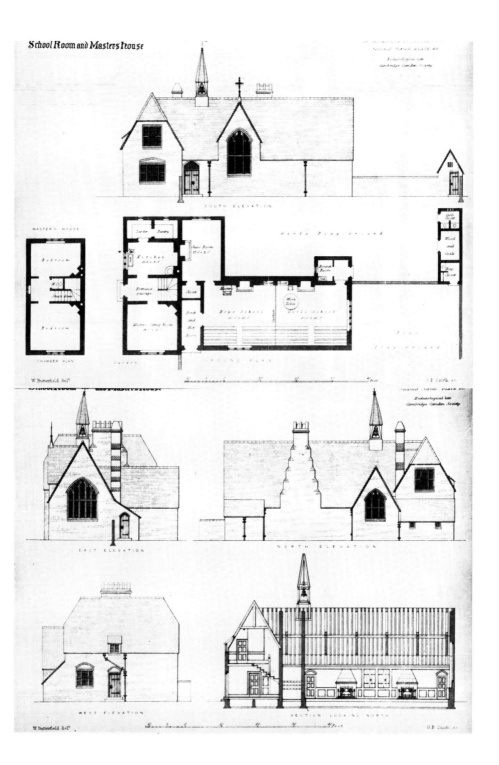

235 *Roman Catholic parish school, Spetchley, Worcestershire, by A. W. N. Pugin, 1841.*

[*197, 234*]. The elevations, as well as the planning, are frequently extremely plain. William White's little school at Probus in Cornwall (1849) could hardly be simpler: the materials are local granite rubble with dressed stone used very sparingly, and there is none of the elaborate Gothic detailing that would have been regarded as essential for a church.

Street followed up this use of local materials and rustic simplicity with a few Gothic details in the small school he built in 1850 at Inkpen in Berkshire. He uses the local materials – in this case flint and red brick – in a way that follows closely the vernacular architecture of the area. The tile roof has half-hipped dormers and wooden window frames are set beneath relieving arches with tile-hanging filling the tympana above them. The building is quiet and unassertive. It cost a modest £250. *The Ecclesiologist* praised its design and noted the use of red brick. In some cases Street's schools form part of an ecclesiastical group. The school and schoolhouse at Boyne Hill near Maidenhead are an important element in the splendid group of buildings begun in 1854, which, as we have seen, also includes a church, vicarage and almshouses [*32*].

Later village schools, such as Norman Shaw's at Church Preen, Shropshire (designed in 1870), show a similar concern with local materials and also with picturesque massing. The schoolroom is lit by tall windows that rise into the roof as dormers. The timber-framed gable of the schoolhouse projects boldly and a tall brick chimneystack adds a vertical accent to the carefully composed design.

The problem of designing parish schools in towns was greater. Often – as at Street's school for St James the Less, Westminster in London – they are not unlike village schools. But where space was limited, as it frequently was, multi-storeyed buildings were necessary. An influential Gothic design was that by J. W. Wild for the Northern District School of St Martin's-in-the-Fields, London (1849–50,†) [*236*]. It was constructed of brick and had arcades of Gothic arches in a manner reminiscent of Northern Italy. The teaching accommodation was on the first two floors and the top storey was occupied by a covered playground. The school was praised by Ruskin and is one of the first secular Victorian designs in an Italian Gothic style – a style which was to become popular in the 1850s and 1860s. (We have already seen how this school served as a model for commercial buildings: p. 131.)

To fit the required accommodation on to a restricted town site required great skill. Butterfield was faced with this

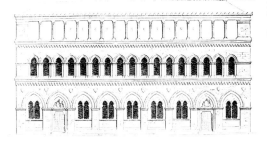

236 *St Martin's-in-the-Fields Northern District School, London, by J. W. Wild, 1849–50.* (Builder, *1849*)

problem at All Saints', Margaret Street in London, and was forced to build high [*195*]. His choir school (1850–53) faces the clergy house across the small courtyard which fronts the church, and has a dormitory, master's study, classroom and refectory. Even higher is the building of the St Giles's National Schools in Endell Street, London, by E. M. Barry (1860) [*237*]. By piling up five storeys on the constricted corner site, Barry was able to accommodate no less than 1,500 pupils.

Board schools

The Elementary Education Act of 1870 called for large numbers of schools, mainly in crowded urban areas, to be built with public rather than private money. London, for example, had over 400 Board schools by 1895. Many of them were designed by E. R. Robson, who was the first architect of the London School Board. He had worked in the office of George Gilbert Scott and subsequently formed a partnership with J. J. Stevenson, whose 'Queen Anne' Red House has been mentioned ([*10*] and p. 65), and who also had a hand in the design of some of the early Board schools. Robson's work was influential, partly because in 1874 he published *School Architecture*, a book in which he illustrated a number of London Board schools (including one by Basil Champneys) and also foreign examples.

Because of their cramped sites the London Board schools are usually multistorey buildings [*238*]. In their planning they retain the large schoolroom, but the provision of classrooms is greater than was usual [*239*]. The members of the School Boards were more secular in their thinking than the builders of the earlier parish schools: though some designers used the Gothic style, Robson argued that 'a continuation of the semi-Ecclesiastical style . . . [of] National schools would appear to be inappropriate and lacking in anything to mark the great change which is coming over the education of the country'. He found in the 'Queen Anne' manner a style with all the freedom of planning which he

237 St Giles's-in-the-Fields National Schools, London, by E. M. Barry, 1860.

required. The Board schools are usually built of yellow London stock brick with red brick used as quoins and for dressings. The white-painted window frames are placed under segmental arches and the windows have glazing bars. But the most characteristic features are the brick gables, which give the buildings a varied and lively skyline, further enhanced by tall chimney-stacks and, usually, a crowning bellcote or cupola. Many of the early London Board schools have been replaced or altered, but Robson's Bonner Street School in Hackney, built in 1875, survives with little external alteration [*238*].

In Birmingham, the firm of Chamberlain and Martin produced 41 Board schools between 1873 and 1898, most of them in a more Gothic style, carrying on the early idea of expressing different functions by separate roofs, resulting in extremely lively compositions.

239

238, 239 Bonner Street Primary School, Hackney, London, by E. R. Robson, 1875: an early photograph of the building, and Robson's working plans for the second floor – the boys' floor – and the master's room a half-level higher (from the Greater London Council archives). The boys' floor is the one lit through tall gables in the photograph; the wall on the right there appears at the bottom in the plan. A large school room and three smaller classrooms are provided, as well as a cloakroom. The master has his own w.c. In the final building, Robson extended the boys' classrooms (upper left in the plan) beyond the stairs, producing the triple set-off seen in the photograph.

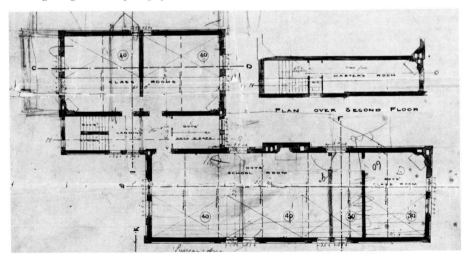

Public schools

Secondary and university education was almost entirely the preserve of the upper and middle classes during the Victorian period. The ancient public schools, which had in many cases been in a depressed state during the eighteenth century, were transformed into suitable places for the education of Christian gentlemen. Dr Thomas Arnold, the famous headmaster of Rugby, was the prophet of the new public-school philosophy. He stated his priorities: 'first religious principles, secondly gentlemanly conduct, thirdly intellectual ability'. These principles appealed to the middle classes, and the demand for this type of education was such that most of the old public schools were extended or rebuilt and many new schools were founded.

The most notable religious foundations were those of Nathaniel Woodard, who was curate for New Shoreham in Sussex when he set up the first of his schools, which later became Lancing College [*240*]. By the time of his death in 1891 he had established fifteen schools. His idea was to complete the system of religious education so that it served the needs of children of all ages and of all classes. The poor were catered for in the system of National Schools, the rich by the older public schools. Woodard set about founding schools for the middle classes. They were categorized as upper, middle or lower schools for the sons of, respectively, 'clergy and other gentlemen', 'substantial tradesmen, farmers, clerks and others of similar station', and 'petty shopkeepers, skilled mechanics and other persons of very small means'.

The Gothic style was the most widely favoured, although not the only architectural mode employed in the construction of public schools. Both Oxford and Cambridge became bastions of the Gothic Revival. As we have seen, the Oxford Movement preached the revival of the Anglican Church and the return to ancient forms of ritual, and the Cambridge Camden Society advocated a return to Gothic architecture and the arrangement of churches along medieval lines. For public schools Gothic was the natural choice to express these enthusiasms. Only later in the period did Renaissance styles become equally popular.

Important developments took place in planning. For public schools a distinction can be drawn between day schools and the boarding schools which had more complex accommodation requirements. Changes also took place in the arrangement of teaching space. At the beginning of the period teaching still took place in large schoolrooms containing many different groups of pupils. By the end, the classroom system had become the norm, and numerous classrooms for smaller groups of pupils were provided.

The first major new public school was the King Edward VI School in Birmingham, by Charles Barry (1833–7,†). Its traditional symmetrical façade was decorated with Perpendicular Gothic motifs designed by Pugin. Pugin soon propagated a very different kind of school: his model was the monastic layout of the medieval English college, with cloisters, dormitories, outbuildings, all clearly differentiated in plan and elevation, and dominated by a large and ornate chapel. The two major buildings of this type that he was able to build are both in Leicestershire: part of Ratcliffe College (1843), and Mount St Bernards Abbey (1839–44), an actual monastery, where he chose a striking simplicity for most of the parts. However, as we shall see, Pugin was not allowed to build Balliol College in Anglican Oxford.

For most Anglican boarding public schools, too, Gothic architecture and a large chapel emphasized the place of religion in the pupils' daily lives. Indeed, the chapel is often the dominant feature of the whole school. This is perhaps truest of Lancing College, Sussex [*240*], designed by R. C. Carpenter, a follower of Pugin who was favoured by the Ecclesiologists (see p. 199). Building began in 1854; Carpenter died in 1855, but the work was

240 Lancing College, Sussex, begun in 1854 by R. C. Carpenter and continued by William Slater and R. H. Carpenter. In the centre is the dining hall, on the right the chapel, begun in 1868 by the younger Carpenter.

carried on by his pupil William Slater (1819–72), and by his son R. H. Carpenter (1841–93). The residential and teaching accommodation, of stone and local flint, is in a restrained Gothic, but the great chapel – only recently completed – is in the early Decorated style, lit by large windows with Geometrical tracery. Massive buttresses support its vault which rises to 94 feet, 20 feet higher than the vault of Lincoln Cathedral and approaching the height of Westminster Abbey. Rising up from the Sussex downs, it is a landmark for miles around.

Lancing is essentially Early Victorian in its architectural detail. Butterfield's work at Rugby from 1858 onwards epitomizes the High Victorian approach to public school design. He was called in by Dr Temple, the headmaster, who was to become Archbishop of Canterbury. In 1867–70 the New Quad was built: it is most elaborate architecturally, in Butterfield's very personal version of Gothic, executed in brick of different colours banded with stone. The chapel (1870–72) towers over the school and rises to a steeple with massive broaches, an octagonal top storey and a pyramid roof. Butterfield also designed a swimming bath, a gymnasium and racquets courts – all in the Gothic style.

The Gothic style continued to be employed for public schools into the Late Victorian period. St Paul's School, Hammersmith, London [241], begun in 1881 to designs by Waterhouse (now demolished except for the High Master's house), was a forceful if somewhat harsh building in Waterhouse's personal version of Gothic, executed in his favourite red brick and terracotta. In layout it did not follow a monastery or college, but instead had a compact E-shaped plan with classrooms on a number of storeys arranged along corridors. It had similarities to a German Gymnasium or grammar school – a building type which had been illustrated in Robson's School Architecture.

Amongst the schools and colleges which did not follow the Gothic pattern the most important were Marlborough in Wiltshire, founded in 1843, where an existing house of the period gave Edward Blore (1787–1879) a reason for employing the William and Mary style in his additions after 1844, and Wellington College, Berkshire, founded in 1853 as a national memorial to the Duke who had died in the previous year [242]. Wellington, built in 1856–9, was less closely associated with the Established Church, and a Classical style, inspired perhaps by Wren's Chelsea Hos-

241 St Paul's School, Hammersmith, London, by Alfred Waterhouse, 1881–4.

pital, seemed appropriate. The architect, John Shaw (1803–70), arranged the school around courtyards. His buildings, of red brick with stone dressings, with mansard roofs and oval dormers, have a slight French flavour, and are very close to the style used by Nesfield for Kinmel Park some ten years later [42].

The *Rundbogenstil* (see p. 196) provided another alternative to Gothic for public schools, and was used by Charles Barry, junior (1823–1900), eldest son of Sir Charles, for the new Dulwich College, built in 1866–70. It was designed for the system of teaching based on small classrooms. The plan is arranged in three blocks: the centre contains a large hall that was used for morning assembly and prayers, and the flanking blocks have classrooms with space for 600 pupils. The blocks are joined by open cloisters. Barry may have been influenced by German schools, both in his planning and in his choice of the *Rundbogenstil* for the elevations.

242 Wellington College, Berkshire, by John Shaw, 1856–9.

243 *Fellows' residences, warden's lodge and chapel of St Augustine's College, Canterbury, by William Butterfield, 1844–73.*

Colleges and universities

Higher education at the start of Queen Victoria's reign was largely in the hands of the ancient universities and under the eye of the Established Church. The notable exception was the newly founded London University, in Gower Street, which expressed its secularism with a Classical building by William Wilkins (begun in 1827 but never finished). Later, a number of civic universities were founded: here the new natural sciences were taught, as well as the traditional subjects which still formed the basis of teaching at Oxford and Cambridge.

Colleges and universities tended to be traditionally arranged around courtyards, though Butterfield and Waterhouse were to use corridor plans. In 1843 Pugin submitted a design for Balliol College, Oxford, in which he tried to recreate a medieval college. A gate tower is flanked by three-storeyed ranges, rather flat but boldly punctuated by gabled chimney-stacks from the tops of which rise four separate chimneys. There was to be an oriel window over the gateway and others at the sides of the façade. But 1843 was the year when Newman resigned from St Mary's, Oxford, soon to join the Roman Catholic Church: religious battle was in the air, and Pugin's own Catholicism

influenced the Balliol dons in the rejection of his design. He had the consolation of realizing some of the ideas at Ratcliffe College, begun in 1843, and a gateway by him was built at Magdalen College, Oxford (1843–4,†).

Butterfield's first college, St Augustine's at Canterbury, incorporates actual medieval buildings, but the result is characteristic of the architect [243]. The college was founded to train missionaries for overseas work; the site was part of St Augustine's monastery. Butterfield received the commission from Beresford-Hope, President of the Cambridge Camden Society. The buildings, which were begun in 1844, are grouped around a courtyard open on one side, each given emphasis according to its importance. The chapel and the library are the most elaborate structures; the dormitory is a design of great simplicity. Inside the dormitory block the rooms for students are arranged along a corridor, a departure from the traditional arrangement of student rooms around numerous staircases.

George Gilbert Scott was also to the fore in college design. He followed Pugin and the Ecclesiologists in choosing the Middle Pointed style for the chapel of Exeter College, Oxford, built in 1856–60. (Nearby is his Martyrs' Memorial of 1841–4, based on an Eleanor Cross.) The chapel is a miniature Sainte-Chapelle – very high, apsed, with large windows filled with Geometrical tracery, and a flèche on the roof. In 1863–9 he added a large chapel to St John's College in Cambridge. Like the Oxford chapel it is apsed, but in addition it has a tall tower based on that of Pershore Abbey, which had been one of Scott's restoration jobs. Glasgow University (designed 1865, begun 1868) is one of his largest works [244]. Its main front is over 600 feet in length and has a tall tower; stepped gables give the Gothic a Scottish flavour.

Scott's college designs have none of the originality of those of Butterfield at Keble College, Oxford [245]. John Keble's Assize sermon of 1833 had sparked off the

244 Glasgow University, by Sir George Gilbert Scott, begun in 1868; Bute Hall and Spire redesigned by Oldrid Scott, 1878–84.

245 Chapel range of Keble College, Oxford, by William Butterfield, 1867–83.

Oxford Movement. On his death in 1866 an appeal was launched to found a college in his memory. William Gibbs, a rich Tractarian whose firm had made a fortune importing guano from South America, gave £50,000 to build the chapel. Work on the college was begun in 1867 and finished in 1883. It sums up much of what Butterfield felt was important in architecture and typifies the high ideals and hard thinking of the Oxford Movement. One of his most bold decisions was to use red brick in Oxford, where for centuries the colleges had been built of stone. He told the Warden of Keble that his principle was not to be bound by tradition – 'to take the responsibility of thinking for myself, and to use the materials, whatever they may be, which the locality and this age supply'.

The rooms are arranged around quads

246 High Street façade of the Examination Schools, Oxford, by Sir T. G. Jackson, 1876–82.

in the traditional manner, but the general effect is governed by the restless small-scale variation of the college wings. The hall and the library are on the first floor of a block set at right angles to the entrance gate, whereas the usual medieval arrangement was for the hall to be opposite the entrance. The staircase to these upper rooms is lit by a large oriel window. Facing the library is the chapel, singled out by its architectural treatment, which soars above the roofs, and with its large windows completely dominates the whole complex. Here the polychromy which enlivens all the college buildings reaches a climax of elaboration. The interior is particularly ornate, decorated with marble, encaustic tiles and stained glass. Rich and busy patterns cover floor, walls and vault.

Butterfield surprisingly built nothing in Cambridge. His place is filled by Waterhouse, who had already designed the front range of Balliol College, Oxford, in Gothic (1867–77). In a number of his

247 *The dining hall, Newnham College, Cambridge, by Basil Champneys, 1888.*

248 *Westminster College, Cambridge, by H. T. Hare, 1899.*

Cambridge buildings Waterhouse turned to the French Renaissance style. His Tree Court at Caius College (1868) is designed in the manner of the Early Renaissance François I work at Blois, stone-faced, with a tower on the front facing King's Parade. At Pembroke College he went back to the Late Gothic of the Charles VIII wing at Blois. The block facing Trumpington Street, begun in 1871, is of red brick and stone. Girton College, the first women's college in Cambridge, also chose Waterhouse: for its buildings, begun in 1872, he reverted to the Gothic style and his favourite red brick and red terracotta, and used a corridor plan.

This combination of Gothic details with red brick and terracotta was extensively used by Waterhouse in the colleges and universities that he built in the North of England, and the epithet 'Red Brick Universities' is probably due more to him than to any other architect. Typical of his work of this type is the Yorkshire College of Science, now part of Leeds University (begun in 1877), and Liverpool College (begun in 1889), now the Victoria Building of Liverpool University. Manchester University, begun in 1869 as Owen's College, is in a similar style, but built of stone – as was Waterhouse's contemporary Town Hall in the city.

Both Oxford and Cambridge in Late Victorian times shrank from the assertive and vigorous architecture of Butterfield and Waterhouse. At Oxford T. G. Jackson won approval in 1876 for his design for the Examination Schools building in a seventeenth-century Renaissance style. It was built of stone and completed in 1882 [246]. In the following year the dons of Pembroke College, Cambridge, having had enough of Waterhouse, employed George Gilbert Scott the younger to build their New Building in a similar Renaissance style. Stone rather than brick was used. Newnham College, Cambridge, a women's college, employed Basil Champneys for their buildings [247]: he provided them, in the years following 1875, with accommodation in the 'Queen Anne' style. Gothic was still employed in the Late Victorian period, but it was very different from High Victorian Gothic. Hare's Westminster College, Cambridge [248], a Presbyterian training college, was built in 1899 in a Tudor Gothic style, of red brick but without any of Waterhouse's assertiveness. At the side is a low tower capped by a squat cupola which echoes the horizontal lines of the main façade.

Perhaps the most spectacular of all Late Victorian educational establishments is the Royal Holloway College at Egham,

Surrey [*249*]. Another early college for women, it was founded by Thomas Holloway (see p. 111), and built in 1879–87 by W. H. Crossland. The building is large – 550 by 376 feet – and made to seem even larger by Crossland's external treatment. The whole structure is a most daring attempt to recreate the effect of a château of the period of François I. (Crossland went specially to the Loire valley to fill his sketchbook with appropriate details.) Red brick is used, with lavish stone dressings. The rooms are ranged around two courtyards. At the corner of each court is an elaborate pavilion enlivened with bay windows, tourelles, chimneys and cupolas. The gate towers are even more fantastic and are piled high with masonry embellishments.

It is perhaps not insignificant that what is in many ways the most interesting stylistically of all Victorian educational buildings is an art school in Glasgow [*250*].

249 Royal Holloway College, Egham, Surrey, by W. H. Crossland, 1879–87.

A competition for the Glasgow School of Art was held in 1896 and was won by Charles Rennie Mackintosh (1868–1928). His design was to gain international renown. Although the building may be regarded as foreshadowing the Modern Movement, it may also be seen as the product of Late Victorian design techniques. The north front, built in 1896–9, might be compared to the work of Norman Shaw, where asymmetrical elements are frequently introduced into a basically symmetrical design [*129*]. The size and spacing of the windows is varied, and a bay window and a small turret appear to the left of the centrally placed doorway; moreover, the doorway itself with its curved pediment has a flavour of the 'Queen Anne' fashion. Much of the general character of the building, its bareness and sheer verticality, owes a debt to Scottish vernacular. Mackintosh's handling of the masonry is very severe, and the character of the façade is largely determined by the enormous studio windows which are treated as simple rectangles divided by their metal mullions

250 Detail of the north front of the Glasgow School of Art, by Charles Rennie Mackintosh, 1896–9.

and transoms. In contrast to this is the delicate attenuated ironwork and the flowing sculptural decoration, which are part of the international Art Nouveau movement.

The architecture of education mirrors the development of Victorian architecture as a whole. Its patronage is largely middle-class. The approach to planning ranges from Classical formality to the picturesque expression of functional arrangements.

Each style, from the Neo-Classical to the Neo-Gothic, from the Neo-Renaissance to the Neo-Vernacular, is represented. Moreover, the schools and colleges clearly illustrate the high ideals which lie behind so much of Victorian architecture. For the Victorians, architecture not only served structural, functional and aesthetic needs: it had a didactic mission. As Nathaniel Woodard said of the mighty chapel of his Lancing College [240], 'no system of education would be perfect which did not provide for the cultivation of the taste of the pupil through the agency of the highest examples of architecture'.

Further reading

Unless otherwise stated, the place of publication is London

A SHORT LIST

This first section contains a necessarily limited selection of the important sources and of the many books which were influential in the nineteenth century or may serve as modern introductions to different aspects of the subject.
Periodicals: *The Architectural Review*; *The Builder*; *The Building News*; *Country Life*.
Exhibition catalogues: *Marble Halls, Drawings and Models for Victorian Secular Buildings* (Victoria and Albert Museum, London, 1973); *Victorian Church Art* (Victoria and Albert Museum, London, 1971).
E. Aslin, *The Aesthetic Movement* (1969); P. Collins, *Changing Ideals in Modern Architecture* (1965); H. J. Dyos, *Victorian Suburb, A study of the growth of Camberwell* (Leicester 1961); C. L. Eastlake, *A History of the Gothic Revival* (1872; reprint, Leicester 1970); M. Girouard, *The Victorian Country House* (Oxford 1971); G. L. Hersey, *High Victorian Gothic. A study in Associationism* (Baltimore, Md., 1972); H.-R. Hitchcock, *Early Victorian Architecture* (New Haven and London 1954; reprint 1972); J. C. Loudon, *An Encyclopaedia of Cottage, Farm and Villa Architecture and Furniture* (1st pub. 1833); R. Macleod, *Style and Society, Architectural Ideology in Britain 1840–1914* (1971); S. Muthesius, *The High Victorian Movement in Architecture, 1850–1870* (1972); N. Pevsner, *Some Architectural Writers of the Nineteenth Century* (1972); N. Pevsner and others, *The Buildings of England* series (Harmondsworth, Mx., 1951ff.); D. Pilcher, *The Regency Style* (1947); A. W. N. Pugin, *Contrasts* (1836, 1841; reprints), and *The True Principles of Pointed or Christian Architecture* (1841; recent reprints); J. Ruskin, *The Seven Lamps of Architecture* (1st pub. 1849), and *The Stones of Venice* (1st pub. 1851–3); R. N. Shaw and T. G. Jackson, eds., *Architecture, a Profession or an Art?* (1892); J. Summerson, *Victorian Architecture, Four Studies in*

Evaluation (New York and London 1970); D. Ware, *A Short Dictionary of British Architects* (1967).

ON INDIVIDUAL ARCHITECTS

V. Fiddes and A. Rowan, *David Bryce* (Edinburgh 1976); P. Thompson, *William Butterfield* (1971); D. Watkin, *The Life and Work of C. R. Cockerell* (1974); A. Nash, *A. E. Cogswell* (Polytechnic, Portsmouth, Hants, 1975); H. Hobhouse, *Thomas Cubitt – Master Builder (1971)*; D. McAra, *Sir James Gowans, Romantic Rationalist* (Edinburgh 1974); D. Watkins, *Thomas Hope 1769–1831 and the Neo-Classical Idea* (1968); G. Rubens, *W. R. Lethaby, his Life and Work* (1978); A. Preedy and I. Stewart, *T. E. Owen, Southsea Architect* (Polytechnic, Portsmouth, Hants, 1972); G. F. Chadwick, *The Works of Sir Joseph Paxton* (1961); J. Anthony, *Joseph Paxton. An illustrated Life 1803–1865* (Aylesbury, Bucks., 1973); P. Stanton, *Pugin* (London and New York 1971); J. G. Harries, *Pugin. An illustrated Life of Augustus Welby Northmore Pugin 1812–1852* (Aylesbury, Bucks., 1973); J. D. Kornwolf, *M. H. Baillie Scott and the Arts and Crafts Movement* (Baltimore, Md., 1972); A. Saint, *Richard Norman Shaw* (New Haven and London 1976); Jane Fawcett, ed., *Seven Victorian Architects* (Burn, Hardwick, Smirke, Pearson, Bodley, Waterhouse, Lutyens) (1976).

ON PLACES

C. E. B. Brett, *The Buildings of Belfast* (1967); A. Crawford and R. Thorne, *Birmingham Pubs 1890–1939* (Centre for Urban and Regional Studies, Birmingham 1976); D. Hickman, *Birmingham* (1970); B. Little, *Birmingham Buildings* (Newton Abbot, Devon, 1971); C. Crick, *Victorian Buildings in Bristol* (Bristol 1975); J. B. Hilling, *Cardiff and the Valleys* (1973); R. Newton, *Victorian Exeter* (Leicester 1968); A. Gomme and D. Walker, *Architecture of Glasgow* (1968); D. Linstrum, *Leeds* (Newcastle-on-Tyne 1969); Q. Hughes, *Seaport, Architecture and Townscape of Liverpool* (1964); J. Summerson, *The Architecture of Victorian London* (Charlottesville, Va., 1976); P.

Metcalf, *Victorian London* (1972); D. J. Olsen, *The Growth of Victorian London* (1976); B. F. L. Clarke, *Parish Churches of London* (1966); M. H. Port, ed., *The Houses of Parliament* (New Haven and London 1976); F. H. W. Sheppard, ed., *Survey of London*, esp. vol. 27 and 28, *North and South Kensington* (1973, 1975); P. Atkins, *Guide across Manchester* (Civic Trust for the North West, Manchester, 1976); C. Stewart, *The Stones of Manchester* (1956), and *The Architecture of Manchester, Index* (Manchester Libraries 1956); B. Allsopp, *Historic Architecture of Newcastle-upon-Tyne* (Newcastle 1967); L. Wilkes and G. Dodds, *Tyneside Classical* (on Newcastle) (1964); D. W. Lloyd, *Buildings of Portsmouth and its Environs* (Portsmouth City Council 1974); P. Nuttgens, *York* (1970); B. de Breffny and G. Mott, *The Churches and Abbeys of Ireland* (1976); H. Dixon, *An Introduction to Ulster Architecture* (Belfast 1975).

OTHER WORKS OF INTEREST

Periodicals: *The Architectural Magazine*; *Publications of the Royal Institute of British Architects*; *The Ecclesiologist*; *The Architect*; *The British Architect*; *Academy Architecture*; *The Studio*; *Architectural History*; *Journal of the Society of Architectural Historians of Great Britain*; *Architectura*.
Catalogue of the Drawings Collection of the Royal Institute of British Architects in London, 1969ff.
The Dictionary of Architecture (Architectural Publication Soc., 1853–92); *The Art Journal Illustrated Catalogue of the Great Exhibition* (1851; recent reprints); E. Aslin, *Nineteenth-century English Furniture* (1962); J. Barnard, *The Decorative Tradition* (1973); S. Barton, *Monumental Follies. An Exposition on the Eccentric Edifices of Britain* (1972); P. Beaver, *The Crystal Palace. 1851–1936* (1970); J. Betjeman, *Ghastly Good Taste* (1st pub. 1934), and *London's Historic Railway Stations* (1972); G. Biddle, *Victorian Stations. Railway Stations in England and Wales 1830–1913* (Newton Abbot, Devon, 1973); T. S. R. Boase, *English Art 1800–1870* (Oxford 1959); M. Bow-

ley, *Innovations in Building Materials* (1960); H. A. N. Brockman, *The British Architect and Industry 1841–1940* (1974); K. Clark, *The Gothic Revival* (1st pub. 1928); B. F. L. Clarke, *Church Builders of the Nineteenth Century. A Study of the Gothic Revival in England* (1938; reprint); H. M. Colvin, *Biographical Dictionary of British Architects 1660–1840* (1954); W. Creese, *The Search for Environment, The Garden City* (New Haven and London 1966); J. S. Curl, *Victorian Architecture. Its Practical Aspects* (1973); G. Darley, *Villages of Vision* (1975); H. J. Dyos and M. Wolff, eds., *The Victorian City* (1973); J. T. Emmett, *Six Essays* (1891; reprint), J. Fawcett, ed., *The Future of the Past, Attitudes to Conservation 1147–1974* (1976); P. Ferriday, ed., *Victorian Architecture* (1963); R. Furneaux Jordan, *Victorian Architecture* (Harmondsworth, Mx., 1966); E. Gauldie, *Cruel Habitations. A History of Working-Class Housing 1780–1918* (1974); G. Germann, *The Gothic Revival in Europe and Britain* (1972); M. Girouard, *Victorian Pubs* (1975); V. Glasstone, *Victorian and Edwardian Theatres* (London and Cambridge, Mass., 1975); G. Godwin, ed. A. D. King, *Town Swamps and Social Bridges* (reprint with preface, Leicester 1972); H. S. Goodhart-Rendel, *English Architecture since the Regency* (1953); H.-R. Hitchcock, *Architecture: Nineteenth and Twentieth Centuries* (Harmondsworth, Mx., and Baltimore, Md., 1958); J. R. Hix, *The Glass House* (1974); T. G. Jackson, *Recollections 1835–1924* (Oxford 1950); S. Jervis, *High Victorian Design* (Victoria and Albert Museum catalogue, 1974–75); R. Kerr, *The Gentleman's House* (1864; reprint 1972); W. R. Lethaby, *Architecture, Mysticism and Myth* (1891; reprint 1974); K. Lindley, *Seaside Architecture* (1973); B. Little, *Catholic Churches since 1623* (1966); J. Macauley, *The Gothic Revival 1745–1845* (1975); N. Pevsner, *Pioneers of Modern Design* (1st pub. 1936), *Studies in Art, Architecture and Design*, vol. 2 (London and New York 1969), *Ruskin and Viollet-le-Duc. Englishness and Frenchness in the Appreciation of Gothic Architecture* (1969), and *A History of Building Types* (Princeton, N.J., and London 1976); N. Pevsner and J. M. Richards, eds., *The Anti-rationalists* (1973); A. Raistrick, *Industrial Archaeology* (1972, Frogmore, Herts. 1973); J. M. Richards, *The Functional Tradition in Early Industrial Buildings* (1958); E. R. Robson, *School Architecture* (1874; reprint 1972); D. Rubinstein, ed., *Victorian Homes* (1974); M. Seaborne, *The English School. Its Architecture and Organisation 1370–1870* (1971); A. R. Sennett, *Garden Cities in Practice* (1905); G. G. Scott, *Remarks on Secular and Domestic Architecture* (1858), and *Personal and*

Professional Recollections (1879); J. Steegman, *Victorian Taste. A study of the Arts and Architecture from 1830–1870* (1970); G. E. Street, *Brick and Marble in the Middle Ages* (1855); J. Summerson, *Heavenly Mansions* (1st pub. 1949), and *The London Building World of the Eighteen-Sixties* (1973); J. N. Tarn, 5% *Philanthropy, An Account of Houses in Urban Areas 1840–1914* (Cambridge 1975); D. Taylor and D. Bush, *The Golden Age of British Hotels* (1974); P. Thompson, *The Work of William Morris* (1967); William White, *Architecture and Public Buildings, their relation to school, academy and state in Paris and London* (1884).

FURTHER INFORMATION

Indices of architects and periodicals in the Library of the Royal Institute of British Architects, London; *Annual of the Victorian Society of Great Britain*, London. Information on theses, existing and in preparation, may be obtained from the Society of Architectural Historians of Great Britain, Newcastle-upon-Tyne, and from *Urban History Year Book*, pub. by the Department of Economic History, University of Leicester.

ADDITIONS TO THE BIBLIOGRAPHY (1984)

M. Binney (SAVE), *Satanic Mills: Industrial Architecture in the Pennines* (1979); E. Blau, *Ruskinian Gothic: The Architecture of Deane and Woodward* (Princeton 1982); *Decimus Burton* (exhib. cat., Building Centre Trust, London 1981); D. Cole, *The Work of Sir George Gilbert Scott* (1980); J. M. Crook, *Victorian Architecture: A Visual Anthology* (1971) and *William Burges and the High Victorian Dream* (1981); C. Cunningham, *Victorian and Edwardian Town Halls* (1981); J. S. Curl, *The Life and Work of Henry Roberts* (Chichester 1983); P. Davey, *Arts and Crafts Architecture* (1980); R. Evans, *The Fabrication of Virtue: English Prison Architecture 1750–1840* (Cambridge 1982); B. Ferrey, *Recollections of Pugin* (1861, new ed. 1978); J. Franklin, *The Gentleman's Country House and its Plan* (1981); K. Garrigan, *Ruskin and Architecture* (Madison, Wis., 1973); M. Girouard, *Sweetness and Light: The Queen Anne Movement* (Oxford 1977) and *Alfred Waterhouse and the Natural History Museum* (1981); A. Gomme, M. Jenner and B. Little, *Bristol: An Architectural History* (1979); A. King, ed., *Buildings and Society: Essays on the Social Development of the Built Environment* (1980); W. R. Lethaby, *Philip Webb and His Work* (1935, new ed. 1979); D. Linstrum, *West Yorkshire* (1980); R. McFadzean, *The Life and Work of Alexander Thomson* (1979); S. Muthesius, *The English Terraced House* (1982); D. Pearce and M. Binney, *Railway Archi-*

tecture (1979); A. Quiney, *John Loughborough Pearson* (1979); J. M. Robinson, *The Wyatts: An Architectural Dynasty* (1979); J. Sheehy, *J. J. McCarthy and the Gothic Revival in Ireland* (Belfast 1977) and *The Rediscovery of Ireland's Past . . . 1830–1930* (1980); F. M. L. Thompson, ed., *The Rise of Suburbia* (Leicester 1982); J. Unrau, *Looking at Architecture with Ruskin* (1978).

ADDITIONS TO THE BIBLIOGRAPHY (1993)

J. Allibone, *A. Salvin* (1988) and *G. Devey* (Cambridge 1991); J. Bassin, *Architectural Competitions in 19th C. England* (Ann Arbor, 1984); British Architectural Library (RIBA), *Directory of British Architects: 1834–1900* (1993); R. Brigden, *Victorian Farms* (Bodmin 1986); C. Brooks, *Signs for the Times* (1984) and *Mortal Remains: the Victorian and Edwardian Cemetery* (Exeter 1989); M. W. Brooks, *John Ruskin and Victorian Architecture* (1989); D. B. Brownlee, *The Law Courts: The Architecture of G. E. Street* (Cambridge, Mass. 1984); J. Mordaunt Crook, *The Dilemma of Style, Architectural Ideas from the Picturesque to Post-Modern* (1987); J. Mordaunt Crook and C. A. Lennox-Boyd, *Axel Haig* (1984); C. Cunningham and P. Waterhouse, *A. Waterhouse* (Oxford 1992); J. S. Curl, *Victorian Architecture* (Newton Abbot 1990); intr. K. Downes, *The Architectural Outsiders* (1985); B. Elliott, *Victorian Gardens* (1986); R. H. Harper, *Victorian Architectural Competitions, An Index to British and Irish Architectural Competitions in* The Builder *1843–1900* (1983); J. Hatcher, *The Industrial Architecture of Yorkshire* (Chichester 1985); P. Howell and I. Sutton, eds, *Faber Guide to Victorian Churches* (1989); S. Jervis, *High Victorian Design* (Woodbridge 1983); Edgar Jones, *Industrial Architecture in Britain 1750–1939* (1985); H. Long, *The Edwardian House* (Manchester 1993); A. Mitchell, *T. Earp, Master of Stone* (Buckingham 1989); J. Orbach, *Blue Guide, Victorian Architecture in Britain* (1987); L. F. Pearson, *The People's Palaces: Britain's Seaside Pleasure Buildings 1870–1914* (Buckingham 1991); C. M. Smart, Jr., *Muscular Churches, Ecclesiastical Architecture of the High Victorian Period* (Fayetteville, Ark. 1989); G. Stamp and C. Amery, *Victorian Buildings of London 1837–1887* (1980); M. Stratton, *The Terracotta Revival* (1993); M. Swenarton, *Artisans and Architects: The Ruskinian Tradition in Architectural Thought* (1989); R. Thorne, *The Iron Revolution: Architects, Engineers and Structural Innovation* (1990); I. Toplis, *The Foreign Office, An Architectural History* (1987); G. Williams, *Augustus Pugin versus Decimus Burton: A Victorian Architectural Duel* (1990); N. Yates, *The Oxford Movement and Anglican Ritualism* (1983).

A short dictionary of architects

This is a selection of some of the more important Victorian architects and some of their works. Others are mentioned in the text, so the general index should be consulted first. A star (★) denotes a cross-reference, a dagger (†) demolition.

Adams, Maurice Bingham (1849–1933). *Worked for Sir William Emerson. Joined staff of 'Building News' 1872, later became architectural editor. Well known as a draughtsman.*
1881 †Bedford Pk, Mx.: Chiswick School of Art; 1896–8 London: Passmore Edwards Art Gallery, Camberwell; 1899 Acton, Mx.: Passmore Edwards Library.
Aitchison, George, sen. (d. 1861). *Architect to St Katharine Dock Co. and London and Birmingham Railway Co.*
1838 Tring, Herts.: station; 1852 London: 'I' Warehouse (Ivory House), St Katharine Dock.
Aitchison, George, jun. (1825–1910). *Travelled abroad with W. Burges★. Partner of father (above) 1859. Professor of architecture at R.A. 1887–1905. RIBA President 1896–9. RIBA Gold Medal 1898.*
In London: 1864–5 Nos. 59–61 Mark Lane; 1865ff. Leighton House, Kensington; 1877–8 Founders' Hall, St Swithin's Lane; 1885 Royal Exchange Assurance Co. offices, Pall Mall.
Aldridge and Deacon. See Deacon.
Allom, Thomas (1804–72). *Articled to Francis Goodwin. Noted architectural draughtsman. Partner of H. F..Lockwood★ in Hull.*
1850s London: work on the N. part of Ladbroke Estate, Kensington (e.g. Lansdowne Rd 1850–55); 1855 London: St Peter, Kensington Pk Rd; 1857 Liverpool: William Brown Library and Museum (altered); 1864 Harwich, Essex: Town Hall (former Gt Eastern Hotel). *See also Lockwood.*
Anderson, Sir Robert Rowand (1834–1921). *Worked under Sir G. G. Scott★. Knighted 1902. RIBA Gold Medal 1916.*
1866–78 Edinburgh: All Saints; 1873–94 Edinburgh: Catholic Apostolic Church; 1875–97 Edinburgh: Medical School and McEwan Hall, University; 1877ff. Mount Stuart,

Bute (for Marquis of Bute); 1882 Edinburgh: Conservative Club, Princes St; 1884 Glasgow: Central Station Hotel; 1885–90 Edinburgh: National Portrait Gallery; 1891–2 Edinburgh: Free Church, Morningside (south).
Andrews, George Townsend (1804–55).
1840 York: Yorkshire Insurance, St Helen's Sq.; 1840–42 York: former Station; 1844 York: St Leonard's Pl. (Cres.) (with P. F. Robinson); 1845 Scarborough, Yorks.: station; 1846–9 Hull: Paragon Station and Hotel; 1849 Newton-upon-Ouse, Yorks.: All Saints; 1849 Richmond, Yorks.: Richmond School; 1853 Flaxton-on-the-Moor, Yorks.: St Lawrence; 1853 York: Station Hotel.
Ashbee, Charles Robert (1863–1942). *Articled to Bodley★ and Garner★. Founded Guild and School of Handicraft 1888. Moved to Chipping Campden, Glos., 1902. Architect, designer and writer, Arts and Crafts ideologist.*
In London: 1894 †Magpie and Stump House, 37 Cheyne Walk; 1897 †Nos. 72–4 Cheyne Walk; 1899 Nos. 38–9 Cheyne Walk.
Ashlin, G. C. See E. W. Pugin.
Ashpitel, Arthur (1807–69). *Writer on baths, washhouses, etc.*
In London: 1845–51 St Barnabas, Homerton High St; 1853 †Lambeth Baths (with J. Whichcord★).
Austin. Hubert James. See Paley.
Baines, George. *Worked later with his son **Reginald Palmer B.** (d. 1962). Specialist in Nonconformist commissions.*
1874 Accrington, Lancs.: Baptist Church; 1901–3 London: Muswell Hill Presbyterian Church; 1903 Little Ilford, Essex: Congregational Church.
Baird, John, 'No. 1' (1798–1859). *No relation to the lesser known John Baird 'No. 2' (for whom see A. Thomson).*
Later work: 1855 Glasgow: Gardner's warehouse, 36 Jamaica St.
Ball, J. H. (1861–1931). *Pupil of A. Waterhouse★.*
1891 Eastleigh, Hants: Parish Hall, Grantham Rd; 1893–5 Portsmouth: St Agatha, Landport (decoration by Heywood Sumner); 1896 Hindhead, Surrey: Undershaw House (for Conan Doyle).
Barbour, James (1835–1912).

In Dumfries: 1877 Nos. 24–36 Buccleuch St; 1877 Militia Barracks, 109–13 English St.
Barclay, Hugh (1828–92). *Pupil of W. Spence. Partner of brother, **David B.** (1846–1917), a school specialist.*
1858 †Glasgow: Ewing Pl. Church; 1886 Glasgow: St George's in the Fields; 1881–9 Greenock: Municipal Buildings; 1891–1901 Glasgow: Coats Thread Agency, Bothwell St; 1899 Glasgow: Hunter Barr's, Queen St.
Barnes, Frederick, *of Ipswich, Suffolk.*
1847–9 Stations on Ipswich–Bury St Edmunds line, Suffolk, e.g. Stowmarket and Needham Market.
Barry, Sir Charles (1795–1860). *RIBA Gold Medal 1850. See p. 12.*
1824–8 Brighton: St Peter, Victoria Gdns; 1824–35 Manchester: City Art Gallery; 1829–32 London: Travellers' Club, Pall Mall; 1833–7 †Birmingham: King Edward VI School (ornament by Pugin); 1834–42 †Trentham Hall, Staffs.; 1834–57 Bowood House, Wilts., alterations and additions; 1835 London: Royal College of Surgeons, Lincoln's Inn Fields; 1835–9 Kingston Lacy, Dorset, alterations; 1837–9 Manchester: Athenaeum; 1837–9 Manchester: Unitarian Chapel, Upper Brook St; 1837–41 London: Reform Club, Pall Mall; 1835 (competition), 1837–67 London: Houses of Parliament (ornament by Pugin); 1838–43 London: Lancaster House, alterations; 1841 London: Pentonville Prison façade; 1842 Highclere Castle, Hants, alterations; 1843–5 Hurstpierpoint, Sx.: Holy Trinity; 1844–50 Dunrobin Castle, Sutherland; 1845ff. London: Board of Trade (also known as Treasury), Whitehall; 1847–57 London: Bridgewater House, St James's; 1849–54 Shrubland Park, Suffolk, alterations and additions; c.1850 Kiddington Hall, Oxon., remodelling; 1850–51 Cliveden, Bucks.; 1854–5 Canford Manor, Dorset, additions; 1855 Dowlais, Glam.: schools; 1859–63 Halifax Town Hall.
Barry, Charles, jun. (1823–1900). *Eldest son and pupil of above. Partner of Robert Richardson Banks (1813–72) 1847–72. RIBA President 1876–9. RIBA Gold Medal 1877.*
1849–51 Bylaugh Hall, Norfolk;

1866–70 London: Dulwich College; 1868–82 London: St Stephen, Dulwich; 1869–73 London: Burlington House, Piccadilly front, 1869–74 Stevenstone House, Devon (partly †).

Barry, Edward Middleton (1830–80). *Third son of Sir Charles B.★ In office of T. H. Wyatt★ before joining his father, whose practice he took over in 1860. Professor of Architecture at King's College, London, 1873–80. R.A.*
1855, 1863 †Birmingham: Birmingham and Midland Institute; 1856 London: St Saviour, Hampstead; 1857 London: Royal Opera House, Covent Gdn; 1857–8 London: Floral Hall, Covent Gdn; 1860 London: National Schools, Endell St; 1861 †London: Cannon St Station Hotel; 1864 Richmond, Surrey: Mansion Hotel (now Star and Garter, renamed after destruction of Phipps's★); 1864 London: Charing Cross Station Hotel: 1866–71 Crewe Hall, Ches.; 1870–75 Cambridge: staircase in Fitzwilliam Museum; 1871–4 Wykehurst Park, nr. Slaugham, Sx.

Basevi, George (1794–1845). *Pupil of Soane. Fell to his death while inspecting the W. tower of Ely Cathedral.*
1837ff. Cambridge: Fitzwilliam Museum; 1839–41 Twickenham, Middlesex: Holy Trinity; 1843–5 London: Conservative Club, St James's (with S. Smirke★); 1845–6 Eye, Hunts.: St Matthew.

Batterbury, Thomas (d. 1922), *in partnership with Huxley.*
1877 London: houses in Hampstead Hill Gdns; 1894 †Warnham, Surrey: Warnham Lodge.

Bazalgette, Sir Joseph William (1819–91).
In London: 1858–75 Metropolitan Drainage System, including Crossness Sewage Works (1865) and Abbey Mills Pumping Station (1867); 1862–74 Thames Embankment; 1884–7 Hammersmith Bridge.

Beattie, William Hamilton (1840–98).
In Edinburgh: 1865 Paper warehouse, W. Register St; 1893–5 Jenners Department Store, 47–52 Princes St; 1896–1900 North British Hotel, Princes St; 1898 Carlton Hotel, North Bridge.

Beckett, Sir Edmund, see Grimthorpe.

Belcher, John (1841–1913). *Son and pupil of John B., a London architect and surveyor. Partner of father 1865ff., and of J. J. Joass 1905ff. RIBA President 1904–6. RIBA Gold Medal 1907. R.A. 1909.*
1870 London: Mappin and Webb, Poultry (with his father); 1885 †London: Rylands and Sons warehouses, Wood St; 1888, 1890–93 London: Institute of Chartered Accountants, Great Swan Alley; 1894 Wargrave, Berks.: Convent of the

Good Shepherd; 1897–8 Pangbourne, Berks · Pangbourne Tower; 1898–1902 Colchester Town Hall.

Bellamy, Pearson, *of Lincoln. Partner of J. Spence Hardy c. 1855ff.*
1854 Louth, Lincs.: Town Hall; 1854 Spalding, Lincs.: Old Corn Exchange; 1856 Hull: Corn Exchange (now Transport Museum); 1863 Grimsby, Lincs.: Town Hall; 1864 E. Retford Town Hall; 1867 Ipswich Town Hall; 1880 Lincoln: Corn Exchange.

Bentley, John Francis (1839–1902). *Pupil of Clutton★. Converted to Roman Catholicism in 1862.*
1861 London: St Francis of Assisi (R.C.), Notting Hill (begun by Clutton); 1875–88 London: Convent of the Sacred Heart (R.C.), Hammersmith; 1883, 1900 Watford, Herts.: Holy Rood (R.C.); 1885 London: Corpus Christi (R.C.), Brixton; 1886–8 Old Windsor, Berks.: St John's Preparatory School, Beaumont; 1895–1903 London: Westminster Cathedral (R.C.).

Bidlake, William Henry (1862–1938). *Pupil of Bodley★ and Garner★.*
In Birmingham: 1892–9 St Oswald, Small Heath; 1899 Branch School of Art, Moseley Rd; 1898–1901 St Agatha's Church and Vicarage, Sparkbrook; 1901 Garth House, Edgbaston Pk Rd, Edgbaston; 1904 Bishop Latimer Church, Handsworth.

Billings, Robert William (1813–74). *Architectural draughtsman, antiquarian and restorer. Pupil of John Britton.*
1854 Crosby-on-Eden, Cumb.: St John the Evangelist; 1859 Dalziel Castle, nr Motherwell, Lanark, restoration.

Blanc, Hippolyte Jean (1844–1917). *Pupil of R. Matheson★.*
1876–9 Edinburgh: Mayfield North Church; 1885–9 Paisley: Coats Memorial Church; 1886 Edinburgh: Edinburgh Café, 70–71 Princes St; 1903 Edinburgh: 60 Princes St.

Blomfield, Sir Arthur William (1829–99). *Son of the Bishop of London. Pupil of P. C. Hardwick★. Knighted 1889. RIBA Gold Medal 1891. One of his early pupils was Thomas Hardy.*
1859–60 London: St Paul, Shoreditch; 1861 Torquay, Devon: St Luke; 1863–4 Windsor, Berks.: All Saints; 1880–81 London: All Saints, Fulham; 1882–9 Cambridge: Selwyn College; 1884–9 Portsmouth: St Mary, Portsea; 1890–94 London: Royal College of Music.

Blore, Edward (1787–1879). *Son of a Derbyshire antiquary. Began his career illustrating topographical and architectural books.*
1838–44 Merevale Hall, Warw.; 1840–45 †Worsley Hall, Lancs.; 1842–3 London: St James the Great, Bethnal Grn; 1843–7 London: chapel, St Mark's College, Chelsea; c.1844–50

Marlborough College, Wilts.; 1846–7 London: Buckingham Palace, E. front.

Blount, Gilbert Robert.
1858 Bromsgrove, Worcs.: St Peter (R.C.); 1860–68 Gloucester: St Peter (R.C.), London St.

Bodley, George Frederick (1827–1907). *Related to Sir G. G. Scott★ and trained in his office. Partner of Thomas Garner★ 1869–97. RIBA Gold Medal 1899.*
1855–7 France Lynch, Glos.: St John the Baptist; 1858–62 Brighton: St Michael; 1859–62 Selsley, Glos.: All Saints; 1861–3 Scarborough, Yorks.: St Martin; 1863 Dedworth, Berks.: All Saints; 1863–5 Hayward's Heath, Sx.: St Wilfred; 1863–9 Cambridge: All Saints; 1865–70 Dundee: St Saviour; 1867 Scarborough, Yorks.: St Martin's vicarage; 1868–70 Liverpool: St John the Baptist, Tue Brook; 1870–74 Pendlebury, Lancs.: St Augustine; 1872–6 Hoar Cross, Staffs.: Holy Angels; 1883–4 Cardiff: St Germain, Roath; 1884–91 Hewell Grange, Worcs.; 1886–9 Clumber, Notts.: church; 1889, 1908–9 Epping, Essex: St John the Baptist; 1890–91 Cambridge: Queens' College Chapel; 1894–9 Eccleston, Ches.: St Mary; 1902 London: Holy Trinity, Prince Consort Rd; 1906ff. Washington, D.C.: Cathedral of SS. Peter and Paul.

Botterill, William.
In Hull: 1865–6 Exchange (now Royal Insurance), Low St; c.1880 Beverley Rd Board school; 1889 Hymers College, Hymers Ave.

Boucher and Cousland: *James Boucher (1832–92), in partnership with James Cousland (c. 1832–66).*
In Glasgow: 1857 †Renfield Free Church, Bath St; 1864 †St George's Free Church, Elderslie St; 1875 Teacher Building, 18 St Enoch Sq.; 1877 No. 998 Great Western Rd.

Bowman and Crowther: *Henry Bowman (1814–81), of Manchester in partnership with Joseph Stretch Crowther (1832–93).*
1846–8 Hyde, Ches.: Unitarian Church, Stockport Rd; 1847–8 Leeds: Mill Hill Unitarian Chapel, Park Row; 1856–8 Manchester: St Mary, Hulme; 1857–64 Manchester: St Alban, Cheetham; 1871–6 Bury, Lancs.: St Mary; 1873–6 Manchester: St Wilfrid, Northenden.

Boyce, Philip.
1856 Barnsley, Yorks.: St John; 1858–9 Maltby, Yorks.: St Bartholomew.

Brakspear, William Hayward (1818/19–98), *of Manchester.*
1863–5 Blackburn, Lancs.: Exchange (now cinema).

Brandon, David (1813–97). *Studied at R.A. Schools. Partner of T. H. Wyatt★ 1838–51.*
1840–46 Wilton, Wilts.: SS Mary and Nicholas (with Wyatt); 1846–7 London: 16 Kensington Palace Gdns

(with Wyatt); 1853–6 Colesbourne House, Glos.; 1854 Wallingford, Berks.: St Mary; 1866 †London: Junior Carlton Club, Pall Mall; 1879 Sidbury Manor, Devon.

Brandon, Raphael (1817–77). *Not related to above. Worked with his brother* **Joshua Arthur B.** *(1821–47); with him pub. 'An Analysis of Gothick Architecture' (1844, 1847).*
1844–5 Epsom, Surrey: Croydon and Epsom Atmospheric Railway Station; 1851–5 London: Christ the King (former Catholic Apostolic Church), Gordon Sq. (unfinished); 1858–60 Datchet, Bucks.: St Mary.

Brodrick, Cuthbert (1822–1905). *Trained with H. F. Lockwood*★.
1853–8 Leeds Town Hall; 1860 Ilkley, Yorks.: Hydropathic Establishment (now College of Housecraft); 1861–3 Leeds: Corn Exchange; 1862 †Hull: Town Hall (parts reused in memorial at Brantingham, Yorks.); 1863–7 Scarborough, Yorks.: Grand Hotel; 1865 Leeds: Mechanics' Institute (now Art School); 1866 †Leeds: Turkish Baths, Cookridge St.

Brooks, James (1825–1901). *Son of a Berkshire farmer. Influenced by Pusey. Moved to London 1847. Pupil of Lewis Stride; entered R.A. Schools 1849. Set up practice 1851. RIBA Gold Medal 1895.*
1856 Henley-on-Thames, Oxon.: parish school; 1860 Wantage, Berks.: Baptist Chapel; 1861–2 London: The Grange, 42 Clissold Cres., Stoke Newington; 1863–5 London: St Michael, Shoreditch; 1864 Headington Quarry, Oxon.: parish school; 1865–6 †London: St Saviour, Hoxton; 1867–70 Plaistow, Essex: St Andrew; 1868–9 London: St Chad, Haggerston; 1868–9 London: St Columba, Kingsland Rd; 1868–70 Chislehurst, Kent: Annunciation; 1871–2 Wolstanton, Staffs.: National Schools; 1872ff. London: St John the Baptist, Holland Rd; 1872 Mortomley, Yorks.: St Saviour; 1875 Kiltegan, Wicklow, Ireland: W. W. F. Hume Dick Mausoleum; 1875–6 Marston Meysey, Wilts.: St James; 1876ff. London: Ascension, Lavender Hill; 1877–8 Doune, Perth: St Modoc; 1880–86 London: Transfiguration, Lewisham; 1883–5 St Leonard's-on-Sea, Sx.: St Peter; 1889–1901 London: Holy Innocents, Hammersmith; 1891–3 Dover, Kent: SS. Peter and Paul; 1892ff. London: All Hallows, Gospel Oak.

Brown, John (1805–76), *of Norwich. Norfolk County Surveyor from 1835.*
1835 Stamford, Lincs.: St Michael; 1836 Norwich: Bignold's Yarn Mill (now Jarrolds), Cow Gate; 1836 Swainthorpe, Norfolk: workhouse (Vale Hospital); 1839–41 London: St Margaret, Lee Ter., Lewisham (altered by J. Brooks★); 1841 Norwich: Christ Church, New Catton; 1843 Bridgwater, Som.: St John, Eastover.

Browne, Sir George Washington (1853–1939). *Pupil of Sellars*★. *Worked with Stevenson*★, *Blomfield*★, *Nesfield*★ *and Anderson*★.
1887–9 Edinburgh: Central Library; 1892 †Edinburgh: Redfern's shop, Princes St; 1897 Glasgow: Miss Cranston's Tea Rooms (now Clydesdale Bank), 91 Buchanan St; 1905 Edinburgh: British Linen Bank, 69 George St.

Brunel, Isambard Kingdom (1806–59). *Engineer and entrepreneur, especially of the Great Western Railway Line.*
1829 Bristol: Clifton Suspension Bridge; 1837 Bristol: Great Western Hotel (with R. S. Pope★); 1838 Maidenhead, Berks.: railway bridge; 1839–40 Bristol: Temple Meads Station (see also M. D. Wyatt); 1852–4 London: Paddington Station (with M. D. Wyatt).

Bryce, David (1803–76). *Pupil of Burn*★, *then his partner 1841–50.*
1841 Edinburgh: Edinburgh and Leith (now Clydesdale) Bank; 1846–51 Edinburgh: British Linen Bank, St Andrew's Sq.; 1846 †Edinburgh: Western Bank (later Scottish Widows' Fund), St Andrew's Sq.; 1854 †Farnell, Angus: Kinnaird Castle, reconstruction; 1855, 1875 Innerleithen, Peebles: The Glen; 1857 Edinburgh: Queen's Theatre; 1864 Lockerbie, Dumfries: Castlemilk; 1864–70 Edinburgh: Bank of Scotland; 1868 Dublin: Post Office, College Grn; 1870–79 Edinburgh: Infirmary; 1874–8 Edinburgh: Union Bank (now Bank of Scotland), 62–6 George St.

Bryce, John (c. 1805–51).
1835 Glasgow: Necropolis, Cathedral Sq.

Brydon, John McKean (1840–1901). *Trained under D. Bryce*★ *in Edinburgh. Assistant to Shaw*★ *and Nesfield*★.
1883 Pickhurst, nr Chiddingfold, Surrey; 1885–7 London: Chelsea Town Hall; 1891–5 London: Chelsea Polytechnic; 1898–1912 London, Government Offices, Parliament Sq.

Buckeridge, Charles (1832/3–73). *Pupil of Sir G. G. Scott*★.
1865–8 Oxford: Holy Trinity Convent (now St Anthony's College).

Buckler, Charles Alban (1824–1905). *Son of J.C.B.*★
1858 Stroud, Glos.: Our Lady of the Immaculate Conception (R.C.); 1874 London: St Dominic's Priory (R.C.), Southampton Rd, Hampstead; 1890–1903 Arundel Castle, Sx., rebuilding.

Buckler, John Chessell (1793–1894). *Antiquarian writer and church restorer. Son of* **John B.** *(1770–1851), the architectural draughtsman.*
Later works: 1845 Butleigh Court, nr Glastonbury, Som.; 1847 Wisbech, Cambs.: Museum; 1849–51 Oxford:

Choristers Hall, Magdalen College (now Library); 1854–6 Oxford: Turl St front of Jesus College.

Bucknall, Benjamin (c. 1833–c. 1895). *Translator of some of the writings of Viollet-le-Duc.*
1858 Abergavenny, Mon.: Our Lady and St Michael (R.C.); c. 1858 Woodchester Park, Glos.; 1861 Taunton, Som.: St George (R.C.); 1868 Swansea, Seamen's Church.

Bunning, John Bunstone (1802–63). *Son and pupil of a London surveyor. Architect to the City of London 1843–63.*
In London: 1844 chapels and lodges, Nunhead Cemetery; 1847–9 †Coal Exchange; 1849–52 †Holloway Prison; 1855 †Caledonian Market, Islington.

Burges, William (1827–81). *Son of a civil engineer. Trained first as an engineer, then with Blore*★ *and M. D. Wyatt*★. *See pp. 44, 214.*
1855 design for Lille Cathedral (unexecuted); 1857 design for Crimean Memorial Church, Constantinople (unexecuted); 1859–60 Gayhurst House, Bucks., additions; 1861–2 Fleet, Hants.: All Saints; 1863ff. Cork, Ireland: St Finn Bar Cathedral; 1866 London: warehouse, 46 Upper Thames St; 1867 Lowfield Heath, Surrey: St Michael; 1868–81 Cardiff Castle; 1869–71 Knightshayes Court, Devon; 1871–2 Skelton, Yorks.: Christ Church; 1871–8 Studley Royal, Yorks.: St Mary; 1873–80 Hartford, Conn., U.S.A.: Trinity College; 1875–81 Castell Coch, Glam.; 1876–81 London: Tower House (own house), 9 Melbury Rd.

Burn, William (1789–1870). *Son of the Scottish architect Robert B. Pupil of R. Smirke*★. *Took over his father's practice c. 1820. Partner of D. Bryce*★ *in Edinburgh until 1844, then moved to London and set up on his own. Later in partnership with J. Macvicar Anderson.*
1838–55 Harlaxton Manor, Lincs., additions; 1839–41 Stoke Rochford Hall, Lincs.; 1851–3 Buchanan House, Stirling; 1856 Fonthill Abbey, Wilts. (for Marquis of Westminster); 1857–9 †London: Montague House, Whitehall Gdns.

Burnet, Frank (1848–1923),· and **W. J. Boston** (1861–1937).
In Glasgow: 1898 St Vincent Chambers, St Vincent Pl.; 1898 Castle Chambers, Renfield and W. Regent Sts; 1900 St George's Rd/Woodlands Rd junction; 1906 Gordon Chambers, Mitchell St.

Burnet, John (1814–1901).
In Glasgow: 1856 Elgin Pl. Congregational Church, Bath St; 1870–73 Clydesdale Bank, St Vincent Pl.; 1874 Stock Exchange.

Burnet, Sir John James (1857–1938). *Worked first with his father (above), then 1885–98 with John Archibald Campbell (1859–1909).*
Early works: 1876 Glasgow: Lanark-

shire House, Ingram St; 1879–80 †Glasgow: Fine Art Institute, Sauchiehall St; 1886 Glasgow: Barony Church, Castle St; 1890 Dumbarton: Garmoyle House (with Campbell); 1891 Glasgow: Athenaeum (now Music Academy), St George's Pl.; 1891 Glasgow: Charing Cross Mansions, Sauchiehall St; 1894 Glasgow: Savings Bank, Ingram St; 1896–1900 Brechin: Garner Memorial Church; 1897 Glasgow: Albany Chambers, Sauchiehall St; 1899 Glasgow: Atlantic Chambers, 43–7 Hope St; 1904–14 London: British Museum, King Edward VII Wing.

Burton, Decimus (1800–81). *Tenth son of James B., the architect. Trained in his father's office and with George Maddox.*

1828–52 Tunbridge Wells, Kent: Calverley Estate; 1829–30 London: Athenaeum Club, Pall Mall; 1835–43 Fleetwood, Lancs.: Northpier, St Peter, and hotel; 1837–9 Eastbourne, Sx.: Holy Trinity; 1844–8 Kew Gdns, Surrey: Palm House; 1845–6 †London: Winter Gdn, Regent's Pk (with R. Turner); 1856–7 London: museum, Kew Gdns; 1860 London: Temperate House, Kew Gdns (date of design).

Bury, Thomas Talbot (1811–77). *Pupil of A. Pugin. Assisted A. W. N. Pugin★ and O. Jones★ with engravings for their books. Partner of Charles Lee 1845–9.*

1837 Chipperfield, Herts.: St Paul; 1852–5 Welford, Berks.: St Gregory; 1861–3 Burgess Hill, Sx.: St John; 1864–7 E. Molesey, Surrey: St Mary.

Butterfield, William (1814–1900). *Son of a London chemist. Pupil of E. L. Blackburne 1833–6. Worked for W. and H. Inwood. Set up own practice in 1840. From 1842 involved with Cambridge Camden Society, contributing designs to 'The Ecclesiologist' and illustrations to 'Instrumenta Ecclesiastica'. RIBA Gold Medal 1884.*

1842 Bristol: Highbury Chapel; 1844–5 Coalpit Heath, Glos.: St Saviour and vicarage; 1844–73 Canterbury, Kent: St Augustine's College; 1848–9 Yealmpton, Devon: St Bartholomew, rebuilding; 1849 Alfington, Devon: SS. James and Anne; 1849–50 Ottery St Mary, Devon: St Mary, restoration; 1849–51 Cumbrae, Bute: Cathedral of the Isles; 1849 (planned), 1850–59 London: All Saints, Margaret St, with vicarage and choir school; 1850ff. Plymouth: St Dunstan's Abbey; 1853–6 Milton Ernest Hall, Beds.; 1853–4 Wykeham, Yorks.: All Saints, with vicarage and school; 1853–4 Cowick, Hensall, Pollington (Balne), Yorks.: churches, vicarages and schools; 1854–5 Braishfield, Hants: All Saints; 1854–5 Langley, nr Maidstone, Kent: church and school; 1854–6 Milton, nr Banbury, Oxon.: St Mary; 1854–7 Oxford: Balliol College Chapel; 1855–7 Waresley, Hunts.: St

James; 1855ff. Baldersby St James, Yorks.: church (1855–7), vicarage and school (1857), and cottages (about 1855); 1856–8 Etal, Northumb.: St Mary; 1856–60 Bamford, Derbys.: church; c. 1857 Trumpington, Cambs.: school house; c. 1858 St Mawgan-in-Pydar, Corn.: rectory; 1858–84 Rugby School, Warw.: additions including chapel (1870–72); 1859–62 London: St Alban, Holborn (only B.'s tower survives); 1859–64 Castle Hill, Devon: school; 1863–8 Winchester: Royal Hampshire County Hospital; 1864–6 Penarth, Glam.: St Augustine; 1865–6 Dropmore, Bucks.: St Anne; 1865–8 Elerch, Card.: church; 1865–74 Babbacombe, Devon: All Saints; 1867–83 Oxford: Keble college; 1870–77 London: St Augustine, Queen's Gate; 1876–91 Belfast: St Mark Dundela; 1877–87 Exeter, Devon: Grammar School; 1877–91 Melbourne, Australia: St Paul's Anglican Cathedral; 1878 Axebridge, Devon: St Michael's Home; 1880–83 Ottery St Mary, Devon: The Chanter's House.

Byrne, Patrick (1783–1864).

In Dublin: 1835–7 St Paul (R.C.), Arran Quay; 1841–6 St Audoen (R.C.), High St; 1850 Rathmines Parish Church (R.C.).

Caröe, William Douglas (1857–1938). *Son of Danish Consul. Pupil of Pearson★. Worked for Ecclesiastical Commissioners. Partner of J. H. Christian and later of Herbert Passmore.*

1889–90 Huyton, Lancs.: Congregational Church; 1890–94 Liverpool: Martins Bank, Brunswick/Castle St; 1897–1900 Exeter, Devon: St David; 1903 London: Church Commissioners' offices, 1 Millbank.

Carpenter, Richard Cromwell (1812–55). *Articled to John Blyth. Friend of A. W. N. Pugin★. Closely associated with the Cambridge Camden Society. Worked with W. Slater★.*

1838–42 London: Lonsdale Sq., Islington; 1844–6 Birmingham: St Andrew, Bordesley; 1846–8 Brighton: St Paul; 1848 Chichester, Sx.: St Peter; 1849–52 London: St Mary Magdalene, Munster Sq.; 1851–3 Hurstpierpoint, Sx.: St John's College; 1852 Bovey Tracey, Devon: St John; 1854–6 Burntisland, Fife: parsonage, and design for St Stephen and school (unbuilt); 1854ff. Lancing College, Sx.

Carpenter, Richard Herbert (1841–93). *Son of above. Pupil of W. Slater★ and afterwards his partner. Later, partner of Benjamin Ingelow.*

1864 Ardingly College, Sx. (with Slater); 1868ff. Lancing College, Sx.: chapel; 1876–83 Ellesmere, Salop.: Ellesmere College (with Ingelow); 1879–87 Denstone, Staffs.: Denstone College Chapel (with Ingelow).

Cawston, Arthur (1857–94).

1883–4 London: Ascension Church and vicarage, Malwood Rd, Balham;

1887–9 Carlisle: Market, Fisher St (with J. Graham); 1886–90 Bromley, Kent: St Luke, Bromley Common.

Chamberlain, John Henry (1831–83). *Pupil of H. Goddard of Leicester. In Italy 1856. Strongly influenced by Ruskin; trustee of Ruskin's St George's Guild. Partner of W. Martin★ 1864–83. Designed 41 Birmingham Board schools 1873–98.*

In Birmingham: 1856 †Nos 28–9 Union St; c. 1858 Eld House, Ampton/Carpenter Rds, Edgbaston; 1870 St Stephen, Serpentine Hill, Selly Oak; c. 1870–80 Longbridge Pumping Station; 1873 St Cyprian, Acock's Grn; c. 1875 School Board Offices (now City Treasurer's Dept), Edmund St; 1877 Oozells St School (now Food and Domestic Arts College); 1877 †The Grove, Harborne (interior, 'Harborne Room', in Victoria and Albert Museum, London); 1879 Highbury, Yew Tree Rd, King's Heath; 1880 Chamberlain Memorial, Chamberlain Sq.; 1880–82 †Central Library; 1881 †Midland Institute, Paradise St, additions; 1881–5, 1893 School of Art (now College of Arts and Crafts); 1883 Library, Constitution Hill. *See also W. Martin.*

Champneys, Basil (1842–1935). *Son of the Dean of Lichfield. Articled to Prichard★. RIBA Gold Medal 1912.*

1868–70 London: St Luke, Kentish Town; 1873 London: Harewood Rd School, Fulham; 1875–1935 Cambridge: Newnham College; 1878–9 Cambridge: Selwyn Divinity School; 1878–82 Bedford: Girls' High School; 1883–96 Oxford: Indian Institute; 1886 Harrow, Mx.: Butler Museum, Harrow School; 1890–99 Manchester: John Rylands Library.

Chantrell, Robert Dennis (1793–1872). *Pupil of Soane.*

In Leeds: 1823–5 Christ Church, Meadow Lane; 1841 St Paul, Shadwell; 1839–41 parish church of St Peter.

Chatwin, Julius Alfred (1829–1907). *Pupil of Sir C. Barry★.*

In Birmingham: 1864 Lloyds Bank, Temple Row; 1868–76 St Augustine, Lyttelton Rd, Edgbaston; 1871 †Lloyds Bank, Colmore Row; 1879 SS. Peter and Paul, Aston; 1883 St Philip's Cathedral, chancel; 1883–5 Christ Church, Summerfield Cres., Winson Grn.

Christian, Ewan (1814–95). *Articled to M. Habershon★. Later worked with W. Railton★ and J. Brown★ of Norwich. Set up practice 1842. Architect and architectural adviser to Ecclesiastical Commissioners from 1850. RIBA President 1884–6. RIBA Gold Medal 1887.*

1858–60 Rochester, Kent: St Peter; 1865 Market Lavington, Wilts.: manor house; 1869–72 Leicester: St Mark; 1880 Scarborough, Yorks.: Holy Trinity; 1884–5 London: St Dionis, Ful-

255

ham; 1890–95 London: National Portrait Gallery. *See also J. Clarke.*

Clark, John K.
1844 Ipswich: Customs House.

Clarke, George Somers Leigh, sen. (1825–82), *Pupil of Sir C. Barry★. With J. Johnson, illustrated 'The New Palace of Westminster' (1849).*
1854–62 Cowley Manor, Glos.; 1860 †London: Printing and Publishing Co., W. Smithfield; 1861 Wanstead, Essex: Merchant Seamen's Orphan Asylum; 1866 London, General Credit and Discount Co. (now Overseas Bankers' Club), Lothbury; 1872–6 Wyfold Court, Oxon.

Clarke, George Somers, jun. (1841–1926). *Son of the Town Clerk of Brighton and nephew of G. S. Clarke sen.★ Pupil of Sir G. G. Scott★. Partner of J. T. Micklethwaite★ 1876–92. Surveyor of St Paul's Cathedral 1896–1906.*
1871–5 Brighton: St Martin; 1887 Ardington, Berks.: Holy Trinity.

Clarke, Joseph (1819–88). *Pub. 'Schools and School-Houses' (1852). Diocesan Architect for Canterbury, Rochester, St Albans.*
1840 Burwood, Surrey: Mental Hospital; 1851–2 Bishops Stortford, Herts.: Hockerill Training College; 1852 Culham, Oxon.: Teachers' Training College; 1852–4 Cockermouth, Cumb.: All Saints; 1869 †London: Architectural Museum and Architectural Association building, 18 Tufton St (with E. Christian★). *See also Underwood.*

Clarke, Thomas Chatfeild (1829–95).
In London: 1862 †Unity (Unitarian) Church, Upper St, Islington; 1869 No. 25 Throgmorton St; 1877 Nos 3–5 Bishopsgate; 1880 Nos 66–7 Cornhill; 1889 Nos 385–97 Oxford St; 1891 Central Foundation School for Girls, Stepney; *c.* 1897 Nos 77–8 Gracechurch St.

Clarke, William (*c.* 1812–89), and **George Bell** (1814–97). *Pupils of Burn★ and D. Bryce★.*
1842–71 Glasgow: City and County Buildings, Wilson St.

Clutton, Henry (1819–93). *Pupil of Blore★. Friend of Burges★, with whom he won first place in the Lille Cathedral competition in 1856. Converted to Roman Catholicism in 1856. Not to be confused with Henry Clutton (1814–95), architect and member of Ecclesiastical Commissioners Agency.*
1857 Quantock Lodge, Som.; 1858–62 Minley Manor, Hants (additions by Devey★); 1859–60 London: St Francis of Assisi (R.C.), Notting Hill (completed by Bentley★); 1860 Birmingham: Oratory cloisters; 1861–5 Leamington, Warw.: St Peter (R.C.); 1865–7 Tavistock, Devon: St Mary Magdalene (R.C.); 1865–8 Woburn, Beds.: St Mary; 1868 Apsley Heath, Beds.: St Michael.

Cockerell, Charles Robert (1788–1863). *Second son and pupil of S. P. Cockerell. Assistant to R. Smirke★ 1809. Travelled in Italy and Greece 1810–17. First recipient of RIBA Gold Medal 1848. RIBA President 1860.*
1836–42 Cambridge: University Library; 1837 †London: London and Westminster Bank, Lothbury; 1839–42 †London: Sun Fire and Life Assurance, Threadneedle St; 1840–41 Killerton Park, Devon, chapel; 1841–5 Oxford: Ashmolean Museum and Taylorian Institute; 1842–5 †Caversfield House, Oxon.; 1844–7 Bristol, Liverpool and Manchester: Bank of England branches; 1846–9 †Liverpool: Bank Chambers, Cook St; 1847–56 Liverpool: completion of St George's Hall; 1855–7 Liverpool: London and Globe Insurance, Dale St (with F. P. Cockerell).

Cockerell, Frederick Pepys (1833–78). *Son of above. Pupil of P. C. Hardwick★ 1854–5.*
1865–8 London: Highgate School; 1871–3 Down Hall, Essex; 1876 Woodcote Hall, Salop.; 1877 Crawley Hall, Hants.

Coe, Henry Edward (1825/6–85). *Pupil of Sir G. G. Scott★. Partners: H. H. Hofland, F. Peck of Cambridge, Goodwin, Stephen Robinson, Arthur Catt.*
1856 first prize in War Office Competition (unexecuted); 1861–2 London: Agricultural Hall, Islington (ironwork by Heaviside of Derby); 1862 Cambridge: Guildhall (now part of Public Library) (by Coe, Peck and Stevens).

Collcutt, Thomas Edward (1840–1924). *Worked in office of Street★. Set up practice 1873. Partner of Stanley Hamp. RIBA Gold Medal 1902.*
1877 Wakefield, Yorks.: Town Hall; 1887–93 London: Imperial Institute († except for tower); 1889 London: Savoy Hotel (altered); 1889 London: Royal English Opera House (now Palace Theatre); 1890 London: 45–7 Ludgate Hill; 1890 London: Wigmore Hall; 1892 Wraysbury Hall, Bucks.; 1895 Totteridge, Herts.: The Croft; 1900 London: Lloyd's Register of Shipping, Lloyds Ave./Fenchurch St.

Colling, James Kellaway (1816–1905). *Worked in offices of W. Brooks, M. Habershon★, J. Brown★ of Norwich, and Sir G. G. Scott★ and Moffatt. Pub. 'Gothic Ornaments' (1848–50).*
1856 Liverpool: Albany Building, Old Hall St; 1858–62 Hooton, Ches.: St Paul; 1861 Coxwold Hall, Lincs.

Corson, George (1829–1910).
In Leeds: 1869 Scottish Widows Assurance, Park Row; 1877 †Sun Buildings, Park Row; 1878–9 Grand Theatre; 1878–84 Municipal Buildings.

Cousin, David (1809–78). *Pupil of Playfair★.*

1841, 1854 Greenock: West (now Old) Kirk; 1847 †Edinburgh: Corn Exchange; 1858 Edinburgh: Reid School of Music; 1864 Edinburgh: India Buildings, Victoria St.

Crickmay, G. R. (1830–1907), *of Weymouth. Later joined by his son* **G. L. C.** *(1858–1921). (Thomas Hardy worked in their office 1869–72.) From the 1880s on the firm also had an office in London.*
1880 Dorchester, Dorset: Eldridge Pope Brewery, Weymouth Ave.; 1886 London: Horns Public House, Kennington; 1887 Salisbury: Church House, Crane St; 1887 Weymouth, Dorset: Holy Trinity; 1898 Lytchett Heath, Dorset: St Aldhelm.

Crossland, William H. (1823–1909). *Pupil of Sir G. G. Scott★.*
1861ff. Akroydon, Yorks., model town (in succession to Scott); 1861 Bradley, Yorks.: St Thomas; 1863–5 Copley, Yorks.: St Stephen; 1865 Ossett, Yorks.: Holy Trinity; 1866–71 Rochdale, Lancs.: Town Hall; 1871–84 Virginia Water, Surrey: Holloway Sanatorium; 1879–87 Egham, Surrey: Holloway College.

Crowther, Joseph Stretch. See Bowman.

Cubitt, Lewis (1799–1883). *Brother of Thomas and William C. Pupil of H. E. Kendall sen.★ Designed many of the houses built by his brothers.*
1841–3 London: houses on S. side of Lowndes Sq.; 1842–4 †London: Bricklayers' Arms Station, Bermondsey; 1851–2 London: King's Cross Station.

Cundy, Thomas II (1790–1867). *Son and pupil of* **Thomas Cundy I** *(1765–1825), whom he succeeded as surveyor of the Grosvenor Estates, London.*
In London: 1840–43 St Paul, Wilton Pl.; 1844–6 Holy Trinity, Paddington (partly †); 1846 St Michael, Chester Sq.

Cundy, Thomas III (1820–95). *Third son of above. Succeeded to his father's practice and surveyorship of the Grosvenor Estates.*
1868 London: Grosvenor Gdns, Grosvenor Pl., Belgrave Mansions; 1870 Park Place House, Berks.

Currey, Henry (1820–1900). *Pupil of D. Burton★.*
1852 Buxton, Derbys.: Baths (altered); 1859–61 †London: London Bridge Terminus Hotel; 1861 Buxton: Hardwick St Congregational Church; 1868–71 London: St Thomas's Hospital (partly †).
In Eastbourne, Sx., Duke of Devonshire's Estate: 1870, 1874, 1889 Eastbourne College; 1894–6 St Peter, Meads Rd.

Darbishire, Henry Astley. *Not to be confused with Alfred Darbyshire (1839–1908), of Manchester.*
In London: 1857–60 †Columbia Sq. flats, Bethnal Grn; 1861 Victoria Pk Fountain; 1862–4 Peabody flats, Com-

mercial St, Spitalfields; 1865 Peabody flats, Greenman St, Islington; 1865 Holly Village, Swain's Lane; 1866–8 †Columbia Market; 1881 Peabody flats, Wild St, Strand.

Daukes (not Dawkes), **Samuel Whitfield** (1811–80). *Articled to J. P. Pritchett of York. Practiced mainly in Gloucester and Cheltenham, specializing in railway stations and churches.*
1845–7 London: St Andrew, Wells St (re-erected at Kingsbury, Mx., 1933); 1846ff. Cirencester, Glos.: Royal Agricultural College; 1847–9 Cheltenham: St Peter; 1847–51 Colney Hatch, Mx.: Lunatic Asylum (now Friern Hospital); 1848 Tetbury, Glos.: St Saviour; 1850–52 Horsted Place, Sx.; 1851–2 London: Christ Church, Hampstead; 1855 Witley Court, Worcs. (gutted).

Davis, Henry David (1838/9–1915). *Later partner of Ernest R. Barrow Emmanuel (1868–1948).*
In London: 1870 Synagogue, Upper Berkeley St; 1879 City of London School for Boys, Victoria Embankment; c.1887 No. 63 St James's St (Mastersingers' Club).

Deacon, Charles E. (1844–1927). *Pupil of W. Emerson. Partner of Aldridge.*
In Liverpool: 1886–7 St Benedict, Everton; 1886–9 St Dunstan, Wavertree; 1898 City Education Offices, 14 St Thomas St.

Deane, Sir Thomas (1792–1871). *From Cork, Ireland. Mayor of Cork, knighted 1830. Partner of Benjamin Woodward (1815–61), and of his son* **Thomas Newenham D.** (1828–99), *who was knighted in 1890.*
1845–9 Cork: Queen's College (now University College).
With Woodward and T. N. D.: 1854–60 Dublin: Trinity College museum; 1855–60 Oxford: Museum of Natural History; 1855–8 †London: Crown Life Insurance Offices, Bridge St; 1856 †Llysdulas (house), nr Llanwennlyfo, Anglesey; 1856–7 Oxford: Union Society Rooms; 1858–61 Dublin: Kildare St Club; 1858–62 Kilkenny Castle, alterations.
By Thomas Newenham D.: 1861–4 Tuam, Galway: Cathedral (Church of Ireland); 1862–5 Oxford: Meadow Building, Christ Church.
By T.N.D. and his son **Thomas Manly D.:** 1885–90 Dublin: National Library and Museum.

Denison, Sir Edmund. See Grimthorpe.

Derick, John Macduff (d. 1861).
1839–45 Leeds: St Saviour (for Pusey); 1845 Manchester: St James, Danes Rd, Rusholme; 1846–9 Pensnett, Staffs.: St Mark.

Devey, George (1820–86). *See p. 50.*
1850 Penshurst, Kent: cottages by the church; 1856–82 Betteshanger House, Kent; 1861 Benenden, Kent: parish school; 1864 Wickwar, Glos.: Old

Rectory; c.1867–78 Akeley Wood, Bucks.; 1870, 1886 Gaunts House, Dorset; 1871–5 Denne Hill, Kent; 1871–6 Hall Place, Kent; 1871–7 Goldings, Herts.; 1874–8 St Alban's Court, Kent; 1874–88 Ascott, Bucks.; 1875–8 †Ashfold, Handcross, Sx.; 1876–9 Blakesware, Herts.; 1876–9 Eythrope, Bucks.; 1886 Minley Manor, Hants, additions.

Dobson, John (1787–1865).
Later works: 1831 Newcastle-upon-Tyne: Royal Arcade (attrib.); c.1834–40 Newcastle-upon-Tyne: E. side of Grey St (with Richard Grainger; see also J. Green and G. Walker); 1837 Warwick, Cumb.: Holme Eden Hall; 1837–41 Corbridge, Northumb.: Beaufront Castle; 1884 N. Shields Town Hall; 1846–65 Newcastle-upon-Tyne: Central Station; 1847 Newcastle-upon-Tyne: High Level Bridge (with R. Stephenson★); 1858 Otterburn, Northumb.: St John; 1858 Newcastle-upon-Tyne: Jesmond parish church; 1860 Sudbrooke, Lincs.: St Edward.

Dodgshun. See Unsworth.

Doll, Charles Fitzroy (1851–1929).
In London: 1898 Russell Hotel, Russell Sq.; 1905–11 †Imperial Hotel, Russell Sq.; 1907 Dillon's Bookshop block, Torrington Pl.

Donaldson, Thomas Leverton (1795–1885). *Son and pupil of James D. Studied at R.A. Schools under Soane. Travelled to Italy, Greece and Asia Minor with J. M. W. Turner. Co-founder of the Institute of British Architects 1835. First Professor of Architecture, University College, London, 1842–62. RIBA Gold Medal 1851. RIBA President 1863–4.*
1848 London: Dr Williams's Library, Gordon Sq.; 1848 London: University College, interior of Great Hall and Library; 1853 Leonards Lee (house), Sx.; 1865 London: German Hospital, Hackney.

Donthorn, William John (c.1799–1859).
Later works: c.1830–34 Highcliffe Castle, Hants; c.1844–50 Holkham Hall, Norfolk: Leicester Column.

Douglas, Campbell (1828–1910). *Pupil of Rochead★. Worked for Dobson★ in Newcastle. Partner of Stevenson★ and Sellars★.*
1858 Ayr: Alloway Church; 1859 †Glasgow: Briggate Free Church; 1859 †Cove, Scotland: Hartfield House.

Douglas, John (1829–1911), *of Chester. Pupil of E. G. Paley★. Partner of Fordham 1885, of Minshull 1898.*
1866 Aldford, Ches.: St John; 1867 Sandiway, Ches.: Oakmere Hall; 1868–70, 1909 Helsby, Ches.: St Paul; 1872 Great Sughall, Ches.: Shotwick Pk; 1873 Broxton Old Hall, Ches.; 1874 Whitegate, Ches.: St Mary; 1876 Moulton, Ches.: St Stephen; 1876, 1902 Chester: St Paul, Broughton;

1879 Hopwas, Staffs.: St Chad; 1881–4 Pulford, Ches.: St Mary; 1882 Eaton Hall, Ches.: Flemish Gateway; 1883 Eccleston, Ches.: The Paddocks; 1884 Wygfair House, Flints.; 1886 Over Wyresdale, Lancs.: Abbeystead House; 1891 Haydock, Lancs.: St James; 1892 The Wern House, Caernarvon; 1893 Glangwna House, Caernarvon; 1895–9 Chester: St Werburgh St; 1897 Chester: Dee Banks (own house); 1902 Sandiway, Ches.: St John the Evangelist.

Doyle, J. Francis (1840/41–1913). *Worked with Shaw★ in Liverpool.*
1879–93 Widnes, Lancs.: St Ambrose; 1896–1903 Liverpool: Royal Insurance, Dale St; 1900–1914 Liverpool: St Barnabas, Allerton Rd.

Drew, Sir Thomas (1838–1910), *of Dublin. Restored many churches.*
1887–91 Dublin: Ulster Bank, College Grn; 1899–1902 Dublin: Graduates Memorial Building, Library Sq.; c.1899 (design) Belfast: St Anne's Cathedral (continued by W. H. Lynn★); 1908 Castle Archdale, Fermanagh: church.

Duff, Thomas, *of Newry, Co. Down.*
1840ff. Armagh: R.C. Cathedral (compl. by McCarthy★).

Dunn, Archibald Matthias (c.1833–1917). *Trained in Bristol under C. F. Hansom★. Partner of H.'s son Edward Joseph H. 1871–1900.*
1872ff. Downside Abbey, Som., church transept; 1879–81 Bath: Our Lady Help of Christians (R.C.); 1887–90 Cambridge: Our Lady and the English Martyrs (R.C.); 1887–95 Newcastle-upon-Tyne: Medical College (now Dental Hospital); 1891 Newcastle-upon-Tyne: St Michael (R.C.).

Dyer, Charles (1794–1848).
1839 Bristol: Victoria Rooms (later additions).

Edgar, Robert (1837/8–73). *Partner of J. L. Kipling.*
1863–9 Stoke-on-Trent, Staffs.: Wedgwood Memorial Institute, Burslem.

Edis, Col. Sir Robert William (1839–1927). *Colonel of the Artists' Corps of Volunteers. Pub. 'Decoration and Furniture of Town Houses (1881). Knighted 1919.*
1881, 1883 Sandringham House, Norfolk, additions including ballroom; 1883 London: 100 Piccadilly; 1884 London: Constitutional Club, Northumberland Ave.; 1897–9 London: Great Central Railway Hotel (now B.R. offices), Marylebone Station.

Ellis, Peter (1804–84).
In Liverpool: 1864 Oriel Chambers, Water St; 1866 No. 16 Cook St.

Elmes, Harvey Lonsdale (1814–47). *Son and pupil of James E. Assistant to H. E. Goodridge★ of Bath 1834. Died of consumption in Jamaica.*
In Liverpool: 1840–43 Collegiate In-

stitute, Shaw St; 1841ff. St George's Hall; 1847 Lancashire County Lunatic Asylum, Rainhill; 1847 †Allanhouse Towers (house), Woolton Rd.

Elmslie, E. W. *Partners: F. C. Cope, C. Eales, Franey, Haddon.*
1845–6, 1857 Winchester: SS. Thomas and Clement; 1860–61 Great Malvern, Worcs.: Imperial Hotel (now Girls' School), and Station; 1860–62 †Great Malvern: Link Hotel; 1860–62 Whitbourne Hall, Here.; 1861–2 Worcester: Lloyds Bank, High St.

Emden, Walter (1847–1913).
1875 Livorno, Italy: Hotel Anglo-Americano; 1888 London: Garrick Theatre; 1899 London: Grand Hotel and Brasserie de l'Europe, 10–15 Leicester Sq.

Emerson, Sir William (1843–1924). *Pupil of W. G. Habershon★ and A. R. Pite★, worked for Burges★. To India 1864. Winner of first competition for Liverpool Cathedral 1886. RIBA President 1899–1902. Knighted 1902.*
1865–71 Bombay: Markets; 1877–9 Brighton: SS. Mary and James; 1898–1901 London: Hamilton House, Victoria Embankment; 1904–21 Calcutta: Victoria Memorial.

Emmanuel, Ernest R. Barrow. See Davis.

Emmett, John T. (1828–98).
1849 London: Congregational College, St John's Wood; 1851 Glasgow: New Independent Church, Bath St, Blythwood.

Fergusson, James (1808–86). *Architectural historian. Went to India as a merchant. Pub. 'Illustrated Handbook of Architecture' (1859), 'History of Architecture' (1865) and 'Indian and Eastern Architecture' (1876). RIBA Gold Medal 1871.*
1882 London: M. North Gallery, Kew Gdns.

Ferrey, Benjamin (1810–80). *Pupil of A. Pugin sen. Worked with W. Wilkins. RIBA Gold Medal 1870. Pub. 'Recollections of A. N. Welby Pugin, and his Father Augustus Pugin' (1861).*
1843–5 Dorchester, Dorset: All Saints; 1847–50 London: St Stephen, Rochester Row, Westminster; 1852–3 London: St John, Angell Town, Brixton; 1853–63 Buckland St Mary, Som.: St Mary; 1857–8 London: All Saints, Blackheath; 1869 Huntsham Hall, Devon.

Fletcher, Sir Banister Flight (1866–1953). *Son of Banister F. (1833–99), surveyor to many institutions and author, whose practice he joined in the 1880s. Educated at Ecole des Beaux Arts, Paris. Pub. 'A History of Architecture on the Comparative Method' (1st ed. 1896).*
Early works, in London: 1890s Nos 20, 46 Harley St and 30 Wimpole St; 1897 †Goslett's, Charing Cross Rd.

Flockton, Thomas James (1825–1900). *Son of William F.★ Partner of Abbot, then E. M. Gibbs.*

In Sheffield: 1866 Williams Deacon's Bank, Church St; 1867 Cutlers Hall, interior; 1877–9 Firth College (now Central Schools) (with E. R. Robson★); 1886–8 Mappin Art Gallery; 1887–9 St John, Ranmoor Pk Rd.

Flockton, William (1804–64). *Father of above.*
In Sheffield: 1837 Wesley Grammar School (now Edward VII School); 1858 Savings Bank.

Foster, John, *of Bristol. (a) Partner of Joseph Wood (d. 1905).*
In Bristol: c. 1850 Victoria Sq., S.W. side; 1857–81 Trinity Almshouses, Old Market St; 1861–83 Foster's Almshouses, Colston St; 1867, 1873 Colston Hall (altered).
(b) With A. Ponton. See Ponton.

Fothergill, Watson (1841–1928). *Changed name from Fothergill Watson 1892. Worked with A. Blomfield★ 1862 and with J. Middleton of Cheltenham 1864.*
In Nottingham: 1873 Nos 5–7 Lenton Rd; 1876, 1899 Nottingham Express Offices, Parliament St; 1880–82 Nottingham and Notts. (now National Westminster) Bank, Thurland St; 1884 Baptist Church, Woodborough Rd; 1895 own office, 15 George St; 1896–7 former Jessop's Store, King St/Long Row.
In Chipping Ongar, Essex: c. 1882 Budworth Hall.

Fowke, Capt. Francis (1823–65). *Commissioned in Royal Engineers 1842. Inspector of Department of Science and Art 1853.*
1859–60 Plymouth: Raglan Barracks, Devonport; 1859–60 Dublin: National Gallery; 1859ff. London: Victoria and Albert Museum quadrangle; 1860–61 Edinburgh: Royal Scottish Museum; 1861 †London: Royal Horticultural Society gdns and greenhouse, S. Kensington; 1861–2 †London: 1862 Exhibition building; 1864 (design), 1867–71 (construction by H. Y. D. Scott★) London: Royal Albert Hall.

Fowler, Charles (1791–1867). *Apprenticed in Exeter. To London 1814, worked for D. Laing. Set up practice c. 1818. A founder of the Institute of British Architects.*
1827 London: Covent Garden Market; 1831–3 †London: Hungerford Market; 1837–8 Honiton, Devon: St Paul; 1837–8 Exeter, Devon: Higher Market; c. 1839 Maristow, Devon: lodges; 1843–6 Exminster, Devon: County Lunatic Asylum; c. 1848 Powderham Castle, Devon, additions.

Fowler, C. Hodgson (1840–1910), *of Durham. Pupil of Sir G. G. Scott★. Did many restorations.*
1866 Tudhoe, Durham: Holy Innocents; 1879 Bearpark, Durham: St Edmund; 1885 W. Hartlepool, Durham: St Paul, Grand Rd; 1888 Middlesbrough, Yorks.: St Barnabas; 1894 Norton, Yorks.: St Peter; 1897

Hepple, Northumb.: Christ Church; 1901 E. Retford, Notts.: St Alban, London Rd; 1904–8 Rochester, Kent: Cathedral restoration.

Fowler, James (1829–92), *of Louth, Lincs. Diocesan Architect for Lincoln.*
In Lincolnshire: 1863 Louth: St Michael; 1864 Ludford Magna: SS. Mary and Peter; 1866 Snitterby: St Nicholas; 1866 Langton-by-Partney: Langton Hall; 1869–87 Lincoln: St Swithun; 1875 Spridlington: St Hilary; 1875 Gedney Hill: Holy Trinity.

Fowler, Sir John (1817–98).
1876–9 Manchester: Central Station; 1882–90 Firth of Forth Br. (with Sir B. Baker and others).

Francis, Frederick John (1818–96) *and Horace* (1821–94).
1853–5 Ringwood, Hants: St Paul; 1854–5 London: school, Broomhouse Lane, Fulham; 1854–5 London: Christchurch, Lancaster Gate; 1857 London: National Discount Offices, Cornhill; 1866 Oxford: Westminster Bank, High St; 1868, 1873 †London: Holborn Restaurant; 1879 London: Grand Hotel Charing Cross.

Fraser, Patrick Allan (1813–90). *Amateur architect.*
c. 1843–53 Arbroath, Angus: Hospitalfields House; c. 1855–70 Blackcraig, Perth: house and fortified bridge; 1873–84 Arbroath: Mortuary Chapel.

Freeman, R. Knill (1838/9–1904), *of Bolton.*
1878 Derby: Library and Museum.

Garner, Thomas (1839–1906). *Pupil of Sir G. G. Scott★.*
(a) In partnership with G. F. Bodley 1869–97: see Bodley.
(b) Alone:
1896 London: Moreton House, Holly Walk, Hampstead; 1901–5 Downside Abbey, Som.: chancel of church.

George, Sir Ernest (1839–1922). *Articled to Samuel Hewitt. Partner of Thomas Vaughan 1861–c. 1875, later of Harold Peto (1828–97), and finally of Alfred B. Yeates. RIBA Gold Medal 1896. Knighted 1908. RIBA President 1908–10. R.A.*
c. 1870 Rousdon, Devon: St Pancras; 1874 Rousdon House, Devon; c. 1879 Uplyme, Devon: Woodhouse; 1881–3 Stoodleigh Ct, Devon; 1882 Newark, Notts.: Ossington Coffee Tavern; 1882 London: 39 Harrington Gdns; 1889–90 Shiplake Ct, Oxon.; 1894–7 London: Claridges Hotel.

Gibson, James Sievewright (1861–1951). *Pupil of Collcutt★. Partner of S. B. Russell. Early works:*
1894–8 Wakefield, Yorks.: W. Riding County Offices; 1912–13 London: Middlesex Guildhall, Storey's Gate.

Gibson, John (1817–92). *Pupil of J. A. Hansom★ in Birmingham. Later worked for Sir C. Barry★. Set up practice 1844. Architect to National Provincial Bank 1864ff. RIBA Gold Medal 1890.*

1845 8 London: Central Baptist Chapel, Bloomsbury St; 1846 †London: Imperial Insurance Office, Threadneedle St; 1847–9 Glasgow: National Bank (now Langside Hall), Queen's Pk; 1853 Shenstone, Staffs.: St John the Baptist; 1856 Bodelwyddan, Flint: St Margaret; 1860–75 Todmorden, Yorks.: Town Hall; 1865 London: National Provincial (now National Westminster) Bank, Bishopsgate; 1866–9 Dobroyd Castle, Yorks.; 1869 Todmorden: Unitarian Church; 1876–9 London: SPCK Building, Northumberland Ave.; 1877 Stockton, Durham: National Provincial (now National Westminster) Bank; 1879 London: Child's Bank, Fleet St.

Gimson, Ernest (1864–1919). *Also craftsman. On advice of Morris, worked with J. D. Sedding★ 1886–8.*
1897 Leicester: The White House, North Ave.; 1899 Charnwood Forest, Leics.: Stoneywell Cottage; 1900 Charnwood Forest: Lea Cottage; *c.*1901 Sapperton, Glos.: The Leasowes Cottage.

Gingell, William Bruce (1818/19–1900), *of Bristol. Partner of T. R. Lysaght.*
1852 Leeds: Leeds and Yorkshire Assurance (now Leek and Westbourne Building Soc.), Commercial St; 1852–7 Bristol: General Hospital, Guinea St; 1854 Bristol: West of England and South Wales Bank (now Lloyds Bank), Corn St (later extensions); *c.*1865 †Bristol: warehouse, 12 Temple St (attrib.).

Goddard, Joseph (1839/40–1900). *Partner of Paget, then of Catlow.*
1866 Tur Langton, Leics.: St Andrew; 1868 Leicester: Clock Tower; 1870 Leicester: Leicestershire (now Midland) Bank, Granby St; 1879 Caldecote Hall, Warw.; 1879 Radcliffe-on-Trent, Notts.: St Mary.

Godwin, Edward William (1833–86). *Son of a Bristol decorator. Practised there, with partner Henry Crisp, until 1865 when he came to London. Friend of Burges★.*
1860–64 Northampton Town Hall; 1862 Bristol: Anderson's Warehouse, 104 Stokes Croft; 1864–7 Congleton, Ches.: Town Hall; 1865 Northampton: St Martin's Villas, 43–4 Billing Rd; 1866–73 Dromore Castle, Limerick; 1867–8 Castle Ashby, Northants.: gatehouse lodge; 1867–70 †Glenbergh Towers, Kerry; 1872 †Harpenden, Herts.: Fallows Green (for Ellen Terry); 1870–74 Plymouth: Guildhall; 1871–4 Beauvale House, Notts.; 1873 Greasley, Notts.: The Manse; 1877–9 †London: The White House, 35 Tite St (for Whistler); 1882–4 London: 34 Tite St, remodelling (for Oscar Wilde; altered).

Godwin, George (1815–88). *Editor of 'The Builder' 1844–83. For part of his career worked with younger brothers*

Henry and Sidney G.
In London. 1850 St Mary, Boltons; 1870 St Jude, Collingham Gdns; 1872 St Luke, Redcliffe Sq.

Goldie, George (1828–87). *Pupil and partner of M. E. Hadfield and J. G. Weightman★. Later worked with his son Edward G. (d. 1921).*
1858 Scarborough, Yorks.: St Peter (R.C.); 1861 Greenock, Renfrew: St Mary (R.C.); 1862–4 York: St Wilfrid (R.C.); 1864 Stamford, Lincs.: St Augustine (R.C.); 1875 London: Assumption (R.C.), Kensington Sq.

Goodridge, Henry Edmund (*c.*1800–63).
1825–6 Bath: Lansdowne Tower (for Beckford); 1837–9 Frome, Som.: Holy Trinity; 1839 Bristol: The Apostles Cathedral (R.C.) (altered and contd. by C. Hansom★ 1847–8); 1842 Devizes Castle, Wilts.; 1848 Bath: Lansdowne Cemetery entrance; 1854 Bath: Percy Chapel, Charlotte St (with A. S. Goodridge).

Gough, Alexander Dick (1804–71). *Pupil of B. Wyatt. Partner of R. L. Roumieu★ 1836–48. Charles and Hugh Roumieu G.★, his sons, worked with him.*
*c.*1840 London: Milner Sq., Islington (with Roumieu); 1850 †London: St Matthew, Essex Rd; 1853–4 London: St Mark, Tollington Pk, Islington; 1853–5 Chatham, Kent: St Paul.

Gough, Hugh Roumieu (1843–1904). *Third son of above, with whom he worked.*
In London: 1882–7 St Paul, Hammersmith (with J. P. Seddon★); 1884–8 St Cuthbert, Philbeach Gdns.

Gowans, Sir James (1821–90). *Scot, mainly active as railway and building contractor.*
In Edinburgh: 1858 †Rockville (own house), 3 Napier Rd; 1859 Lammerburn House, 10 Napier Rd; 1866–70 Nos. 25–36 Castle Ter.

Graham, James Gillespie (1776–1855).
Later works: 1829ff. Murthly House, Perth; 1836 designs for Houses of Parliament, London (with A. W. N. Pugin★; unexecuted); 1844 Edinburgh: St John's Tolbooth (with Pugin).

Green, John (1787–1852) and **Benjamin** (d. 1858), *of Newcastle. Partners c.1830–44.*
Later works: 1836–7 Earsdon, Northumb.: St Alban; 1837 Tynemouth: Tyne Master Mariners' Asylum; 1837 Newcastle-upon-Tyne: Town Hall and Corn Market (completed 1858–63 by John Johnston).

Greene, G. T. *Director of Engineering and Architectural Works for the Admiralty.*
At Sheerness, Kent: 1856 factory smithery; 1857 foundry, ship fitting shop, boatstore.

Gregan, John Edgar (1813/14–55).

In Manchester: 1845–6 St John, Longsight; 1848–9 Heywood's Bank (now Williams Deacon's Bank), St Ann Sq.; 1850 †warehouse, Portland St/Parker St; 1854 Mechanics' Institution (now College of Commerce).

Griffiths, William, *of Llanelli.*
1885 (design), 1893 Llanelli, Carmarthen: Town Hall.

Grimthorpe, Lord (1816–1905). *Also known as Edmund Beckett and Edmund Denison. Created Baron Grimthorpe 1886. Amateur architect. Designed clock for the Houses of Parliament and devised specifications for Big Ben bell.*
1858 Doncaster, Yorks.: St James; 1880–85 St Albans, Herts.: Abbey restoration; 1885 Doncaster: St Mary.

Habershon *family and partners, of London and Newport, Mon.* **Matthew H.** (1789–1852). *Father of* **William Gillbee H.** (1818–92) and **Edward H.** (*partners 1849–58). Partners of W. G. H.: Alfred Robert Pite★ 1860–78, J. Follett Fawkner 1870, W. Yorke. Partner of Edward H.: E. P. L. Brock (1833–95).*
1828 Derby Town Hall; 1842 Rakeworth, Yorks.: St Thomas; 1842–3 Jerusalem: St James's Anglican Cathedral and mission buildings; 1856–7 London: Stanhope Institute, St Marylebone Grammar School; 1867 Cardiff: Hannah St Congregational Chapel; 1885 Cardiff: Park Hotel, Park Pl.

Hadfield, M. E. See Weightman.

Hakewill, Edward Charles (1812–72). *Son of architect Henry H. Brother of John Henry H. (1811–80). Pupil of P. Hardwick★ 1831–8.*
1840–41 London: St James, Lower Clapton; 1845–8 London: St John of Jerusalem, S. Hackney; 1861–2 Thurston, Suffolk: St Peter.

Hamilton, David (1768–1843) and **James** (*c.*1807–62).
In Glasgow: 1829–30 Royal Exchange (now Stirling's Library); 1840 British Linen Bank, Queen St/Ingram St; 1841 Western Club, Buchanan St.

Hamilton, James, *of Glasgow. Not known whether related to above. Worked for A. Kirkland★. Joined by his son* **John H.** *Irish partner until 1866, Frank Stirrat.*
1858–60 Belfast: Ulster Bank; 1863 Sligo: Ulster Bank; 1871–3 Belfast: Henry Matier Mansion, Fort William.

Hamilton, Thomas (1784–1858).
In Edinburgh: 1825–9 Royal High School; 1830 (compl.) Burns Monument; 1833 Dean Orphanage; 1845 Royal College of Physicians, 9 Queen St.

Hansom, Charles Francis (1816–88). *Brother of J. A. H.★*
1860–80 Bristol: Clifton College. *See also below.*

Hansom, Edward Joseph. See Dunn.

Hansom, Joseph Aloysius (1803–82). *Inventor of the 'Patent Safety Cab'. Founded 'The Builder' 1842. Part-*

ner at different times of Edward Welch, his brother **Charles H.★**, E. W. Pugin★, and his sons **Henry John H.** and **Joseph Stanislas H.**

1832–60s Birmingham Town Hall; 1845 Leicester: Particular Baptist Chapel, Belvoir St (now part of Adult Education Centre); 1850 Preston, Lancs.: St Walburga (R.C.); 1858 Plymouth: SS. Mary and Boniface Cathedral (R.C.); 1863, 1871 Abbotskerswell, Devon: priory and nunnery (R.C.); 1869 Manchester: Church of the Holy Name (R.C.); 1870–73 Arundel, Sx.: St Philip Neri (now R.C. cathedral); 1876 London: St Mary's Priory (R.C.), Fulham Rd; c.1885 Ushaw, Durham: St Cuthbert's College (chapel by Pugin 1842).

Hardwick, Philip (1792–1870). *Son and pupil of Thomas H. R.A. 1841. RIBA Gold Medal 1854.*

1829–35 London: Goldsmiths' Hall, Foster Lane; 1832–3 London: City Club, Old Broad St; 1835–9 †London: Euston Station (Great Hall, booking hall, etc., with P. C. Hardwick★ 1846–8); 1838 Birmingham: Curzon St Station; 1842 London: house of Lord Sefton, S.E. corner of Belgrave Sq. (now Seaford House); 1843–3 London: Hall and Library, Lincoln's Inn (with assistance of P. C. Hardwick★).

Hardwick, Philip Charles (1820–90). *Son of above. Pupil of Blore★. Joined his father's practice in 1843, taking over in 1847.*

1846–8 †London: Euston Station, Great Hall; 1848–51 Aldermaston Court, Berks.; 1851–3 London: Great Western Hotel, Paddington; 1856–61 Limerick: St John's Cathedral (R.C.); 1858–62 Limerick: St Alphonsus (R.C.); 1865–72 Charterhouse School, Surrey.

Hare, Henry Thomas (1860–1921). *Articled to C. A. Bury of Scarborough 1876. Studied at Ecole des Beaux Arts, Paris. RIBA President 1917–19.*

1893–5 Stafford: County Hall; 1893–7 Oxford Town Hall; 1897 London: Passmore Edwards Library and Baths, Shoreditch; 1899 Cambridge: Westminster College; 1900 Henley, Oxon.: Town Hall; 1908–9 London: Public Library, Fulham.

Harris, Thomas (1830–1900). *Pub. 'Victorian Architecture' (1860).*

1873–7 Bingley, Yorks.: Milner Field (for Sir T. Salt); 1884 Bedstone Court, Salop.; 1889 Stokesay Court, Salop.

Hartley, Jesse (c.1780–1860). *Trained as stonemason and bridgemaster. Surveyor and engineer of Liverpool docks and harbour walls 1824–60.*

Liverpool docks and harbour walls: 1832 Brunswick Dock (except tower); 1834 Waterloo Dock; 1841–5 Albert Dock; 1848 Victoria Tower, nr Stanley Dock; 1850–57 Stanley Dock; 1855 Wapping Dock; 1858 West Canada Dock.

In Hull: 1846 †Railway Dock and Castle St Warehouse.

Hawkins, Major Rhode (1821–84). *Pupil of Blore★.*

1857 London: Royal Victoria Patriotic School, Wandsworth; 1867–8 Exeter: St Michael; 1875 Holmwood, Surrey: St John, N. Holmwood.

Hay brothers: John, William Hardie (1813/14–1901), and **James Murdoch** (1823/4–1915).

1847 Liverpool: Holy Trinity, Breck Rd (John H.); 1855 †Greenock: Academy; 1856 Brechin, Angus: E. Free (now Baptist) Church; 1856 Bridge of Allan, Stirling: Chalmers Church; 1857 Edinburgh: Buccleuch and Greyfriars Free Church, E. Crosscauseway; 1857 St Helens, Lancs.: Holy Trinity, Traverse St; 1859–61 Edinburgh: Augustine-Bristo Congregational Church, George IV Br.; 1886 project for Liverpool Cathedral (unexecuted).

Hay, William (1818–80). *Pupil of J. Henderson★. Worked for Sir G. G. Scott★ 1847–50. In Canada 1853–60. Partner of G. Henderson (1804–1905, son of J. H.★; in Australia 1868–78).*

1853 Peterhead: St John's Longside (Hay); 1871–84 Edinburgh: St Giles's Cathedral, restoration (Hay); 1881–1906 Edinburgh: Old St Paul's Episcopal Church; 1885 Hamilton, Bermuda: Government House; 1885–1905 Hamilton: Holy Trinity Cathedral; 1889, 1901 Edinburgh: Craiglockhart Church (Henderson).

Haycock *of Shrewsbury:* **John Hiram H.**, *his son* **Edward H.** (b. c.1792) **sen.**, *and grandson* **Edward H. jun.**

Later works of E. Haycock sen.: 1840 Shrewsbury: Music Hall, The Square; 1841 Cressage, Salop.: Christ Church; 1845 Dorrington, Salop.: St Edward; 1854–8 Netley Hall, nr Longnor, Salop.

Hayward, John (1808–91), *and his son and partner* **Pearson Barry H.** (1838–88).

1856 Ilfracombe, Devon: SS. Philip and James; 1865–6 Exeter: Albert Memorial Museum.

Healey. See Mallinson.

Heathcote, Charles H. (1851–1938). *Pupil of C. Hansom★.*

Early works in Manchester: 1898 No. 107 Piccadilly (London St); 1902 Parr's (now Westminster) Bank, Spring Gdns.

Heiton, Andrew (1823–94). *Pupil of his father and of D. Bryce★.*

1867 Perth: St Mary's Monastery; 1867 †Dundee: Castleroy, Broughty Ferry; 1872 Perth: Victoria Buildings, 36–44 Tay St; 1878 Pitlochry, Perth: Atholl Palace (Hydropathic).

Henderson, John (1804–62). *Pupil of T. Hamilton★.*

1836 Edinburgh: 3 George IV Br.;

1837 Montrose: Natural History Museum; 1838 Dumfries: St Mary; 1843–51 Glenalmond, Perth: Trinity College; 1854 Arbroath: St Mary's Episcopal Church.

Hibbert, James (c.1833–1903), *of Preston, Lancs.*

In Preston: 1857 Fishergate Baptist Church; 1882–93 Harris Museum and Library.

Hill, William (1827–89), *of Leeds.*

1863–4 Sheffield: Methodist College, Ranmoor; 1866–73 Bolton, Lancs.: Town Hall; 1886–90 Portsmouth: Guildhall.

Hine, Thomas Chambers (1813–99). *Joined in 1867 by his son, **George Thomas H.***

1849 Mansfield, Notts.: Bentinck Memorial; 1850 Nottingham: Corn Exchange, Thurland St; 1850ff. Nottingham: Park Estate; 1851–4 Flintham Hall, Notts.; 1854–5 Nottingham: Thos. Adams Warehouse, Stoney St; 1856 Nottingham: Christ Church, Basfield; 1862–4 †Cranfield Court, Beds.; 1867–8 Nottingham: St Matthias, Sneinton; 1875–8 Nottingham: conversion of castle into museum; 1898 Nottingham Station.

Holding, Matthew Henry (d. 1910). In Northampton: 1880s Nos 81–7 St Giles's St; 1885 St Mary, Towcester Rd; 1889–92 Town Hall extension (with Jeffery★); 1890 St Paul, Semilong Rd; 1891–4 St Matthew, Kettering Rd; 1909 Holy Trinity, Balmoral Rd (with **E. de W. Holding**).

Honeyman and Keppie: *John Honeyman (1831–1914), in partnership 1885ff. with John Keppie (1863–1945), a pupil of J. L. Pascal in Paris. Joined by C. R. Mackintosh★ as draughtsman 1889, partner 1901.*

1862 Glasgow: Lansdowne Church, Gt Western Rd, Woodside; 1866 Paisley: Museum; 1872 Glasgow: Ca' d'Oro warehouse, 41–55 Gordon St (altered); 1880 Glasgow: Westbourne Church, Kelvinside; 1890 Glasgow: Fairfield Offices, Govan (by Keppie); 1893 Glasgow: *Glasgow Herald* building, 60–76 Mitchell St (by Mackintosh).

Horsley, Gerald Callcott (1862–1917). *Pupil of Shaw★.*

1889 Colwyn Bay, N. Wales: Bron y Nant House; 1903–4 Longsdon, Staffs.: St Chad.

Humbert, Albert J. (1822–77).

1854–62 Whippingham, I.o.W.: St Mildred; 1862–8 Windsor, Berks.: Mausoleum for Prince Albert, Frogmore; 1870ff. Sandringham House, Norfolk (for Edward, Prince of Wales).

Hunt, H. A.

1847ff. Stoke-on-Trent, Staffs.: station and North Stafford Hotel.

I'Anson, Edward, jun. (1812–88). *Surveyor to Merchant Taylors' Co. and St Bartholomew's Hospital, London.*

In London; 1842–4 †Royal Exchange Buildings, Freeman's Pl.; 1866 British and Foreign Bible Soc., Queen Victoria St; 1881 Corn Exchange, Seething Lane.

Jackson, Thomas, *of Waterford.* 1840–44 Belfast: St Malachy's (R.C.).

Jackson, Sir Thomas Graham (1835–1924). *Educated at Wadham College, Oxford. Articled to Sir G. G. Scott★ 1858. Set up practice 1862. RIBA Gold Medal 1910. R.A., Baronet 1913.* 1868 Walkden, Lancs.: Ellesmere Memorial; 1872–4 Hornblotton, Som.: St Peter; 1876–82 Oxford: Examination Schools; 1877–82 Thorne House, Som.; 1879 Oxford: Girls' High School (now Dept of Metallurgy), Banbury Rd; 1880–81 Oxford: Boys' High School (now College of Further Education), George St; 1880–89, 1909–11 Oxford: New Buildings, Brasenose College; 1893 London: 2–3 Hare Court, Temple; 1897 Giggleswick, Yorks.: school chapel.

James, Joseph (1828–75). *Pupil of Daukes★.* 1854–6 Barnsley, Yorks.: Congregational Church; 1855–7 Halifax, Yorks.: Square Congregational Church (partly †); 1859 †Sheffield: Congregational Chapel, Cemetery Rd; 1862 London: Arundel Sq. Congregational Church, Barnsbury.

James, Seward and Thomas. See Seward.

Jearrad, Robert William and C. (active 1813–46). In Cheltenham: 1836–9 Queen's Hotel; 1838–40 Christ Church (interior 1883); 1838–41 Lansdown Parade; *c.* 1845 Lypiatt Ter. (attrib.)

Jeckyll (or Jeckell), **Thomas** (1827–81). *Also designed metalwork.* 1866 Norwich: St Andrew, Thorpe; 1870–71 Lilley, Herts.: St Peter; 1876 London: 'Peacock Room', 49 Princes Gate (painted by Whistler) (now in Freer Gallery of Art, Washington, D.C.); 1880 †Norwich, 'Pagoda', cast-iron music pavilion in Chapel Field Gdns.

Jeffery (A. W.) and Skiller, *of Hastings, Sx.* 1870–73 Winchester Guildhall (extensions by J. B. Colson 1892–3).

Jones, Sir Horace (1819–87). *Architect and Surveyor to City of London Corporation.* 1852–3 Cherry Burton, Yorks.: St Michael; 1853 Cardiff: 'Old' Town Hall. In London: 1866 Smithfield Market; 1870ff. †Marshall and Snelgrove Store; 1875–7 †Billingsgate Market; 1880 Temple Bar Memorial; 1881 Leadenhall Market; 1886–94 Tower Bridge.

Jones, Owen (1809–74). *Pupil of Vulliamy★. Travelled in Greece, Egypt and Spain. Pub. 'Grammar of Ornament'*

(1856). *RIBA Gold Medal 1857.* 1845–c.1849 London: ?1 Kensington Palace Gdns; 1851 †London: Crystal Palace, interior decoration; 1852–4 †London: courts in Crystal Palace, Sydenham; 1856 †London: St James's Concert Hall, Piccadilly; 1856–60 †London: Osler's Gallery, Oxford St; *c.*1872 Abbotsfield House, Som.

Keane, John B. (d. 1859). *c.* 1833 Nenagh, Tipperary: Courthouse; 1847–9 Galway: Queen's College (now University College); *c.* 1849 (compl.) Waterford: Courthouse.

Keeling, Enoch Bassett (1837–86). In London: 1862–3 St Mark, Notting Hill; 1864 †Strand Music Hall; 1864 St Andrew, Glengall Rd.

Kendall, Henry Edward, sen. (1776–1875). *Pupil of Thomas Leverton. A founder of RIBA. c.*1830 London: 24 Belgrave Sq. (now Downshire House).

Kendall, Henry Edward, jun. (1805–85). *Son and pupil of above. Partner of Frederick Mew.* 1843–4 London: St John, Kensal Grn; 1853 Brentwood, Essex: lunatic asylum; 1858 Hove, Sx.: St Patrick; 1859 Haywards Heath, Sx.: St Francis's Hospital.

Kennedy, Henry (d. *c.*1897), *of Bangor.* 1844–5 Ffestiniog, Merioneth: church; 1864–6 Bangor: St James.

Kerr, Robert (1823–1904). *A founder and first President of the Architectural Association 1847–8. Professor of the Arts of Construction, King's College, London. Pub. 'The Gentleman's House' (1st ed. 1864).* 1865–74 Bear Wood, Berks.; 1868 Ford Manor, Surrey; 1868 Ascot Heath House, Berks.

Kibble, John. 1872 Glasgow: Crystal Art Palace, Botanic Garden.

Kirkland, Alexander (*c.* 1824–92 (not 1901)). In Glasgow: 1850–55 St Vincent Cres.; 1851 Suspension Bridge; 1854 †Nos 37–51 Miller St.

Knight, William, *of Nottingham.* 1872–7 Bexleyheath, Kent: Christ Church.

Knightley, Thomas Edward (1823–1905). *c.*1866 Eastbourne, Sx.: Cavendish Hotel; 1891 †London: Queen's Hall, Langham Pl. (with Phipps★); 1895–6 †London: Birkbeck (later Westminster) Bank, Holborn.

Knowles, James Thomas, sen. (1806–84). 1854–5 London: 191–2 Fleet St; 1860–62 London: Grosvenor Hotel (*with his son: see below*); 1865–8 Hedsor House, Bucks.

Knowles, Sir James Thomas (1831–1908). *Son and pupil of above. Founded 'The Nineteenth Century' review. Friend of Tennyson. Knighted 1903.*

1860 London: Cedars Estate, Clapham; 1862–4 London: Thatched House Club; 1863–6 London: Park Town Estate, Battersea; 1867–8 London: St Philip, Queenstown Rd; 1868–9 Blackdown, Sx.: Aldworth (for Tennyson).

Lamb, Edward Buckton (1806–69). *Pupil of Cottingham. Contributed illustrations to works by Loudon★ and to 'The Builder'.* 1841 Elkington Hall, Lincs.; 1848–50 Thirkleby, Yorks.: All Saints; 1854 W. Hartlepool, Durham: Christ Church; 1856 Castle Douglas, Dumfries: Episcopal Church; 1856–9 Englefield Green, Surrey: SS. Simon and Jude; 1857 Eye, Suffolk: Town Hall; 1857–8 Braiseworth, Suffolk: St Mary; 1858 Berkhampstead, Herts.: Town Hall; 1862–5 London: St Martin, Gospel Oak; 1863–6 Hughenden Manor, Bucks., alterations; 1868 Croydon, Surrey: St Mary Magdalene, Addiscombe.

Lanchester, Henry Vaughan (1863–1953). *Son and Pupil of H. J. L., a London architect. Set up practice 1894. Partner of James Stewart (d. 1902) and E. A. Rickards (1872–1920). RIBA Gold Medal 1934.* Early works: 1897 designs for Civic Centre, Cardiff; 1900–1903 London: Deptford Town Hall; 1906 (compl.) Cardiff: City Hall and Law Courts.

Lanyon, Sir Charles (1813–89). *Partner of W. H. Lynn★ until 1872; also of his son* **John Lanyon.** 1839 Belfast: Palm House, Botanic Gdns; 1849 Belfast: Queen's College (Univ.); 1849–51 Killyleagh Castle, Down; 1857 Belfast: Sinclair Seamen's Church; 1869 Belfast: Richardson Sons and Owden warehouse (now Water Offices); 1872–5 Belfast: Carlisle Memorial Church.

Leeming and Leeming: John L. (*c.*1849–1931), *in partnership with his brother* **Joseph,** *starting at Halifax 1872.* 1884, 1894–5 London: Admiralty, Whitehall; 1895 Halifax, Yorks.: Borough Market; 1903 Leeds: City Markets, front block.

Leiper, William (1839–1916). *Pupil of Boucher★ and Cousland, worked for Pearson★ and others in London.* 1865 Glasgow: Dowanhill Church; 1869–70 Auchterarder: Colearn; 1871 Helensburgh: Cairndhu; 1878 Glasgow: Camphill Church; 1889 Glasgow: Templeton's Factory, Glasgow Grn; 1892 Glasgow: 147–51 W. George St.

Lethaby, William Richard (1857–1931). *Pupil and principal assistant of Shaw★. Set up practice 1891. Chief promoter and first principal of Central School of Arts and Crafts, London, founded 1894. Pub. 'Architecture, Mysticism and Myth' (1892), etc.* 1891 Avon Tyrrell, Hants; 1898 Melsetter House, I. of Hoy, Orkney; 1898

High Coxlease, Lyndhurst, Hants; 1900 Birmingham: Eagle Insurance Co., Colmore Row; 1901–2 Brockhampton, Here.: All Saints.
Livesay, Augustus Frederick (1807–79), of Portsmouth.
1838 Trowbridge, Wilts.: Holy Trinity; 1840–46 Andover, Hants: St Mary (compl. by S. Smirke★).
Lockwood, Henry Francis (1811–78). Partner of Richard (1834–1904) and William Mawson in Bradford, Yorks., 1849–74, then moved to London.
1843 Hull: Great Thornton St Chapel (with Allom★); c.1850 Bradford: warehouses, Drake St; 1851–2 Bradford: St George's Hall; 1851–76 Saltaire, Yorks.: mills and model town; 1864–7 Bradford: Wool Exchange; 1871, 1873 Bradford: warehouses, 62 and 65 Vicar Lane; 1869–72 †Bradford: Kirkgate Markets; 1869–73 Bradford Town Hall.
Lockwood, Thomas Meakin (1830–1900).
1885 Newport, Mon.: Town Hall; 1885–6 Chester: Grosvenor Museum and Schools; 1888 Chester: corner of Bridge St and Eastgate St.
Lorimer, Sir Robert Stoddart (1864–1929). Pupil of R. Anderson★ and H. M. Wardrop, then worked with Bodley★.
Early works: 1893 Edinburgh: Miss Guthrie Wright's house, Colinton; 1898 Briglands House, Kinross; 1903–6 Rowallan House, Ayr; 1906 Ardkinglas, Argyll: house for A. Noble; 1907 St Andrews, Fife: University Library.
Loudon, John Claudius (1783–1843). Son of a Scottish farmer. Set up as landscape gardener in London 1803. Pub. many works on horticulture, landscape gardening and architecture, including 'An Encyclopaedia of Cottage, Farm and Villa Architecture and Furniture' (1833) and 'The Suburban Gardener and Villa Companion' (1838).
1837–8 London: semi-detached villa in Porchester Rd, Bayswater; 1840 Derby: Arboretum (Public Pk).
Lutyens, Sir Edwin Landseer (1869–1944). Pupil of E. George★ 1887. Knighted 1918. RIBA Gold Medal 1921. R.A. President 1938.
Early works: 1890 Farnham, Surrey: Crooksbury Lodge; 1894 Chinthurst Hill, Surrey; 1896 Munstead Wood, Surrey; 1897–8 Varengeville, France: Le Bois des Moutiers; 1898 Abinger, Surrey: Goddards; 1898–9 Godalming, Surrey: Orchards; 1899 Sonning, Berks.: Deanery Garden; 1899 Tigbourne Court, nr Witley, Surrey; 1900–1901 Gullane, E. Lothian: Grey Walls.
Lynn, William Henry (1829–1915). Partner of C. Lanyon★ until 1872.
By Lynn alone: 1864 Chester Town Hall; 1866 Jordanstown, Antrim: St

Patrick; 1878–87 Barrow-in-Furness, Lancs.: Town Hall. See also T. Drew, and Lanyon.
Macartney, Sir Mervyn Edmund (1853–1932). Pupil of Shaw★. A founder of Art Workers' Guild. Knighted 1930.
1889 London: 167 Queen's Gate; 1893 Sandhills, Bletchingley, Surrey; 1893 London: Guinness Trust Flats, Vauxhall Walk, Lambeth; 1900 Northwood, Mx.; Frithwood House.
Mackenzie, Dr Alexander Marshall (1848–1933). Trained with his father Thomas M.'s partner J. Matthews★, then D. Bryce★. Joined Matthews as partner 1877.
1885 Aberdeen: Northern Assurance Buildings, 146 Union St; 1885 Aberdeen: Art Gallery, Museum, War Memorial and Art School; 1892 Aberdeen: Free S. Church, Rosemount Viaduct; 1896–1906 Aberdeen: Marischal College, Broad St front; 1907–8 London: Waldorf Hotel, Aldwych.
Mackenzie, Thomas (1814–54). Pupil of W. M. Mackenzie. Worked for A. Simpson★ and W. Robertson in Elgin.
1842 Elgin: Museum; 1845 Fochabers, Moray: Milne's School; 1847 Inverness: Bank of Scotland, 9–11 High St; 1847 Ballindalloch, Stirling, reconstruction; 1853 Fraserburgh, Aberdeen: Town Hall.
Mackintosh, Charles Rennie (1868–1928). From 1889 draughtsman for Honeyman★ and Keppie; partner in 1901. Earlier work by M. alone: 1893 Glasgow: Glasgow Herald Building, Mitchell St; 1895 Glasgow: Martyrs School, 11 Barony St; 1896–1909 Glasgow: School of Art; 1897 Glasgow: St Cuthbert and Queen's Cross Church, Woodside; 1897–8 Glasgow: Buchanan St Tea Rooms; 1901 Kilmacolm, Renfrew: Windyhill House; 1901–12 Glasgow: Ingram St Tea Rooms; 1902 Helensburgh, Dumb.: Hill House.
Mackison, William (1833–1906). Pupil and then partner of Francis M. (d. 1884) in Stirling. After 1868 in Dundee.
1863 Stirling: 5–17 Clarendon Pl. (large villas); 1871–92 Dundee: 73–97 and 68–110 Commercial St (with J. Lessels of Edinburgh); 1885–99 Dundee: Whitehall St and Cres.
Mackmurdo, Arthur Heygate (1851–1942). Pupil of J. Brooks★ 1873. Travelled with Ruskin to Italy 1874. Set up practice 1875. Founded Century Guild 1882. Pub. 'Wren's City Churches' (1883), editor of 'The Hobby Horse'.
Enfield, Mx.: c. 1883 No. 8 Private Rd. In London: c. 1893–4 No. 25 Cadogan Gdns; 1894 No. 12 Hans Rd.
MacLaren, James (1829–93). Pupil of D. Bryce★. Partner c.1872–8 of G. S. Aitken (1836–1921), later of Edinburgh.
1854 Dundee: Clement Pk, Lochee; 1865 Dundee: Cox's Stack, Camperdown Works, Lochee; 1870 Kinnoull,

Perth: Balthayock House; c.1870 Monifieth, Forfar: Ashludie House; 1877 Dundee: Calcutta Buildings, Commercial St; 1886 Dundee: Cox Bros. (now Sidlaw Industries), Meadow Pl.
MacLaren, James Marjoribanks (1843–90). Pupil of Salmon★, C. Douglas★ and Stevenson★ in Glasgow.
1887–8 Stirling: High School, new wing; 1888–9 London: 22 Avonmore Rd, Kensington; c.1889 Fortingall, Perth: Glenlyon House, farm buildings and cottages; 1889–90 London: 10–12 Palace Court, Bayswater.
Mallinson and Healey, of Bradford and Halifax: James Mallinson (1819–84) and Thomas Healey (1809–62, pupil of R. D. Chantrell★).
1847 Bradford: St Paul, Manningham. Thomas Henry Healey (1839–1910) and Francis Healey (c.1840–1910), sons of Thomas H.
1872 †Leeds: Royal Exchange.
Marrable, Frederick (1818–72). In London: 1860 †Old County Hall, Spring Gdns, Trafalgar Sq.; 1864 Garrick Club, Garrick St; 1866–70 St Peter, Wickham Rd, Deptford (tower by A. Blomfield★).
Martin, William (d. 1899). Partner of J. H. Chamberlain★ 1864–83; worked under the name 'Martin and Chamberlain' after C.'s death.
(a) With C.: see Chamberlain.
(b) After C.'s death.
In Birmingham: 1888 St John the Evangelist, Sparkhill; 1893 Library, Spring Hill; 1893 Library and Baths, Green Lane, Small Heath; 1896 No. 19 Newhall St.
Matcham, Frank (1854–1920).
1879 Newcastle-upon-Tyne: Empire Palace, Newgate St; 1894 Blackpool: Grand Theatre; 1895 Belfast: Grand Opera House; 1898 Leeds: Empire Theatre; 1898–1900 Leeds: County and Cross Arcades (attrib.); 1899–1900 London: Hippodrome; 1900 Portsmouth: Theatre Royal; 1900 London: Hackney Empire; 1903 Buxton, Derbys.: Opera House; 1903 Harrogate: Kursaal; 1904 London: Coliseum Theatre.
Matheson, Robert (1808–77). Pupil of W. Nixon. Government architect.
1855 Edinburgh: Palm House, Botanic Gdns; 1856–62 Edinburgh: New Register House; 1861–5 Edinburgh: Post Office.
Matthews, James (1820–98). Pupil of A. Simpson★. Worked for Sir G. G. Scott★. Partner of T. Mackenzie★, then 1877ff. of A. M. Mackenzie★. Worked also with Lawrie in Inverness.
1861 Aberdeen: Grammar School; 1862 Aberdeen: Town and County (now Clydesdale) Bank, Union St; 1877 Ardo, Deeside, Aberdeen; 1878 Kirkcaldy, Fife: St Brycedale; 1878–82 Inverness Town Hall (with Lawrie).
McCarthy, James J. (1817–82), of

Dublin. (All churches mentioned R.C.).
1852–82 Maynooth College, Kildare, chapel, *c.*1853 82 Armagh Cathedral, completion (interior decoration 1887–1904); 1858 Dublin: St Saviour; 1861–82 Monaghan: St Macarthan's Cathedral; 1862–72 Thurles, Tipperary: Cathedral; 1871 Cahermoyle House, Limerick; 1876 Dungannon, Tyrone: St Patrick; 1879 Kilmallock, Co. Limerick: SS. Peter and Paul.

Medland *of Gloucester:* **James M.** *(1808–94), assistant to S. W. Daukes*★*, then partner of Daukes's former partner, J. Hamilton, and later of A. W. Maberly and* **John M.** *(1840–1913).*
1856 Gloucester: entrance to Eastgate St Market; 1857 Gloucester: cemetery chapels, Cemetery Rd; 1862 Cirencester, Glos.: entrance to Corn Hall.

Micklethwaite, John Thomas (1843–1906). *Pupil of Sir G. G. Scott*★*. Partner of Somers Clarke jun.*★*, then 1893–4 of Sir Charles A. Nicholson (1867–1949). Set up on his own 1896.*
1886–96 London: St Paul, Augustus Rd, Putney; 1896 Bocking, Essex: St Peter. *See also S. Clarke jun.*

Middleton, John (d. 1885). *Partner of H. A. Prothero.*
1847–8 Darlington: St John, Neasham Rd; 1862–7 Cheltenham: St Mark, Lansdown; 1865 †Cheltenham: Abbey Holme (own house) (ceiling at Bowes Museum, Barnard Castle); 1866 Clearwell, Glos.: St Peter; 1868 Cheltenham: All Saints, Pittville; 1873 Cheltenham: St Stephen, Tivoli; 1883 Cheltenham: Christ Church, interior (with others).

Mills and Murgatroyd: *Alexander William Mills (d. 1905), in partnership with James Murgatroyd (d. 1887).*
In Manchester: 1857–9 ★Assembly Rooms, Strangeways (with J. G. Crace); 1869–74 Royal Exchange (theatre now built inside).

Mitchell, Arthur George Sydney (1856–1930). *Pupil of R. R. Anderson*★*.*
Early works, in Edinburgh: 1883 No. 3 Rothesay Pl.; 1884 Well Court; 1889 Craig House (Asylum); 1893–4 Ramsay Gdns (greater part; for Patrick Geddes).

Mitchell, Charles W. *Patron and artist.*
1888 Newcastle-upon-Tyne: St George, Osborne Rd (architect T. R. Spence).

Moffatt, W. B. See Sir G. G. Scott.

Moore, Temple Lushington (1856–1920). *Pupil and later assistant of G. G. Scott jun.*★ *Later in partnership with his son* **Richard M.** *and his nephew-in-law* **Leslie M.** Early works:
1886–94 Peterborough: All Saints; 1892 Lake, I.o.W.: Good Shepherd; 1900 Middlesbrough, Yorks.: St Cuthbert; 1901 Bilbrough, Yorks.: Manor House; 1904–14 Harrogate, Yorks.: St Wilfrid.

Moore, Thomas.
1848 Monkwearmouth, Durham: sta-

tion; 1864 Sunderland: Corby Hall.

Morgan, George, *of Carmarthen*
1872 Carmarthen: English Baptist Church; 1872 (compl.) Haverfordwest, Pemb.: Masonic Hall; 1875 Swansea: Mount Pleasant Chapel.

Mountford, Edward William (1855–1908). *Articled to W. G. Habershon*★ *and A. R. Pite*★ *1872. Set up practice 1881.*
1888–90 London: Battersea Public Library, Lavender Hill; 1888–91 London: St Andrew, Garratt Lane; 1890–94 London: Battersea Polytechnic; 1890–97 Sheffield Town Hall; 1892 London: Battersea Town Hall; 1893–6 London: Northampton Institute, Finsbury; 1900–1907 London: Central Criminal Court, Old Bailey.

Nesfield, William Eden (1835–88). *Son of landscape gardener* **William Andrews N.** *(1793–1881). Pupil of W. Burn*★ *1851–3 and of his uncle A. Salvin*★ *1853–6. Set up practice 1858. Shared office with Shaw*★ *1863; in formal partnership with him 1866–8.*
1860–61 Shipley Hall, Derbys., farm buildings; 1863–5 †Combe Abbey, Warw.; 1864 †London: lodge, Regents Pk; 1865 Crewe Hall, Ches., estate cottages; 1866–8 Cloverley Hall, Salop. (partly †); 1867 Kew Gdns, Surrey: lodge; 1868ff. Kinmel Park, nr Abergele, Denbigh (gutted); 1870 Broadlands, Hants: Southampton Lodge; 1872–8 Calverhall, Salop.: Holy Trinity; 1873–4 Plas Dinan house, Montgomery; 1878 Loughton Hall, Essex; 1878 Newport, Essex: Grammar School.

Newton, Ernest (1856–1922). *Pupil of Shaw*★ *1873. Set up practice 1879. RIBA President 1914–17. RIBA Gold Medal 1918.*
Early works: *c.*1881 Fremlington House, Devon; 1888 Beckenham, Kent: St Barnabas's vicarage; 1894 Red Court (house), Haslemere, Surrey; 1897 Glebeland (house), Wokingham, Berks.

Nicholl, Samuel J. (1826–95). *Pupil of J. J. Scoles*★*. (All churches R.C.).*
1862 London: St Charles, Ogle St, Marylebone; 1879 Preston, Lancs.: St Wilfrid (with Ignatius Scoles).

Norton, John (1823–1904). *Pupil of B. Ferrey*★*.*
1853 St Audries, W. Quantoxhead, Som.: St Etheldreda; 1855 †Bristol: St John Bedminster; 1858 Nutfield, Surrey: house; 1862–4 Tyntesfield, nr Flax Bourton, Som.; 1864–6, 1883 Middlesbrough, Yorks.: St John the Evangelist, Marton Rd; 1870–71 Elveden Hall, Suffolk; *c.*1870–72 St Audries House, Som.; 1872 Southampton: Southwestern Hotel.

Oliver and Leeson: *Thomas Oliver, jun., and Richard John Leeson.*
1886 Wallsend, Northumb.: St Luke; 1899 Newcastle-upon-Tyne: Cooper-

ative Wholesale Society, W. Blandford St; 1900 Newcastle-upon-Tyne: Cathedral Buildings, Dean St.

Owen, Thomas Ellis (1804–62), *Businessman, local politician, developer, architect.*
In Portsmouth: 1835–7 Holy Trinity, Fareham (with his father, Jacob O.); 1845–6 Portland Ter., Southsea; 1850 The Vale (houses), Southsea.

Owen, William (1849/50–1909) and **Segar O.**, *of Liverpool.*
1888ff. Port Sunlight, Ches.: model town for Lord Lever (with many other architects, including J. Douglas★ and Fordham).

Paley, Edward Graham (1823–95). *Partner of Sharpe*★*. In 1868 joined by Hubert James Austin (1841–1915), and later by the latter's son, Henry A. (1865–1946). Firm continued as Austin and Paley.*
1857–9 Lancaster: R.C. Cathedral; 1869–71 Kirkby, Lancs.: St Chad; 1870 Yealand Conyers, Lancs.: Leighton Hall; 1870–75 Liverpool: SS. Matthew and James, Mossley Hill; 1871 Holker Hall, Lancs.; 1875 Bolton, Lancs.: St Thomas, Halliwell; 1879–81 Daisy Hill, Lancs.: St James; 1880–81 Bolton: All Souls, Astley Bridge; 1880–81 Leigh, Lancs.: St Peter; 1882–5 Dalton-in-Furness, Lancs.: St Mary; 1883–7 Pilling, Lancs.: St John; 1891 4 Waterloo, Lancs.: Christ Church; 1892–4 Broughton E., Lancs.: St Peter; 1893–7 Stockport, Ches.: St George, Buxton Rd.; 1894 Wigan, Lancs.: St Matthew, Highfield; 1897 Sedbergh, Yorks.: school chapel.

Parker, Charles (1800–81). *Pupil of Wyatville. Set up practice 1830. Pub. 'Villa Rustica' (1832).*
1846–7 Kingston, Surrey: St Raphael (R.C.); 1850–51 St Albans, Herts.: Christ Church.

Parnell, Charles Octavius (d. 1865).
In London: 1848–51 †Army and Navy Club, Pall Mall (with A. Smith); 1861, 1874 Westminster Bank, Lombard St; 1865 Whitehall Club, Parliament St.

Paull, Henry John (d. 1888), *of Cardiff, London and Manchester. In partnership variously with Aycliffe, Bickerdike, Robinson and Bonella.*
1863–8 Halifax, Yorks.: W. Hill Pk Estate (with Aycliffe); 1866 Manchester: Philips Pk Cemetery, Beswick (with Aycliffe); 1870 †Ashton-under-Lyne, Lancs.: Public Baths, Henry Sq. (with Robinson); 1873–5 †London: Christ Church (Congregational), Westminster Bridge Rd (with Bickerdike); 1882–3 Southport, Lancs.: Promenade Hospital (with Robinson); 1888 London: Islington Chapel, Upper St (with Bonella).

Paxton, Sir Joseph (1803–65). *See p. 12.*
1836–40 †Chatsworth, Derbys.: Great Stove; 1838ff. Edensor, Derbys.: model village; 1842–4 Liverpool: Princes Pk;

1843ff. Birkenhead, Ches.: Birkenhead Pk; 1849–50 Chatsworth, Derbys.: Victoria Regia lily house; 1850–51 †London: Crystal Palace; 1851–4 Mentmore Towers, Bucks. (with G. H. Stokes); 1851–4 †London: re-erected Crystal Palace, Sydenham; 1853–9 Ferrières, nr Paris (Rothschild house).

Peacock, Joseph (1821–93).
1858 London: St Simon Zelotes, Chelsea; 1866 London: St Stephen, Gloucester Rd; 1869 Perth: St Andrew.

Pearce, J. B. (1843/4–1903), *of Norwich*.
1882 Great Yarmouth, Norfolk: Town Hall.

Pearson, John Loughborough (1817–97). *See p. 218. RIBA Gold Medal 1880.*
1846–8 Ellerton, Yorks.: St Mary; 1848–50 Treberfydd House and church, Brecon; 1849–50 Landscove, Devon: St Matthew; 1857 Quar Wood house, Glos. (much altered); 1858–61 Dalton Holme, Yorks.: St Mary; 1860 Daylesford, Glos.: St Peter; 1860 (design), 1863–5 London: St Peter, Vauxhall; 1863–6 Appleton-le-Moors, Yorks.: Christ Church; 1866–8 Sutton Veny, Wilts.: St John the Evangelist; 1868 Roundwick House, Sx.; 1868–73 Freeland, Oxon.: St Mary, vicarage and school; 1870 (design), 1871–c. 1877 London: St Augustine, Kilburn (spire 1897–8); 1879–81 Birmingham: St Alban, Bordesley; 1876, 1880–85 Croydon, Surrey: St Michael; 1880–1910 Truro, Corn.: Cathedral; 1882–4 Cullercoats, Northumb.: St George; 1883–5 Liverpool: St Agnes, Sefton Pk; 1884–5 Thurstaston, Ches.: St Bartholomew; 1895–7 Port Talbot, Glam.: St Theodore; 1901ff.: Brisbane Cathedral.

Peddie and Kinnear: John Dick˙ Peddie (1824–91), *pupil of Rhind★, and* **Charles George Hood Kinnear** (1830–94), *pupil of D. Bryce★.*
1860 Edinburgh: Cockburn St; 1861–6 Aberdeen: Town Hall; 1863–6 Dundee: Morgan Academy; 1869 Glenmayne, Peebles; 1877 Dunblane, Perth: hydropathic; 1877 Glasgow: hotel and arcade complex, 91–115 Hope St; 1878–80 Edinburgh: Craiglockhart Hydropathic (now R.C. college).

Peddie, John More Dick (1853–1921). *Son of John Dick P.★*
Early works: 1884 Edinburgh: Bank of Scotland, 101–3 George St; 1898–1900 Edinburgh: Standard Life, 3 George St; 1899 Glasgow: National (now Royal) Bank, Buchanan St/St Vincent St (with G. W. Browne); 1905–6 Glasgow: Scottish Provident Building, 17–29 St Vincent Pl.

Pennethorne, Sir James (1801–71). *Pupil of Nash and A. Pugin sen. RIBA Gold Medal 1865. Knighted 1870.*
In London: 1851–96 Public Record

Office; 1853–5 Ball Room, Buckingham Palace; 1854 Duchy of Cornwall Offices, Buckingham Gate.

Penrose, Francis Cranmer (1817–1903). *Surveyor of St Paul's Cathedral.*
1855 Castle Cary, Som.: Market House; 1860 London: St Paul's Cathedral, pulpit; 1867 Hornblotton, Som.: rectory (now manor house).

Penson, Richard Kyrke (1816–86). *Active in Chester, Carmarthenshire, Cardiganshire, Oswestry. Partner of A. Ritchie of Chester and Swansea.*
1855–6 Ruthin, Denbigh: College; 1856–8 †Wrexham: St Mark, Hope Rd.

Penson, Thomas, jun. (1791–1859), *of Wrexham and Oswestry.*
1842 Llanymynech, Salop.: St Agatha; 1848 Shrewsbury Station (altered); 1848 Wrexham: Market.

Penson, Thomas Mainwaring (1818–64), *of Chester. Son of above.*
In Chester: 1848–50 Old Cemetery, Grosvenor Rd; 1856 Nos 34 and 36 Eastgate St; 1858 Browns Crypt Buildings, Eastgate St.

Perkin, Henry, *in partnership with George Bertram Bulmer (d. 1915).*
1894 Leeds: Yorkshire Penny Bank, Infirmary St.

Petit, the Rev. John Louis (1801–68). *Influential architectural writer: 'Remarks on Architectural Character' (1846), 'Architectural Studies in France' (1854).*
1862–3 Caerdeon, Merioneth: church.

Phipps, Charles John (1835–97).
1865 Nottingham: Theatre Royal, Upper Parliament St; 1874 †Richmond, Surrey: Star and Garter Hotel; 1881 London: Savoy Theatre; 1888 London: Lyric Theatre, Shaftesbury Ave.; 1891 †London: Queen's Hall, Langham Pl. (with Knightley★); 1891–5 London: Her Majesty's Theatre; 1891 (design), 1897–9 †London: Carlton Hotel.

Picton, Sir James Allanson (1805–89). *Historian, benefactor and architect. Later, partner of his son William Henry P. (1836–1900).*
1834 Hoylake, Ches.: Holy Trinity; 1857 †Liverpool: Richmond Buildings, 26 Chapel St; 1861 Liverpool: Hargreaves Building, 5 Chapel St; 1864–5 Liverpool: The Temple, Dale St; 1878–80 Liverpool: Victoria (Wesleyan) Chapel (now Juvenile Court), Crosshall St.

Pilkington, Frederick Thomas (1832–98). *Trained with his father, Thomas P.*
1861–3 Irvine, Ayr: Trinity Church; 1861–70 Larbert, Stirling: Children's Asylum; 1862–3 Edinburgh: Barclay Church; 1867 Kelso: St John, Edenside; 1875–7 †Moffat, Dumfries: hydropathic; 1881–3 †London: Windsor Hotel, Victoria St.

Pirie, John Bridgeford (c. 1851–92).

Pupil of A. Ellis. Worked for D. Bryce★ and J. Matthews★.
1880 Aberdeen: Queen's Cross Church; 1884 Macduff, Banff: Town Hall; 1884ff. †Aberdeen: Hamilton Pl.; 1885 Drumtochty, Kincardine: St Palladius; 1886 Aberdeen: 50 Queen's Rd.

Pite, Alfred Robert (1832–1911). *Articled to W. G. Habershon★. In office of P. Hardwick★ 1851. Partner of Habershon 1860–78. See Habershon.*

Pite, Arthur Beresford (1861–1934). *Son of above. In office of J. Belcher★. Professor of Architecture at Royal College of Art 1900–23. Known especially for his architectural drawings.*
Early works in London: 1896 No. 82 Mortimer St, Marylebone; 1898–1903 Christchurch, N. Brixton; 1899 No. 37 Harley St.

Playfair, William Henry (1790–1857). *Trained under W. Stark and R. Smirke★ in London and in Scotland.*
Later work: 1822–6, 1832–5 Edinburgh: Royal Scottish Institution; 1838ff. Kelso: Floors Castle, remodelling; 1842–5 Edinburgh: Donaldson's Hospital; 1846–50 Edinburgh: Free Church College; 1850–54 Edinburgh: National Gallery of Scotland.

Plumbe, Sir Rowland (1838–1919).
1872 London: Bryant and May Match Tax Testimonial Fountain, Bow Rd, Poplar; 1881ff. London: Noel Pk Estate, Wood Grn; 1896 Loxwood, Sx.: St John; 1896 London: Nile St council flats, Shoreditch; 1911 †London: YMCA, Great Russell St.

Ponton, Archibald. (a) *Associate of J. Foster★.*
1866–71 Bristol: Museum and Library (now University).
(b) *Partner of W. V. Gough.*
Also in Bristol: c. 1869 †chemist's shop, High St; 1871 Granary Warehouse, Welsh Back; 1871–3 Holy Nativity, Knowle.

Pope, Richard Shackleton (1791–1884).
In Bristol: c. 1835 Vyvyan Ter., Clifton; 1837 Royal Western Hotel (with Brunel★); 1839 St Mary on the Quay (R.C.); 1843 Guildhall, Broad St.

Poulton and Woodman, *of Reading: W. F. Poulton and W. H. Woodman (c. 1822–1879).*
1854 St Helier, Channel Is.: French Congregational Church, Halkett Pl.; 1856–7 Dorchester, Dorset: Congregational Church, South St; 1860 Wokingham, Surrey: Town Hall; 1861–2 Batsford, Glos.: St Mary; 1863–5 London: Westminster Chapel.

Prichard, John (1817–86). *Pupil of Walker, the chief assistant of A. W. N. Pugin★. Llandaff Diocesan Architect c. 1846–86. Partner of J. P. Seddon★ 1853–63 (P. worked in Glamorgan, S. in Monmouthshire).*
1843–82 Llandaff Cathedral, additions;

1857–8 Aberavon, nr Port Talbot, Glam.: St Mary; 1858–63 Ettington Park, Warw.; 1864 Jérez de la Frontera, Spain: house.

Prior, Edward Schroeder (1852–1932). *Pupil of Shaw★. Slade Professor of Fine Art at Cambridge 1912–32.*
Early works: 1883 Harrow, Mx.: Red House, Byron Hill; 1884–6 Cambridge: Henry Martyn Memorial Hall; 1897 Exmouth, Devon: The Barn (house); 1897 Brantham, Suffolk: lychgate; 1901–4 Cambridge: Zoological Laboratory.

Pritchett, James Pigott (1788–1868). *Practiced in York, in partnership with son* **James Pigott P.** *(1830–91), who later worked from Darlington.*
1845 Meltham Mills, Yorks.: St James; 1845–50 Huddersfield Station; 1857–8 Durham: St Nicholas.

Prynne, George Halford Fellowes (1853–1927). *Worked in office of Street★.*
1893 Budleigh Salterton, Devon: St Peter; 1893 Farnborough, Devon: St John the Baptist; 1895 Hadlow Grange, Kent; 1895 London: Holy Trinity, Roehampton.

Pugin, Augustus Welby Northmore (1812–52). *See pp. 12, 184. (All churches mentioned R.C.)*
1833–7 †Birmingham: King Edward VI School, decorative detailing (for Sir C. Barry★); 1835–6 Alderbury, Wilts.: St Marie's Grange; 1836 designs for Houses of Parliament, London (with J. G. Graham★) (unexecuted); 1837ff. London: Houses of Parliament, decorative detailing (for Sir C. Barry★); 1837–9 Derby: St Marie; 1837–45 Scarisbrick Hall, Lancs.; 1838–41 Macclesfield, Ches.: St Alban; 1839 Gorey, Wexford: St Michael; 1839–41 Birmingham: St Chad's Cathedral; 1839–42 Manchester: St Wilfrid, Hulme; 1839–44 Mount St Bernard Abbey, Leics.; 1840–2 Liverpool: St Oswald, Old Swan; 1840–48 London: St George, Southwark (mostly †); 1840ff. Alton, Staffs.: St John's Hospital; 1841 Spetchley, Worcs.: school; 1841–4 Nottingham: St Barnabas's Cathedral; 1841–6 Cheadle, Staffs.: St Giles; 1842ff. Killarney: St Mary's Cathedral; 1843 Ratcliffe College, Leics.; 1843–4 †Oxford: gateway for Magdalen College; 1843–4 Ramsgate, Kent: The Grange; 1844 Wexford: St Alphonsus, Barntown; 1845–6 Rampisham, Dorset: Glebe Farm; 1845–8 Marlow, Bucks.: St Peter; 1845–51 Ramsgate, Kent: St Augustine; 1847–9 Salisbury: St Osmund; 1847–9 London: St Thomas of Canterbury, Fulham; 1850 Bicton, Devon: Rolle Mortuary Chapel.

Pugin, Edward Welby (1834–75). *Son of above. Took over his father's practice 1852 (All churches mentioned R.C.)*
(a) *In England, partner of James Murray*
(1831–63), *from Armagh.*
1853 Shrewsbury: Our Lady of Help Cathedral; 1858 Liverpool: Bishop Eton Monastery, Childwall; 1859 Liverpool: Our Lady of Reconciliation, Vauxhall Rd; 1864 Manchester: St Francis, Gorton; 1874 Carlton-in-Balne, Yorks.: Carlton Towers.
(b) *In Ireland, partner of George Coppinger Ashlin (1837–1921), his brother-in-law. After P.'s death firm continued as 'Ashlin and Coleman'.*
1862ff. Dublin: SS. Augustine and John, St Thomas St; 1866 Dublin: Sacred Heart, Donnybrook; 1868–1919 Queenstown (now Cobh): Cathedral.

Railton, William (1801–77). *Pupil of W. Inwood. Architect to Ecclesiastical Commissioners 1838–40.*
1833–4 Grace-Dieu, Leics.: house and R.C. chapel; 1840–43 London: Nelson's Column; 1848 London: Holy Trinity, Hoxton.

Redmayne, George Tunstall (1840–1912).
In Manchester: 1874 Scottish Widows Fund, Albert Sq.; 1880–81 College of Art, Chorlton-on-Medlock.

Rhind, David (1808–83).
1844–6 Edinburgh: Commercial Bank of Scotland, George St; 1849–53 Edinburgh: Daniel Stewarts College; 1854 Glasgow: Commercial Bank, Gordon St; 1855–9 †Edinburgh: Life Assurance of Scotland, Princes St.

Ricardo, Halsey (1854–1928). *Worked with B. Champneys★ (not with Shaw★), and after 1888 with William De Morgan and the Arts and Crafts Exhibition Society.*
1887 †London: offices in Great George St, Westminster; 1892 competition design for Oxford Town Hall (unexecuted); 1893–4 London: 15–17 Melbury Rd, Kensington; c. 1898 Calcutta: Howrah Station; 1906–7 London: 8 Addison Rd.

Richardson, Charles James (1809–71). *Pupil of Soane. Pub. several books on villas.*
1852 London: 13 Kensington Palace Gdns.

Roberts, Henry (1803–76). *Pupil of C. Fowler★. R.A. Schools 1825. Worked in office of R. Smirke★. Architect to Society for Improving the Conditions of Labouring Classes.*
1831–4 London: Fishmongers' Hall; 1837 Ottery St Mary, Devon: Escott House; 1844–6 †London: first London Bridge Station; 1849–50 London: 'Model Houses', Streatham St, Bloomsbury; 1851 model cottage for Great Exhibition, now in Kennington Pk, London.

Robertson, John Murray (1844/5–1901). *Pupil of A. Heiton★ of Perth.*
In Dundee: 1874 India Buildings; 1874 Beach Tower, Broughty Ferry; 1879–80 Caledonian Insurance, Albert
Sq.; 1880 †The Cottage (later Landsdowne), Lochee; 1882 The Bughties, Broughty Ferry; 1886 former Technical Institute; 1895 Free Library and Baths, Lochee; c. 1895 Fyffe's Buildings, 89 Nethergate; 1899 Royal Victoria Hospital.

Robinson, George Thomas (1828–97), *of Leamington.*
1852–7 Stoke-on-Trent, Staffs.: Old Town Hall, Burslem; 1860 Earlswood, Warw.: St Patrick, tower.

Robson, Edward Robert (1835–1917). *Assistant of J. Dobson★ and Sir G. G. Scott★. Partner of J. J. Stevenson★ 1870–75. Architect to School Board for London 1872–84.*
1858 Durham: St Cuthbert, North Rd; 1864–8 Liverpool: Municipal Offices (with Weightman); 1864 W. Rainton, Durham: St Mary; 1867–70 Liverpool: buildings in Stanley Pk (with E. Kemp); 1875 London: Bonner St Primary School, Hackney; 1876–88 †London: Queen Anne's Mansions, Broadway; 1878 Loftus, Yorks.: Town Hall; 1887–94 Dunstable, Beds.: Grammar School; 1896–8 Cheltenham: Princess Hall, Cheltenham Ladies College.

Rochead, John Thomas (1814–78). *Pupil of D. Bryce★. Worked for D. Hamilton★.*
1855 Glasgow: Grosvenor Ter.; 1859 Glasgow: John St Church, Cochrane St; 1859–69 Abbey Craig, Stirling: Wallace Monument; 1860–61 Edinburgh: St Mary's Free Church, Albany St; 1869 Glasgow: Bank of Scotland, 2 St Vincent Pl.

Rolfe, Clapton Crabb (1845–1907). *Nephew of W. Wilkinson★ of Oxford.*
1866–9 Hailey, Oxon.: church; 1870 Oxford: artisans' houses, Kingston Rd; 1893 Oxford: St Thomas's vicarage.

Ross, Alexander (1834–1925).
1866–8 Inverness: St Andrew's Cathedral; 1870, 1889, 1898 Inverness: market, arcade and premises in Queensgate; 1873–88 Inverness: Ardross St and Ter.; 1875–9 Aberlour, Banff: St Margaret's Episcopal Church.

Roumieu, Robert Lewis (1814–77). *Pupil of B. Wyatt★. Partner of A. D. Gough★ 1836–48.*
1860 Wimbledon, Surrey: No. 70 The Ridgeway; 1866 London: The Priory, Roehampton; 1868 London: Nos 33–5 Eastcheap.

Rushforth, Thomas Henry.
1859 Welsh Bicknor, Here.: St Margaret; 1859 Greetland, Yorks.: St Thomas.

St Aubyn, James Piers (1815–95).
1848 St Agnes, Corn.: St Agnes; 1850–78 St Michael's Mount, Corn., additions; 1865 Reading, Berks.: All Saints; 1884–5 London: Garden Court Building, Middle Temple.

Salmon, James (1805–88). *Pupil of John Brash.*
1849 †Glasgow: St Matthew, Bath St.

Salomons, Edward (1827–1906). *Pupil of J. E. Gregan★.*

1856–7 †Manchester: Crystal Palace, Trafford Pk (Art Treasures Exhibition); 1858 Manchester: Synagogue, Cheetham Hill Rd; 1870–71 Manchester: Reform Club, King St (with Jones); 1877 London: Agnew's, 43 Old Bond St.

Salvin, Anthony (1799–1881). *B. in Co. Durham, son of a general. Worked for Nash. Set up practice 1828.*

1828–30 Mamhead House, Devon; 1831–7 Harlaxton Manor, Lincs.; 1837–44 Scotney Castle, Lamberhurst, Kent; 1840 Kilndown, Kent: alt. to Christ Church; 1844–50 Peckforton Castle, Ches.; 1846–8 Penoyre, Brecon; 1849–50 London: St Stephen, Hammersmith; 1854 Great Yarmouth, Norfolk: Gurney (now Barclays) Bank; 1854–65 Keele Hall, Staffs.; 1856–7 Torquay, Devon: St Mark; 1864–75 Thoresby Hall, Notts.; 1869–72 Paddockhurst (now Worth Priory), Sx.

Scoles, Joseph John (1798–1863). *Pupil of Joseph Ireland 1812. Set up practice in London 1826. (All churches mentioned R.C.)*

1835 London: Our Lady, Lisson Grove, Marylebone; 1843 London: St John the Evangelist, Duncan Ter., Islington; 1844–63 Bath: St Paul, Prior Pk; 1848–50 Great Yarmouth, Norfolk: St Mary, Regent Rd; 1853 London: Oratorians' House, Brompton Oratory.

Scott, Sir George Gilbert (1811–78). *See p. 12. Partner of W. B. Moffatt (1812–87) 1835–46. Knighted 1872. RIBA President 1873–5.*

1835 Old Windsor, Berks.: workhouse (now hospital); 1840 Great Dunmow, Essex: workhouse; 1841–3 Wanstead, Essex: Infant Orphan Asylum (now Royal Wanstead School); 1841–4 Oxford: Martyrs' Memorial; 1842–4 London: St Giles, Camberwell; 1842–4 Reading, Berks.: Gaol; 1842–5 Westwood Heath, nr Coventry: St John the Baptist; 1843–5 West Meon, Hants: St John the Evangelist; 1844 (competition)–c.1860 Hamburg, Germany: Nikolaikirche; 1846ff. St Johns, Newfoundland: St John's Cathedral; 1847–8 Bradfield, Berks.: St Andrew; 1847–50 Alderney, Channel Is.: St Ann; 1854 Ilam, Staffs.: cottages; 1854ff. Doncaster: St George; 1855–9 Halifax: All Souls, Haley Hill; 1856–7 competition design for Government Offices, London (unexecuted); 1856–8 Richmond, Surrey: St Matthias; 1856–60 Oxford: Exeter College chapel; 1857 Sandbach, Ches.: Literary Institute; 1857ff. Lichfield, Staffs.: Cathedral restoration; 1857–8 Crewe Green, Ches.: St Michael; 1857–60 London: St Michael, Cornhill, restoration; 1858–60 Leafield, Oxon.: St Michael; 1858–61 Kelham Hall,

Notts.; 1858–62 Walton Hall, Warw.; 1859 Ranmore Common, Surrey: St Bartholomew; 1861–6 Hafodunos house, Denbigh; 1862 †Preston, Lancs.: Town Hall; 1862–73 London: Government Offices (Foreign Office, etc.), Whitehall; 1863–9 Cambridge: St John's College chapel; 1863–72 London: Albert Memorial; 1864–8 Leeds: Infirmary; 1865 Winchcombe, Glos.: Sudeley Almshouses; 1865, 1868–71 Glasgow University; 1866 †Brighton: Brill's Baths; 1868–74 London: Midland Grand Hotel, St Pancras; 1869–72 London: St Mary Abbots, Kensington; 1872/3 (competition), 1874–9 Edinburgh: Episcopal Cathedral.

Scott, George Gilbert, jun. (1839–97). *Eldest son and pupil of above. Father of Sir Giles G. Scott.*

1870 Cambridge: Peterhouse hall, remodelling and redecoration; 1875 Leamington, Warw.: St Mark's vicarage; 1875–7 Woolton Hill, Hants: rectory; 1876 Leamington, Warw.: St Mark; 1877–9 Hull: 3 and 5 Salisbury St; 1877–9 Ashe, Hants: Holy Trinity and St Andrew; 1879 Cambridge: New Building, Pembroke College; 1884ff. Norwich: St John the Baptist (R.C.) (contd. by his brother John Oldrid S.★ 1891–1910).

Scott, Lieut.-Col., later Major-Gen. Henry Young Darracott, R.E. (1822–83). *Followed Fowke★ as architect of the Department of Science and Art 1865.*

1867–71 London: Science Schools (Huxley Building), Exhibition Rd (with Wild★); 1867–71 London: Royal Albert Hall. *See also Fowke.*

Scott, John Oldrid (1841–1913). *Second son of Sir G. G. Scott★. Entered father's office 1860 and succeeded to his practice.*

1874–82 London: St Sophia, Moscow Rd; 1875–1913 Slough, Bucks.: St Mary; 1876 Chailey, Sx.: St Mary; 1876 Manchester: St Paul, New Cross, Oldham Rd; 1890–1901 Bradfield College, Berks., chapel. See also G. G. S. jun.

Scott, Mackay Hugh Baillie (1865–1945). *Articled to C. E. Davis of Bath 1886.*

Early works: 1892–3 Douglas, I.o.M.: Oakleigh; 1896 Knutsford, Ches.: Bexton Croft; 1898–9 Wantage, Berks.: White Lodge; 1898–9 Bowness-on-Windermere, Westmor.: Blackwell House; 1899–1900 Helensburgh, Dumb.: White House.

Sedding, John Dando (1838–91). *Pupil of Street★ 1858–65. Partner of brother Edmund S. (1836–68) in Penzance, Corn., 1865–8. Came to London 1875. Assisted by Henry Wilson★.*

1871–3 Bournemouth, Hants: St Clement, Boscombe (compl. by Wilson); 1887 Plymouth: All Saints' vicarage; 1887 London: Holy Redeemer, Clerkenwell (tower by Wilson); 1887 Flete,

Devon: lodge; 1887–90 Falmouth, Corn.: All Saints; 1888–90 London: Holy Trinity, Sloane St; 1890 Bristol: Industrial Schools, Knowle.

Seddon, John Pollard (1827–1906). *Pupil of T. L. Donaldson★. Partner of Prichard★ 1853–63, of John Coates Carter 1884–1904.*

1852–62 Southerndown, Glam.: hotel; 1864–90 Aberystwyth: hotel (now University College); 1866 competition design for Law Courts, London (unexecuted); 1869 London: Powell Almshouses, Fulham; c. 1869 Birchington-on-Sea, Kent: Westcliff Bungalow (for D. G. Rossetti) and other bungalows in Spencer Rd, etc.; 1875 Ayot St Peter, Herts.: St Peter; 1880–85 Hoarwithy, Here.: St Catherine, remodelling of 1843 church; 1880–88 London: St Paul, Hammersmith (with H. R. Gough★). *See also Prichard.*

Sellars, James (1843–88). *Pupil of H. Barclay★. Partner of C. Douglas★ 1872–88.*

In Glasgow: 1873 St Andrew's Halls; 1875 Belmont and Hillhead Parish Church (based on scheme by Leiper★); 1877 Belhaven (now St Luke's) Greek Orthodox) Church; 1877 Kelvinside Academy; 1878 Finnieston (now Kelvingrove) Church; 1879 Nos 144–6 W. George St; 1884 Wylie and Lochead's Department Store, Buchanan St.

Seward, Edwin (1853–1924).

In Cardiff: 1882 Central Library (James, Seward and Thomas); 1883–6 Coal Exchange, Mount Stuart Sq. (James, Seward and Thomas); 1896 Central (now Morgan) Arcade.

Sharpe, Edmund (1809–77). *Articled to Thomas Rickman. Partner of Edwin Graham Paley★.*

1842–5 Bolton, Lancs.: St Stephen, Lever Br.; 1843–4 Knowsley, Lancs.: St Mary (additions by Paley 1860, 1871); 1844 Capernwray Hall, Lancs.; 1845–6 Manchester: Holy Trinity, Fallowfield.

Shaw, John (1803–70). *Son and pupil of J. S. sen. (1776–1832). Surveyor of Christ's Hospital, London, and Eton College.*

1841 †London: Christ Church, Watney St, Stepney; 1843–4 London: Goldsmiths' College, Deptford; 1844–6 Eton College, Bucks., New Buildings; 1856–9 Wellington College, Berks.

Shaw, Richard Norman (1831–1912). *See p. 14.*

1866–8 †Bingley, Yorks.: Holy Trinity; 1866–8 Groombridge, Sx.: Glen Andred; 1866 (design), 1868–9 Groombridge, Sx.: Leyswood (partly †); 1867–9 †Lyons, France: English Church; 1870 Church Preen, Salop.: village school; 1870–72 Harrow Weald, Mx.: Grims Dyke; 1871–3 †London: New Zealand Chambers, Leadenhall St; 1870–c. 1885 Cragside,

Rothbury, Northumb.; 1873–5 London: Lowther Lodge, Kensington Gore; 1874–6 London: 196 Queen's Gate; 1875–6 London: 8 Melbury Rd; 1875–6 London: 6 Ellerdale Rd; 1875–7 London: Swan House, 17 Chelsea Embankment; 1876–8 Frensham, Surrey: Pierrepoint; 1876–81 Adcote, Salop.; 1877–80 Bedford Pk, Mx.: work including 24–34 Woodstock Rd and Tabard Inn; 1878–9 Ilkley, Yorks.: St Margaret; 1878–83 Flete, Devon; 1879–82 Bedford Pk, Mx.: St Michael and All Angels; 1879–86 London: Albert Hall Mansions, Kensington Gore; 1884–5 †London: 180 Queen's Gate; 1884–5 London: 39 Frognal; 1887–9 London: Holy Trinity, Latimer Rd; 1887–90, 1900–1907 London: New Scotland Yard; 1888–90 London: 170 Queen's Gate; 1889–94 Bryanston, Dorset; 1890–93 Richards Castle, Salop.: All Saints; 1894–5 Swanscombe, Kent: All Saints, Galley Hill; 1895–8 Liverpool: White Star Offices, 30 James St (with J. F. Doyle).

Shellard, Edwin Hugh (active 1844–64).
1844 Manchester: St Peter, Blackley; 1848 Lees, Lancs.: St Thomas; 1853–5 Preston, Lancs.: St John the Divine.

Simpson, Archibald (1790–1847). *Pupil of D. Laing and R. Lugar of London.*
In Aberdeen: 1833–40 Old Infirmary, Woolmanhill; 1840–42 †New Market; 1842 Marischal College; 1843 Triple Kirks.

Skipper, George John (1856–1948), *of Norwich.*
1894–5 Street, Som.: Crispin Hall and other buildings; 1894–6 Cromer, Norfolk: Hotel de Paris; 1896 Norwich: 7 London St (own office); 1898 Norwich: Royal Arcade; 1901–6 Norwich: Norwich Union Insurance; 1902 Lowestoft; Norfolk and Suffolk Yacht Club House; 1904 †Cambridge: Norwich Union Branch Office, 30 St Andrew's St; 1904 Norwich: Telephone House, St Giles St (former Norwich and London Accident Insurance); 1904–11 Guist, Norfolk: Sennowe Pk.

Slater, William (1819–72). *Pupil and later successor of R. C. Carpenter★, then partner of C.'s son, R. H. Carpenter★, 1863–72.*
1854–5 Loughborough, Leics.: Town Hall; 1856 Earl Shilton, Leics.: SS. Simon and Jude; 1856 design for a model iron church, pub. by Ecclesiological Soc. in *Instrumenta Ecclesiastica*; 1859 Bray, nr Dublin: Christ Church; 1860 Basseterre, St Kitt's, W. Indies: church; 1864ff. Ardingly College, Sx. (with R. H. Carpenter).

Smirke, Sir Robert (1781–1867). *Second son of artist Robert S., R.A. briefly in office of Soane 1796. Knighted 1832. RIBA Gold Medal 1853. R.A.*

Later works: c.1820–35 Drayton Manor, Staffs.; 1823ff. London: British Museum (portico begun 1842).

Smirke, Sydney (1798–1877). *Fifth son of Robert S. R.A. and brother and pupil of above. RIBA Gold Medal 1860. Professor of Architecture at R.A. 1861–5.*
1834 †London: Bazaar, Oxford St; 1838–46 London: Imperial War Museum portico and dome; 1843–5 Conservative Club, St James's (with Basevi★); 1845–56 †London: Carlton Club, Pall Mall; 1846 Loughton, Essex: St John the Baptist; 1846–7 Bury, Lancs.: Athenaeum; 1854–6 Brookwood Cemetery, nr Woking, Surrey (with Tite★); 1854–7 London: British Museum Reading Room.

Smith, John (1781–1852), *of Aberdeen. Trained in London.*
1836 Cluny Castle, Aberdeen; 1839 Forglen House, Banff.

Smith, Samuel Pountney (1812–83), *of Shrewsbury.*
1859–72 Leaton, Salop.: Holy Trinity.

Smith, William (1817–91). *Trained with T. L. Donaldson★. Followed his father John S.★ as City Architect of Aberdeen.*
1853–5 Balmoral Castle III, nr Ballater, Aberdeen; 1869–71 Aberdeen: Boys' and Girls' Hospital (now Institute of Technology School of Navigation), 352 King St.

Snell, Henry Saxon (1830–1904). *Pupil of Pennethorne★. Assistant to Paxton★ and Tite★.*
1869–79 London: Archway Hospital; 1879 London: St Charles Hospital, N. Kensington; 1885 London: Victoria Hospital for Children, Chelsea.

Starforth, John (1823–98). *Pupil of Burn★ and D. Bryce★.*
1867 Dumfries: Greyfriars Church; 1869 Dumfries: Royal Infirmary; 1878 †Peebles: Hydropathic; 1882 Moffat, Dumfries: parish church and manse.

Stephenson, Robert (1803–59). *Engineer, son of George S.*
1835–9 London to Birmingham line; 1845–50 Britannia Bridge, Menai Straits; 1847 London: round house, Chalk Farm Rd (engine house; with R. B. Dockray); 1854–9 Montreal, Canada: Victoria Bridge. *See also Dobson and Thompson.*

Stevenson, John James (1831–1908). *B. in Glasgow. Entered office of D. Bryce★ 1856, then that of Sir G. G. Scott★ 1858. Partner of C. Douglas★, and of E. R. Robson★ 1870–75; designed several elementary schools for London School Board.*
1862 Glasgow: Kelvinside Parish Church; 1871 †London: Red House, 140 Bayswater Rd; 1876–8 London: 42–8 Pont St; 1879–80 Ken Hill, Snettisham, Norfolk; c.1883 London: 1 Fitzjohns Ave.

Stokes, Leonard Aloysius Scott (1858–1925). *Worked for Street★,*

Collcutt★ and Bodley★. RIBA President 1910–12. RIBA Gold Medal 1919.
1883–4 Exeter: Sacred Heart (R.C.); 1888 Liverpool: St Clare (R.C.), Sefton Pk; 1889 Folkestone, Kent: Our Lady Help of Christians (R.C.); 1896 Peterborough: All Souls (R.C.); 1898 Pangbourne, Berks.: Shooters Hill House; 1899–1903 London Colney, Herts.: All Saints' Convent (R.C.); 1903–5 Minterne House, Dorset.

Street, George Edmund (1824–81). *Pupil of Owen Browne Carter of Winchester 1841–4. Worked for Sir G. G. Scott★ 1844–9. Set up practice in London 1849. Moved to Wantage, Berks., 1850, to Oxford 1852, back to London 1856. RIBA Gold Medal 1874. RIBA President 1881. R.A. After his death his son,* **Arthur Edmund S.** (1855–1938), *continued the practice. See also p. 209.*
1847 Par, Corn.: St Mary; 1849–50 Wantage, Berks.: vicarage; 1850 Inkpen, Berks.: schools; 1853 Colnbrook, Bucks.: vicarage; 1854–5 Boyne Hill, Berks.: All Saints, vicarage, school and cottages; 1855 design for Lille Cathedral (unexecuted); 1856 E. Hanney, Berks.: St James the Less; 1856 (competition), 1863–8 Constantinople: Crimea Memorial Church; 1857–8 Watchfield, Berks.: St Thomas; 1857–60 Wolverton, Bucks.: St James, New Bradwell, vicarage and school; 1859 Howsham, Yorks.: St John; 1859–61 London: St James the Less, Westminster; 1859–65 Oxford: SS. Philip and James; 1860–62 Denstone, Staffs.: All Saints, vicarage and school; 1861, 1884–5 Torquay, Devon: St John; 1864–6 Fawley, Berks.: St Mary; 1865–72 Eastbourne, Sx.: St Saviour; 1865–90 East Grinstead, Sx.: convent; 1866 Shipmeadow, Suffolk: chapel of former workhouse; 1866–7 competition design for Law Courts, London; 1866–70 Westcott, Bucks.: St Mary and school; 1867–73 London: St Mary Magdalene, Paddington; 1871–4, 1887–8 London: St John the Divine, Kennington; 1872–6 Rome: American Episcopal Church; 1873–6 Holmbury St Mary, Surrey: Holmedale; 1873–80 Kingston, Dorset: St James; 1874–82 London: Law Courts; 1877–9 Holmbury St Mary, Surrey: St Mary; 1878 Mürren, Switzerland: English Church; 1880–87 Rome: All Saints' English Church; 1880–1906 Paris: American Church.

Sugden, William (1820/21–92), *of Leek, Staffs. In 1881 joined in partnership by his son,* **W. Larner S.** (d. 1901).
In Leek, Staffs.: 1882 former District Bank, Derby St; 1882–4 Nicholson Institute, Stockwell St; 1888 Aintree, nr Liverpool: model houses.

Tarver, Edward John (1842–91). *Pupil of Ferrey★.*
1870 Broadstairs, Kent: Holy Trinity rectory; 1871 Tyringham, Bucks.: St Peter; 1875–9, 1890 Harlesden, Mx.:

267

All Souls, High St; 1879 Hooton, Ches.: St Mary (R.C.).

Tattersall, Robert.
1830–32 Carlisle: Cumberland Infirmary; 1836 Carlisle: Dixon's Mills, Junction St; 1839 Golborne, Lancs.: cotton mill.

Taylor, James Medland (1833/4–1909). *Partner of Henry Taylor.*
1864–5 St Helens, Lancs.: St Peter, Parr; 1865–6 Blackpool: Christ Church; 1867–8 Hyde, Ches.: St Thomas; 1874–6 Haughton Green, Lancs.: St Mary; 1880 Bolton, Lancs.: St George, Daubhill; 1884–5 Manchester: St Agnes, Levenshulme.

Teulon, Samuel Saunders (1812–73). *Brother of* **W. Milford T.** *(1823/4–1900). Pupil of George Legg. Set up practice 1840.*
1849–52 Tortworth Court, Glos.; 1852–3 Angmering, Sx.: St Margaret; 1854 †London: St Andrew, Lambeth; 1854 Windsor, Berks.: cottages for Crown labourers, Layton's Gate; 1854 Curridge, Berks.: chapel school; 1856 Burringham, Lincs.: St John the Baptist; 1856 Wells, Som.: St Thomas, vicarage and schools; 1856–60 Shadwell Park, Norfolk, large additions; 1857–60 Wimbledon, Surrey: Christchurch; 1858–60 Leckhampstead, Berks.: St James; 1859–62 Elvetham Hall, Hants; 1861–3 Huntley, Glos.: St John the Baptist; 1862–4 Bestwood Lodge, Notts.; 1866 London: Buxton Memorial Fountain, Victoria Tower Gdns; 1868–71 London: St Stephen, Rosslyn Hill.

Thomas, John (1813–62). *Also sculptor (Houses of Parliament, etc.).*
1844ff. Somerleyton, Suffolk: Hall, St Mary, model village and school (for Sir M. Peto); 1847ff. Lowestoft: Royal Hotel and houses in Marine Par.; 1850 Aylesford, Kent: Preston Hall (now Chest Hospital).

Thompson, Francis. *Architect to N. Midland Railway 1835ff.*
c.1840 26 stations on Derby–Leeds line (partly †); 1840 Derby: Trijunct Station and N. Midland Hotel; 1845–50 Britannia Bridge, Menai Straits (with R. Stephenson★ and W. Fairbairn); 1847–8 Chester: General Station; 1850 (compl.) Chester–Holyhead line and stations (with R. Stephenson★); 1852 Cambridge Station.

Thomson, Alexander 'Greek' (1817–75). *Worked with J. Baird No. 1★ 1836–49. Partner of J. Baird No. 2 1849–57, and later of his brother* **G. T.** *and R. Turnbull. No relation to Glasgow architect James Thomson★, partner of J. Baird No. 1.*
In Glasgow: 1849 †warehouses, 3–11 Dunlop St; 1856 Hutchesontown and Caledonia Rd Free Church (gutted); 1856 Langside House, 25 Mansionhouse Rd; 1856 Holmwood House, Netherlee Rd, Cathcart; 1857 Walmer Cres., Paisley Rd, W. Ibrox; 1858 St Vincent St U.P. Church; 1859 Nos 1–10 Moray Pl., Strathbungo; 1859–64 Grosvenor Buildings, 68–80 Gordon St; 1860 †Cairney warehouses, Bath St; 1863 Buck's Head warehouse, 63 Argyle St; 1867 †Queen's Pk U.P. Church; 1867 Great Western Ter., Kelvinside; 1871 Egyptian Halls, 84–100 Union St; 1871 Nos 200 and 202 Nitsdale Rd, Pollokshields.
1864 design for Natural History Museum, London (unexecuted).

Thomson, James (1835–1905). *Pupil of James Brown. Assistant and successor to J. Baird No. 1★.*
In Glasgow: 1858–75 Crown Circus, Gdns, Ter., Dowanhill; 1865–71 217–21 Argyle St; 1866 Belhaven Ter.; 1895 Nos 202–12 Sauchiehall St; 1898 London, Liverpool and Globe Buildings, Hope St/W. George St.

Tite, Sir William (1798–1873). *Articled to David Laing 1812. M.P. for Bath 1855–73. RIBA Gold Medal 1856. Knighted 1869. RIBA President 1861–3.*
1838 †London: Nine Elms Station; 1841–4 London: Royal Exchange; 1848 Perth Station; 1851 Windsor, Berks.: station; 1854 Brookwood Cemetery, Surrey (with S. Smirke★); 1859 Gerrards Cross, Bucks.: St James.

Townsend, Charles Harrison (1851–1928). *B. Birkenhead, Ches. Articled in Liverpool to Walter Scott, in London to Lewis Banks. Set up practice c.1888. Master of Art Workers' Guild.*
1892 London: All Saints, Ennismore Gdns, W. front; 1892–4 London: Bishopsgate Institute; c.1894 Blackheath, Surrey: Blatchfield; 1895 Blackheath, Surrey: St Martin; 1895 (design); 1897–9 London: Whitechapel Art Gallery; 1898–1901 London: Horniman Museum; 1902–4 Great Warley, Essex: St Mary the Virgin.

Truefitt, George (1824–1902). *Pupil of Cottingham. Worked for Sancton Wood★. Architect to Tufnell Estate in London. Pub. 'Designs for Country Churches' (1850).*
1859 London: 1 Middleton Grove, N.7; 1868 Manchester: Royal Exchange Assurance Offices, Chancery Lane/Brown St; 1868 London: St George, Tufnell Pk; 1868 Worthing, Sx.: St George; 1870 Altrincham, Ches.: Lloyds Bank; 1880 Bromley, Kent: St John; 1889–90 Davyhulme, Lancs.: St Mary.

Underwood, Henry Jones (1804–52). *Pupil of R. Smirke★.*
1835 Littlemore, Oxon.: SS. Mary and Nicholas (for Newman); 1840 Sibford Gower, Oxon.: Holy Trinity.

Unsworth, William Frederick (1850–1912). *Assistant to Street★ and Burges★. Partners: Inigo Triggs, Dodgshun.*
1876–9 †Stratford-on-Avon: Shakespeare Theatre; 1881 Stratford-on-Avon: Art Gallery and Library; 1887–9 Woking, Surrey: Christ Church; 1893 Woodham, Surrey: All Saints.

Verity, Thomas (1837–91). *Associate of G. H. Hunt, and later partner of his son* **Frank Thomas V.** *(1864–1937).*
1870–74 London: Criterion Theatre and Restaurant (remodelled inside); 1877–80 Scarborough, Yorks.: baths; 1881 London: Comedy Theatre; 1884–8 Nottingham: Guildhall (with Hunt); 1891 London: 96–7 Piccadilly (with F. T. Verity); 1901 London: Imperial Theatre, Westminster (F. T. Verity).

Voysey, Charles Francis Annesley (1857–1941). *Son of a clergyman. Articled to J. P. Seddon★ 1874. Worked for S. Snell★ and G. Devey★. Set up practice in London 1882. RIBA Gold Medal 1940.*
Early works: 1888 Bishops Itchington, Warw.: The Cottage; 1890 Bannut Tree Farm, Castlemorton, Worcs.; 1890 Bedford Pk, Mx.: Forster House; 1890 Elmesthorpe, Leics.: Wentworth Arms and Wortley Cottages; 1898–1900 Cartmel Fell, Lancs.: Broadleys and Moor Crag, on Lake Windermere; 1900 Halwill, Devon: Winsford Cottage Hospital; 1900–1901 Chorleywood, Herts.: The Orchard; 1901 N. Luffenham, Rutland: The Pastures.

Vulliamy, Lewis (1791–1871). *Pupil of R. Smirke★. Worked until 1861 with his nephew,* **George John V.** *(1817–86).*
1834 Richmond, Surrey: Hickey's Almshouses; 1838 London: new front of Royal Institution, Albemarle St; 1846–9 London: All Saints, Ennismore Gdns; 1848–63 †London: Dorchester House, Park Lane.

Walker, George. *Worked with John Wardle for Richard Grainger. (See also Dobson.)*
c.1834–40 Newcastle-upon-Tyne: Clayton St, Grainger St, W. side of Grey St; Central Exchange.

Walker, James Campbell (c.1822–88). *Pupil of Burn★ and D. Bryce★.*
1868 Kincardine, Perth: Blair Drummond; 1875 Dunfermline: Municipal Buildings.

Walters, Edward (1808–72). *In Constantinople 1832–7. In Manchester 1839–65.*
In Manchester: 1839 Cobden Warehouse, 15 Mosley St; 1845 †Silas Schwabe Warehouse; 1847–8 Cavendish St Independent Chapel; 1851–2 †Brown and Son Warehouse, 9 Portland St; 1853 Free Trade Hall; 1857, 1860 warehouses at Nos 34, 10 and 12 Charlotte St; 1860 Manchester and Salford (now Williams Deacon's) Bank, Mosley St.
1860 Bakewell, Miller's Dale and Matlock, Derbys.: stations.

Wardell, William Wilkinson (1823–99). *Friend of A. W. N. Pugin★. To Australia 1857. Inspector-General of Public Works and Buildings in Victoria*

1869–78. (All churches R.C.)
1849 Dorchester, Oxon.: St Birinus;
1849–51 London: Our Lady of Victories, Clapham; 1851 London: Our Lady Star of the Sea, Greenwich; 1858–97 Melbourne: St Patrick's Cathedral; 1859 Sydney: St John's College, Sydney University; 1865 Sydney: St Mary's Cathedral.

Wardrop, James Maitland (1824–82). *Worked for D. Bryce★. Partner of Thomas Brown II.*
1862 Wigtown: County Buildings; 1864 Lochinch House, nr Castle Kennedy, Wigtown; 1869–77 Falkirk: Callander Park, remodelling; 1875 Stirling: Court House; 1880 Beaufort Castle, Beauly, Inverness.

Waterhouse, Alfred (1830–1905). *Joined in partnership by his son* **Paul W.** *(1861–1924) 1891. RIBA Gold Medal 1878. RIBA President 1888–91. See p. 14.*
1856 †Manchester: Fryer and Binyon warehouse; 1856 Hinderton House, Neston, Ches.; 1858 †Manchester: Barcombe Cottage, Fallowfield; 1859ff. †Manchester: Assize Courts; 1861 †Manchester: Royal Insurance, King St; 1864 Darlington, Durham: Market and public offices, and Barclays Bank; 1866 Reading, Berks.: Foxhill, Whiteknights Pk; 1866–8 Manchester: Strangeways Gaol; 1867–70 Liverpool: Allerton Priory (house), Allerton Rd; 1867–77 Oxford: Balliol College, S. front; 1868–77 Manchester Town Hall; 1868 Cambridge: Gonville and Caius College; 1868–71 Liverpool: Lime St Station Hotel; 1869ff. Manchester: Owen's College (now University); 1870–73 Blackmoor House, Hants; 1870–83 Eaton Hall, Ches. (part †); 1871 Knutsford, Ches.: Market Hall and Town Hall; 1872–5 Reading, Berks.: Town Hall; 1871–4 Cambridge: Pembroke College, additions; 1872ff. Cambridge: Girton College; 1873–81 London: Natural History Museum; 1877–1908 Leeds: Yorkshire College of Science (now University); 1878 Iwerne Minster House, Dorset (now Clayesmore School); 1878 Bedford: Assize Courts; 1878 †Yattendon Court, Berks. (own house); 1878, 1885, 1905 London: Prudential Assurance Co., Holborn; 1880 London: 1 Old Bond St; 1881–4 †London: St Paul's School, Hammersmith (Master's house survives); 1881–3 Liverpool: Turner Memorial Home, Toxteth; 1882–3 Reddish, Lancs.: St Elizabeth; 1883 London: Lyndhurst Rd Congregational Church, Hampstead; 1884 London: National Liberal Club, Victoria Embankment; 1885 Nottingham: Prudential Assurance, Queen St; 1886 Liverpool: Prudential Assurance, Dale St; 1886 Liverpool: Royal Infirmary; 1888 Brighton: Hotel Metropole; 1889–91 London: King's Weigh House Chapel, Duke St; 1891 Cambridge: Lloyds Bank; 1893–1913

Manchester: Refuge Assurance, Oxford St (with Paul W.); 1895 Edinburgh: Prudential Assurance; 1897–1906 London: University College Hospital.

Watson, Fothergill. See Fothergill.

Watson, Thomas Lennox (c. 1850–1920). *Pupil of A. Waterhouse★.*
Early works: 1883 Glasgow: Wellington Church, University Ave.; 1886–8 Hunter's Quay: Clyde Yacht Club; 1889 Glasgow: 24 St Vincent Pl.

Watt, Richard Harding (1842–1913). *'A glovemaker with a passion for architecture'.*
In Knutsford, Ches.: 1899–1902 Ruskin Rooms; 1905 High Morland House, Legh Rd; 1907 Gaskell Memorial Tower and King's Coffee House.

Webb, Sir Aston (1849–1930). *Articled to R. R. Banks and C. Barry jun.★ Partner of E. Ingress Bell (1837–1914). RIBA President 1902–4. Knighted 1904. RIBA Gold Medal 1905.*
Early works: 1885–97 London: St Bartholomew the Great, Smithfield, restoration; 1886–95 Birmingham: Assize Courts; 1893–5 London: Royal United Services Institution, Whitehall; 1893–1902 Christ's Hospital, Horsham, Sx.; 1893 (design), 1899–1909 London: Victoria and Albert Museum, Cromwell Rd front; 1899–1905 Dartmouth, Devon: Royal Naval College.

Webb, Philip Speakman (1831–1915). *B. Oxford, son of a doctor. Articled to John Billing of Reading. Worked for Street★ in London, becoming his chief assistant; there met W. Morris. Set up practice in London 1856. Joined Morris's firm 1861. With Morris, founded Society for the Protection of Ancient Buildings.*
1859–60 Bexleyheath, Kent: Red House, Red House Lane; 1860 Sandroyd, Fairmile, nr Cobham, Surrey (now Benfleet Hall School); 1861–3 London: 91–101 Worship St, Shoreditch (shops and houses); 1863 Arisaig house, Inverness; 1868 London: 19 Lincoln's Inn Fields; 1868–9 London: 35 Glebe Pl., Chelsea; 1868–73 London: 1 Palace Green; 1872–6 †Rounton Grange, Yorks.; 1874–8 Brampton, Cumb.: St Martin; 1876–8 Brampton, Cumb.: Four Gables; 1877–9 Smeaton Manor, Yorks.; 1879–91 Clouds, E. Knoyle, Wilts. (altered); 1889–90 Middlesbrough, Yorks.: Bell Bros. Offices, Zetland Rd; 1892–4 Standen, nr E. Grinstead, Sx.

Weightman and Hadfield: *John Grey Weightman (1801–72), assistant of Sir C. Barry★ and C. R. Cockerell★), in partnership 1838–58 with Matthew Ellison Hadfield (1812–85), also pupil to Goldie★. From 1858 firm was M. E. Hadfield; joined 1864 by his son Charles H. Not to be confused with Liverpool Corporation Architect John Weightman.*
1833 Sheffield: Brunswick Chapel, The Moor; 1836 Glossop: All Saints

(R.C.); 1838 Glossop Town Hall; 1843 Rotherham, Yorks.: St Bede (R.C.); 1844–8 Salford. R.C. Cathedral; 1845 Little Crosby, Lancs.: St Mary (R.C.); 1846 Sheffield: St Marie (R.C.); 1846 Burnley, Lancs.: St Mary (R.C.); 1848 Manchester: St Mary (R.C.), Mulberry St; 1850 Leek, Staffs.: Westwood Hall (now Westwood High School); 1851 †Sheffield: Victoria Station; 1861 Sheffield: Victoria Station Hotel; 1879 Grimsby, Lincs.: St Mary (R.C.).

Welland (W. J.) and Gillespie, *of Dublin.*
1870–72 Belfast: St Matthew, Woodvale Rd.

Whichcord, John, jun. (1823–85). *Son of John W. (1790–1860) of Maidstone. RIBA President 1879–81. Early partner: A. Ashpitel★.*
1862–4 Brighton: Grand Hotel; 1863 Dover: Clarence Hotel.

White, William (1825–1900). *Great-nephew of Gilbert White of Selborne. In office of Sir G. G. Scott★. Set up practice in Truro 1847. Not to be confused with his near-contemporary, W. H. White (1838–96), RIBA Secretary.*
1849 Probus, Corn.: parish school; 1849–50 St Columb Major, Corn.: Old Rectory; 1852ff. London: All Saints, Notting Hill; 1853 St Hilary, Corn.: church; 1854 Arley Hall, Ches.: chaplain's cottage; 1855 Audley, Staffs.: shops; 1855 Wantage, Berks.: St Michael's Home; 1855 Hooe, Devon: church and school; c. 1855 St Columb Major, Corn.: Penmellyn (house); 1856 Smannell, Hants: Christ Church; 1856 Hawridge, Bucks.: St Mary; 1857 St Columb Major, Corn.: bank; 1858 Little Baddow, Essex: former vicarage; 1858–69 Lyndhurst, Hants: St Michael; 1860–64 Sowton, Devon: Bishop's Court; 1865 Sowton: St Saviour, Aberdeen Pk; 1866–70 Humewood, Co. Wicklow; 1873 London: St Mark, Battersea Rise.

Wightwick, George (1802–72). *Assistant to Soane. In Plymouth, Devon, continuing J. Foulston's practice, 1829ff. Architectural writer (e.g. in Weale's 'Quarterly Papers on Architecture').*
In Plymouth: 1839 Town Hall; 1846 Christ Church; 1850 new front to Public and Cottonian Libraries.

Wild, James William (1814–92). *Son of artist Charles W. Pupil of Basevi★. Curator of Soane Museum, London, 1878–92.*
1836 Botley, Hants: All Saints; 1838–9 London: Holy Trinity, Blackheath Hill; 1839 Valletta, Malta: St Paul; 1839–42 †Southampton: St Lawrence; 1840–42 London: Christ Church, Streatham; 1844 Newport, I.o.W.: St Paul; 1849–50 †London: St Martin-in-the-Fields Northern District School, Shelton St; 1852 Grimsby, Lincs.: Dock Tower; 1873 London:

Bethnal Grn Museum (using ironwork of old S. Kensington Museum).

Wilkinson, William (1819–1901), *of Oxford. Harry Wilkinson Moore (1850–1915) was his nephew.*

1860ff. Oxford: Norham Manor Estate (1 Norham Gdns 1864, 11 Norham Gdns 1866, 13 Norham Gdns 1868); 1864 Oxford: Randolph Hotel; 1865 Oxford: 60 Banbury Rd; 1869 Upper Heyford, Oxon.: parsonage; 1871–3 Caversfield, Oxon.: Brashfield House.

Wilson, Charles (1810–63). *Worked for D. and J. Hamilton★ 1827–37.*

In Glasgow: 1841 Gartnavel Royal Hospital; 1845 Kirklee Ter.; 1846 Glasgow Academy (later High School); 1854 Faculty of Procurators, St George's Pl.; 1855 Park Circus, Ter., Quadrant, etc.; 1856 Free Church (Trinity) College; 1857 Queen's Rooms, La Belle Place.

In Paisley: 1849 Neilson Institution.

Wilson, Henry (1864–1934). *Also sculptor, metalworker and silversmith. Worked for J. O. Scott★ and J. Belcher★. Chief assistant to J. D. Sedding★, whose practice he took over in 1891.* Early works:

1891 London: Public Library, Ladbroke Grove; c.1893 Bournemouth, Hants: tower of St Clement, Boscombe; 1897–1908 Brighton: furnishings in St Bartholomew.

Wilson, James (1816–1900), *F.S.A., of Bath and London.*

1840–45 Bath: St Stephen, Lansdown Rd (chancel later); 1841–3 Cheltenham: Cheltenham College (many later additions); 1849–51 London: Westminster College, Horseferry Rd (chapel 1872); 1851 Lansdown, Som.: Kingwood School.

Wimperis, John Thomas (1829–1904). *Partner of East 1889.*

1870–75 Braemar, Aberdeen: Invercauld Castle; 1889 London: 27 Grosvenor Sq.; 1891 London: 8 Grafton St.

Withers, Robert Jewell (1823–94).

1848 Poyntington, Dorset: school; 1855 Llanfair Nantgwyn, Pembroke: St Mary; 1859 Cardigan: Municipal Buildings; 1859–60 London: Lavers and Barraud's Painted Glass Works, 22 Endell St; 1862–5 Brussels: Anglican Church of the Resurrection; 1873–4 London: St Mary, Bourne St.

Wood, Sancton (1815–86). *Pupil of S. Smirke★.*

1845 Dublin: Kingsbridge (now Heuston) Station; 1852 †London: Queen's Assurance, Cheapside.

Woodward, B. See Deane.

Woodyer, Henry (1816–96). *Worked with Butterfield★ 1844, later friend.*

1845–7 Wyke, Surrey: St Mark; 1847–52 Highnam, Glos.: Holy Innocents, school, vicarage and lodge; 1853–96 Windsor, Berks.: House of Mercy (now Convent of St John the Baptist), Clewer; 1854–6 Tenbury, Worcs.: St Michael and college; 1860 Lower Whitley, Reading, Berks.: school; 1860 Buckland, Surrey: St Mary; 1861–5 Reading, Berks.: Christ Church, Whitley; 1866–77 Dorking, Surrey: St Martin.

Worthington, Thomas (1826–1909). *Pupil of Bowman★ and Crowther.*

In Manchester: 1852 Overseers' and Churchwardens' Office, Fountain St; 1854 †Botanical Society Building; 1857 Mayfield Baths, Ardwick; 1862–7 Albert Memorial; 1864 Memorial Hall; 1866 Prestwich Union Workhouse (now Withington Hospital); 1868 The Towers, Didsbury (now Shirley Institute); 1868–71 Police Court; 1869–71 Brookfield Unitarian Church, Hyde Rd; 1879 Nicholls Hospital, Hyde Rd.

In Salford: 1870 †Greengate Artisans' Dwellings.

In Liverpool: 1896–9 Sefton Pk Unitarian Church (with Percy Scott W.).

Wray, Christopher George, *of London. Pupil of Joseph Clarke★.*

1868–71 Hull: Dock Offices; 1880 Maidstone, Kent: St Francis (R.C.).

Wyatt, Sir Matthew Digby (1820–77). *Son of Matthew W., who was first cousin of James W. Younger brother and pupil of T. H. Wyatt★. Secretary for Great Exhibition 1851. RIBA Gold Medal 1866. First Slade Professor of Fine Arts at Cambridge.*

1852–4 London: Paddington Station, architectural detailing (for Brunel★); 1857 Little Warley, Essex: garrison chapel; 1864–5 Cambridge: Addenbrooke's Hospital; 1865–78 Bristol: Temple Meads Station, main entrance and shed (see also Brunel); 1866 Possington Manor, Sx.; 1867 London: India Office, Whitehall, interior and Durbar Court (now part of Foreign Office); 1872 †London: Alford House, Princes Gate.

Wyatt, Thomas Henry (1807–80). *Elder brother of above. Articled to P. Hardwick★. Set up practice 1838. Partner of D. Brandon★ 1838–50. RIBA President 1870. RIBA Gold Medal 1873.*

1841 London: St Andrew, Bethnal Grn (with Brandon); 1855–8 Orchardleigh Pk, Som.; 1861 Savernake Forest, Wilts.: St Katherine; 1865 Liverpool: Exchange; 1866 Fonthill Gifford, Wilts.: Holy Trinity; 1875–9 †London: Knightsbridge Barracks; 1878 N. Perrott, Som.: Manor House (now school); 1879 Norwich: Norfolk and Norwich Hospital (with E. Boardman). See also D. Brandon.

Young, William (1843–1900). *Scottish architect, moved to London. Pub. his own designs in 'Town and Country Mansions' (1878).*

1873–4 Holme Wood House, Hunts.; 1876 Oxhey Grange, Herts.; 1879 London: 23 Oakhill Rd, E. Putney; 1880–90 Gosford House, E. Lothian, remodelling; 1883–8 Glasgow: City Chambers; 1893 Elvedon Hall, Suffolk, large additions; 1898 London: War Office, Whitehall.

Acknowledgments for illustrations

In addition to the museums and collections mentioned in the captions, the authors and publishers would like to thank the following: Aerofilms Ltd 11, 93, 103, 114, 167; Architectural Press Ltd 111; Dennis Assinder 171; Gordon Barnes 32, 183, 192; Batsford 134; by courtesy of Ulster Bank Ltd, Belfast 121; Birmingham Public Libraries 161; Metropolitan Bradford Libraries 59; by courtesy of the Chief Librarian, East Sussex County Library, Brighton 79; British Rail, London Midland Region 71; Cambridgeshire Collection, Cambridgeshire Libraries 248; by courtesy of St Augustine's College, Canterbury 243; John Chesshyre 98; Keith Collie 81; Copyright *Country Life* 12, 37, 38, 39, 41, 42, 86, 177; Crown Copyright 88, 148; Roger Dixon 30, 50, 57, 87, 235, 241; by courtesy of Doulton & Co. Ltd 126; Bord Fáilte, Dublin 207; by courtesy of Professor H. J. Dyos 48; by courtesy of Mark Girouard 17, 75, 77, (copyright Mrs J. F. Silcock) 24; Annan, Glasgow 250; Hunterian Art Gallery, University of Glasgow, Birnie Philip Bequest 52; Glasgow University Library 244; G. Leslie Horn 191; by courtesy of Paul Joyce 165; James Semple Kerr 206; A. F. Kersting, 26, 33, 40, 125, 155, 242, 247; Emily Lane 131, 169; Leeds City Council 143; Leeds City Library 110; Elsam, Mann & Cooper Ltd, Liverpool 142; The Greater London Council Photograph Library 55, 63, 66, 74, 123, 237, 238, (GLC Photographic Unit) 239; The Mander and Mitchenson Theatre Collection, London 78; Mansell Collection, London 62, 153; Science Museum, London, from the Fox Talbot Collection 186; Victoria and Albert Museum, London p. 1, 25, 85, 92, 96, 97, 146, 168, 178; Courtauld Institute of Art, University of London 140; Royal Holloway College, University of London 249; John McNamara 27; Manchester Public Libraries 73, 108, 119, 139, 160; George Mott 185; Stefan Muthesius 47, 58, 76, 83, 104, 107, 109, 112, 115, 144, 176, 203; National Monuments Record (England) 13, 21, 23, 35, 36, 53, 65, 68, 72, 82, 84, 95, 113, 117, 120, 129, 138, 154, 156, 166, 170, 172, 174, 175, 188, 189, 194, 195, 209, 213, 218, 219, 222, 226, 245, (the following taken by Gordon Barnes) 190, 193, 197, 202, 204, 205, 211, 212, 217, 223; National Monuments Record (Scotland) 5, 18, 116, 124, 145, 230, 233; by courtesy of Professor Donald Olsen 45; Bodleian Library, Oxford 90; Oxfordshire County Libraries 149, 150, 246; Radio Times Hulton Picture Library 132; H. E. G. Read 56; Walker Studios, Scarborough 70; Edwin Smith 19, 28, 60, 133, 137, 159, 182, 198, 199, 200, 214, 216, 224; by courtesy of Sotheby & Co. 20; by courtesy of Dr Phoebe Stanton 180; by courtesy of Thames Water Authority 105; John H. Thomas 225; Eileen Tweedy 164; D. M. Wrightson 46, 127, 128, 231; P. R. Wrightson 101. Illustration 49 is based on an illustration in S. E. Rasmussen, *London, the unique city* (Penguin Books, Harmondsworth, 1960); illustration 178 is taken from Stephen Ayling, *Photographs from Sketches by Augustus Welby Pugin* (1865), in the Victoria and Albert Museum, London. Ill. 127 is reproduced by courtesy of the Prudential Assurance Company, London.

Index